BURNOUT

Published by DC Comics, 1700 Broadway, New York, NY 10019.

Copyright © 2008 Rebecca Donner and Inaki Miranda.
All rights reserved. MINX and all characters featured in this book,
the distinctive likenesses thereof and related elements are
trademarks of DC COMICS.

The stories, characters and incidents mentioned in this book
are entirely fictional.

Printed in Canada.
DC Comics, a Warner Bros.Entertainment Company.

ISBN: 978-1-4012-1537-8

Cover by Inaki Miranda

BURNOUT

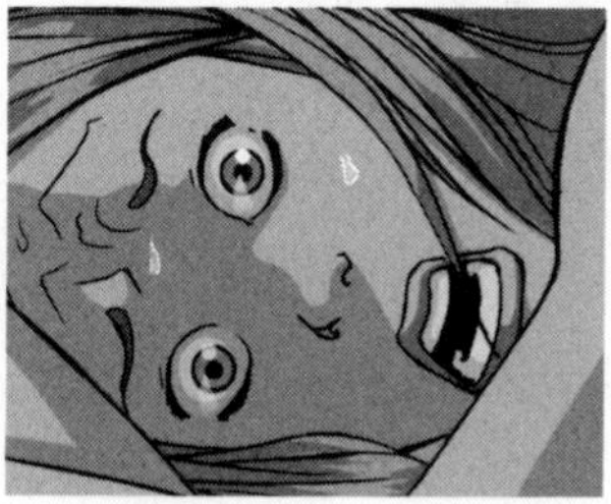

Written by Rebecca Donner

Illustrated by Inaki Miranda

Gray tones by Eva de la Cruz

Lettering by Jared K. Fletcher

minx

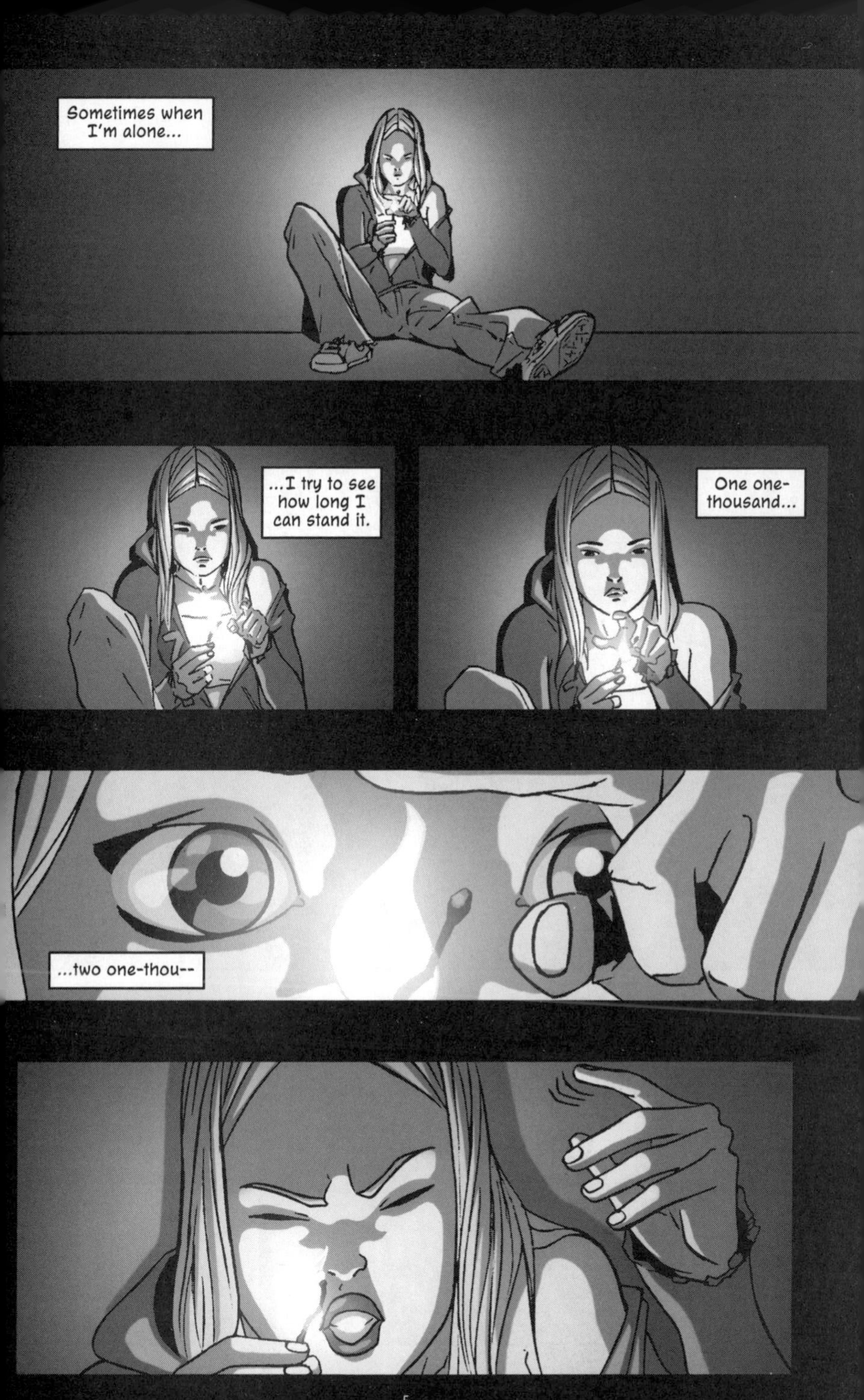
Sometimes when I'm alone...
...I try to see how long I can stand it.
One one-thousand...
...two one-thou--

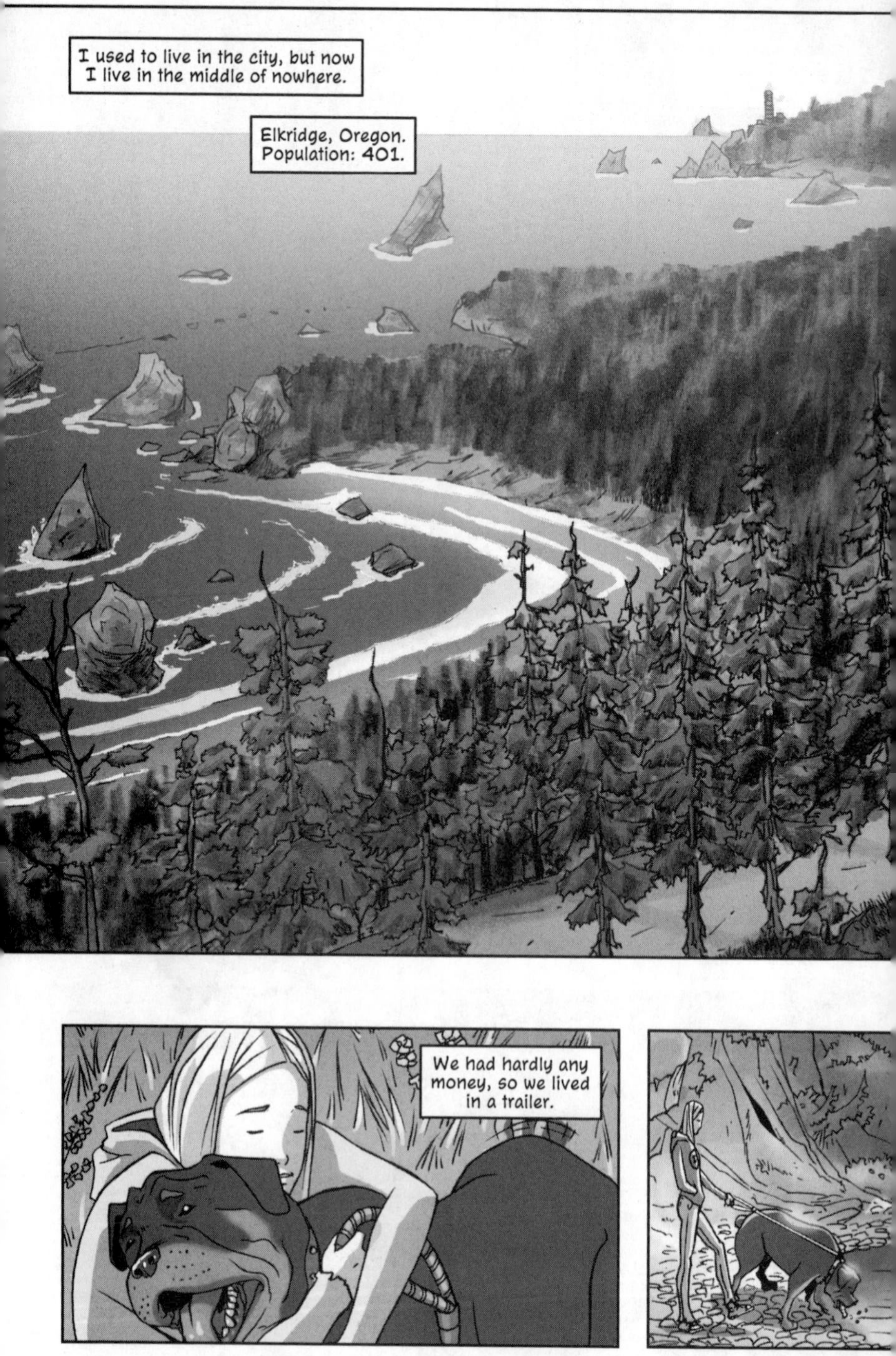
I used to live in the city, but now I live in the middle of nowhere.
Elkridge, Oregon. Population: 401.
We had hardly any money, so we lived in a trailer.

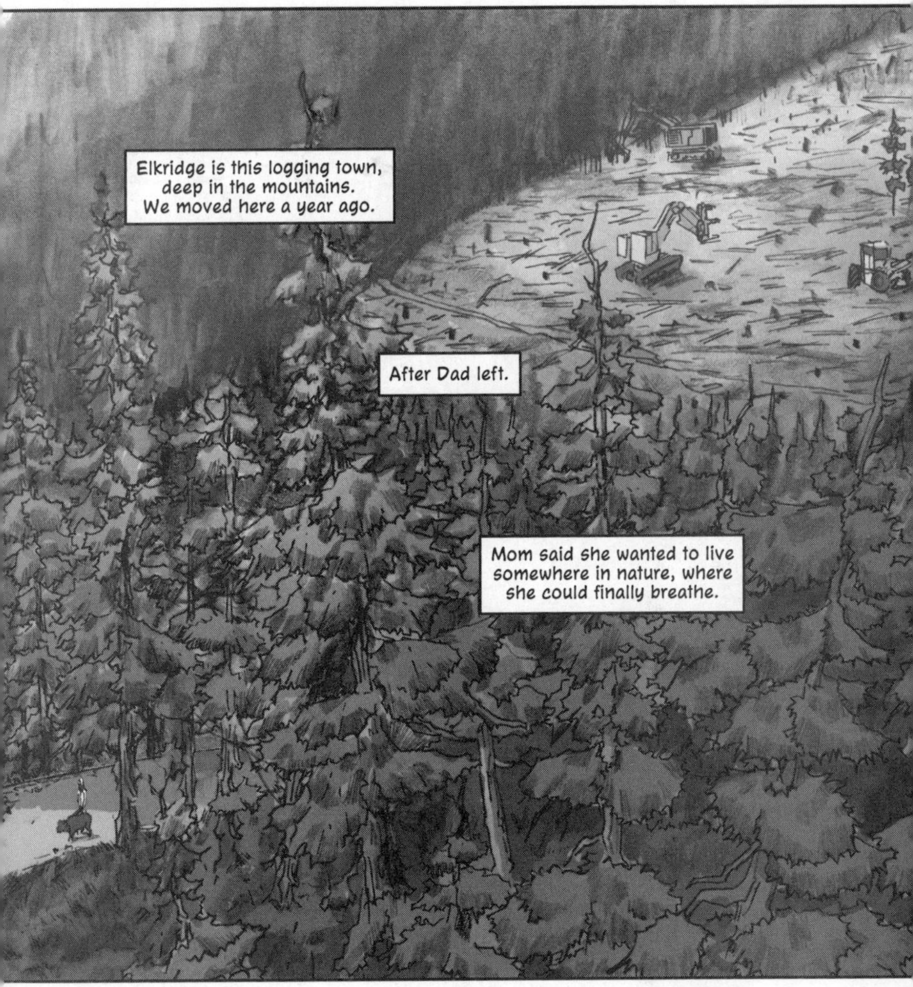
Elkridge is this logging town, deep in the mountains. We moved here a year ago.
After Dad left.
Mom said she wanted to live somewhere in nature, where she could finally breathe.

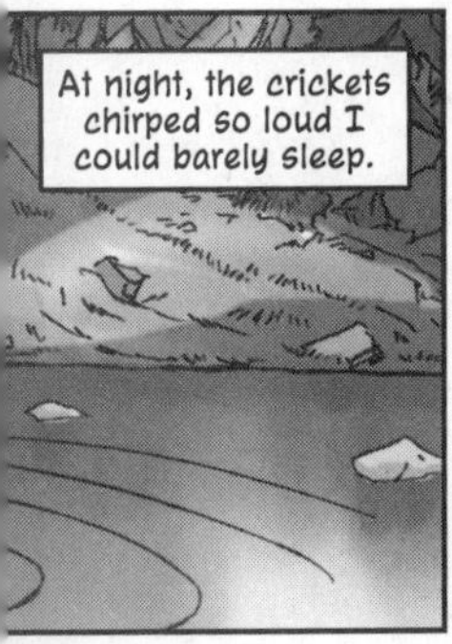
At night, the crickets chirped so loud I could barely sleep.

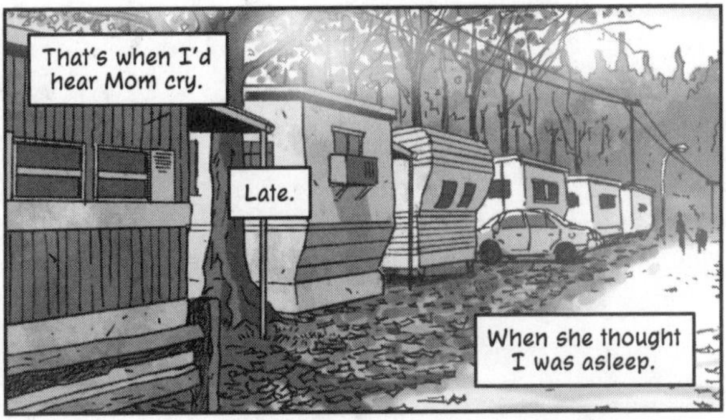
That's when I'd hear Mom cry.
Late.
When she thought I was asleep.

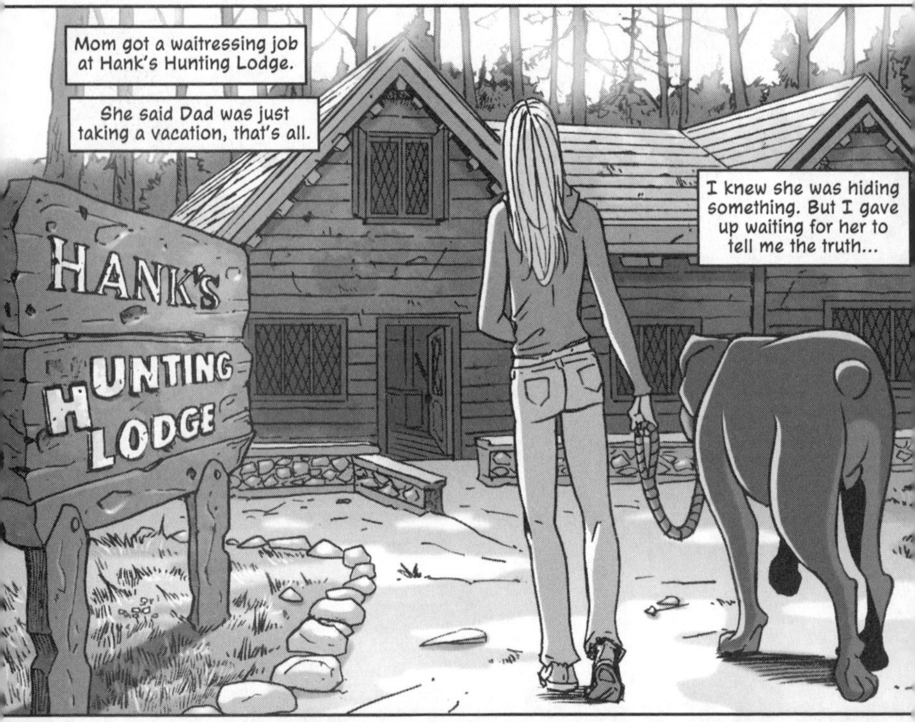
Mom got a waitressing job at Hank's Hunting Lodge.
She said Dad was just taking a vacation, that's all.
HANK'S HUNTING LODGE
I knew she was hiding something. But I gave up waiting for her to tell me the truth...

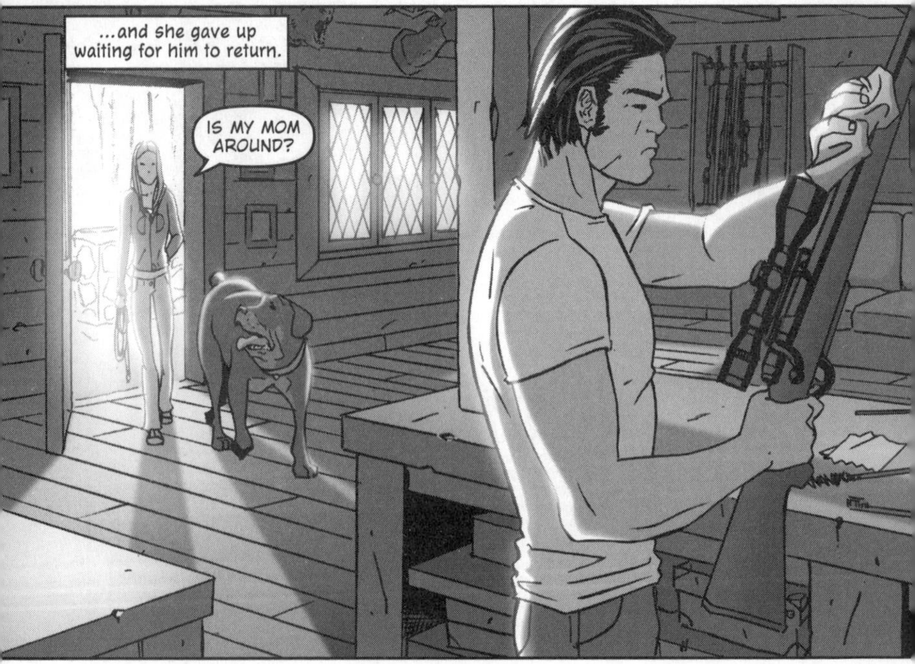
...and she gave up waiting for him to return.
IS MY MOM AROUND?

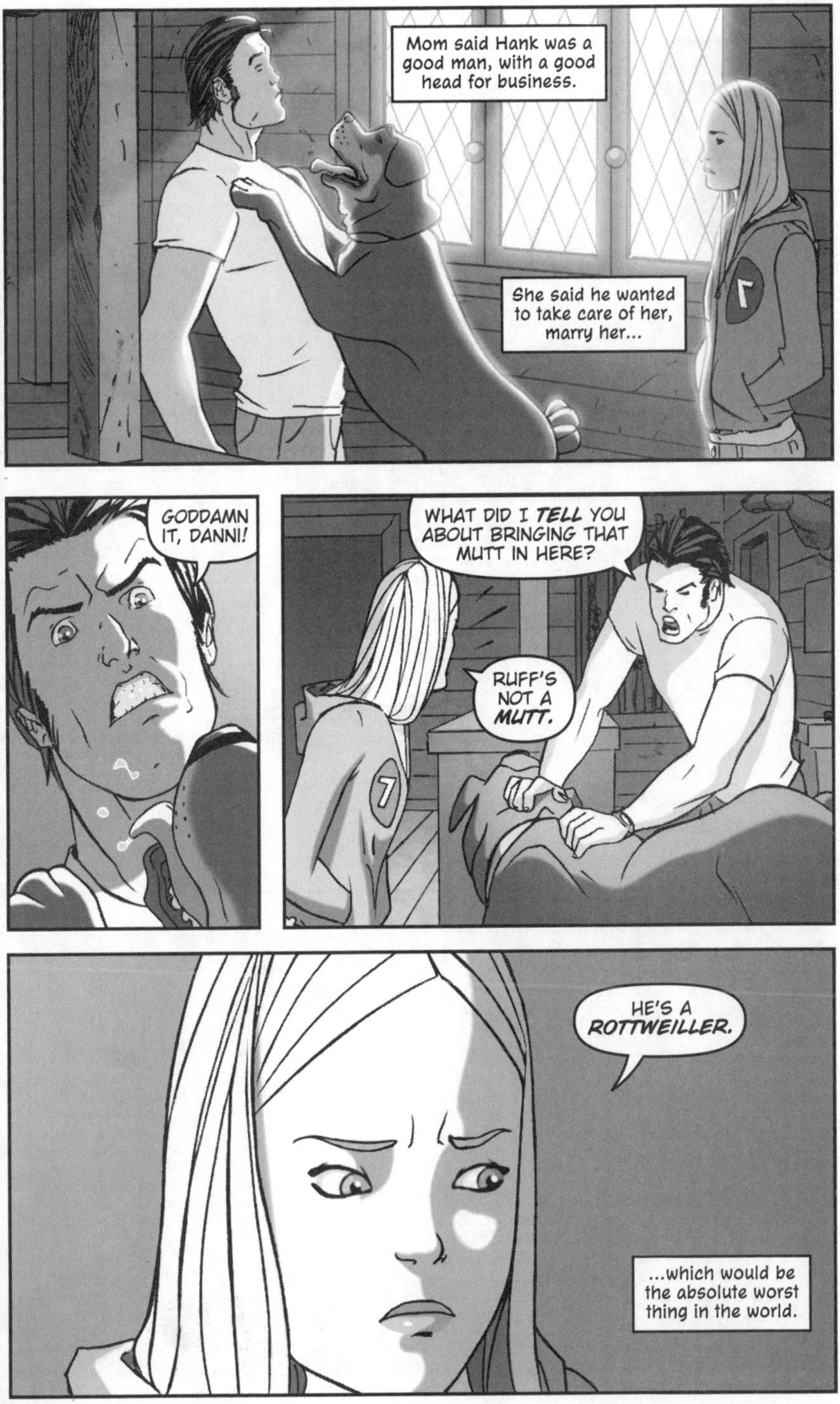
Mom said Hank was a good man, with a good head for business.
She said he wanted to take care of her, marry her...
GODDAMN IT, DANNI!
WHAT DID I *TELL* YOU ABOUT BRINGING THAT MUTT IN HERE?
RUFF'S NOT A *MUTT.*
HE'S A *ROTTWEILLER.*
...which would be the absolute worst thing in the world.

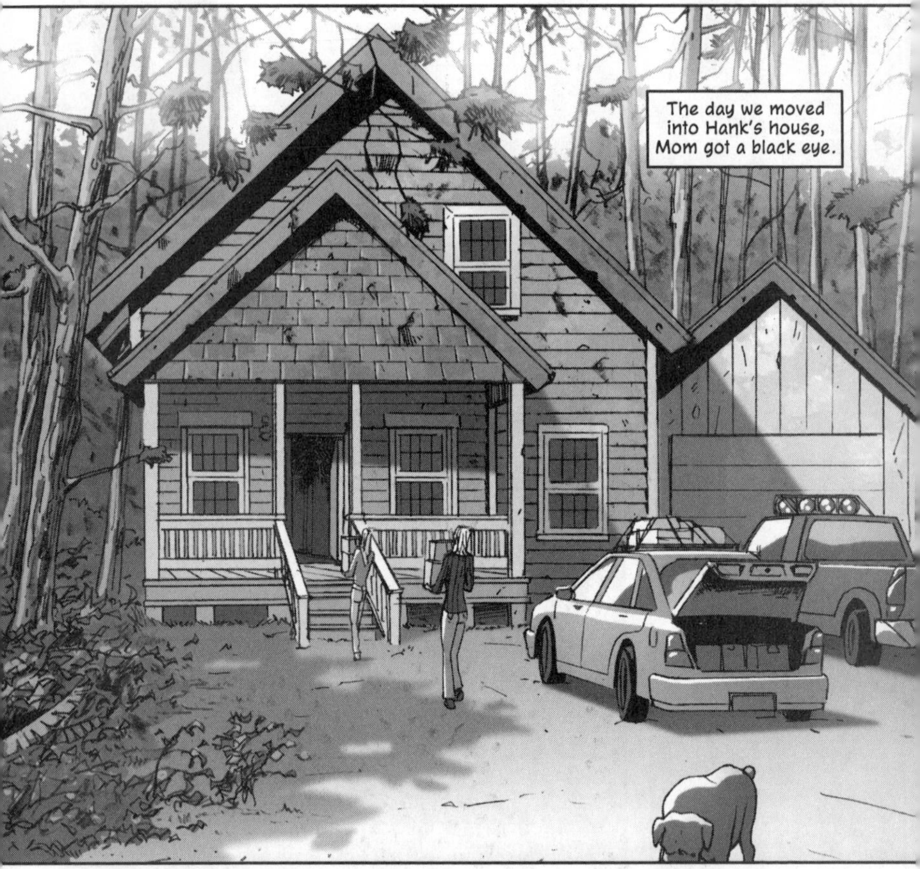
The day we moved
into Hank's house,
Mom got a black eye.

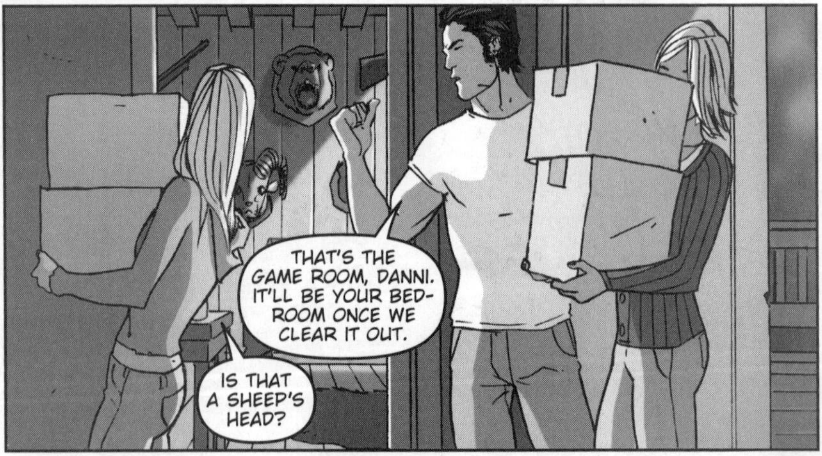
THAT'S THE GAME ROOM, DANNI. IT'LL BE YOUR BED-ROOM ONCE WE CLEAR IT OUT.
IS THAT A SHEEP'S HEAD?

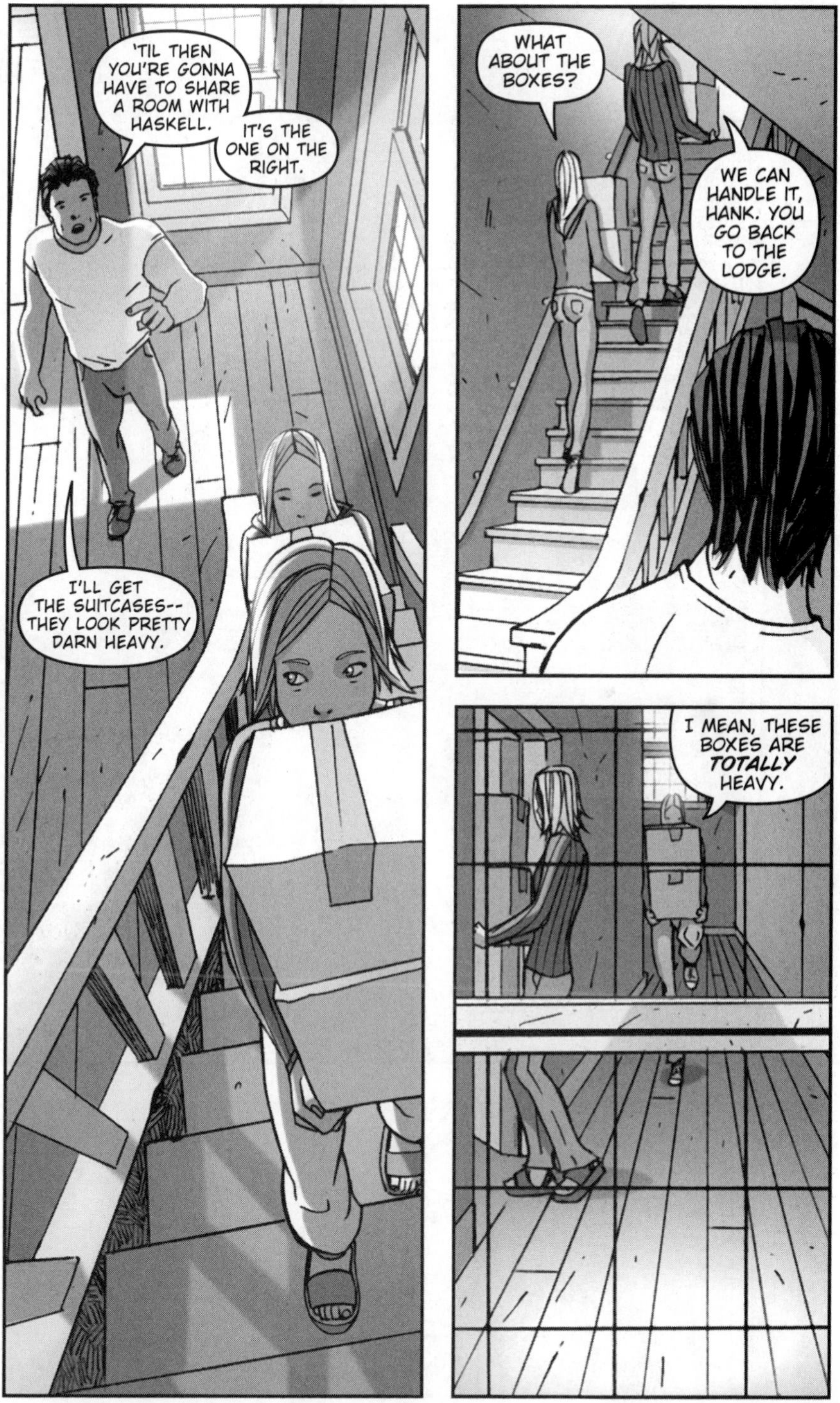
'TIL THEN YOU'RE GONNA HAVE TO SHARE A ROOM WITH HASKELL.
IT'S THE ONE ON THE RIGHT.
I'LL GET THE SUITCASES-- THEY LOOK PRETTY DARN HEAVY.
WHAT ABOUT THE BOXES?
WE CAN HANDLE IT, HANK. YOU GO BACK TO THE LODGE.
I MEAN, THESE BOXES ARE *TOTALLY* HEAVY.

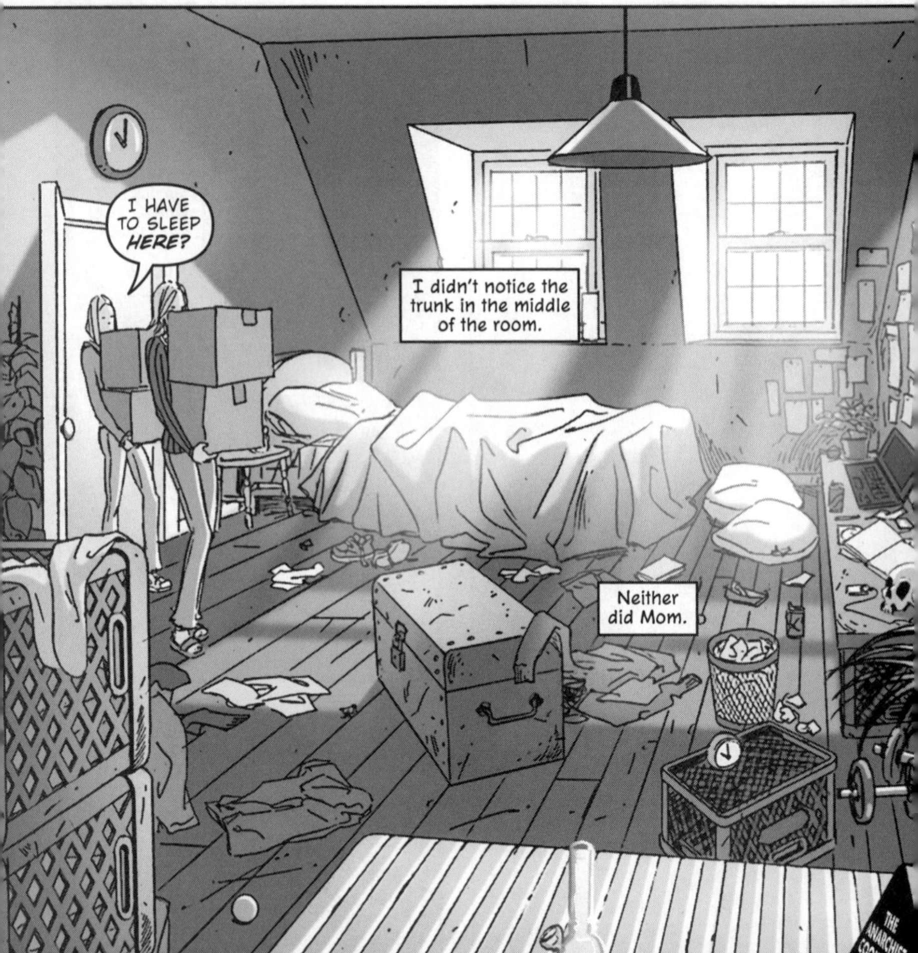
I HAVE TO SLEEP *HERE?*
I didn't notice the trunk in the middle of the room.
Neither did Mom.
ON THE ROAD
JACK KEROUAC
SIDDHARTHA HERMANN HESSE
THE ANARCHIST COOKBOOK

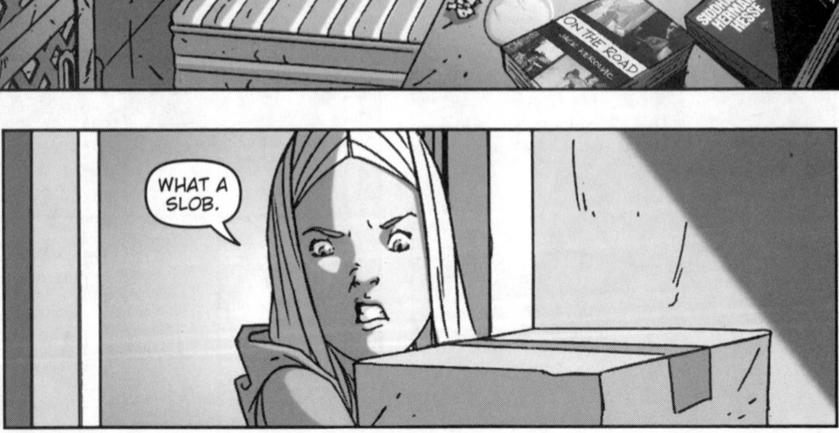
WHAT A SLOB.

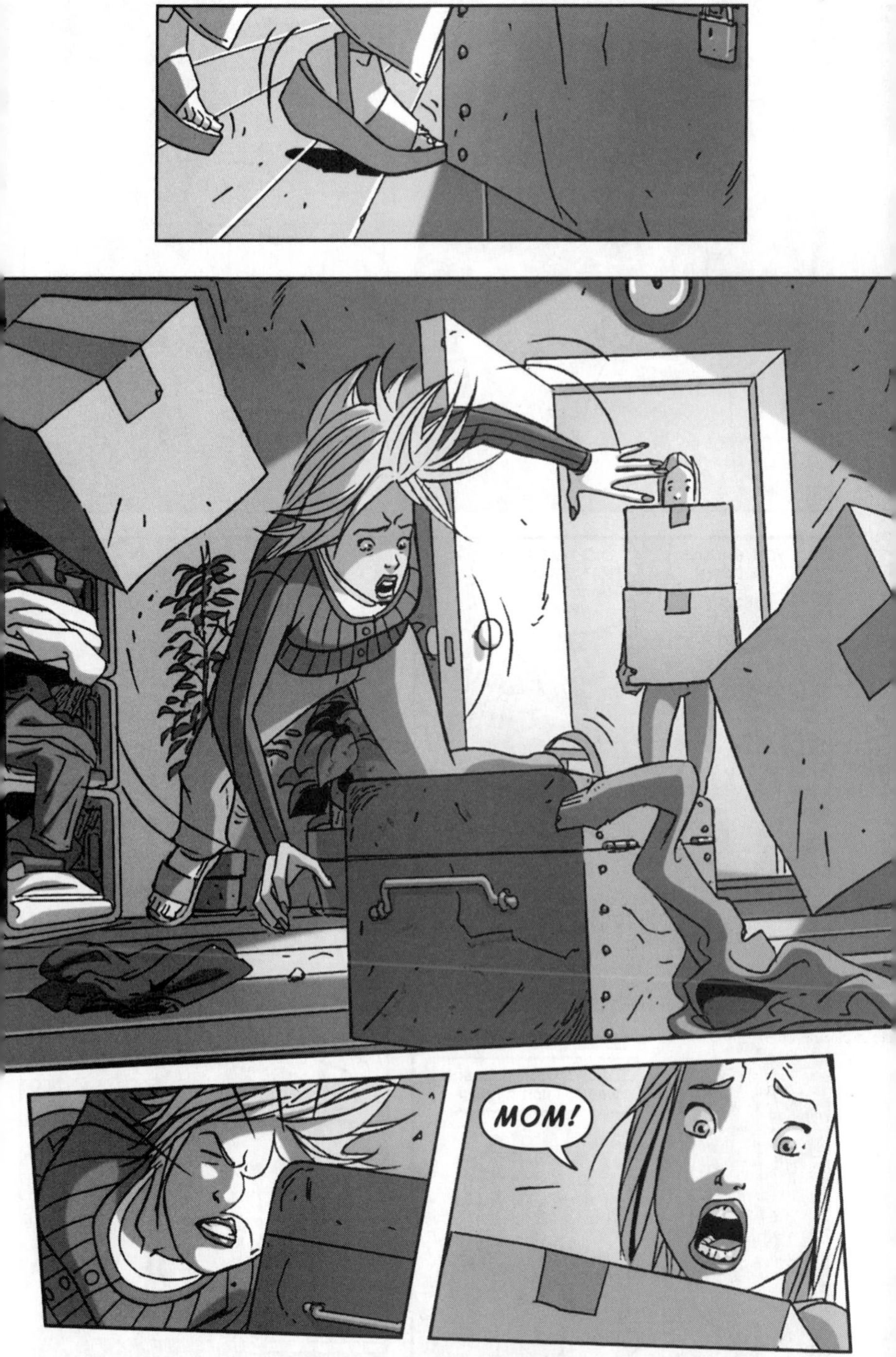
MOM!

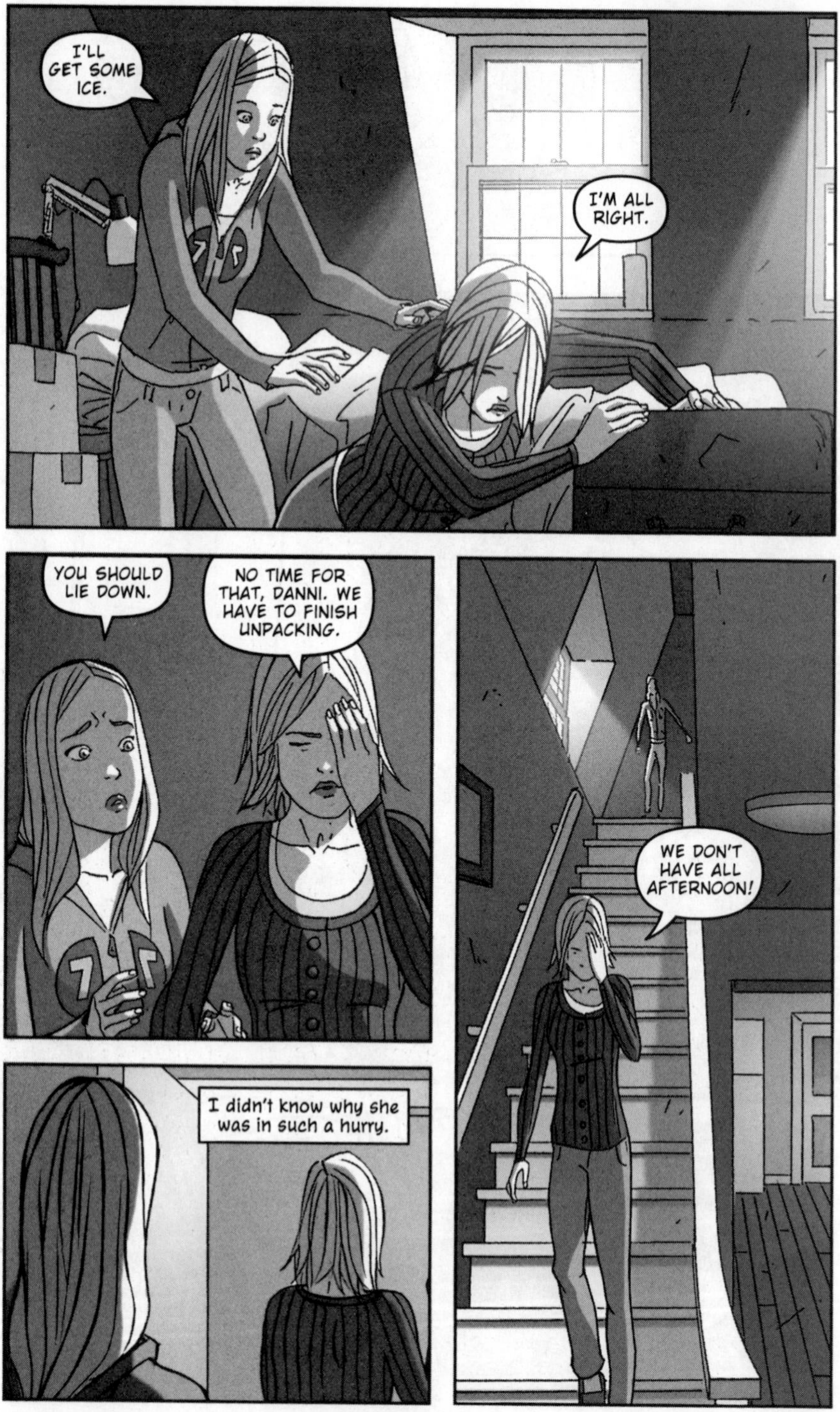
I'LL GET SOME ICE.
I'M ALL RIGHT.
YOU SHOULD LIE DOWN.
NO TIME FOR THAT, DANNI. WE HAVE TO FINISH UNPACKING.
I didn't know why she was in such a hurry.
WE DON'T HAVE ALL AFTERNOON!

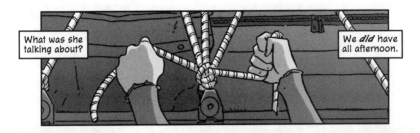

What was she talking about?

We *did* have all afternoon.

DON'T TAKE SO *MANY.* YOU'RE GOING TO *TRIP* AGAIN.

DON'T WORRY, SWEETIE. I'M FINE.

She didn't take a rest even after we were finished unpacking.

SSSSSSS

CRACKLE

She said she had to get dinner on the table before Hank came back.

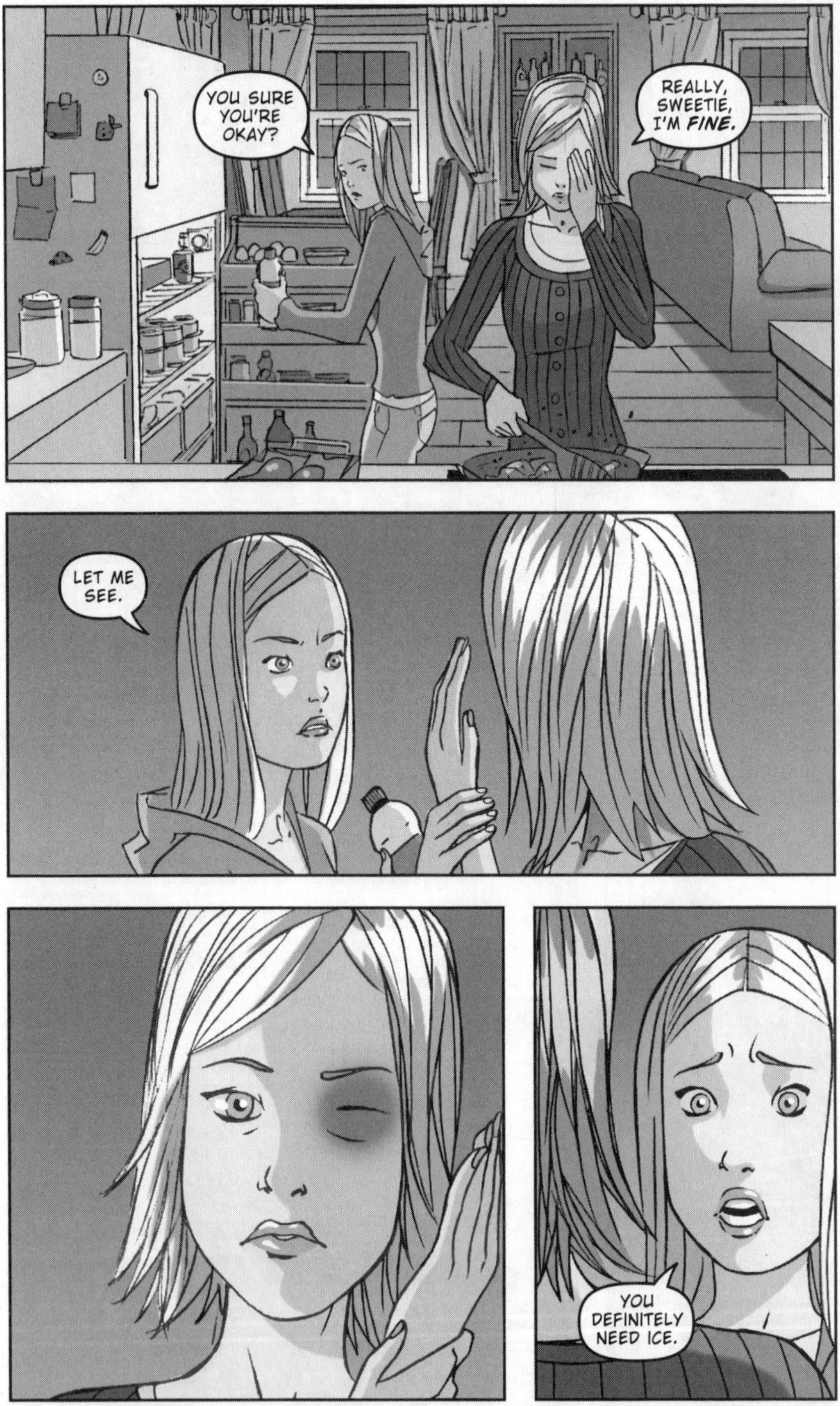
YOU SURE YOU'RE OKAY?
REALLY, SWEETIE, I'M *FINE.*
LET ME SEE.
YOU DEFINITELY NEED ICE.

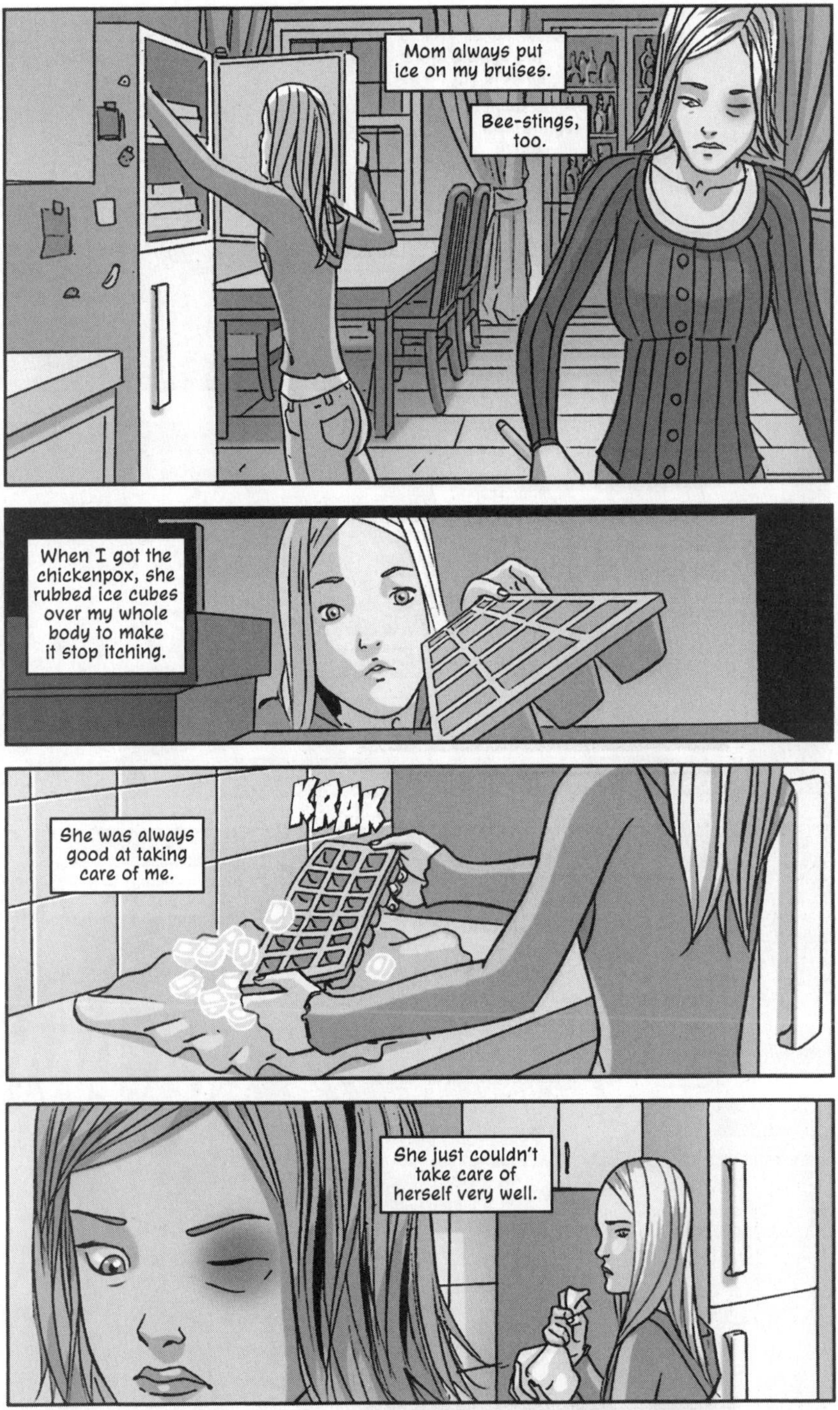
Mom always put ice on my bruises.
Bee-stings, too.
When I got the chickenpox, she rubbed ice cubes over my whole body to make it stop itching.
KRAK
She was always good at taking care of me.
She just couldn't take care of herself very well.

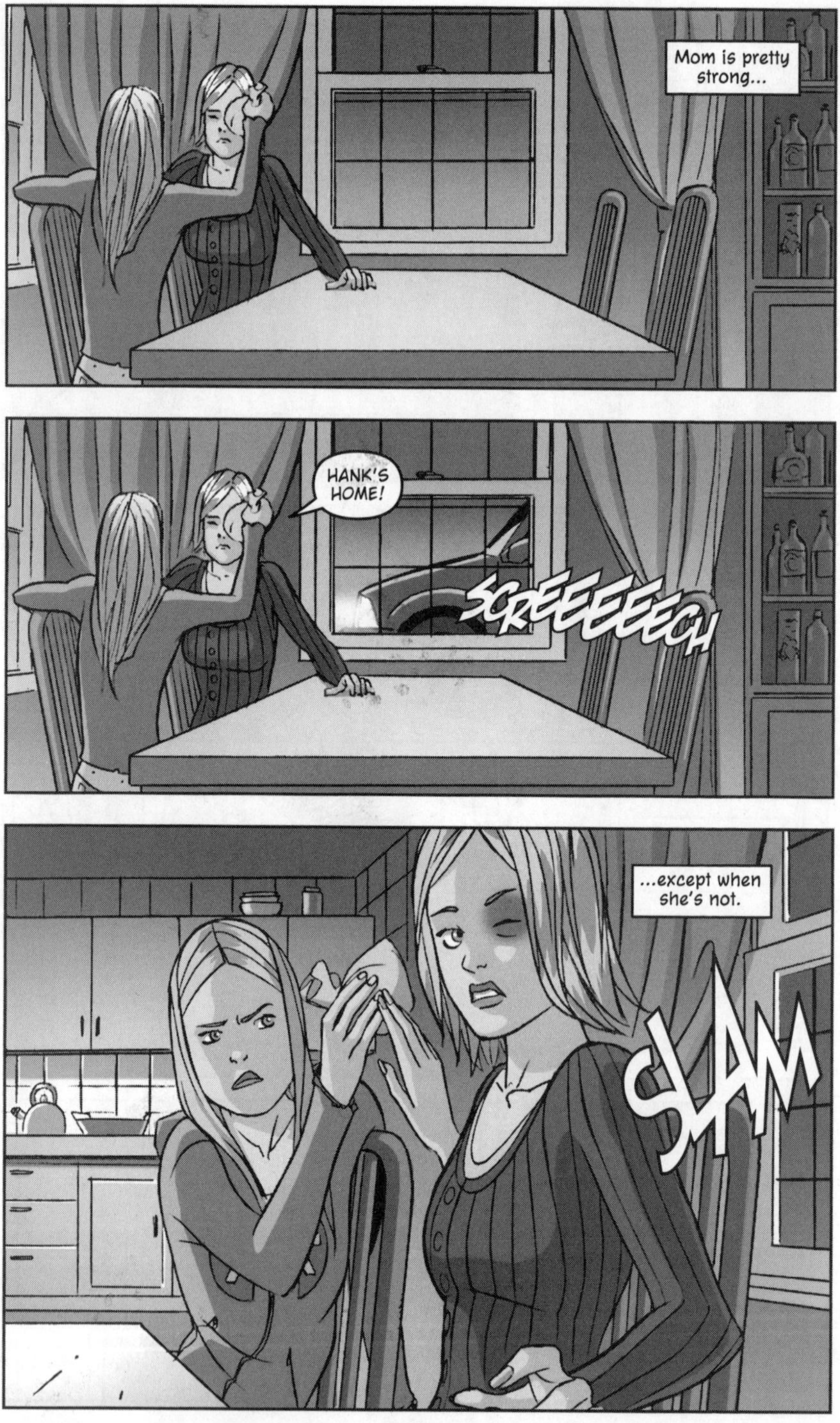
Mom is pretty strong...
HANK'S HOME!
SCREEEEEECH
...except when she's not.
SLAM

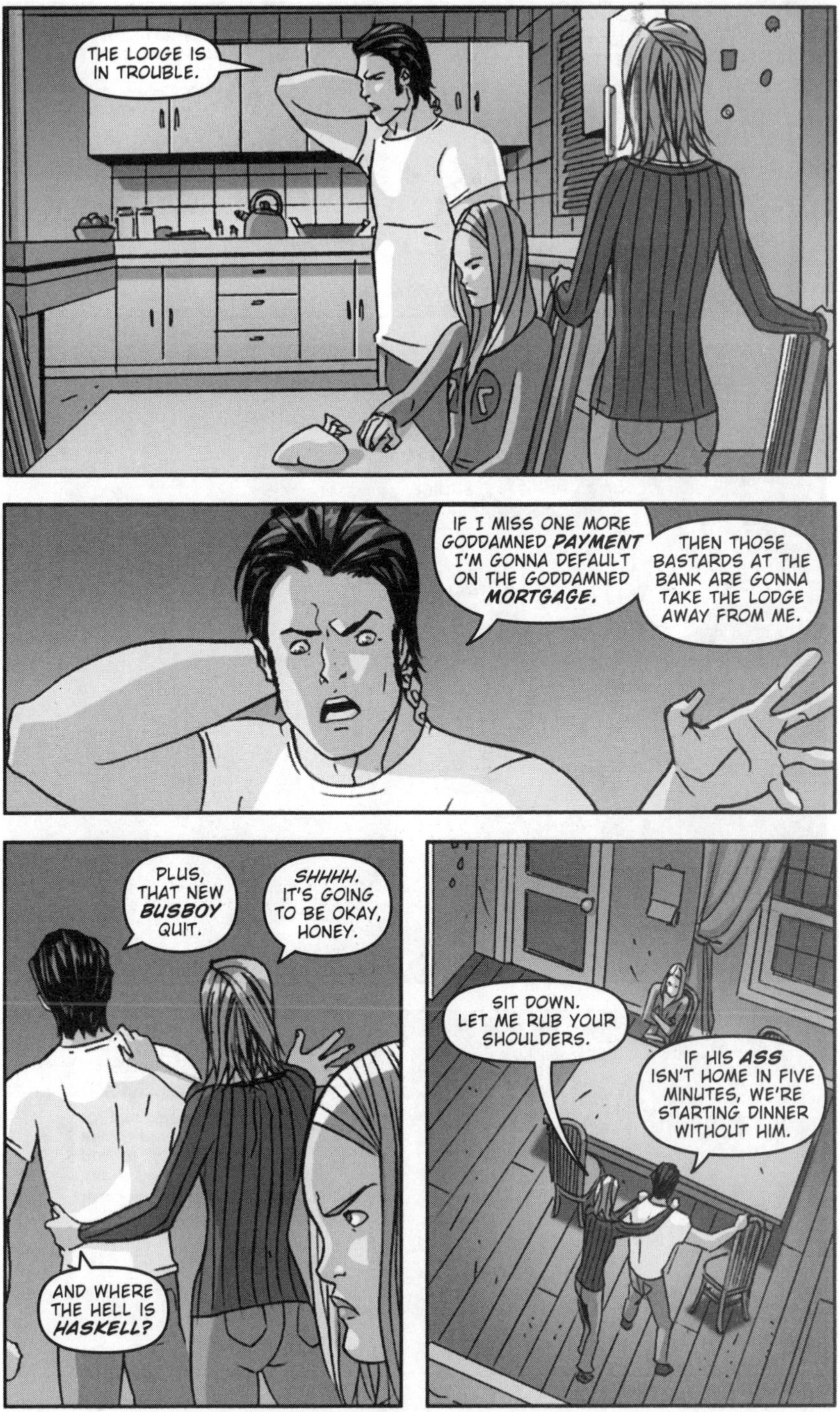
THE LODGE IS IN TROUBLE.
IF I MISS ONE MORE GODDAMNED PAYMENT I'M GONNA DEFAULT ON THE GODDAMNED MORTGAGE.
THEN THOSE BASTARDS AT THE BANK ARE GONNA TAKE THE LODGE AWAY FROM ME.
PLUS, THAT NEW BUSBOY QUIT.
SHHHH. IT'S GOING TO BE OKAY, HONEY.
AND WHERE THE HELL IS HASKELL?
SIT DOWN. LET ME RUB YOUR SHOULDERS.
IF HIS ASS ISN'T HOME IN FIVE MINUTES, WE'RE STARTING DINNER WITHOUT HIM.

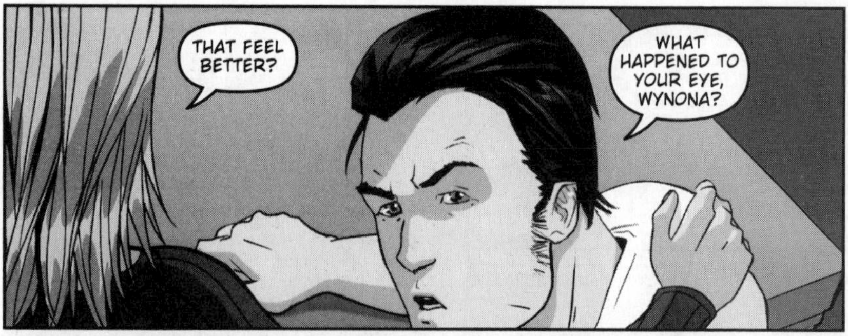
THAT FEEL BETTER?
WHAT HAPPENED TO YOUR EYE, WYNONA?

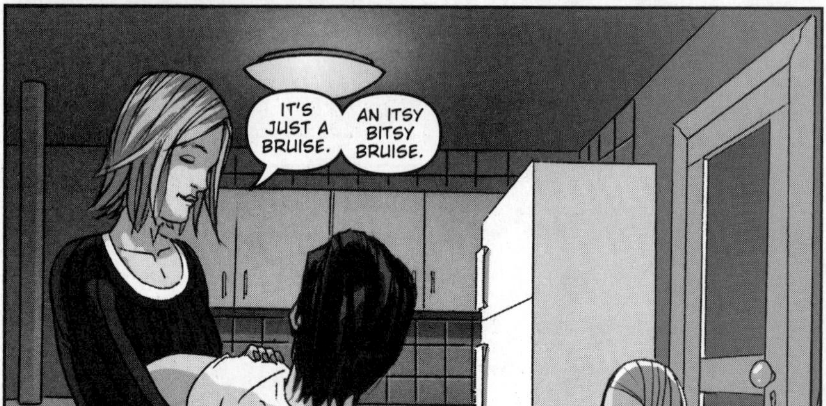
IT'S JUST A BRUISE.
AN ITSY BITSY BRUISE.

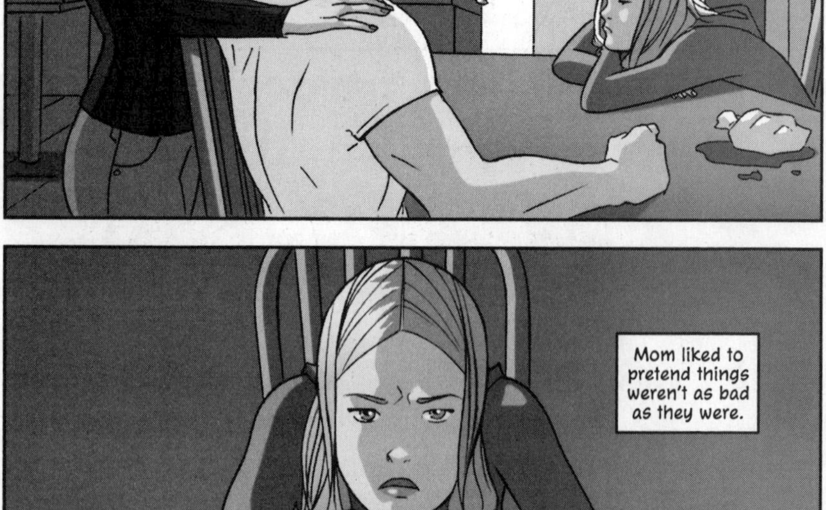
Mom liked to pretend things weren't as bad as they were.

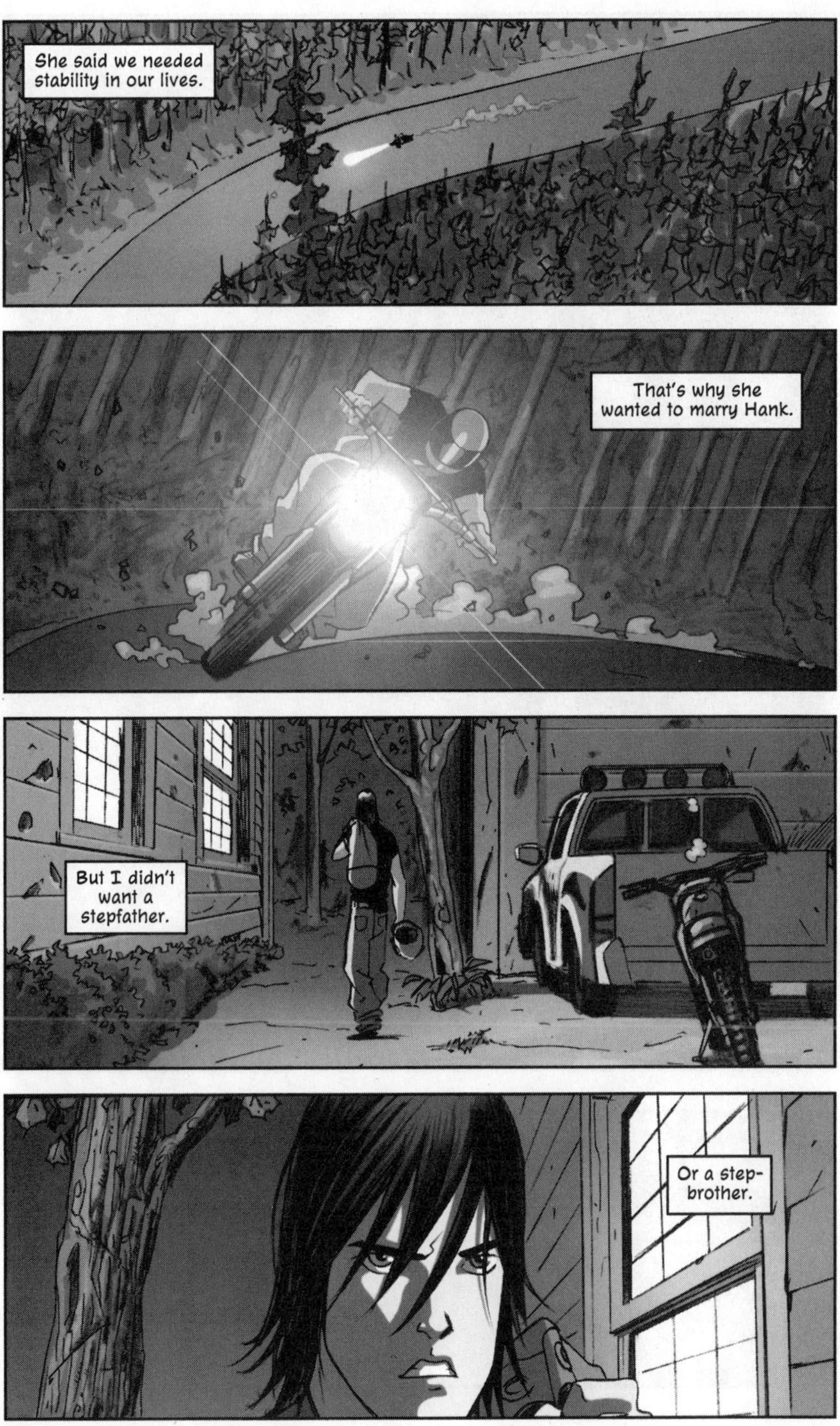
She said we needed stability in our lives.
That's why she wanted to marry Hank.
But I didn't want a stepfather.
Or a step-brother.

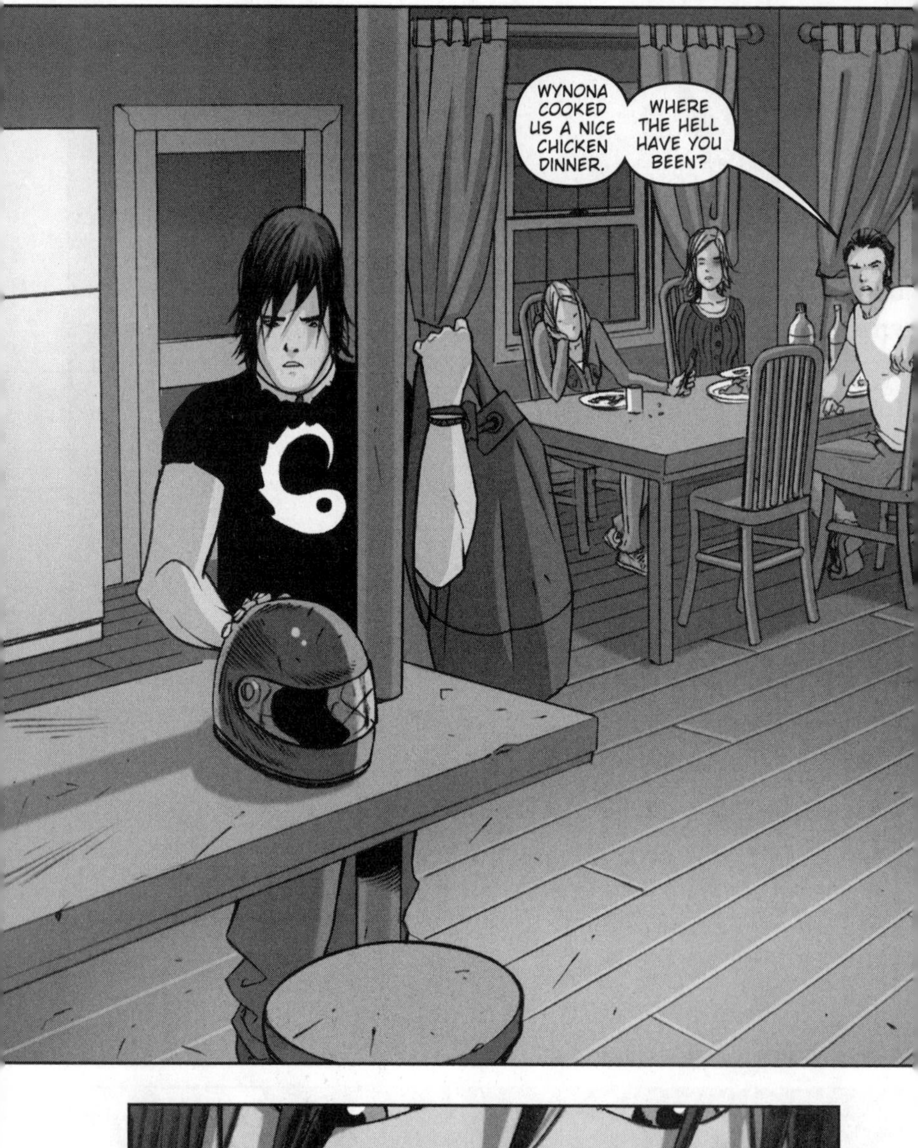
WYNONA COOKED US A NICE CHICKEN DINNER.
WHERE THE HELL HAVE YOU BEEN?

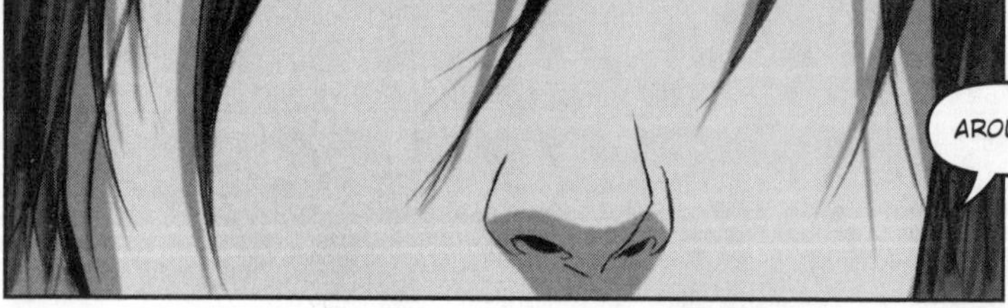
AROUND.

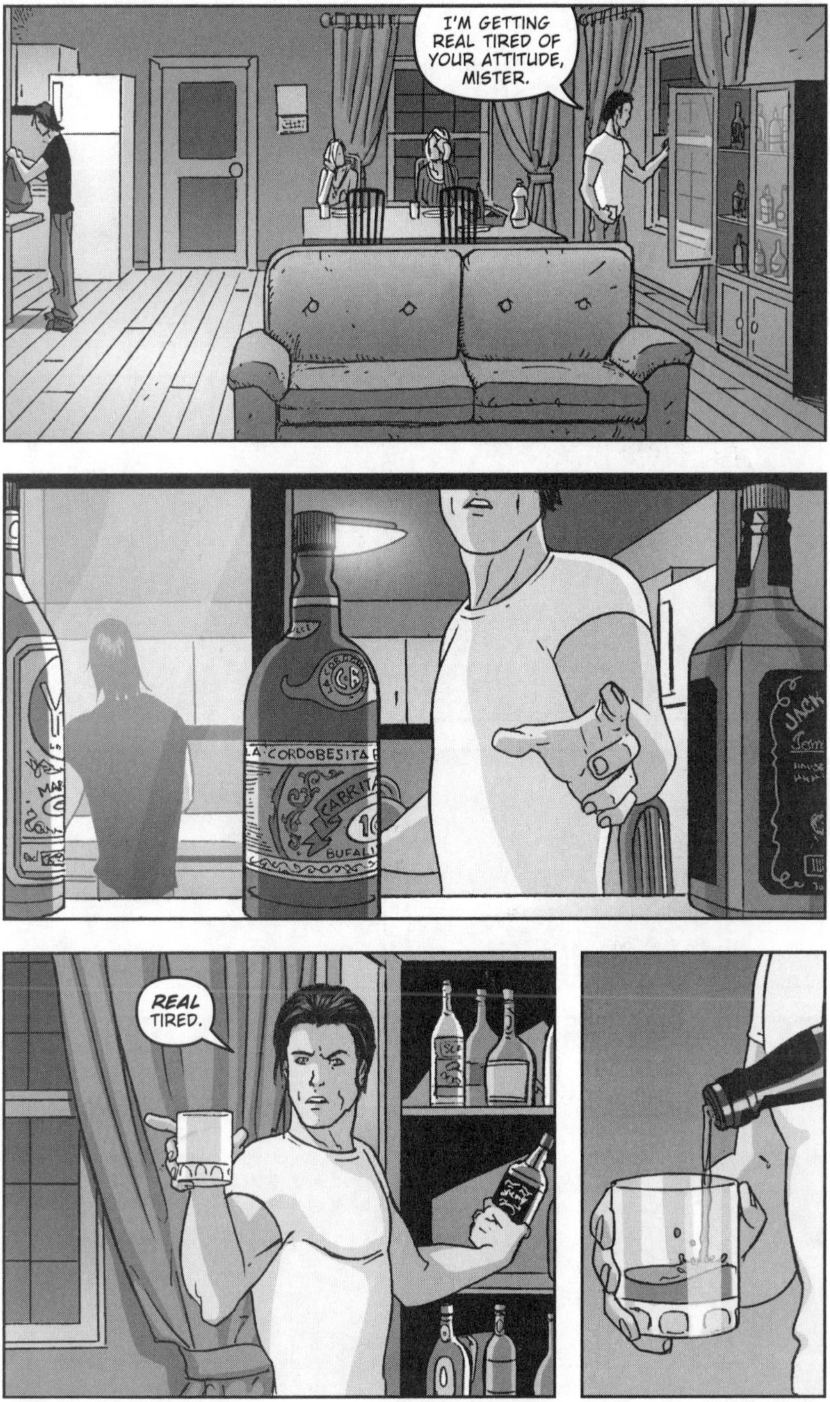
I'M GETTING REAL TIRED OF YOUR ATTITUDE, MISTER.
LA CORDOBESITA
REAL TIRED.

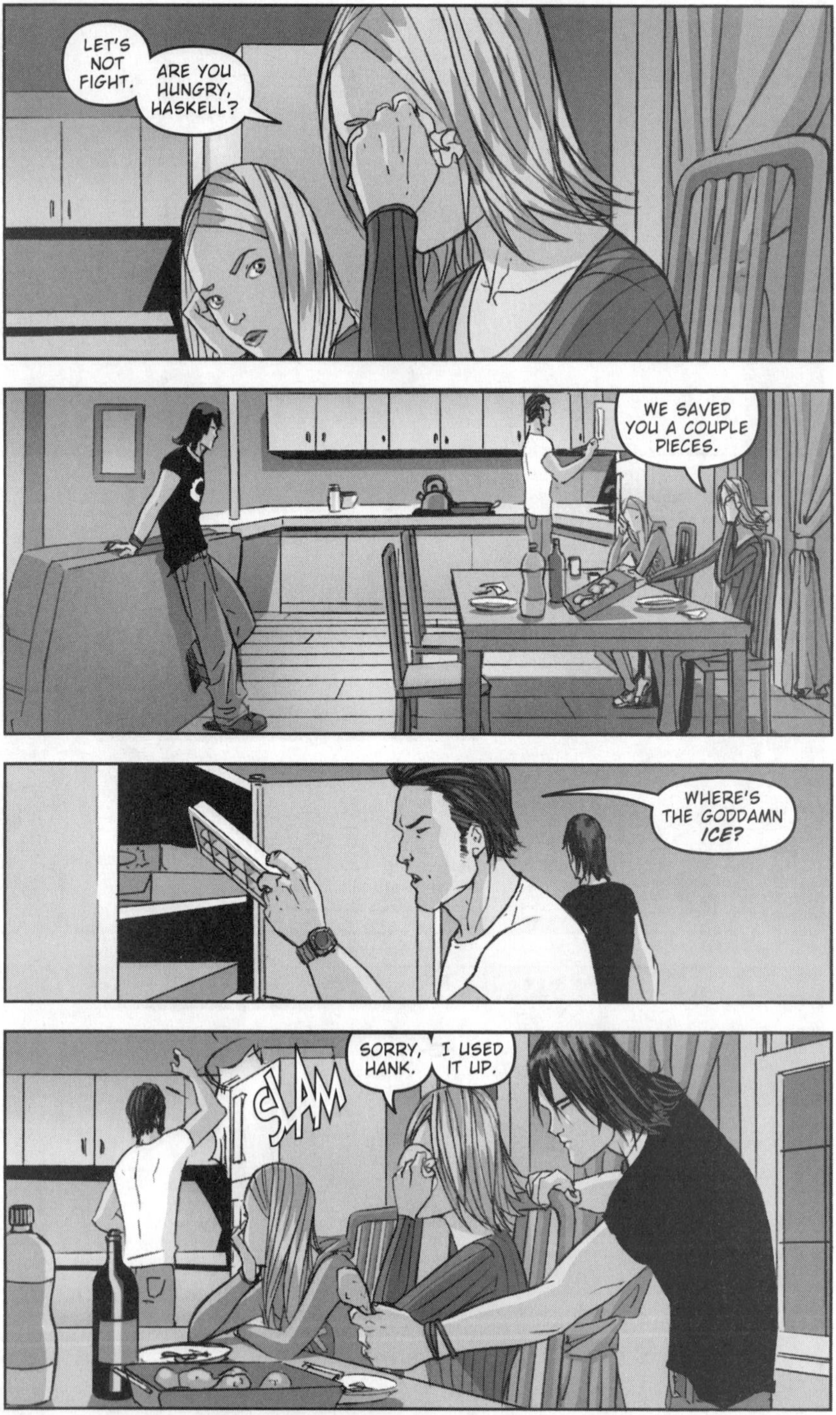
LET'S NOT FIGHT.
ARE YOU HUNGRY, HASKELL?
WE SAVED YOU A COUPLE PIECES.
WHERE'S THE GODDAMN *ICE?*
SLAM
SORRY, HANK.
I USED IT UP.

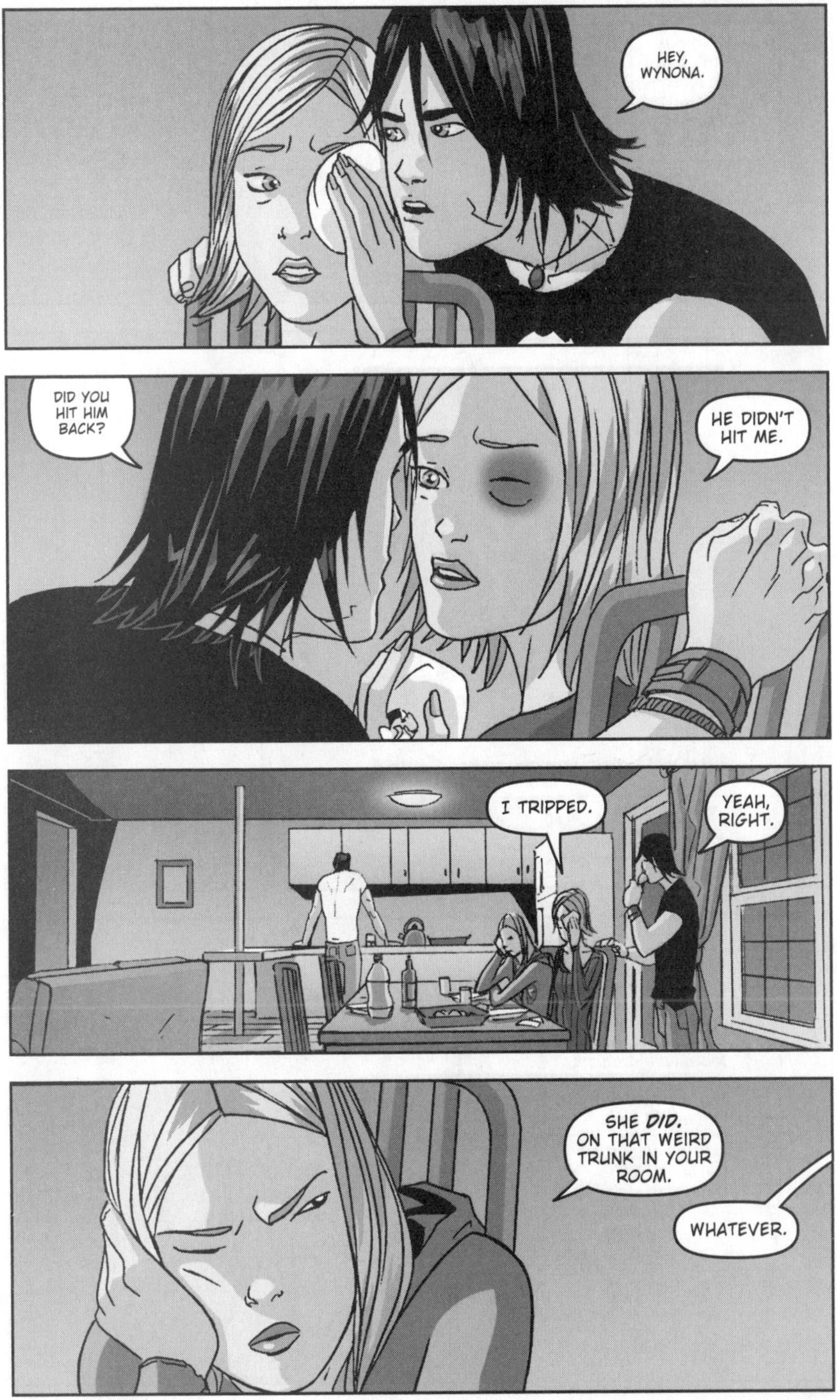
HEY, WYNONA.
DID YOU HIT HIM BACK?
HE DIDN'T HIT ME.
I TRIPPED.
YEAH, RIGHT.
SHE *DID.* ON THAT WEIRD TRUNK IN YOUR ROOM.
WHATEVER.

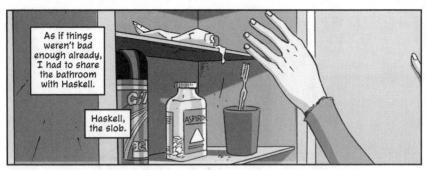

As if things weren't bad enough already, I had to share the bathroom with Haskell.

Haskell, the slob.

GROSS.

I kept telling myself that it was just temporary.

Mom would change her mind about Hank, and then we'd move out of here.

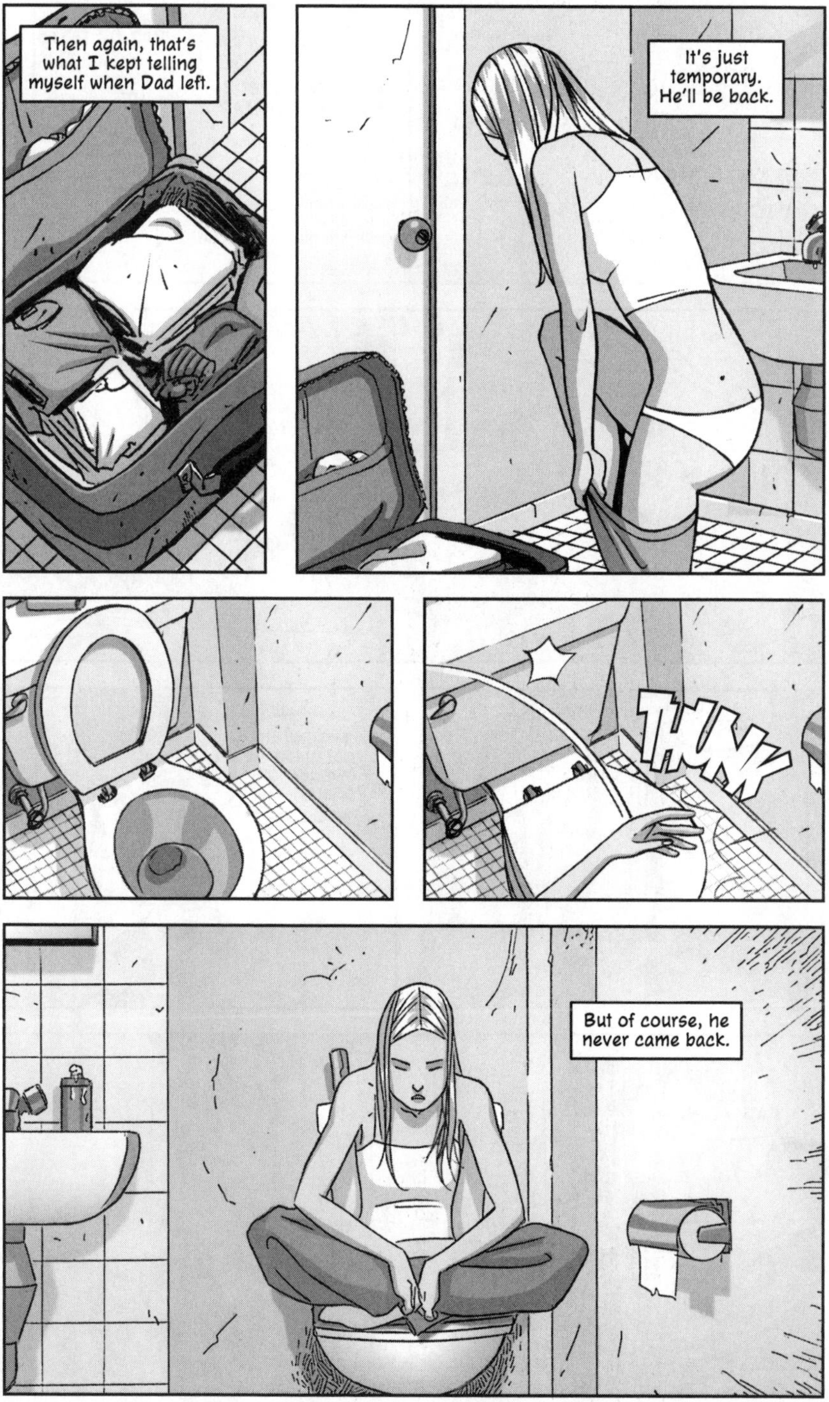
Then again, that's what I kept telling myself when Dad left.
It's just temporary. He'll be back.
THUNK
But of course, he never came back.

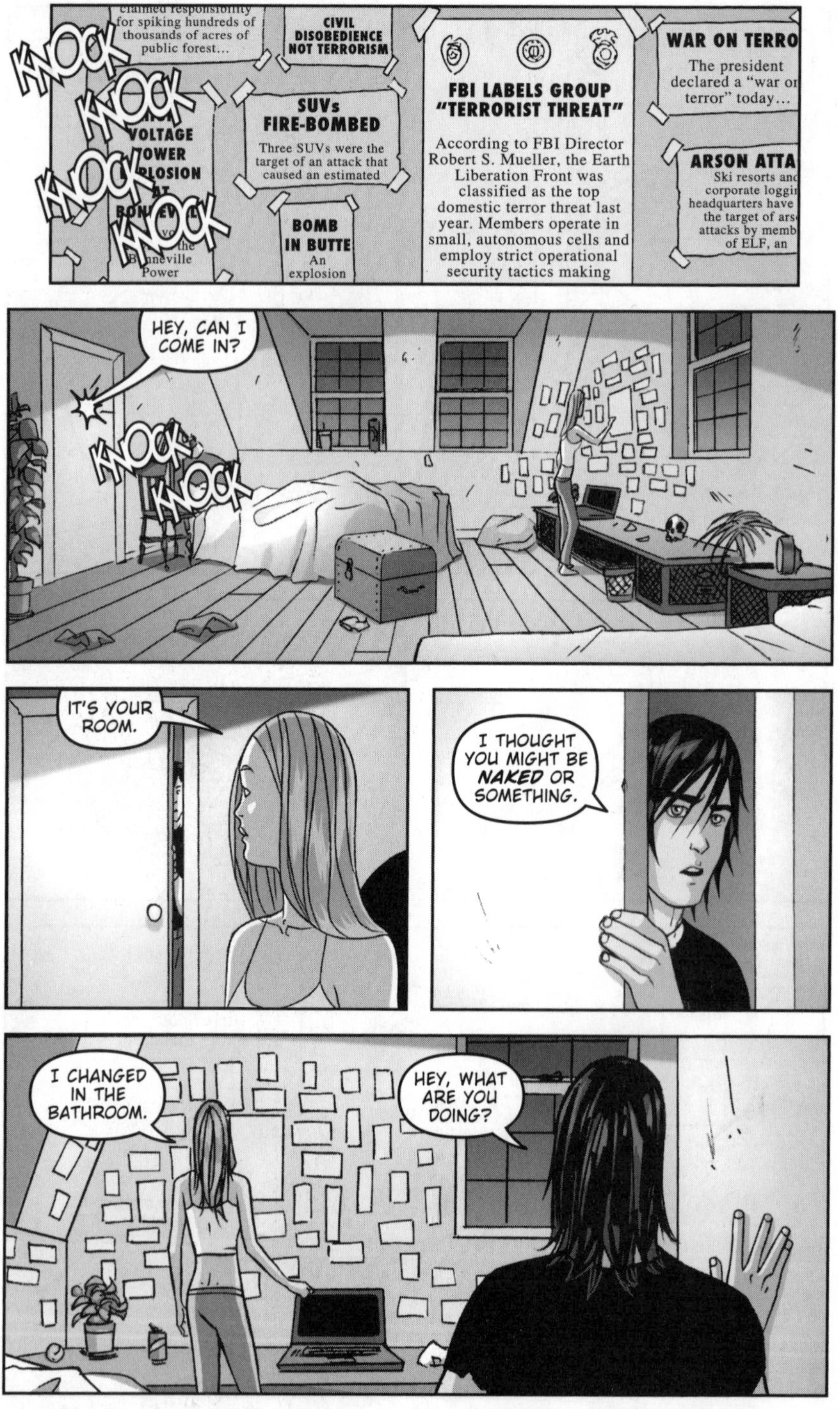
KNOCK KNOCK KNOCK KNOCK
for spiking hundreds of thousands of acres of public forest...
CIVIL DISOBEDIENCE NOT TERRORISM
SUVs FIRE-BOMBED
Three SUVs were the target of an attack that caused an estimated
VOLTAGE TOWER
BOMB IN BUTTE
An explosion
FBI LABELS GROUP "TERRORIST THREAT"
According to FBI Director Robert S. Mueller, the Earth Liberation Front was classified as the top domestic terror threat last year. Members operate in small, autonomous cells and employ strict operational security tactics making
WAR ON TERRO
The president declared a "war o terror" today...
ARSON ATTA
Ski resorts and corporate loggi headquarters have the target of ars attacks by memb of ELF, an
HEY, CAN I COME IN?
KNOCK KNOCK
IT'S YOUR ROOM.
I THOUGHT YOU MIGHT BE *NAKED* OR SOMETHING.
I CHANGED IN THE BATHROOM.
HEY, WHAT ARE YOU DOING?

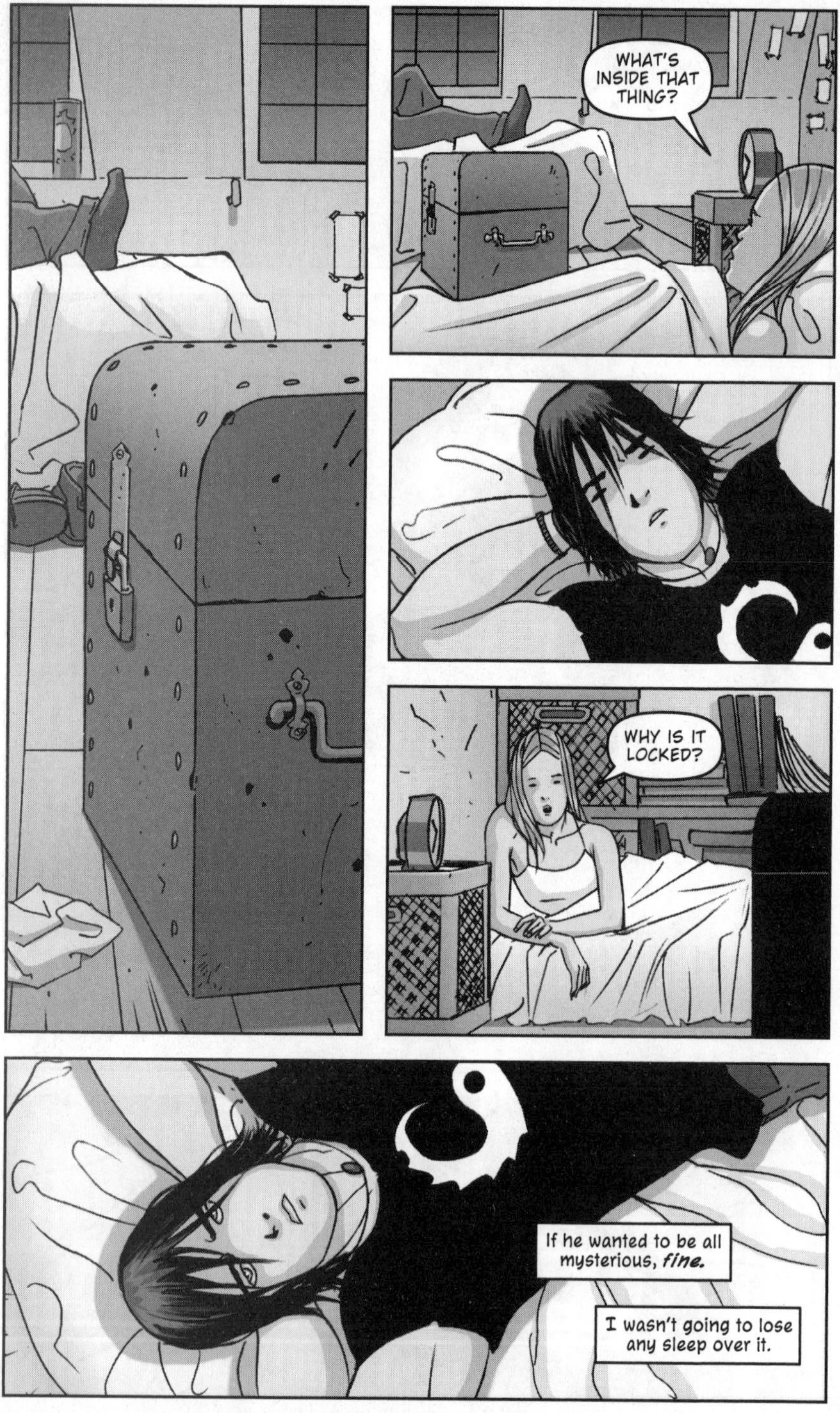
WHAT'S INSIDE THAT THING?
WHY IS IT LOCKED?
If he wanted to be all mysterious, *fine.*
I wasn't going to lose any sleep over it.

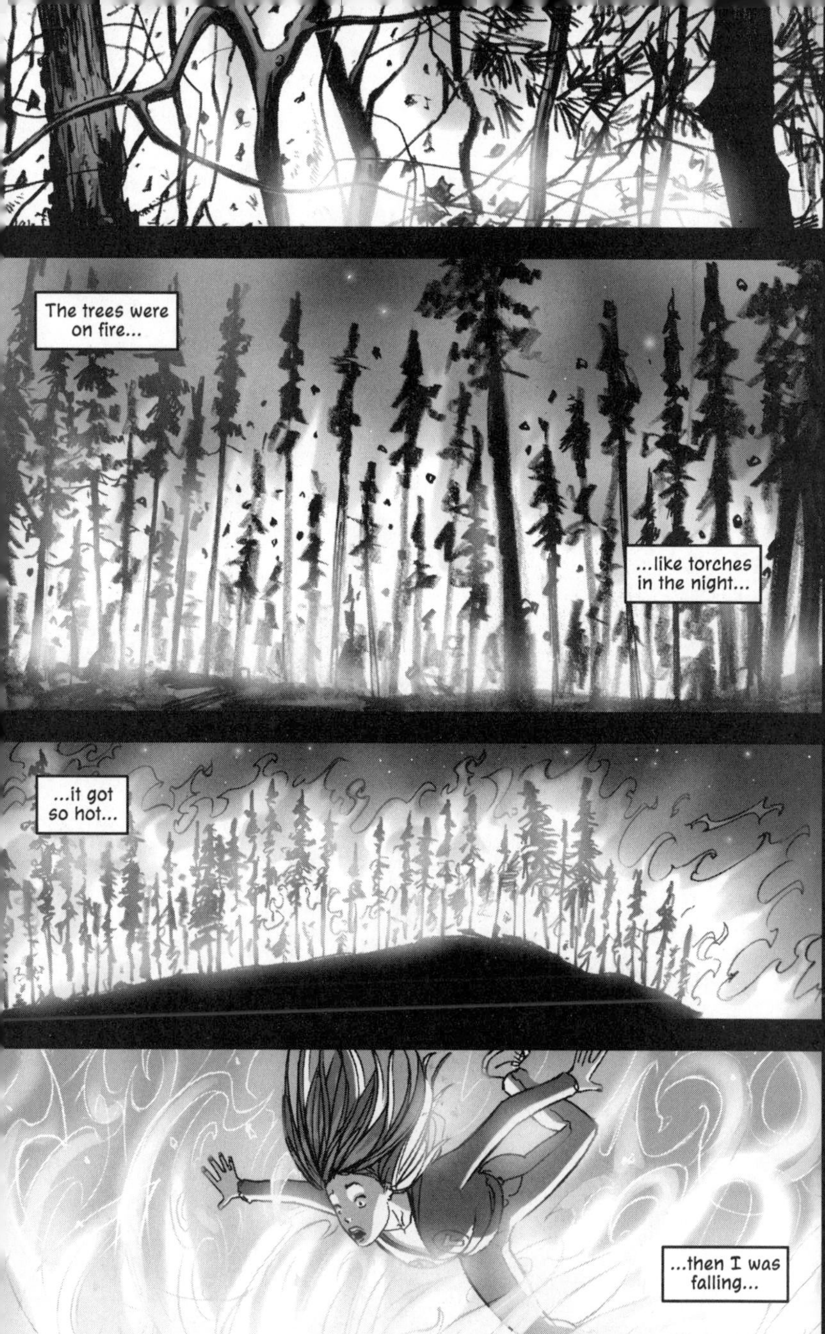
The trees were on fire...
...like torches in the night...
...it got so hot...
...then I was falling...

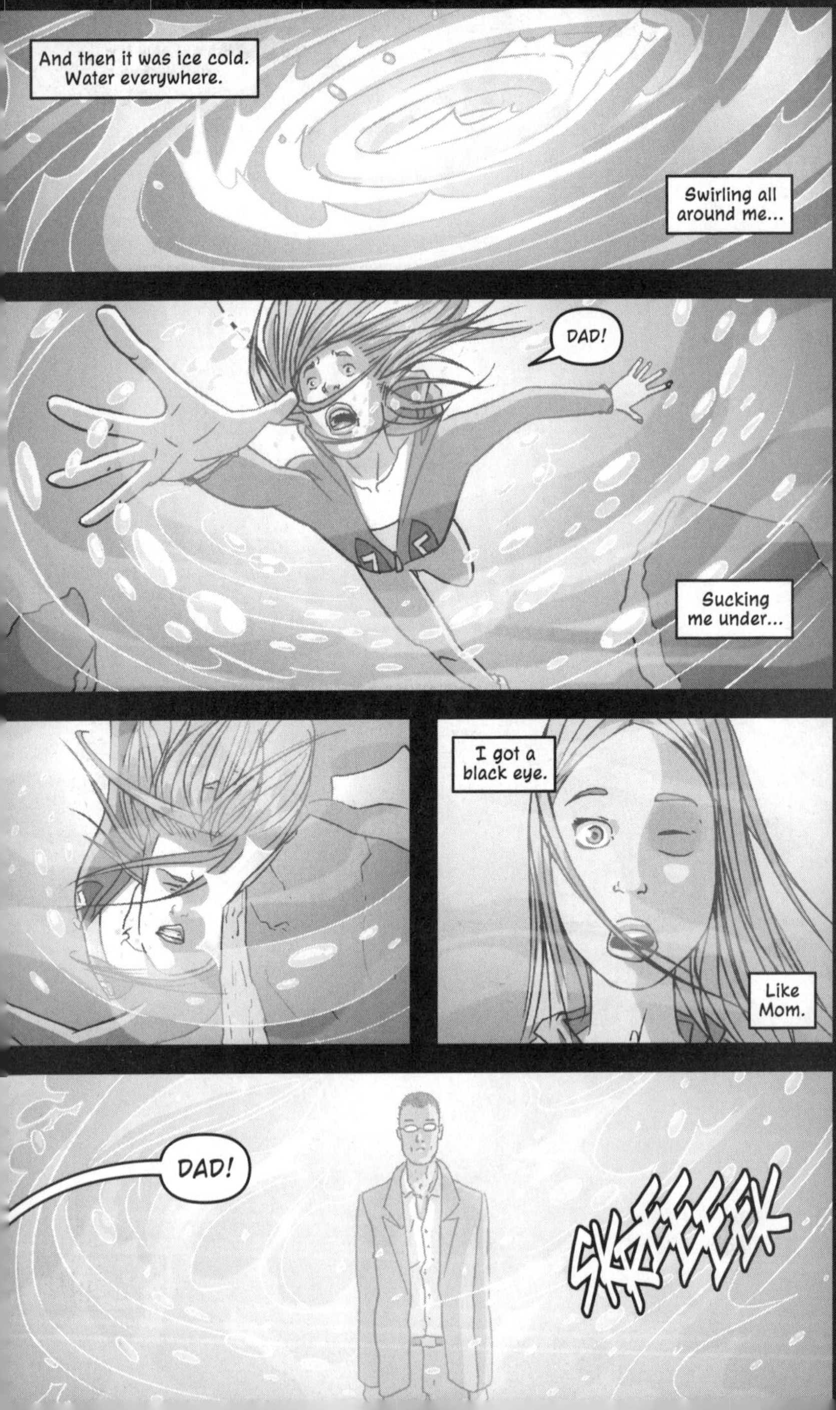
And then it was ice cold. Water everywhere.
Swirling all around me...
DAD!
Sucking me under...
I got a black eye.
Like Mom.
DAD!
SKREEEEK

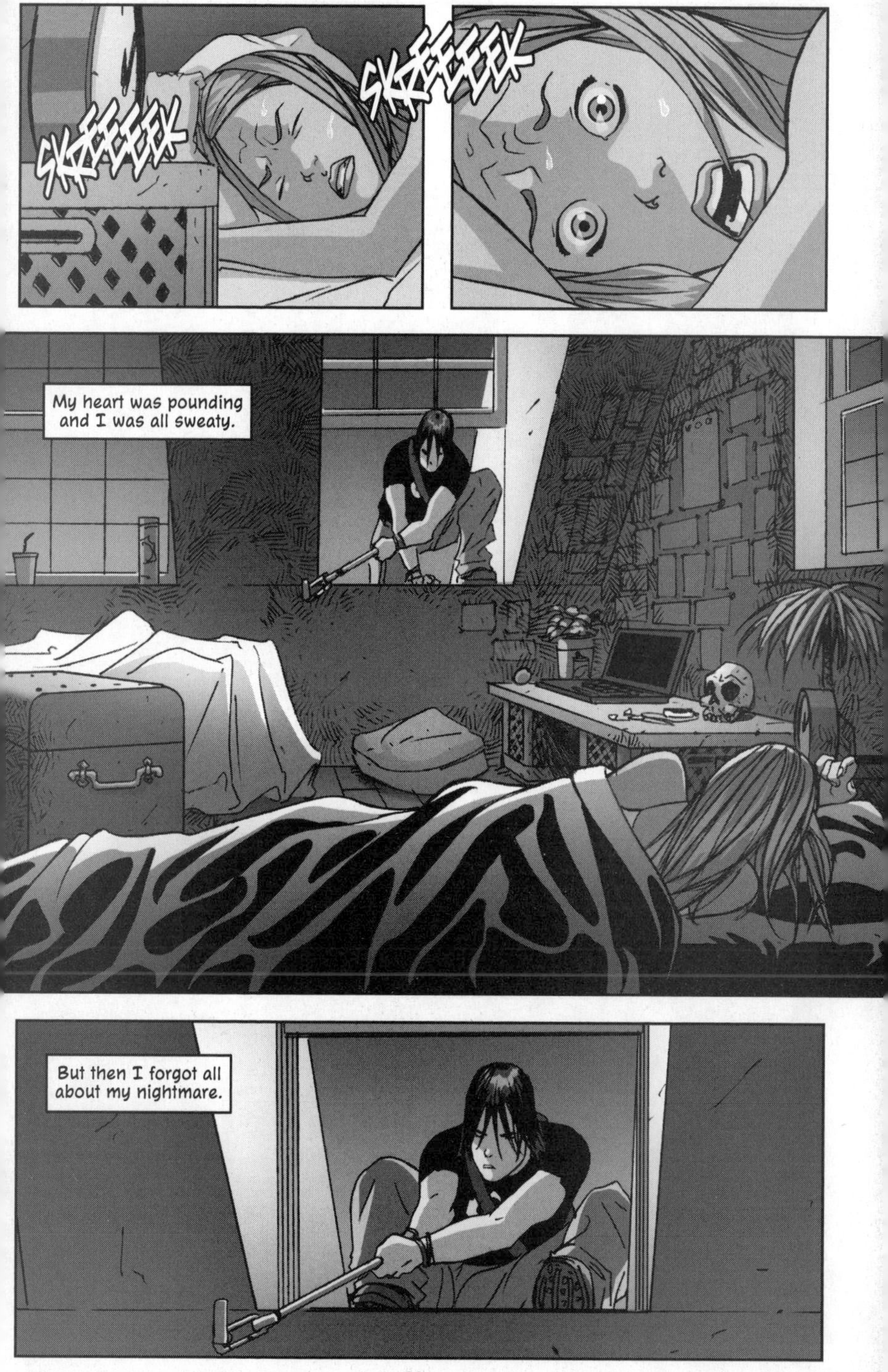
SKREEEEK
SKREEEEK
My heart was pounding and I was all sweaty.
But then I forgot all about my nightmare.

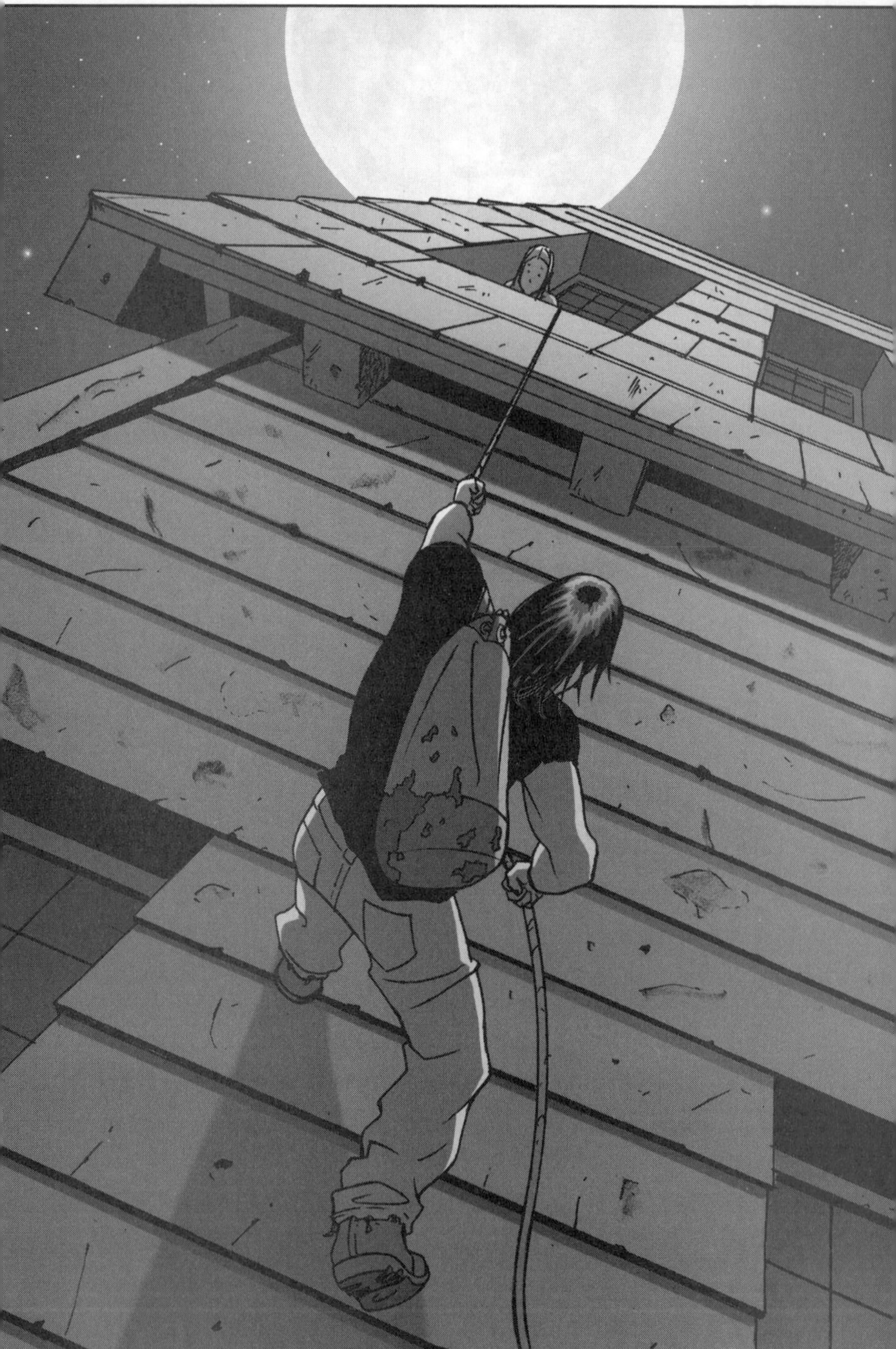

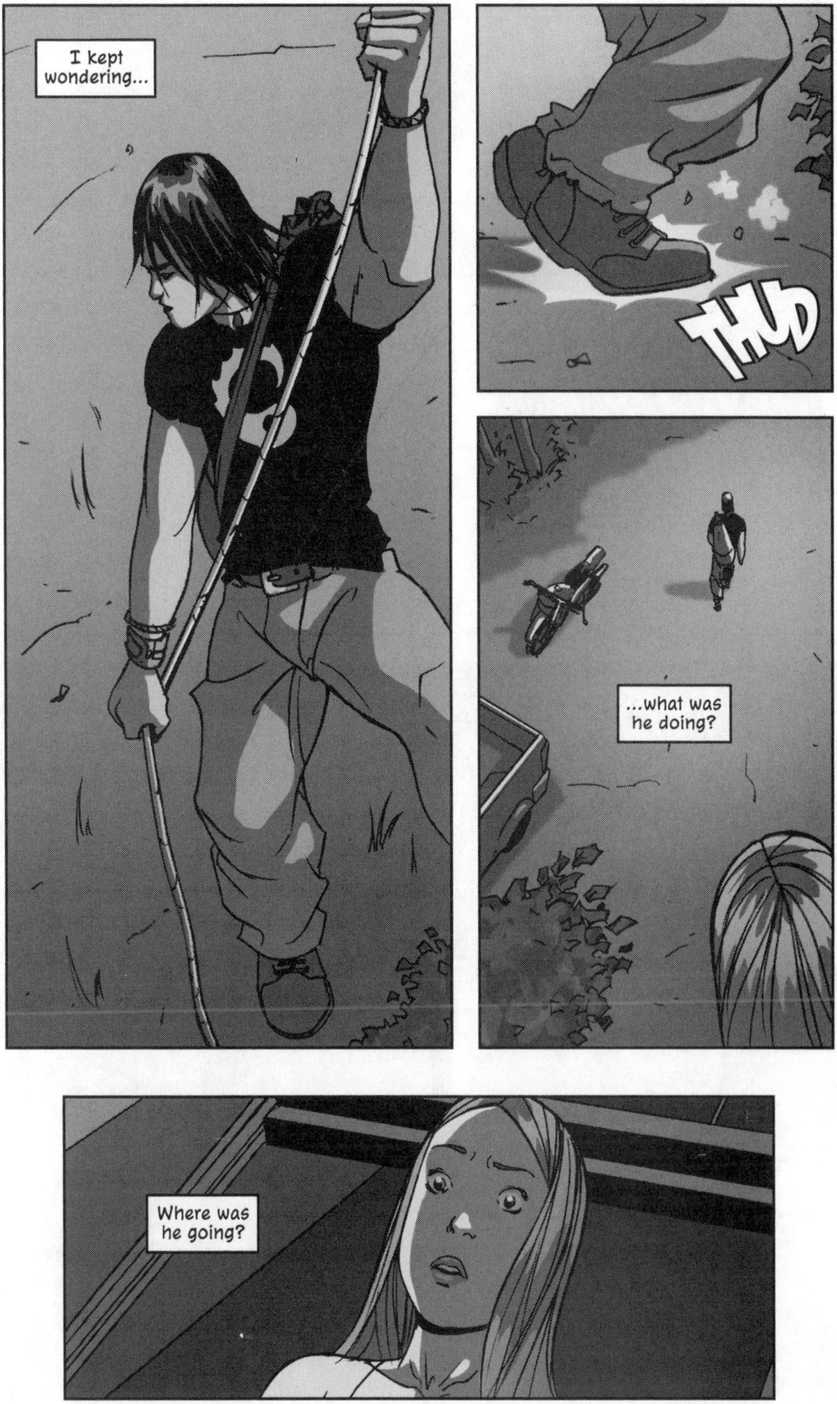
I kept wondering...
THUD
...what was he doing?
Where was he going?

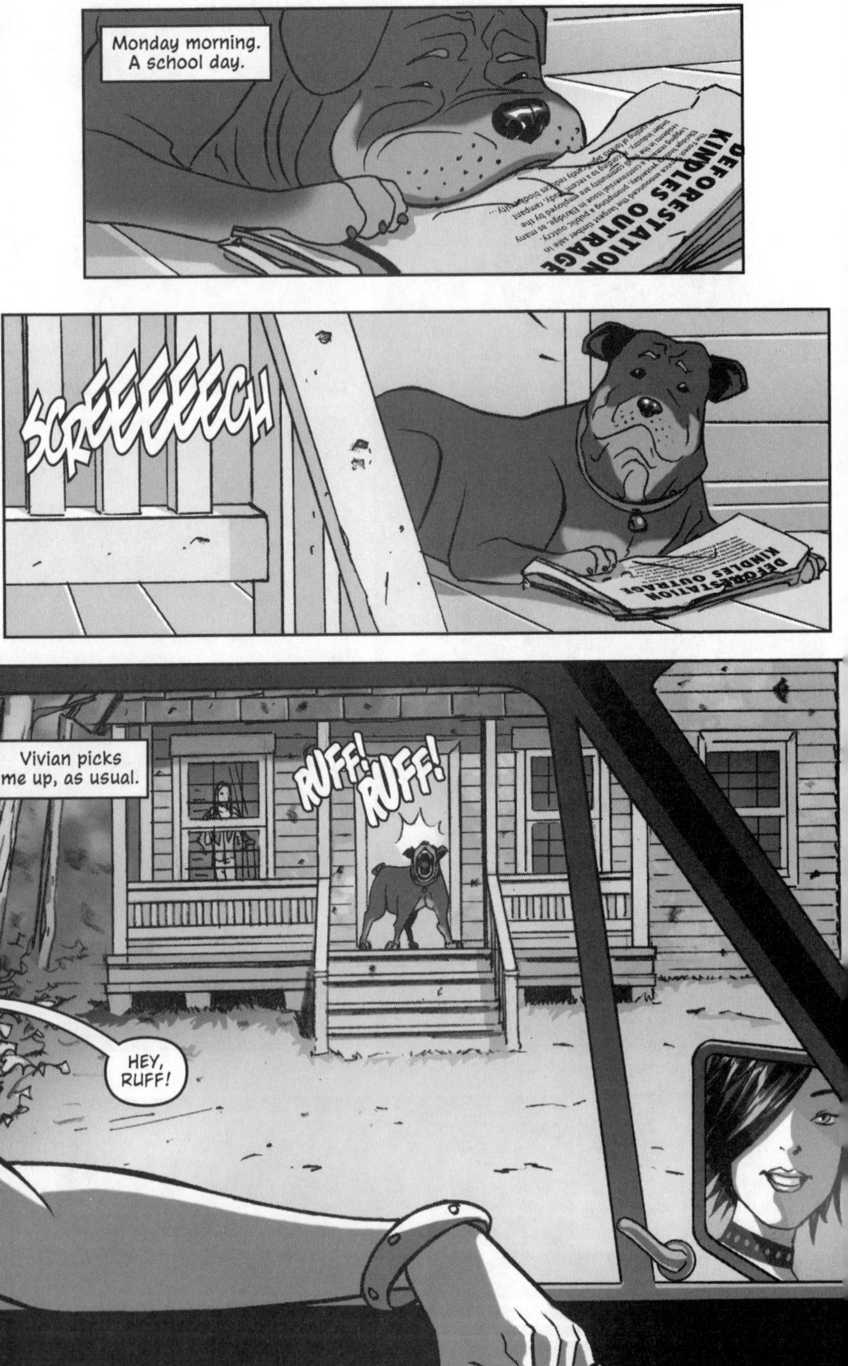
Monday morning. A school day.
DEFORESTATION KINDLES OUTRAGE
SCREEEEEECH
DEFORESTATION KINDLES OUTRAGE
Vivian picks me up, as usual.
RUFF! RUFF!
HEY, RUFF!

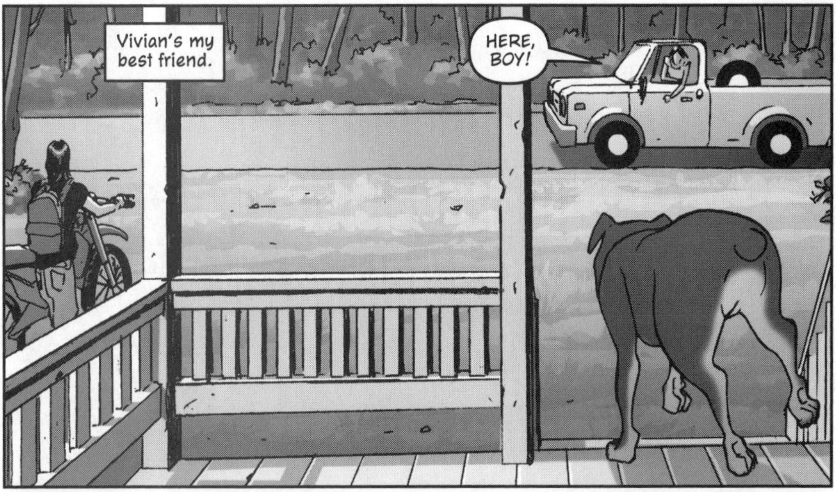
Vivian's my best friend.
HERE, BOY!

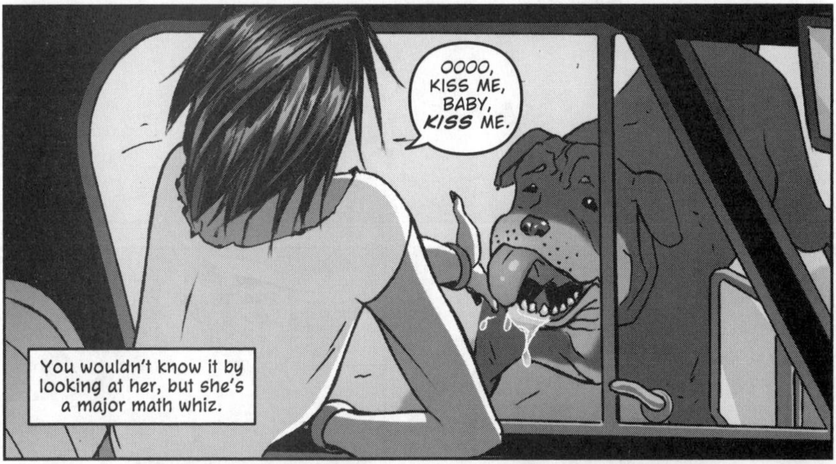
OOOO, KISS ME, BABY, KISS ME.
You wouldn't know it by looking at her, but she's a major math whiz.

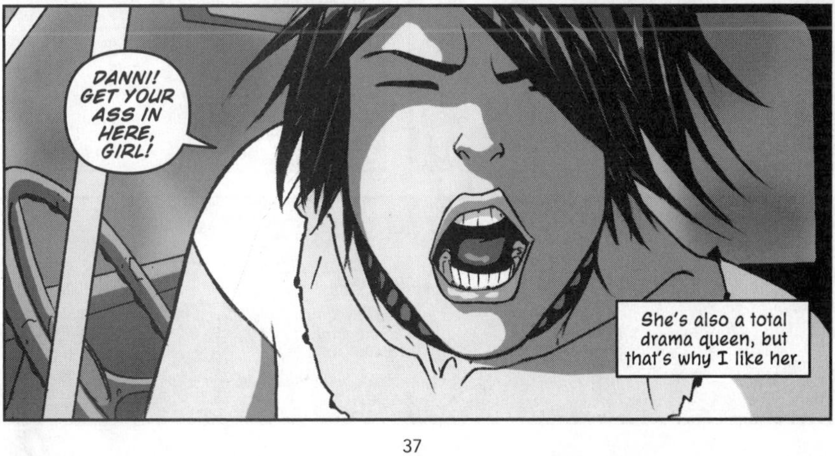
DANNI! GET YOUR ASS IN HERE, GIRL!
She's also a total drama queen, but that's why I like her.

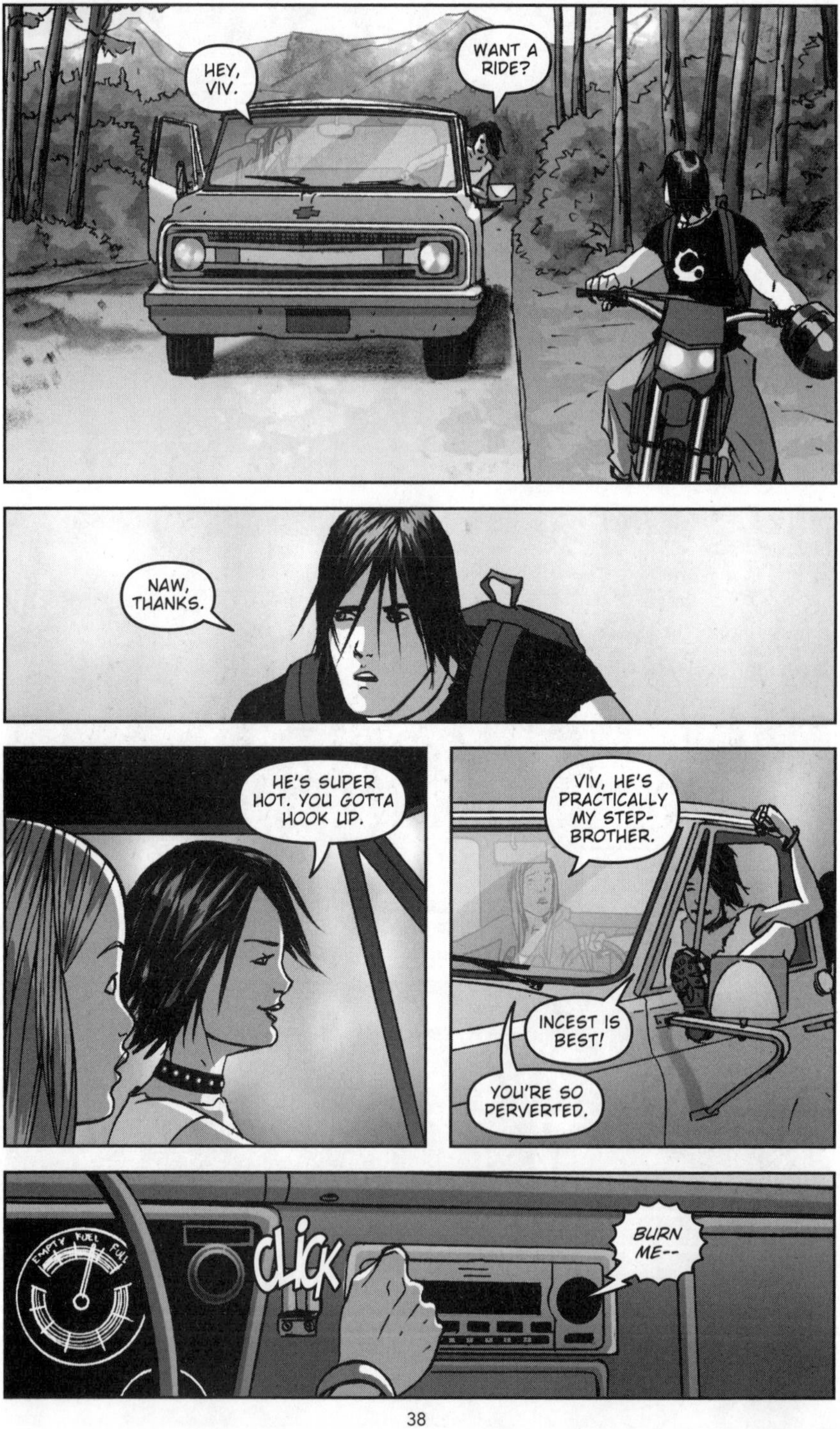
HEY, VIV.
WANT A RIDE?
NAW, THANKS.
HE'S SUPER HOT. YOU GOTTA HOOK UP.
VIV, HE'S PRACTICALLY MY STEP-BROTHER.
INCEST IS BEST!
YOU'RE SO PERVERTED.
EMPTY FUEL FULL
CLICK
BURN ME--

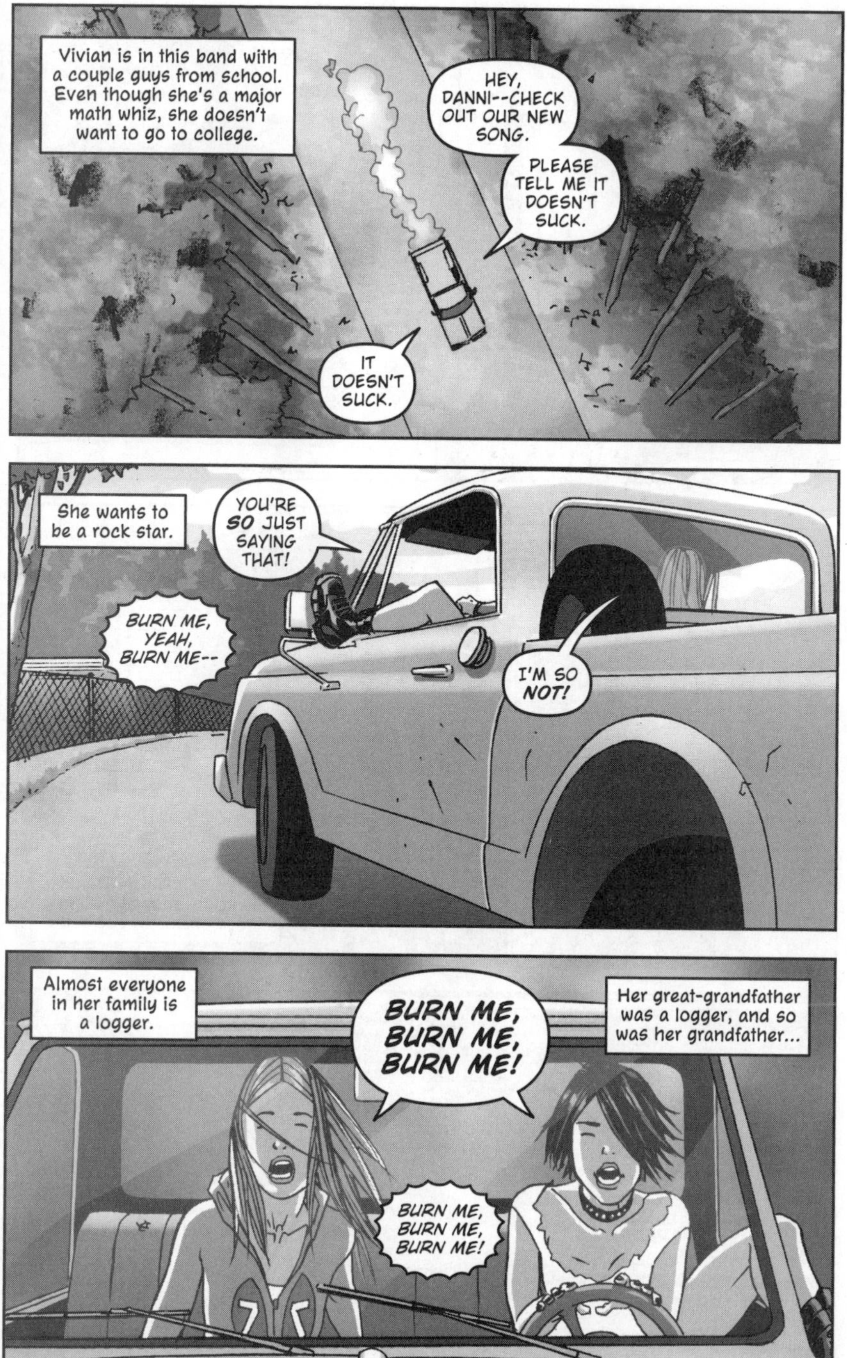
Vivian is in this band with a couple guys from school. Even though she's a major math whiz, she doesn't want to go to college.
HEY, DANNI--CHECK OUT OUR NEW SONG.
PLEASE TELL ME IT DOESN'T SUCK.
IT DOESN'T SUCK.
She wants to be a rock star.
YOU'RE SO JUST SAYING THAT!
BURN ME, YEAH, BURN ME--
I'M SO NOT!
Almost everyone in her family is a logger.
BURN ME, BURN ME, BURN ME!
Her great-grandfather was a logger, and so was her grandfather...
BURN ME, BURN ME, BURN ME!

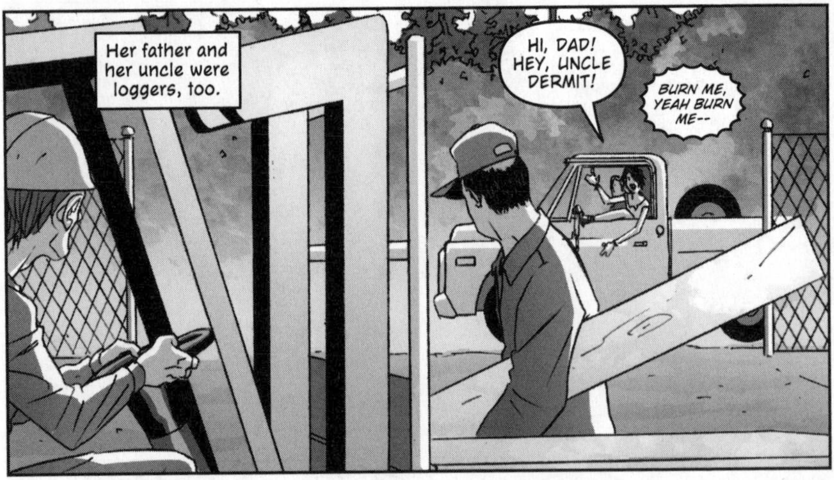
Her father and her uncle were loggers, too.
HI, DAD! HEY, UNCLE DERMIT!
BURN ME, YEAH BURN ME--

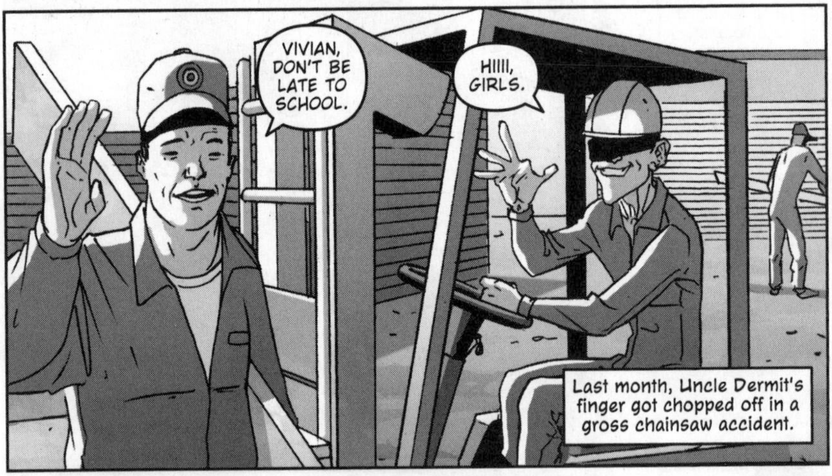
VIVIAN, DON'T BE LATE TO SCHOOL.
HIIII, GIRLS.
Last month, Uncle Dermit's finger got chopped off in a gross chainsaw accident.

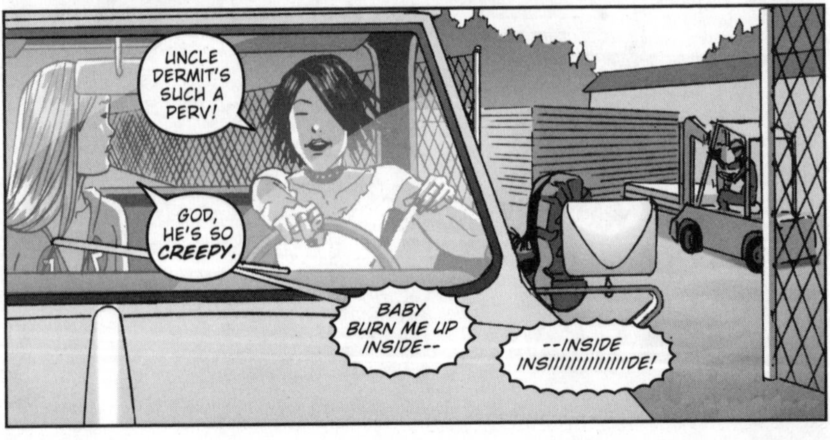
UNCLE DERMIT'S SUCH A PERV!
GOD, HE'S SO CREEPY.
BABY BURN ME UP INSIDE--
--INSIDE INSIIIIIIIIIIIIIIDE!

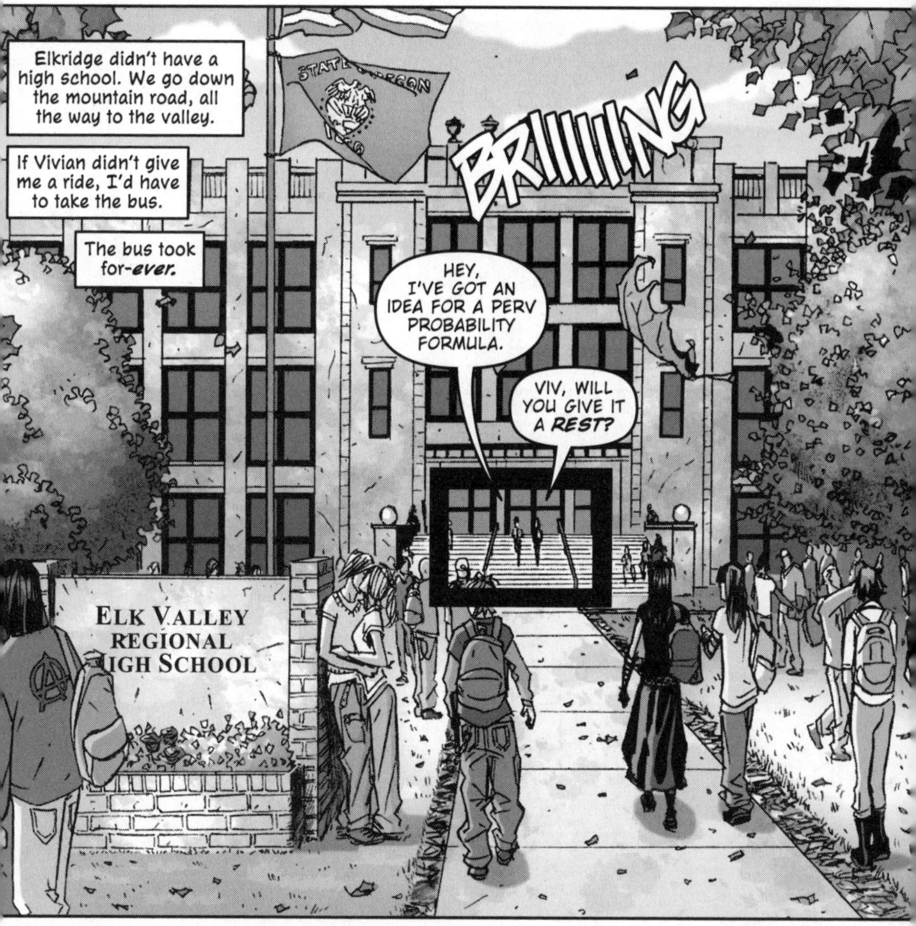
Elkridge didn't have a high school. We go down the mountain road, all the way to the valley.
If Vivian didn't give me a ride, I'd have to take the bus.
The bus took for-*ever.*
BRIIIIING
HEY, I'VE GOT AN IDEA FOR A PERV PROBABILITY FORMULA.
VIV, WILL YOU GIVE IT A *REST?*
ELK VALLEY
REGIONAL
IGH SCHOOL

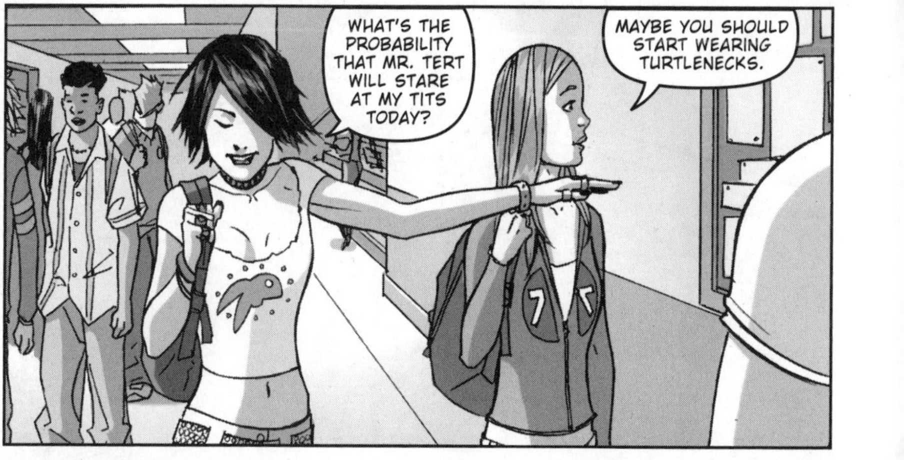
WHAT'S THE PROBABILITY THAT MR. TERT WILL STARE AT MY TITS TODAY?
MAYBE YOU SHOULD START WEARING TURTLENECKS.

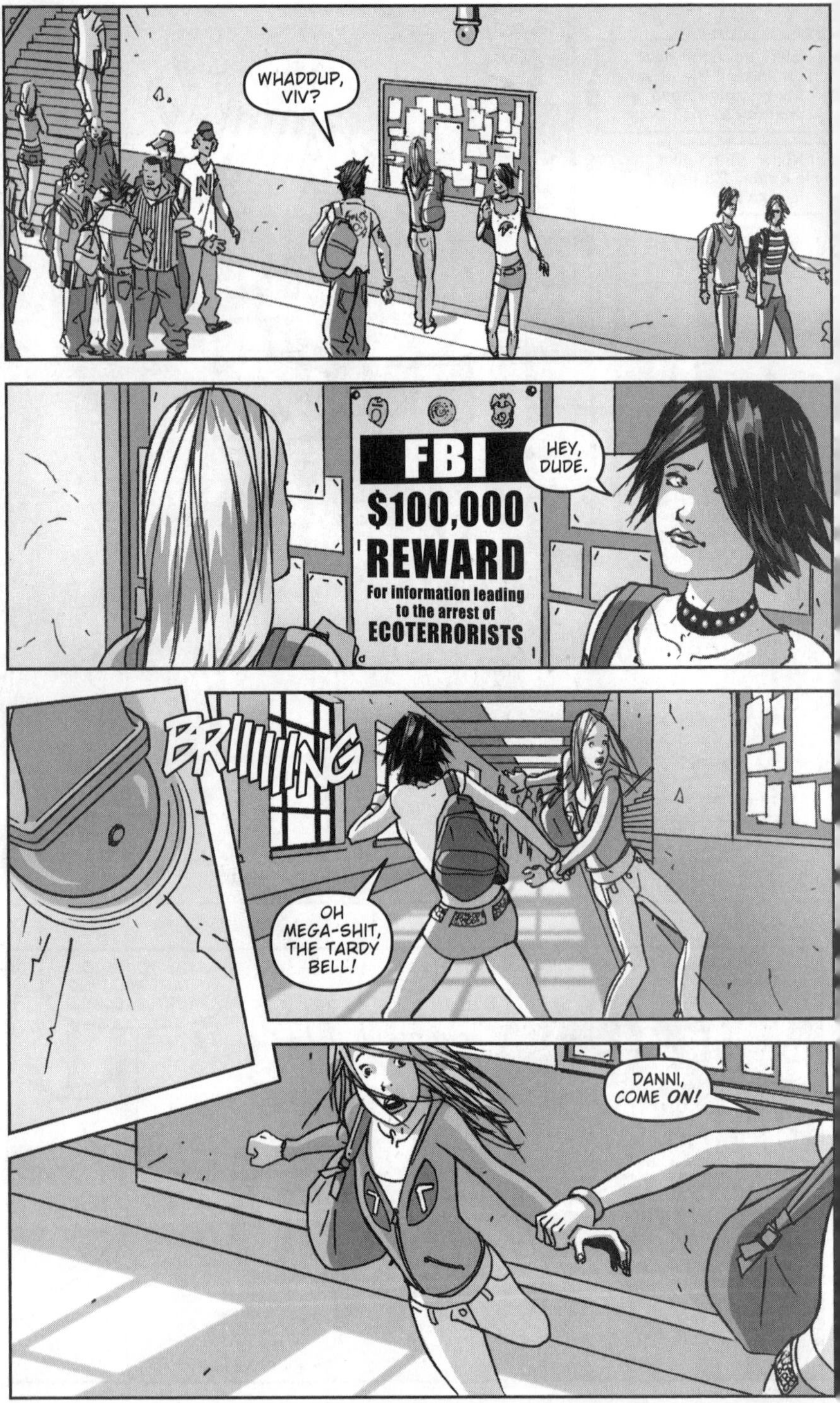
WHADDUP, VIV?
FBI
$100,000
REWARD
For information leading to the arrest of
ECOTERRORISTS
HEY, DUDE.
BRIIIIING
OH MEGA-SHIT, THE TARDY BELL!
DANNI, COME ON!

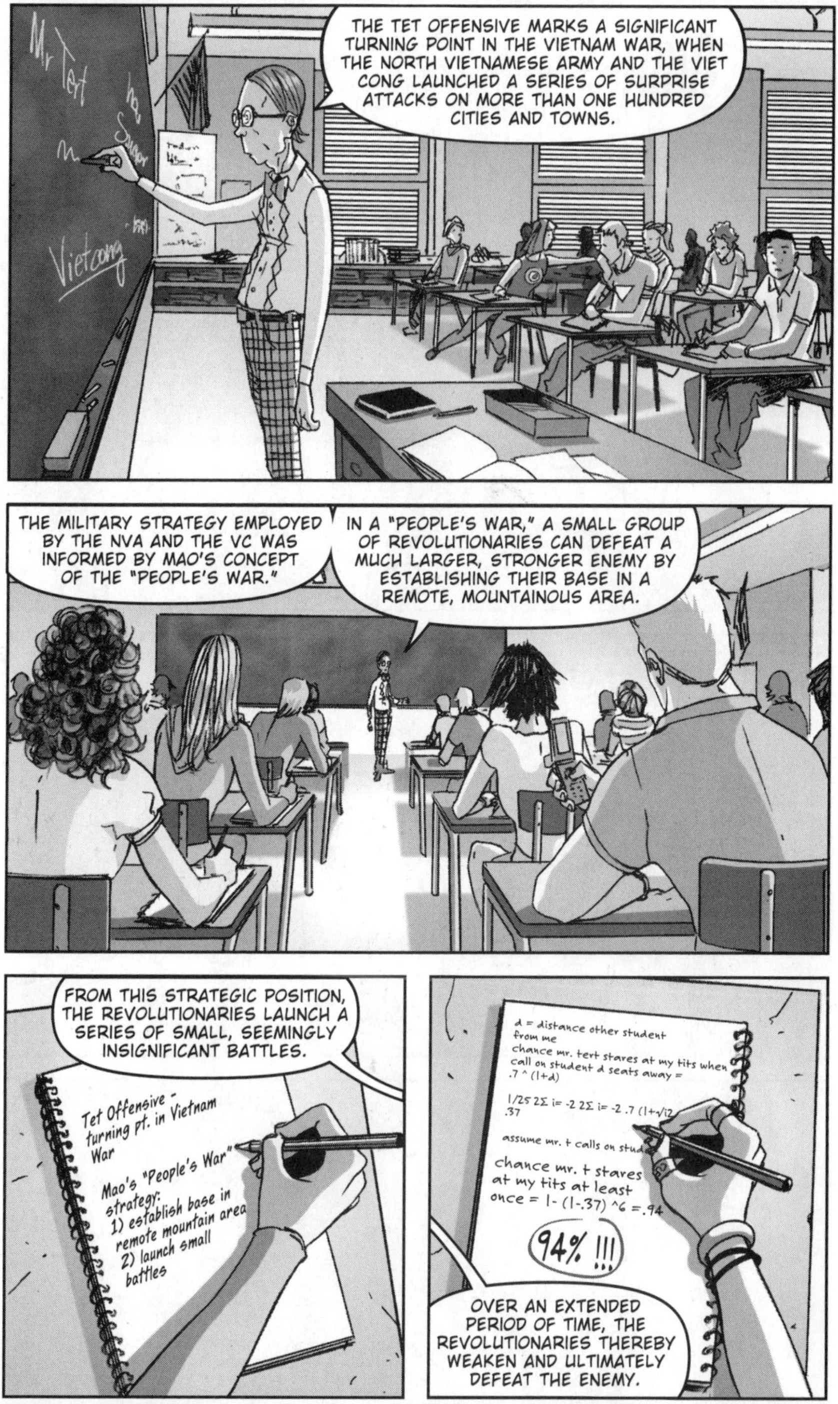
Mr Tert
Vietcong
THE TET OFFENSIVE MARKS A SIGNIFICANT TURNING POINT IN THE VIETNAM WAR, WHEN THE NORTH VIETNAMESE ARMY AND THE VIET CONG LAUNCHED A SERIES OF SURPRISE ATTACKS ON MORE THAN ONE HUNDRED CITIES AND TOWNS.
THE MILITARY STRATEGY EMPLOYED BY THE NVA AND THE VC WAS INFORMED BY MAO'S CONCEPT OF THE "PEOPLE'S WAR."
IN A "PEOPLE'S WAR," A SMALL GROUP OF REVOLUTIONARIES CAN DEFEAT A MUCH LARGER, STRONGER ENEMY BY ESTABLISHING THEIR BASE IN A REMOTE, MOUNTAINOUS AREA.
FROM THIS STRATEGIC POSITION, THE REVOLUTIONARIES LAUNCH A SERIES OF SMALL, SEEMINGLY INSIGNIFICANT BATTLES.
Tet Offensive - turning pt. in Vietnam War
Mao's "People's War" strategy:
1) establish base in remote mountain area
2) launch small battles
d = distance other student from me
chance mr. tert stares at my tits when call on student d seats away = .7 ^ (1+d)
1/25 2Σ i= -2 2Σ i= -2 .7 (1+√i2
.37
assume mr. t calls on stud
chance mr. t stares at my tits at least once = 1- (1-.37) ^6 =.94
94% !!!
OVER AN EXTENDED PERIOD OF TIME, THE REVOLUTIONARIES THEREBY WEAKEN AND ULTIMATELY DEFEAT THE ENEMY.

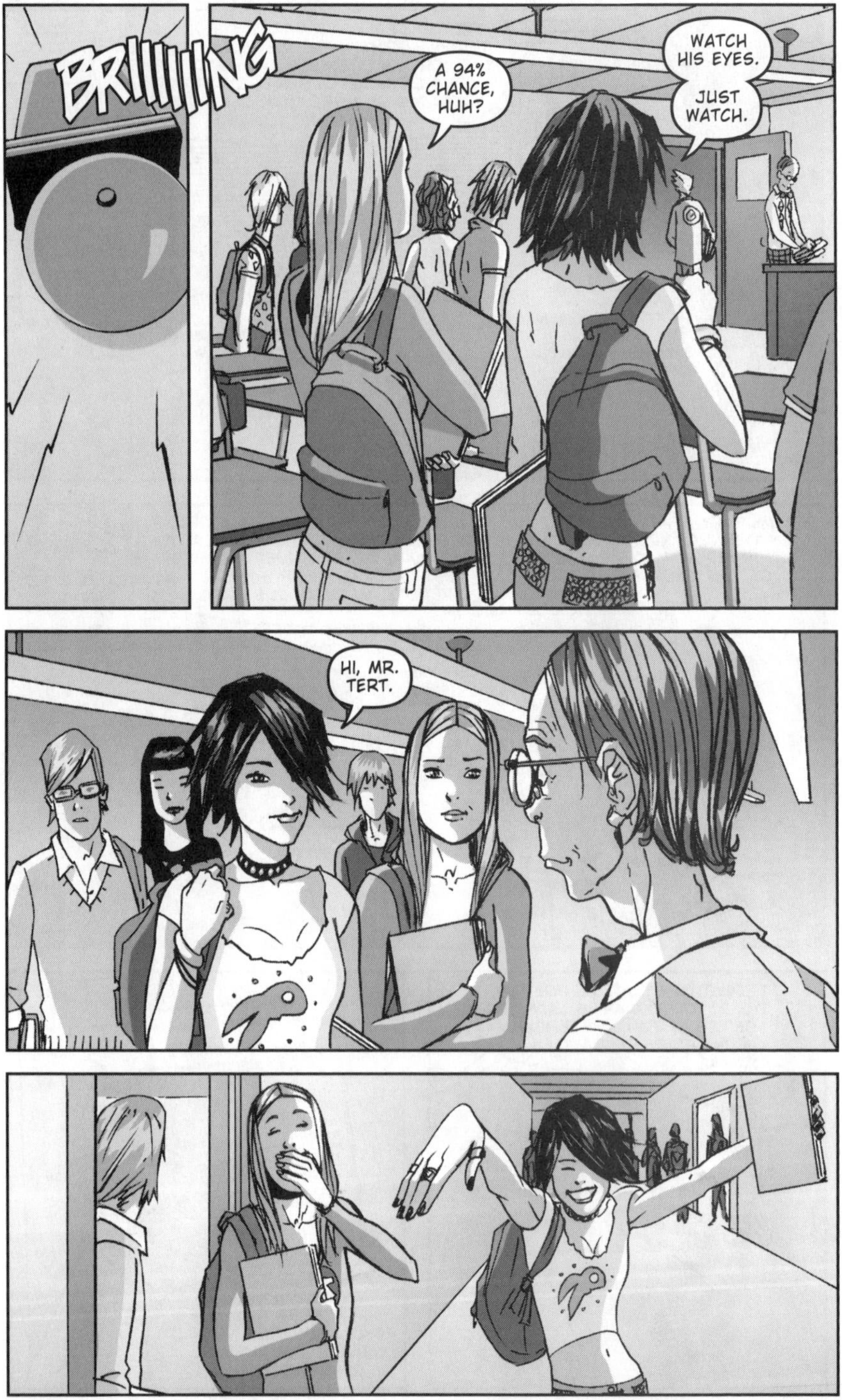
BRIIIIIING
A 94% CHANCE, HUH?
WATCH HIS EYES.
JUST WATCH.
HI, MR. TERT.

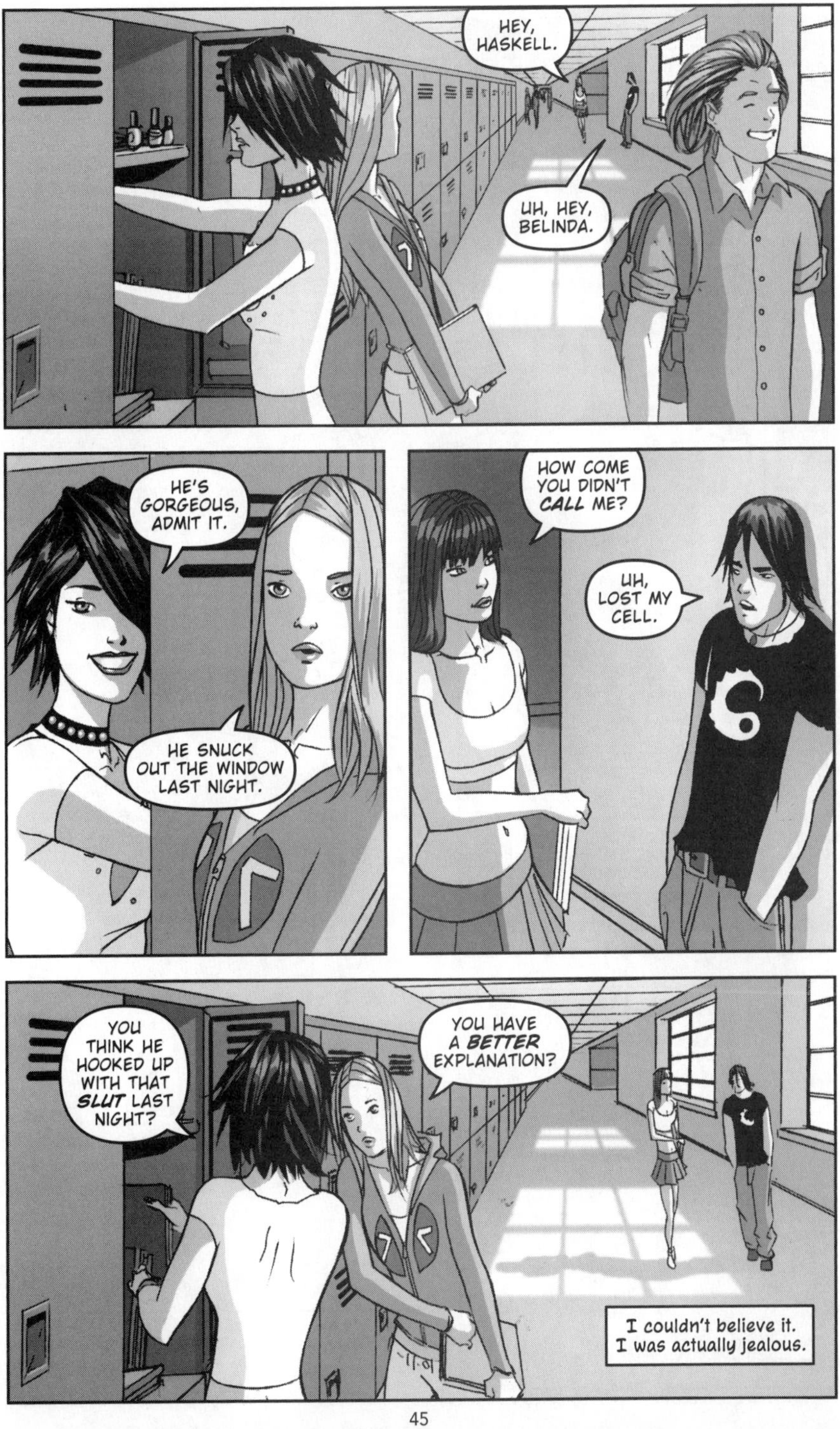
HEY, HASKELL.
UH, HEY, BELINDA.
HE'S GORGEOUS, ADMIT IT.
HE SNUCK OUT THE WINDOW LAST NIGHT.
HOW COME YOU DIDN'T CALL ME?
UH, LOST MY CELL.
YOU THINK HE HOOKED UP WITH THAT SLUT LAST NIGHT?
YOU HAVE A BETTER EXPLANATION?
I couldn't believe it. I was actually jealous.

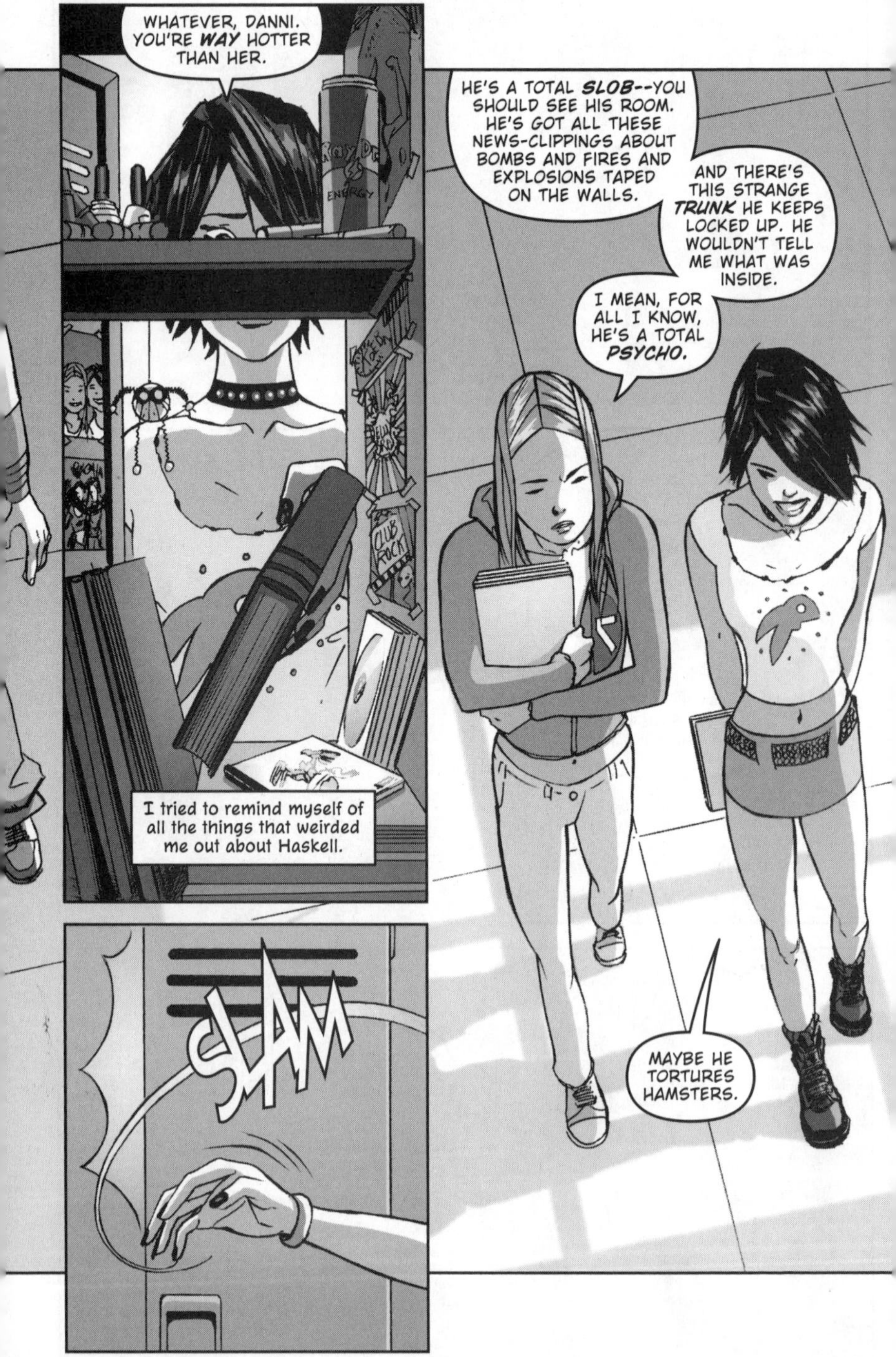
WHATEVER, DANNI. YOU'RE WAY HOTTER THAN HER.
HE'S A TOTAL SLOB--YOU SHOULD SEE HIS ROOM. HE'S GOT ALL THESE NEWS-CLIPPINGS ABOUT BOMBS AND FIRES AND EXPLOSIONS TAPED ON THE WALLS.
AND THERE'S THIS STRANGE TRUNK HE KEEPS LOCKED UP. HE WOULDN'T TELL ME WHAT WAS INSIDE.
I MEAN, FOR ALL I KNOW, HE'S A TOTAL PSYCHO.
I tried to remind myself of all the things that weirded me out about Haskell.
SLAM
MAYBE HE TORTURES HAMSTERS.

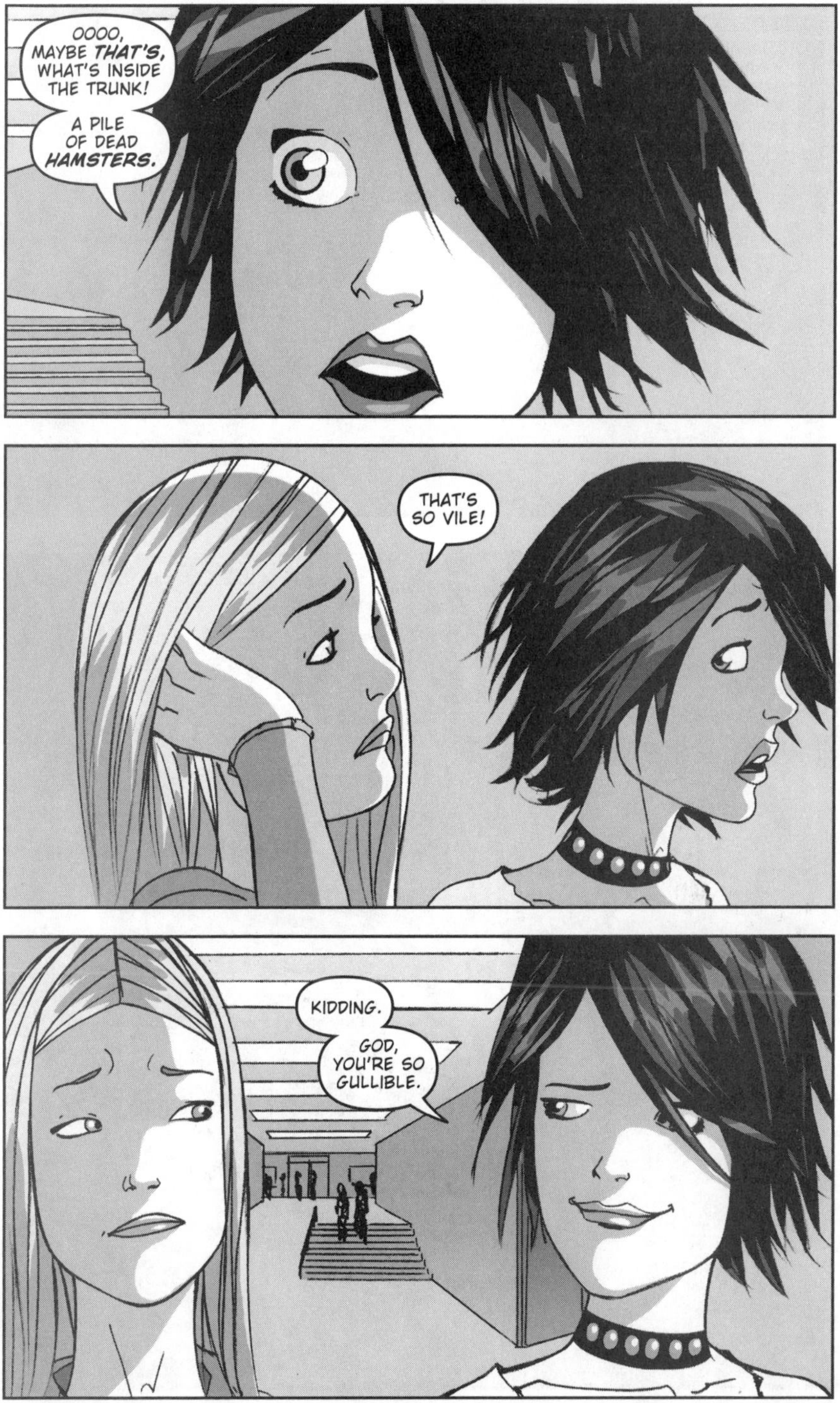
OOOO, MAYBE THAT'S, WHAT'S INSIDE THE TRUNK!
A PILE OF DEAD HAMSTERS.
THAT'S SO VILE!
KIDDING.
GOD, YOU'RE SO GULLIBLE.

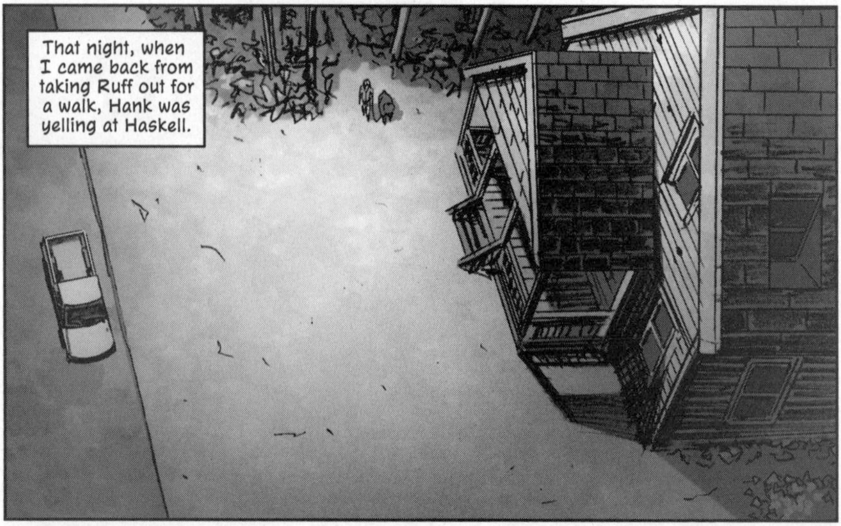
That night, when I came back from taking Ruff out for a walk, Hank was yelling at Haskell.

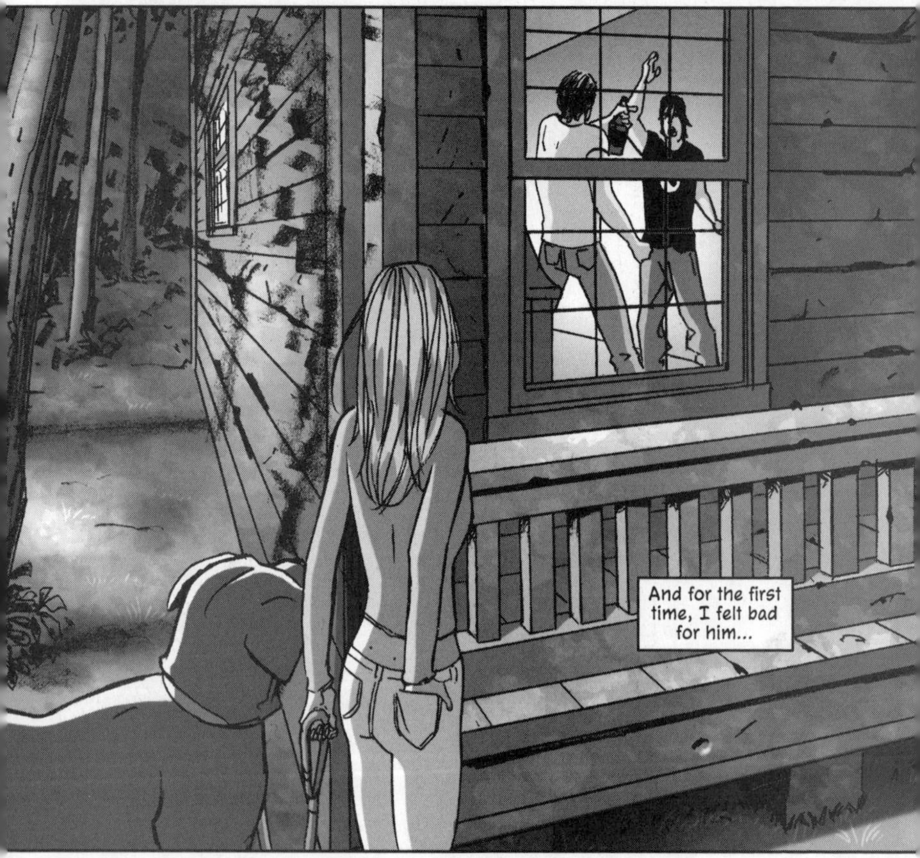
And for the first time, I felt bad for him...

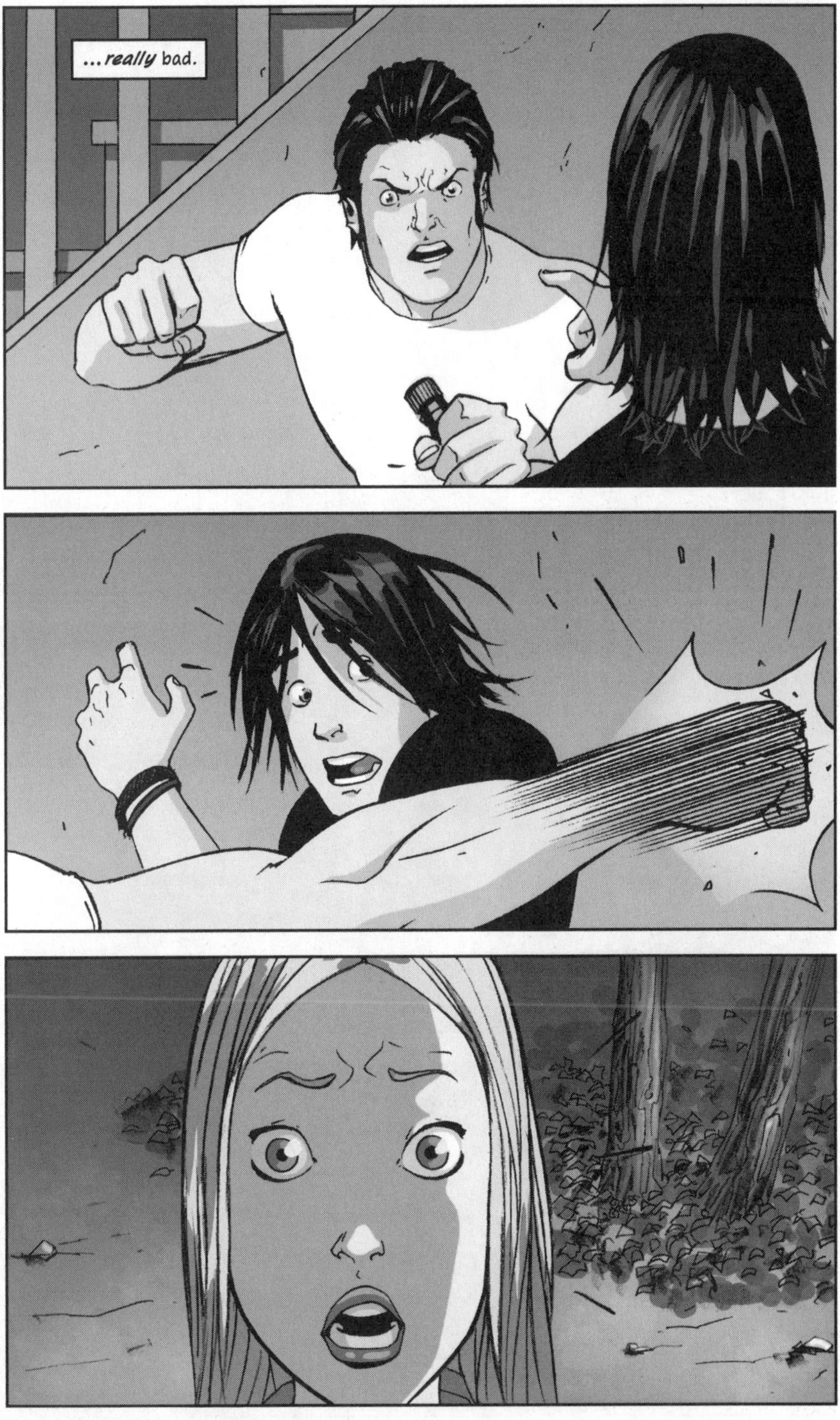
...*really* bad.

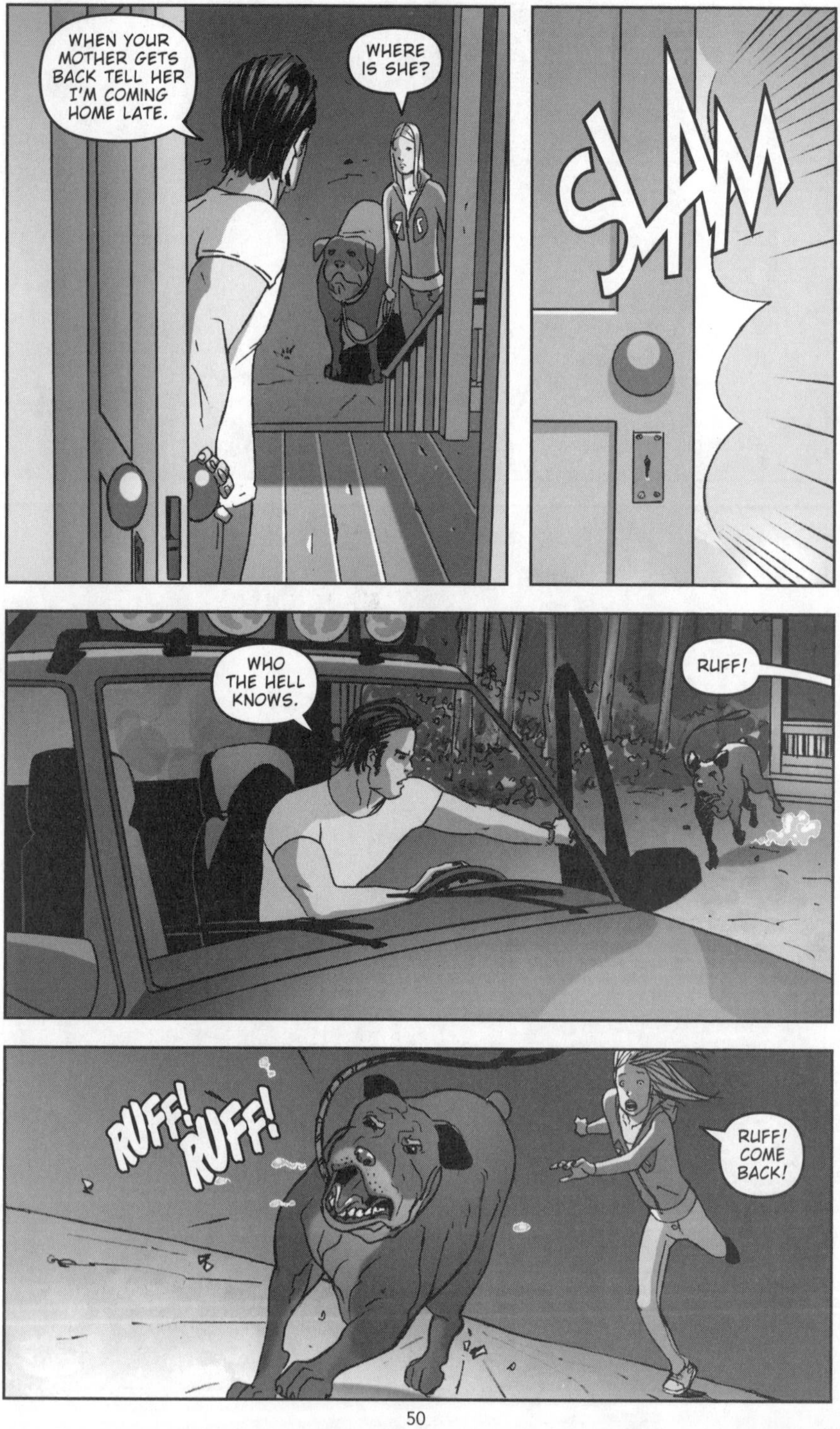

WHEN YOUR MOTHER GETS BACK TELL HER I'M COMING HOME LATE.
WHERE IS SHE?
SLAM
WHO THE HELL KNOWS.
RUFF!
RUFF! RUFF!
RUFF! COME BACK!

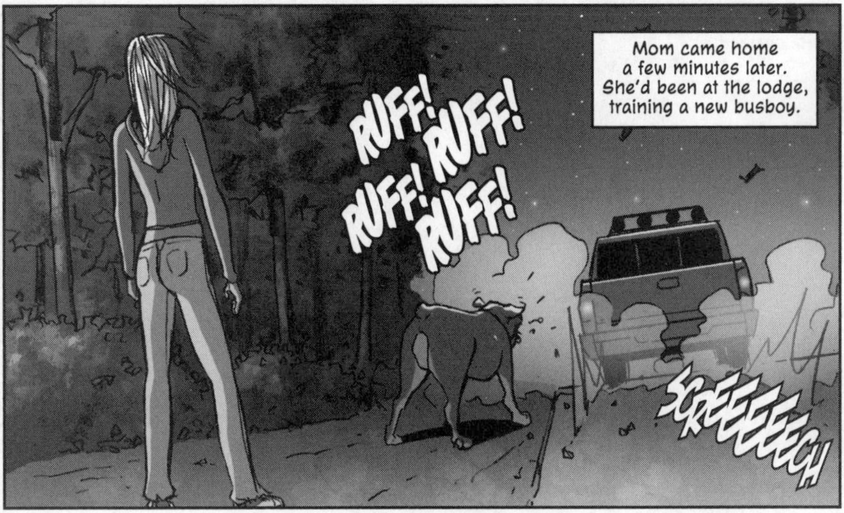
Mom came home a few minutes later. She'd been at the lodge, training a new busboy.
RUFF! RUFF! RUFF! RUFF!
SCREEEEEECH

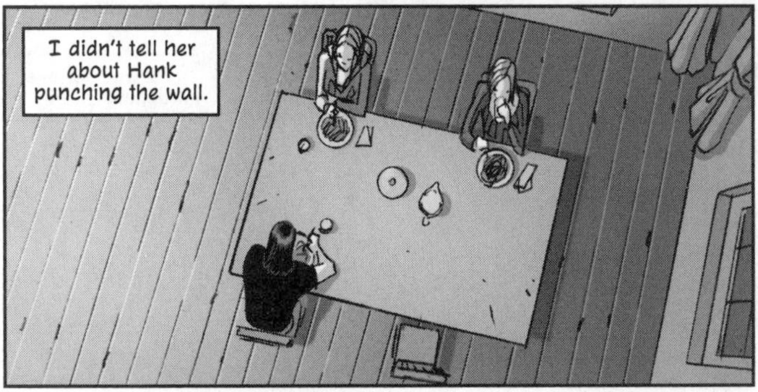
I didn't tell her about Hank punching the wall.

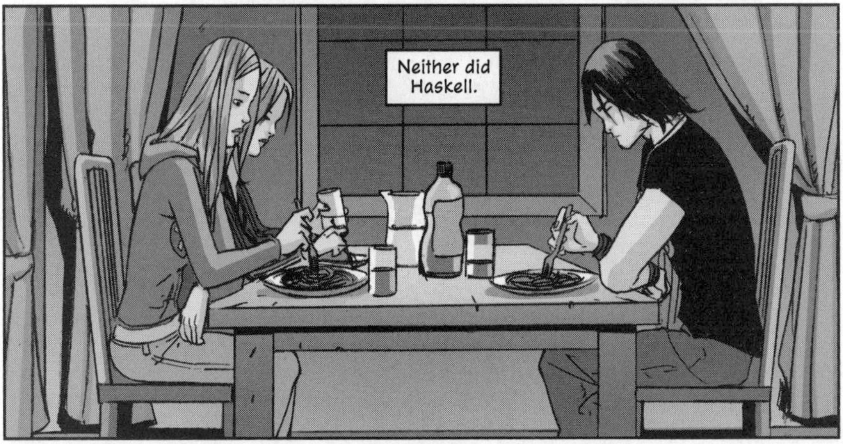
Neither did Haskell.

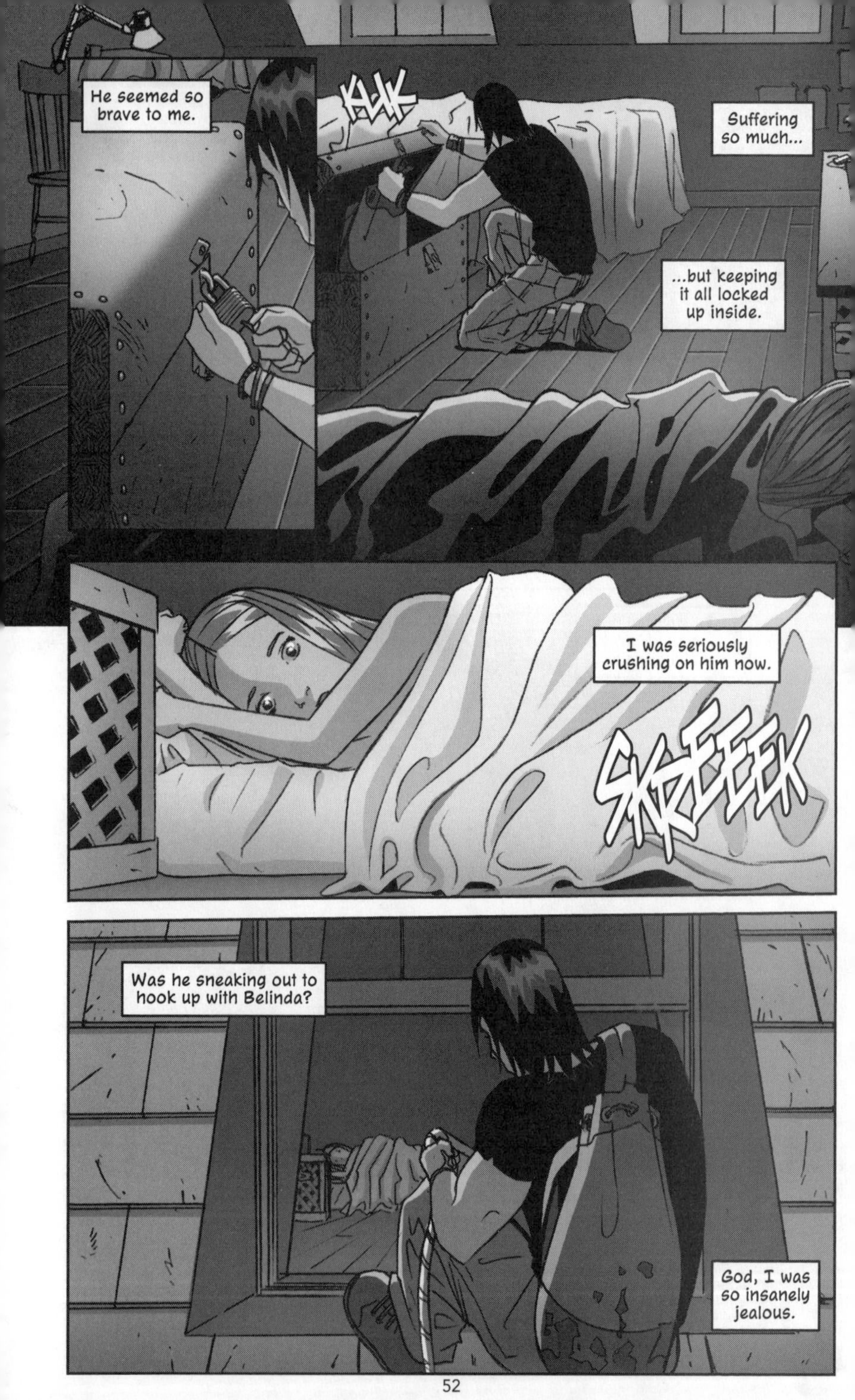
He seemed so brave to me.
KLIK
Suffering so much...
...but keeping it all locked up inside.
I was seriously crushing on him now.
SKREEEK
Was he sneaking out to hook up with Belinda?
God, I was so insanely jealous.

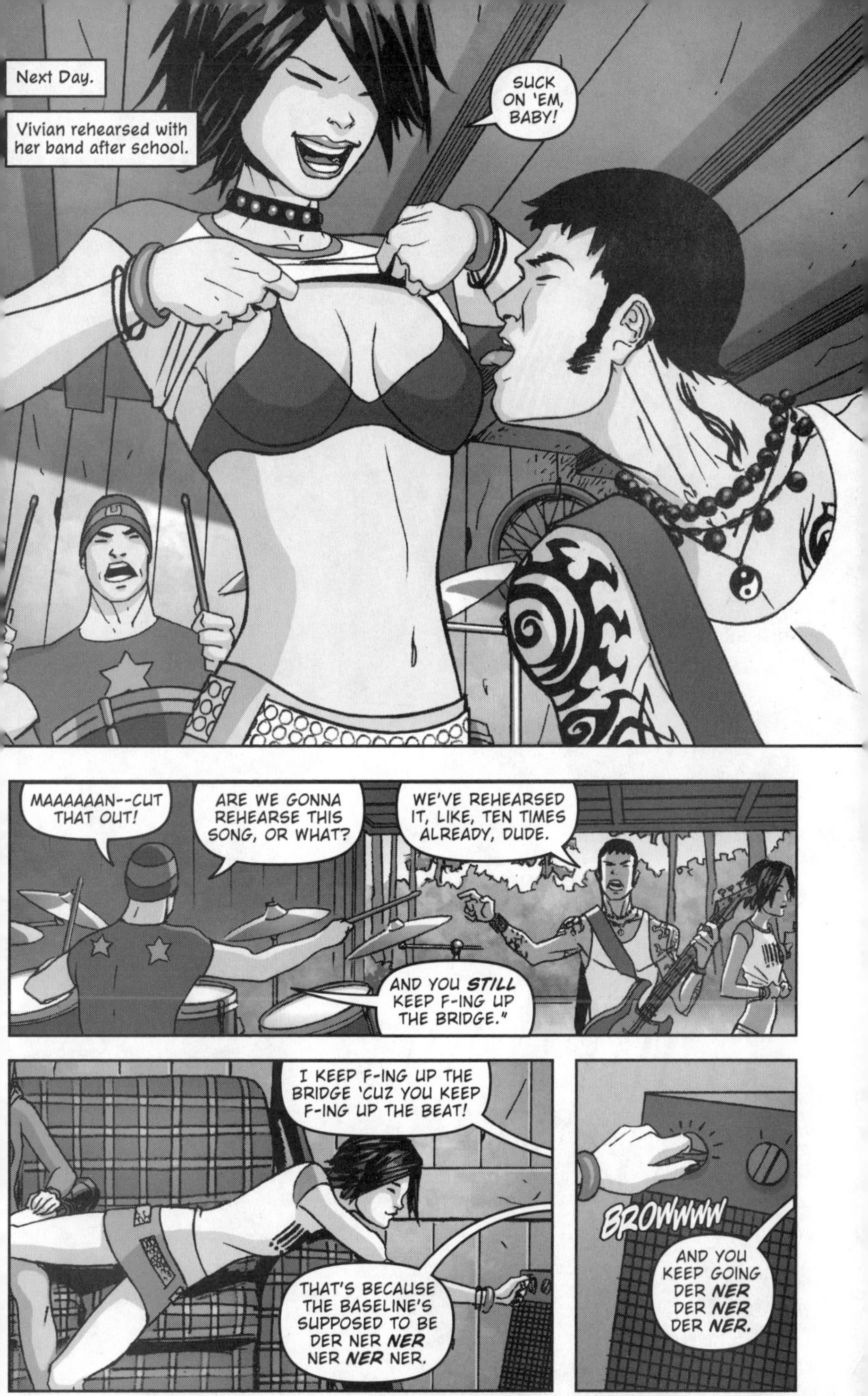
Next Day.
Vivian rehearsed with her band after school.
SUCK ON 'EM, BABY!
MAAAAAAN--CUT THAT OUT!
ARE WE GONNA REHEARSE THIS SONG, OR WHAT?
WE'VE REHEARSED IT, LIKE, TEN TIMES ALREADY, DUDE.
AND YOU STILL KEEP F-ING UP THE BRIDGE."
I KEEP F-ING UP THE BRIDGE 'CUZ YOU KEEP F-ING UP THE BEAT!
THAT'S BECAUSE THE BASELINE'S SUPPOSED TO BE DER NER NER NER NER NER.
BROWWWW
AND YOU KEEP GOING DER NER DER NER DER NER.

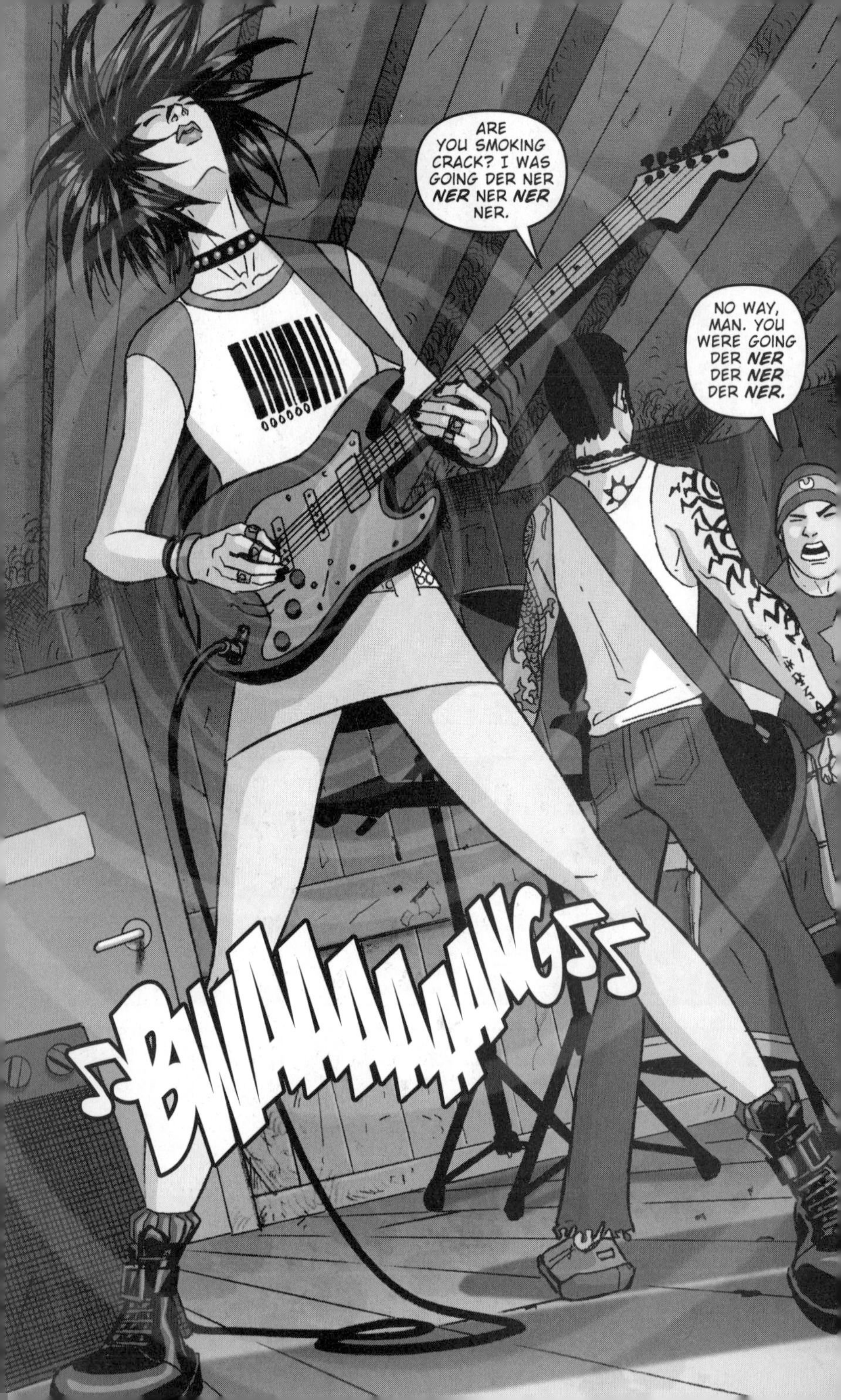
ARE YOU SMOKING CRACK? I WAS GOING DER NER **NER** NER **NER** NER.
NO WAY, MAN. YOU WERE GOING DER **NER** DER **NER** DER **NER.**
BWAAAAAAANG

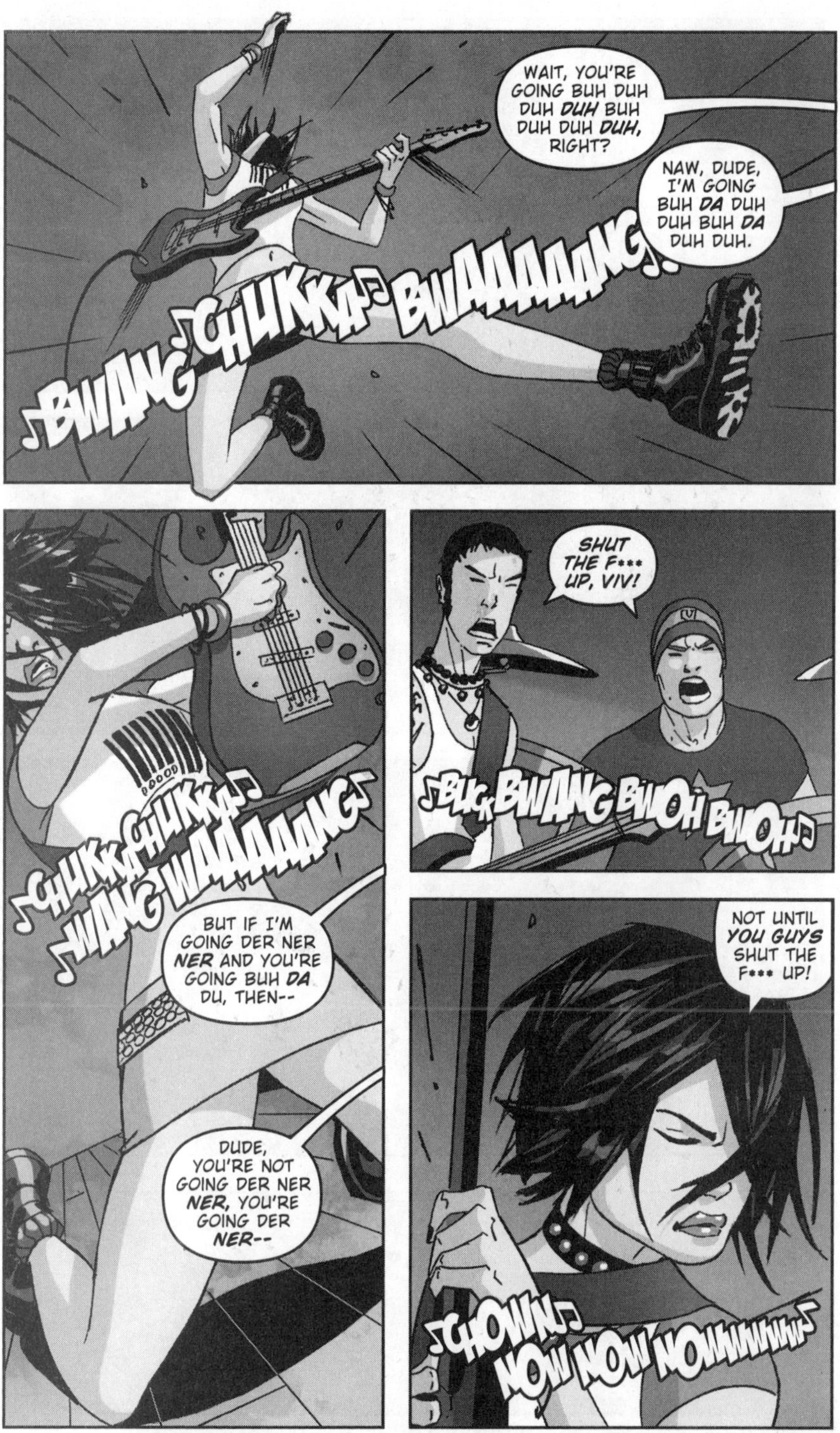

WAIT, YOU'RE GOING BUH DUH DUH *DUH* BUH DUH DUH *DUH*, RIGHT?
NAW, DUDE, I'M GOING BUH *DA* DUH DUH BUH *DA* DUH DUH.
BWANG CHUKKA BWAAAAAANG
CHUKKA CHUKKA WANG WAAAAAANG
BUT IF I'M GOING DER NER *NER* AND YOU'RE GOING BUH *DA* DU, THEN--
DUDE, YOU'RE NOT GOING DER NER *NER*, YOU'RE GOING DER *NER*--
*SHUT THE F*** UP, VIV!*
BUCK BWANG BWOH BWOH
NOT UNTIL *YOU GUYS* SHUT THE F*** UP!
CHOWN NOW NOW NOWWWWW

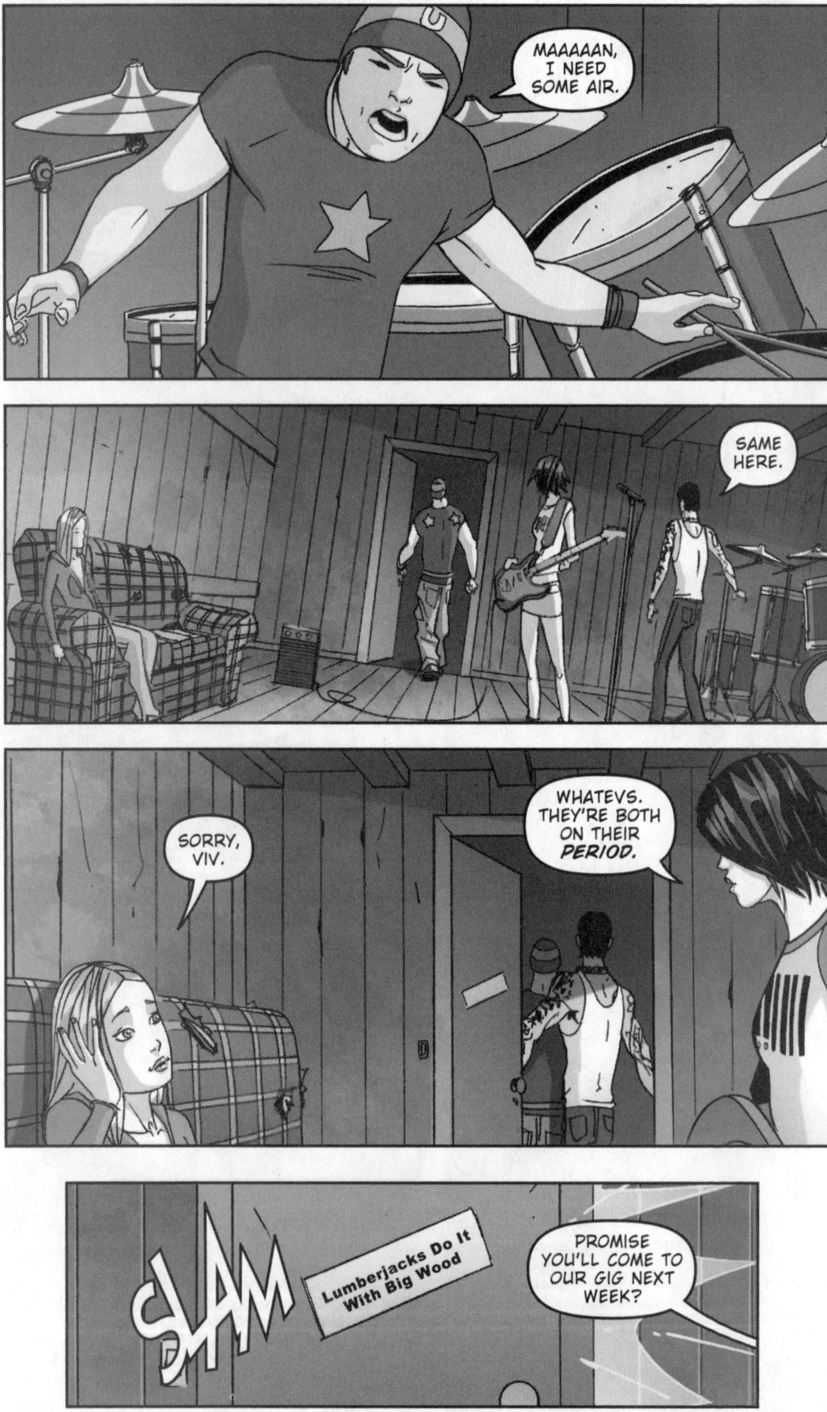
MAAAAAN, I NEED SOME AIR.
SAME HERE.
SORRY, VIV.
WHATEVS. THEY'RE BOTH ON THEIR *PERIOD.*
SLAM
Lumberjacks Do It With Big Wood
PROMISE YOU'LL COME TO OUR GIG NEXT WEEK?

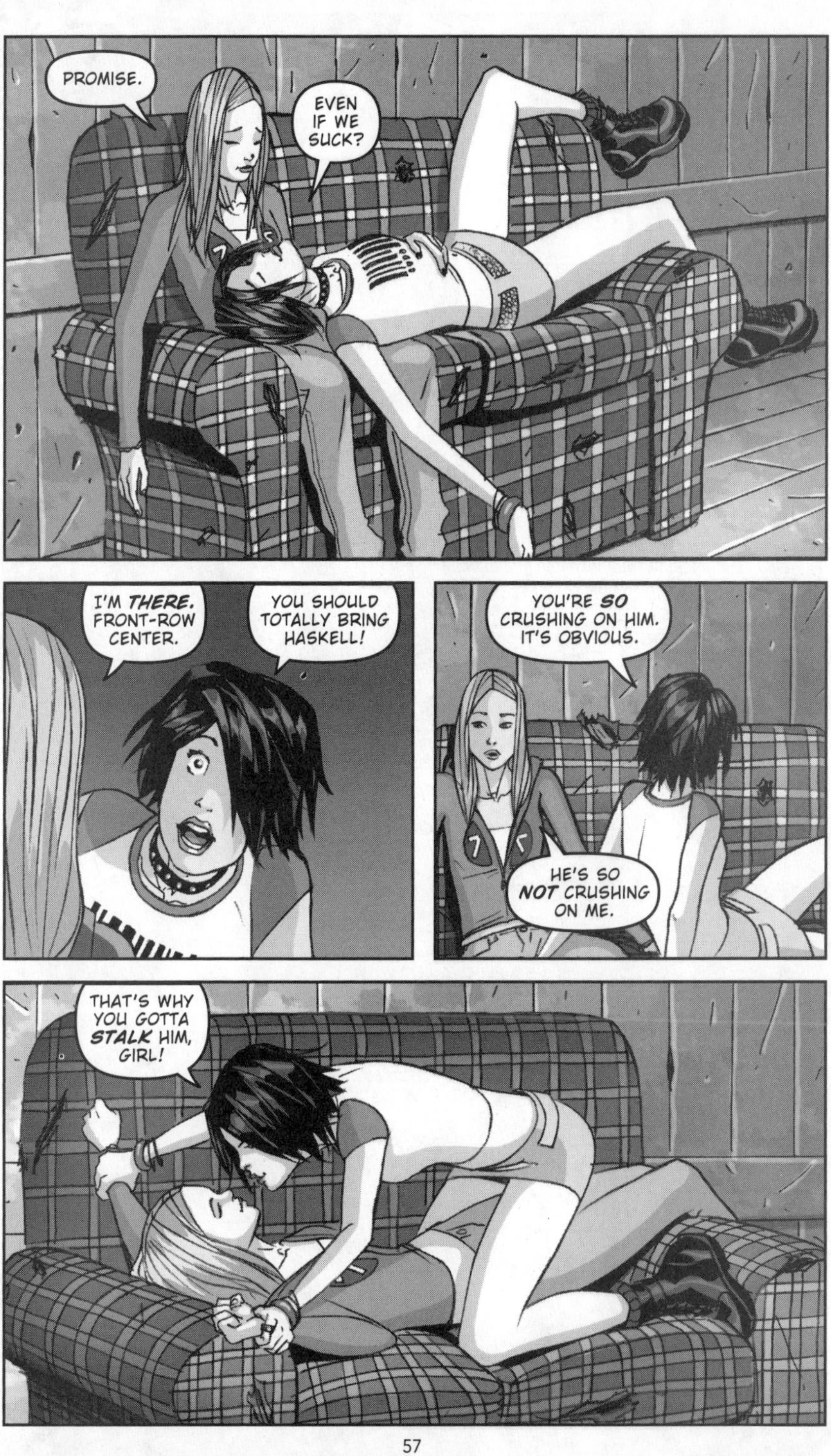
PROMISE.
EVEN IF WE SUCK?
I'M *THERE.* FRONT-ROW CENTER.
YOU SHOULD TOTALLY BRING HASKELL!
YOU'RE *SO* CRUSHING ON HIM. IT'S OBVIOUS.
HE'S SO *NOT* CRUSHING ON ME.
THAT'S WHY YOU GOTTA *STALK* HIM, GIRL!

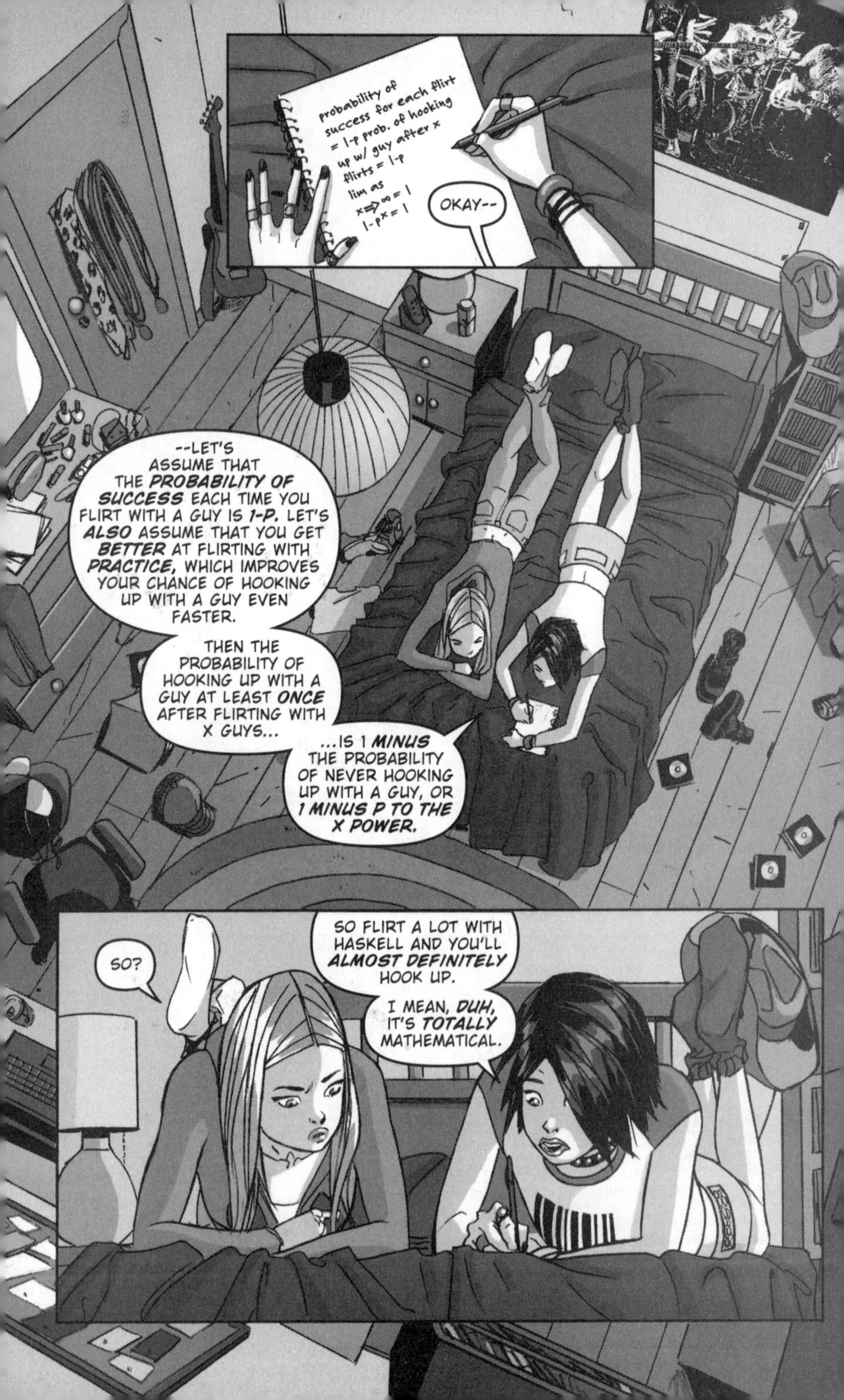
probability of
success for each flirt
= 1-p prob. of hooking
up w/ guy after x
flirts = 1-p
lim as
x⇒∞ = 1
1-p^x = 1
OKAY--
--LET'S ASSUME THAT THE PROBABILITY OF SUCCESS EACH TIME YOU FLIRT WITH A GUY IS 1-P. LET'S ALSO ASSUME THAT YOU GET BETTER AT FLIRTING WITH PRACTICE, WHICH IMPROVES YOUR CHANCE OF HOOKING UP WITH A GUY EVEN FASTER.
THEN THE PROBABILITY OF HOOKING UP WITH A GUY AT LEAST ONCE AFTER FLIRTING WITH X GUYS...
...IS 1 MINUS THE PROBABILITY OF NEVER HOOKING UP WITH A GUY, OR 1 MINUS P TO THE X POWER.
SO?
SO FLIRT A LOT WITH HASKELL AND YOU'LL ALMOST DEFINITELY HOOK UP.
I MEAN, DUH, IT'S TOTALLY MATHEMATICAL.

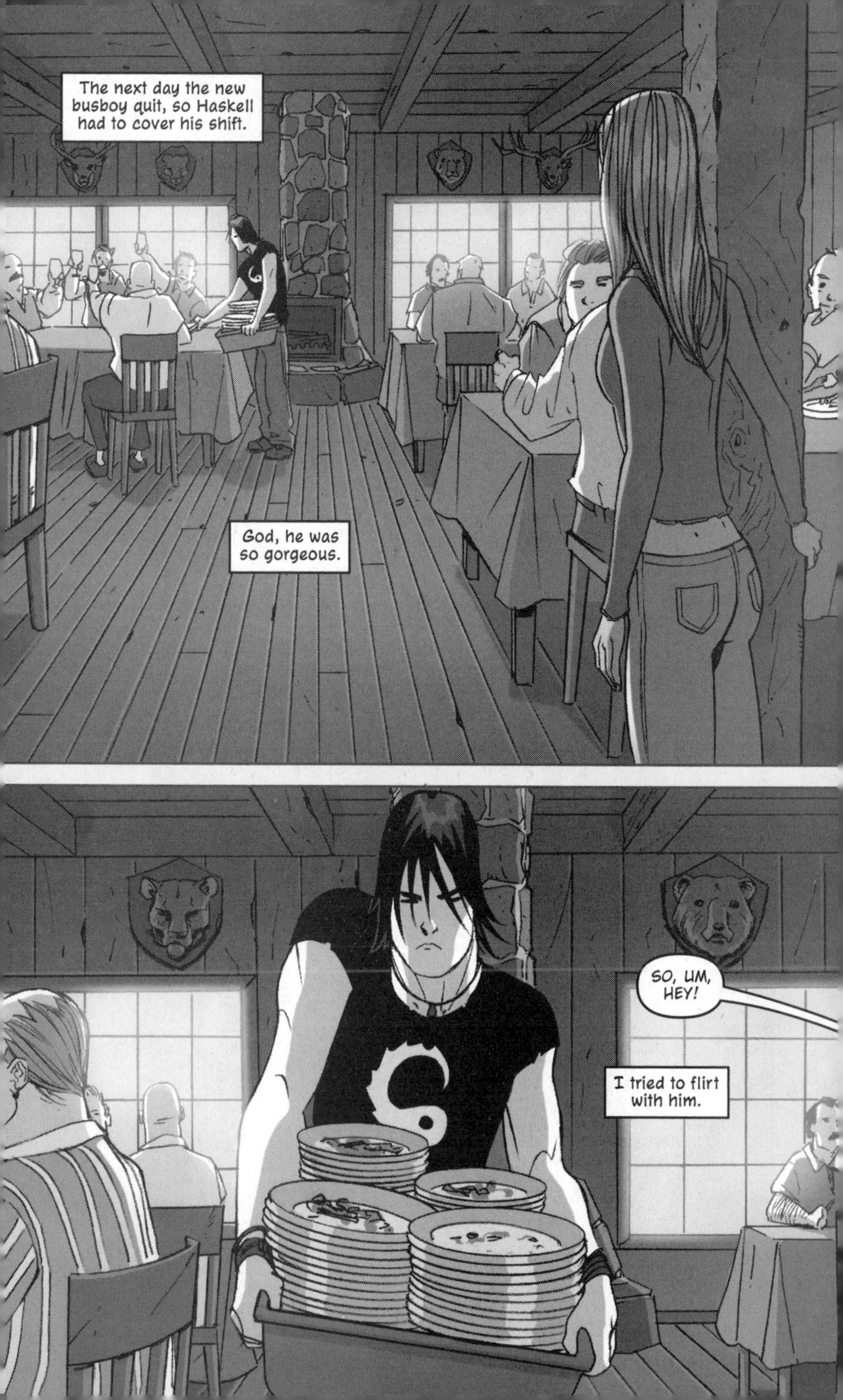
The next day the new busboy quit, so Haskell had to cover his shift.
God, he was so gorgeous.
SO, UM, HEY!
I tried to flirt with him.

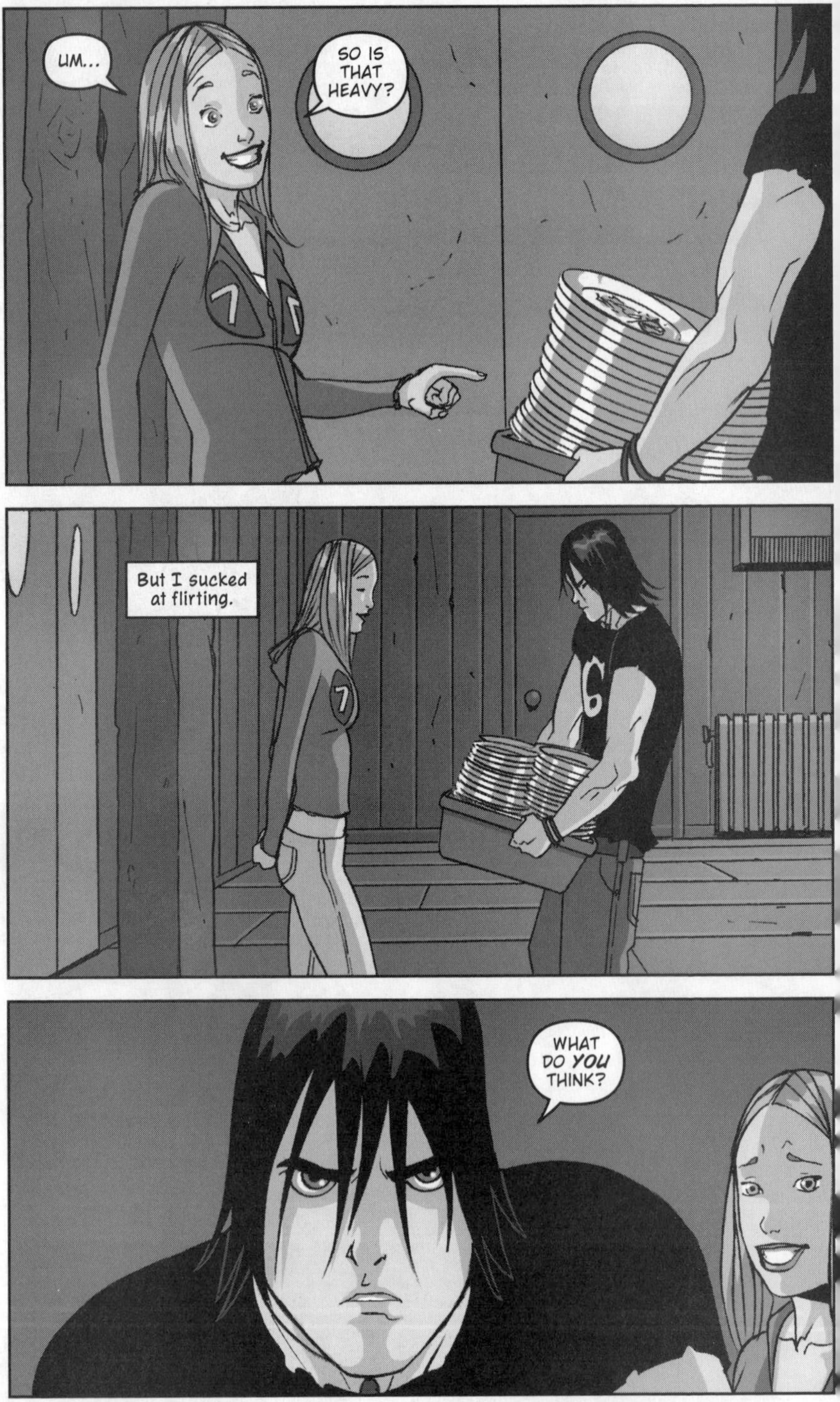
UM...
SO IS THAT HEAVY?
But I sucked at flirting.
WHAT DO YOU THINK?

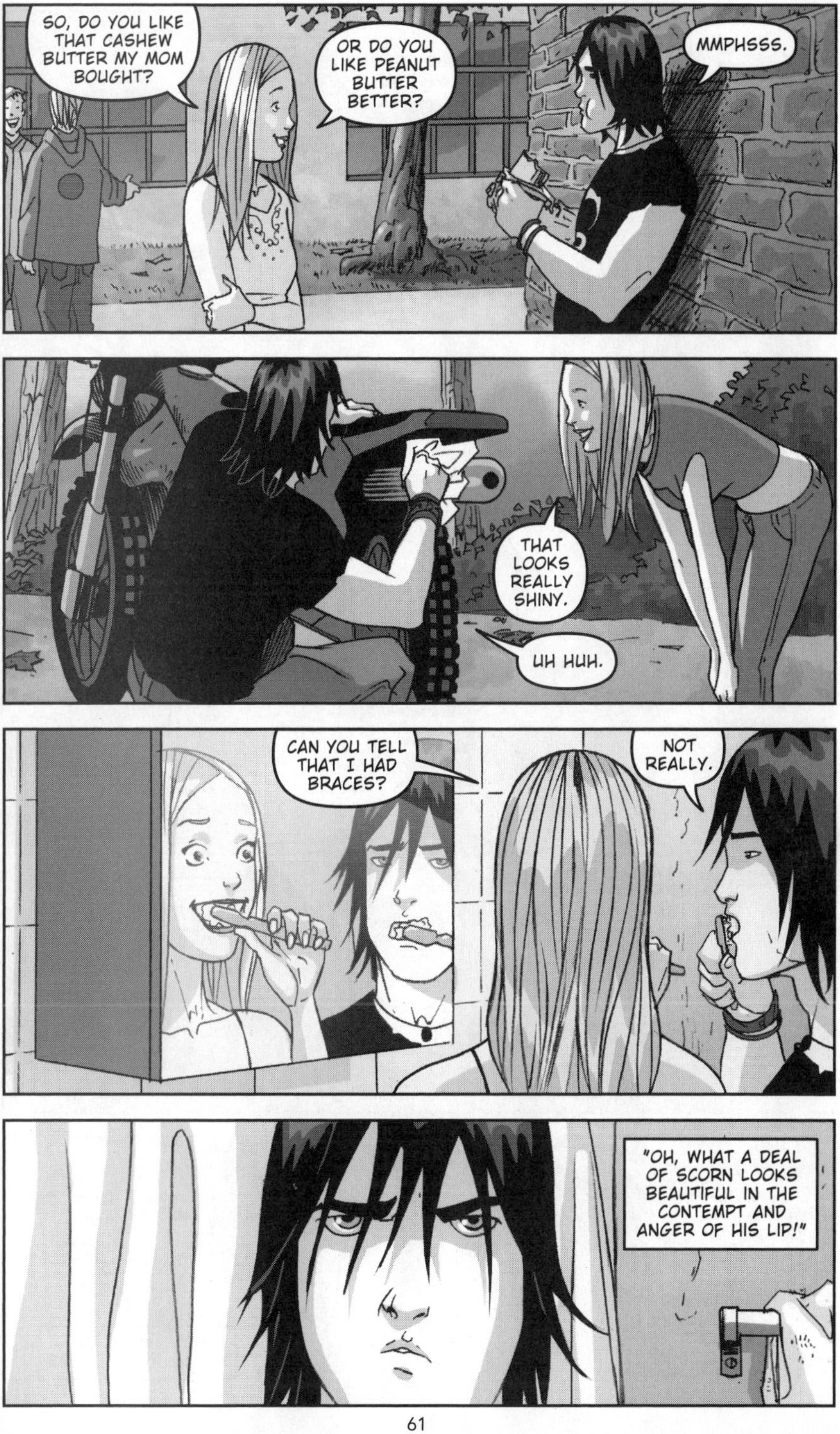
SO, DO YOU LIKE THAT CASHEW BUTTER MY MOM BOUGHT?
OR DO YOU LIKE PEANUT BUTTER BETTER?
MMPHSSS.
THAT LOOKS REALLY SHINY.
UH HUH.
CAN YOU TELL THAT I HAD BRACES?
NOT REALLY.
"OH, WHAT A DEAL OF SCORN LOOKS BEAUTIFUL IN THE CONTEMPT AND ANGER OF HIS LIP!"

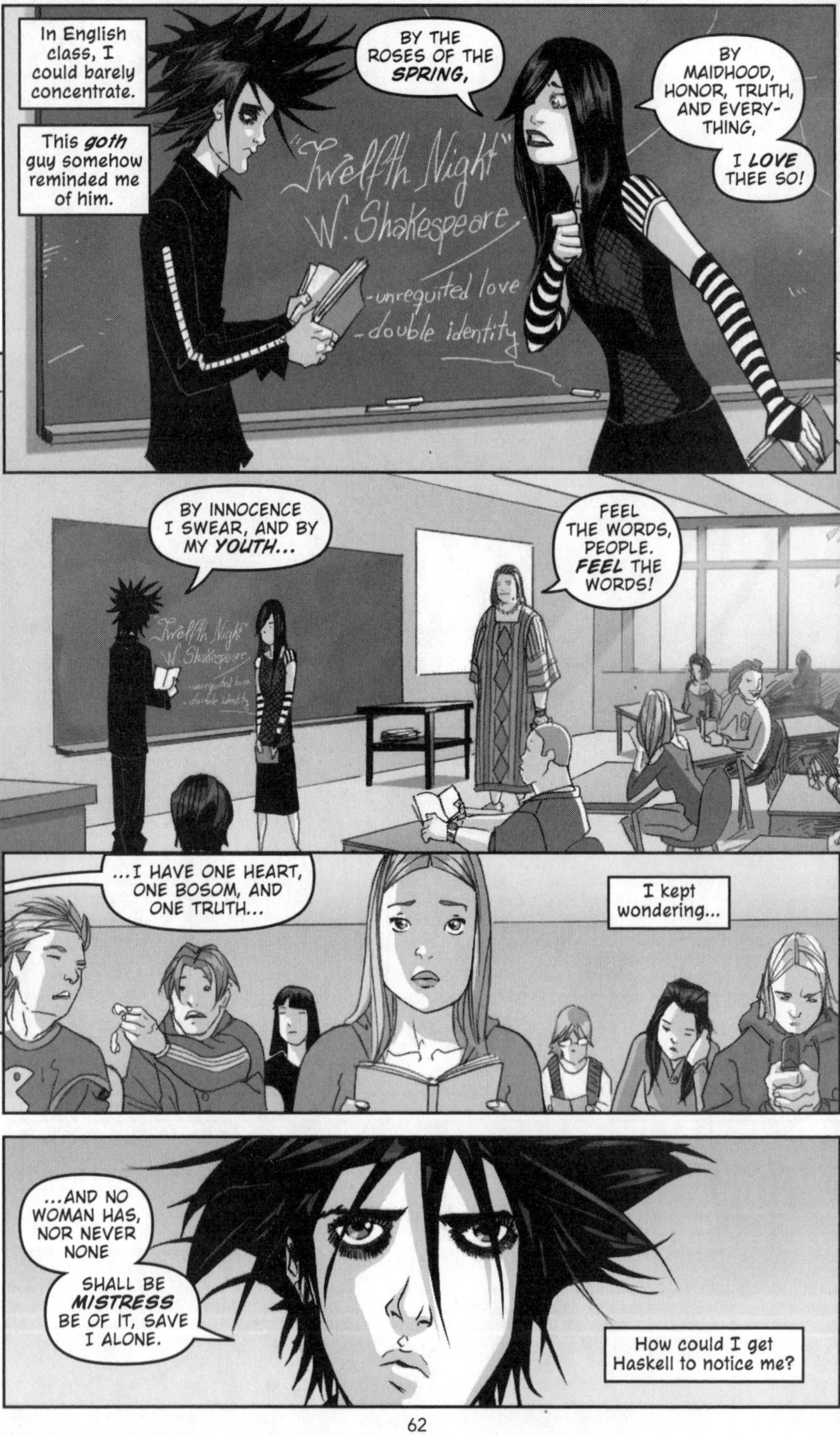
In English class, I could barely concentrate.
This goth guy somehow reminded me of him.
BY THE ROSES OF THE SPRING,
BY MAIDHOOD, HONOR, TRUTH, AND EVERY-THING,
I LOVE THEE SO!
"Twelfth Night"
W. Shakespeare
-unrequited love
-double identity
BY INNOCENCE I SWEAR, AND BY MY YOUTH...
FEEL THE WORDS, PEOPLE. FEEL THE WORDS!
...I HAVE ONE HEART, ONE BOSOM, AND ONE TRUTH...
I kept wondering...
...AND NO WOMAN HAS, NOR NEVER NONE
SHALL BE MISTRESS BE OF IT, SAVE I ALONE.
How could I get Haskell to notice me?

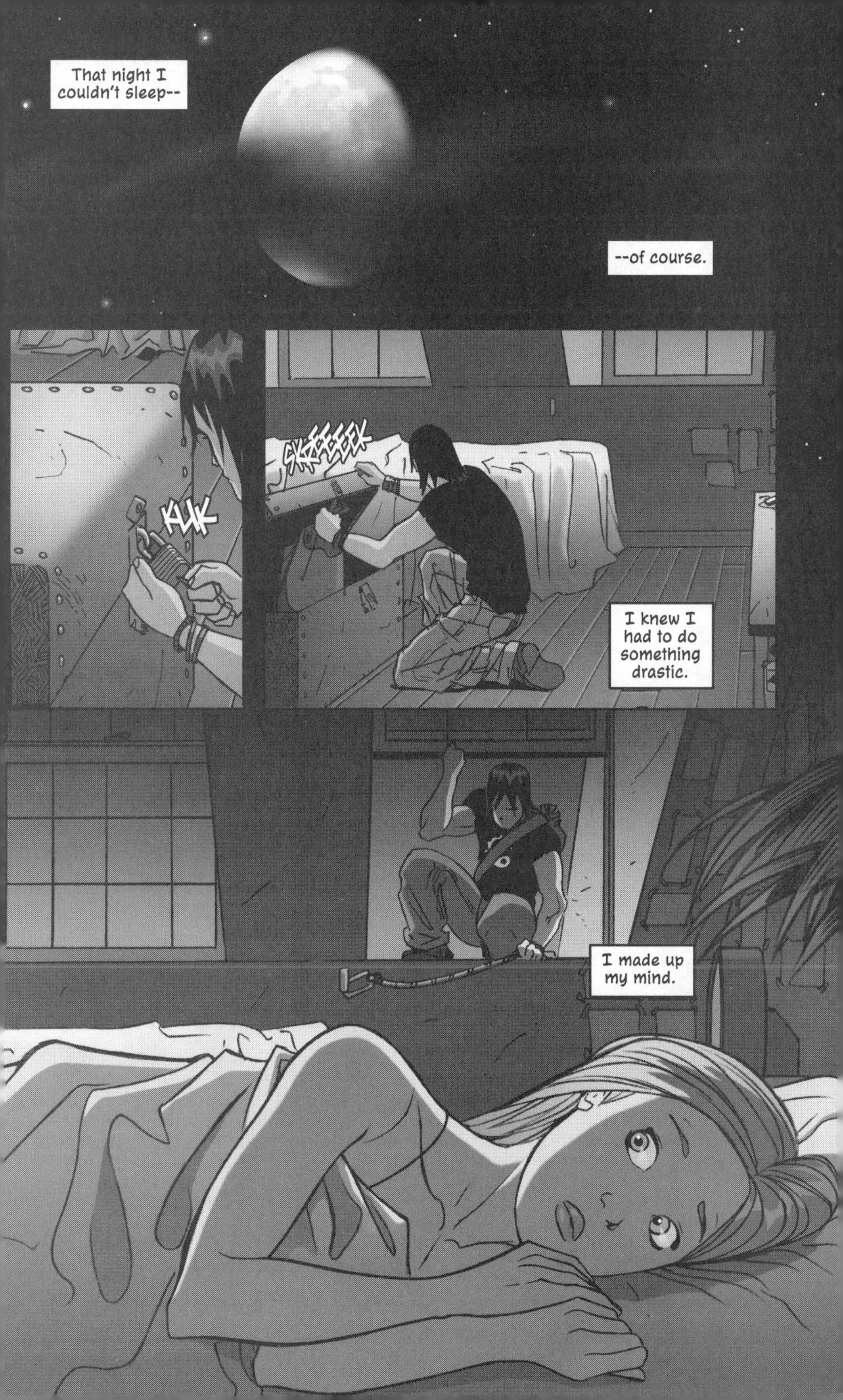
That night I couldn't sleep--
--of course.
KLIK
SKREEEEEK
I knew I had to do something drastic.
I made up my mind.

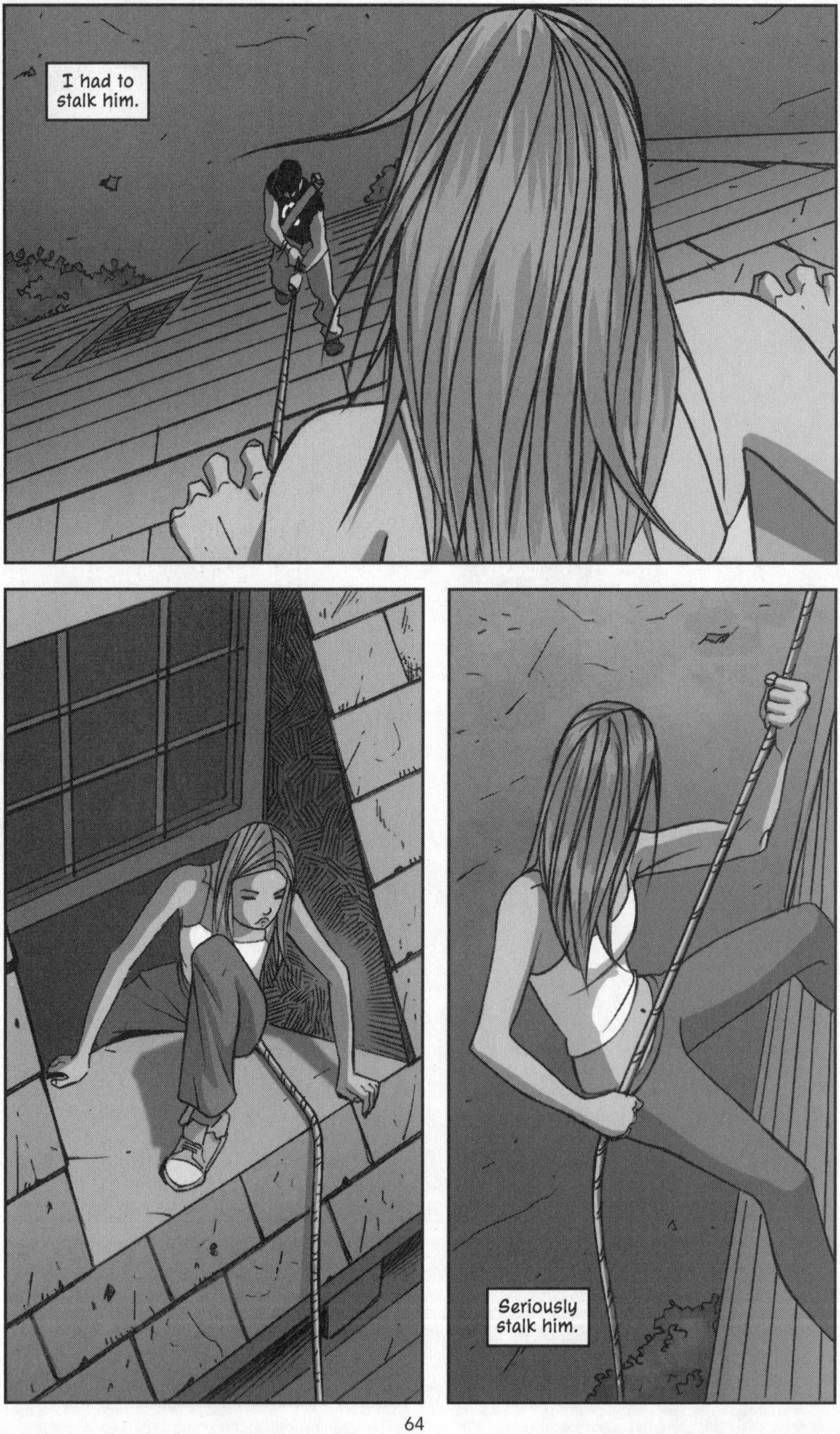
I had to stalk him.
Seriously stalk him.

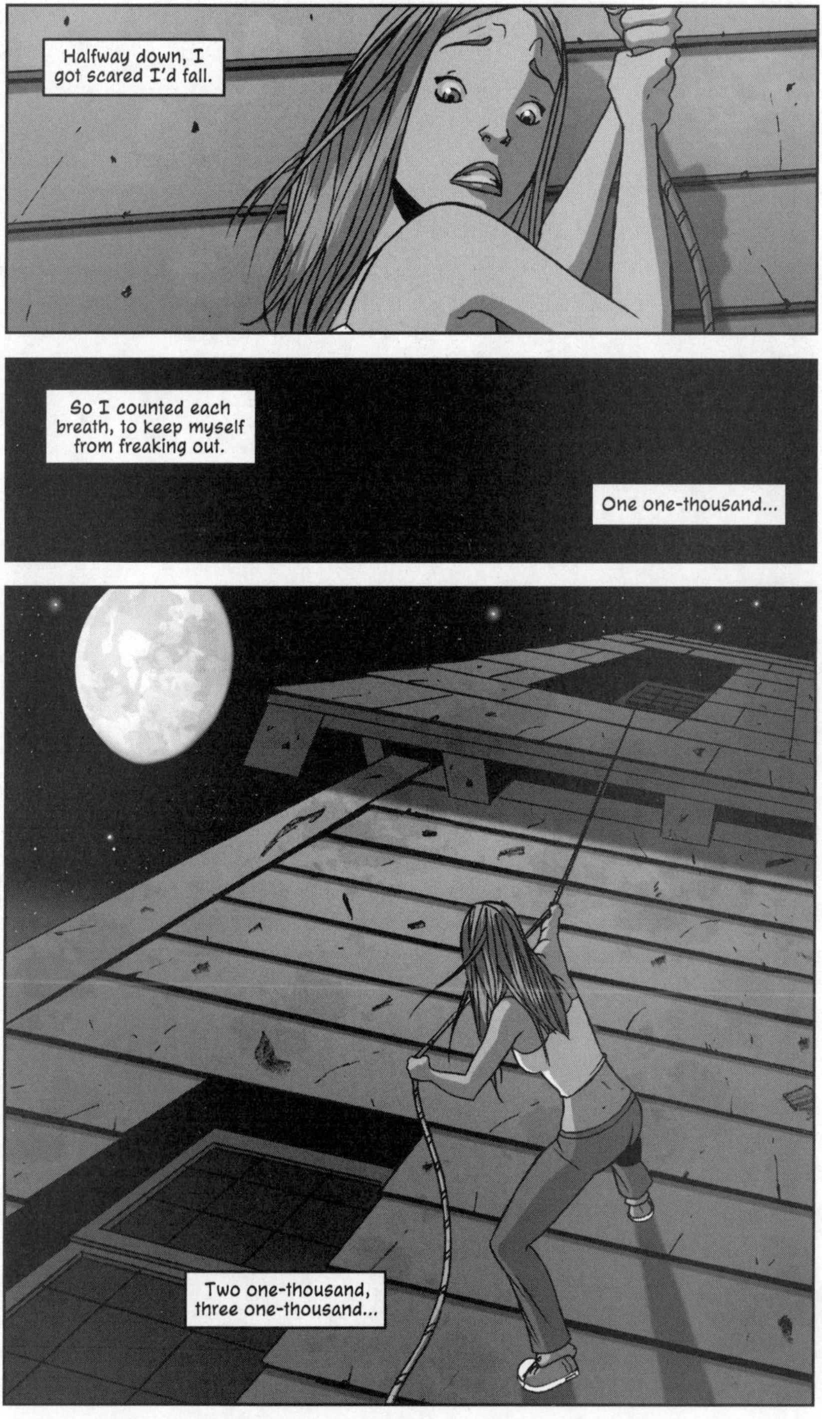
Halfway down, I got scared I'd fall.
So I counted each breath, to keep myself from freaking out.
One one-thousand...
Two one-thousand, three one-thousand...

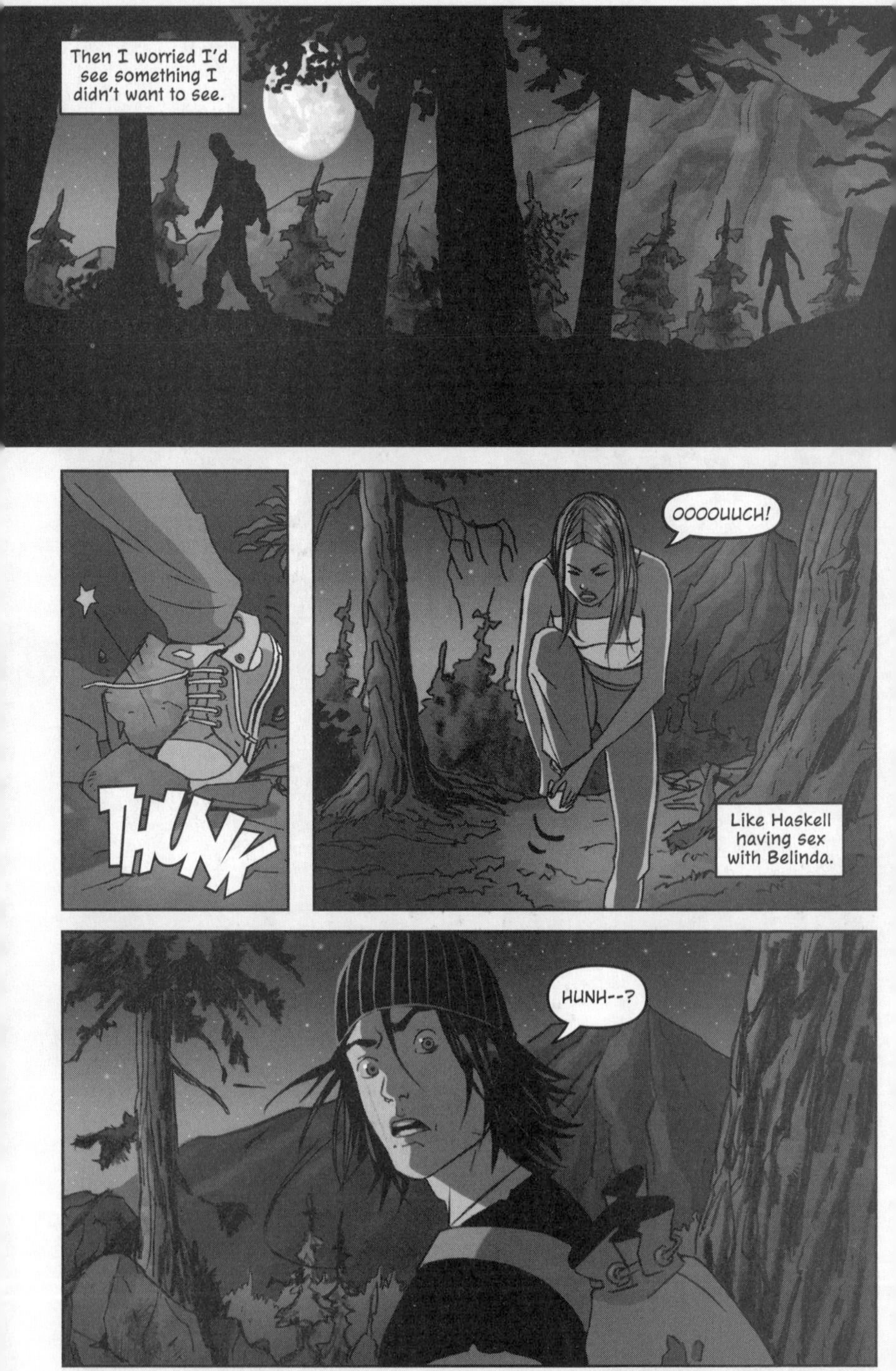
Then I worried I'd see something I didn't want to see.
THUNK
OOOOUUCH!
Like Haskell having sex with Belinda.
HUNH--?

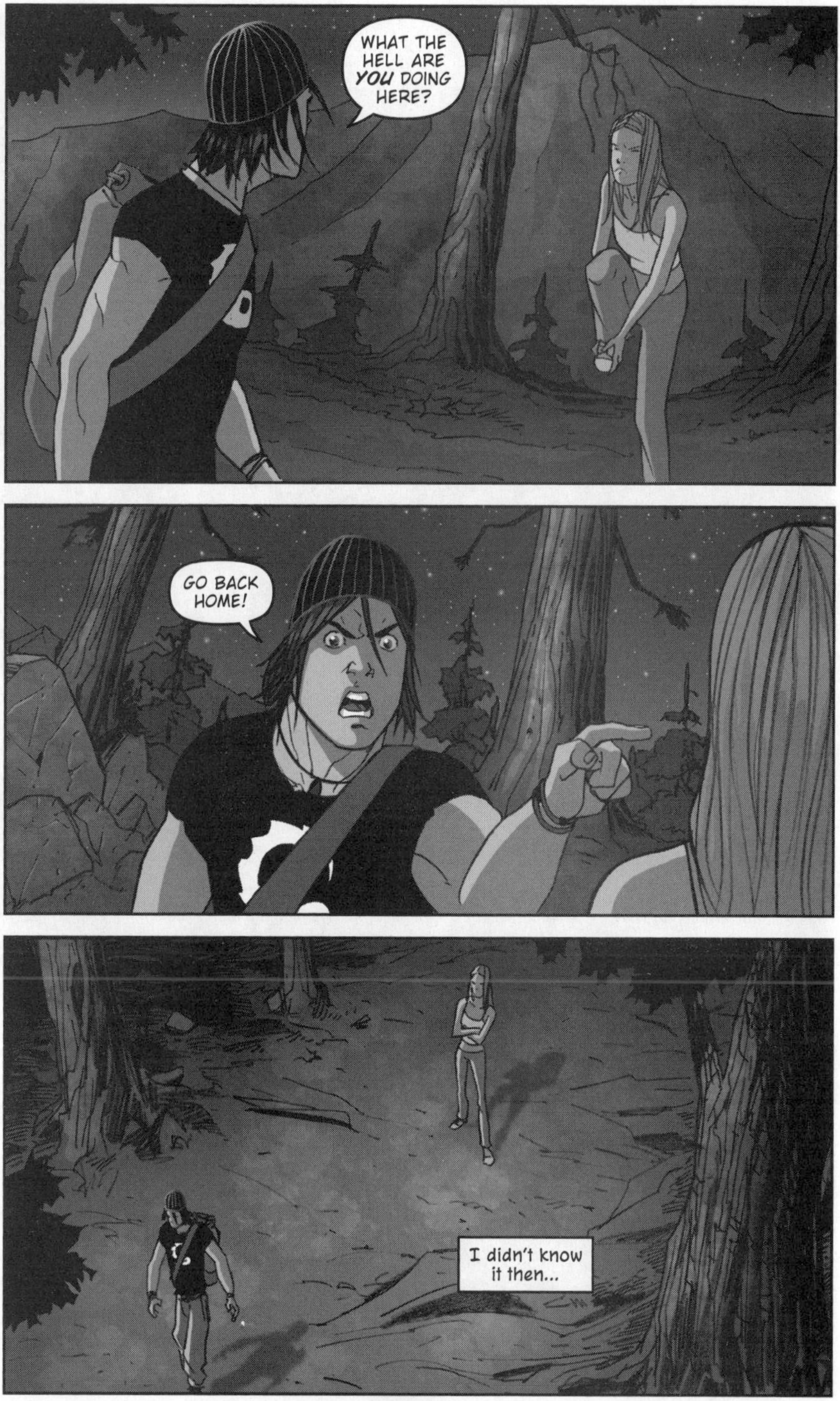
WHAT THE HELL ARE *YOU* DOING HERE?
GO BACK HOME!
I didn't know it then...

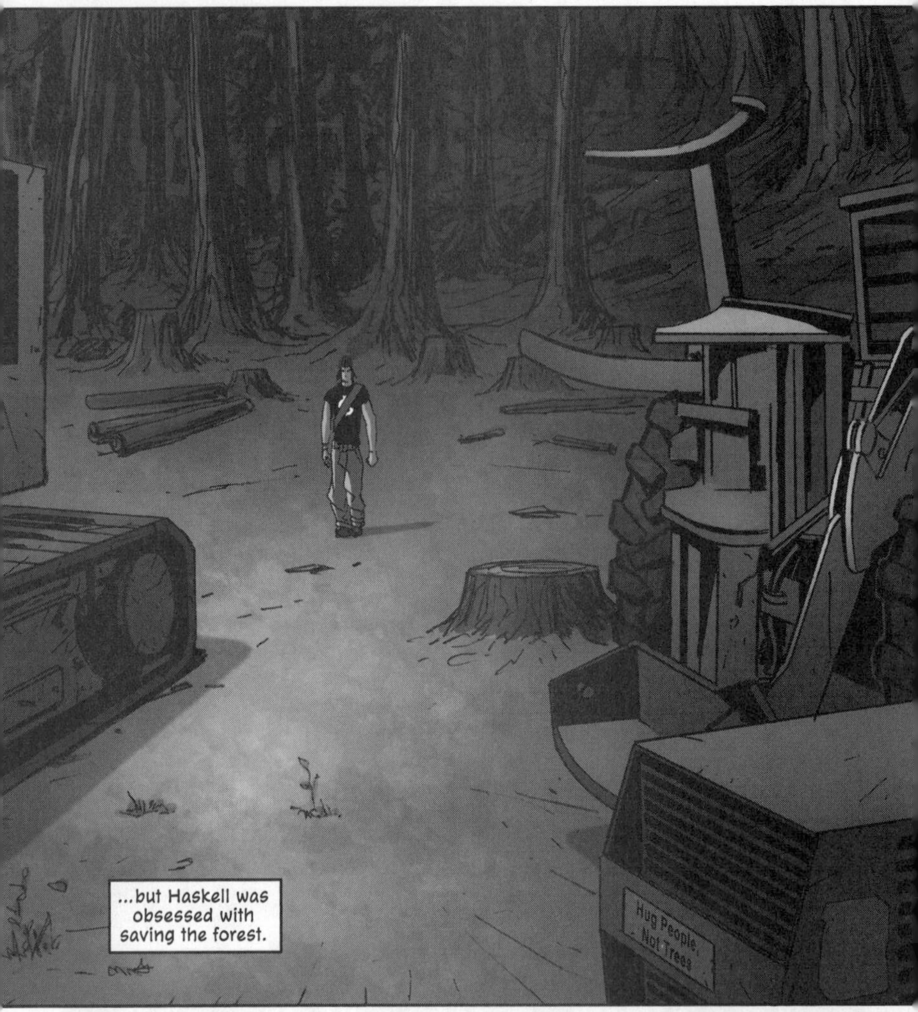
...but Haskell was obsessed with saving the forest.
Hug People, Not Trees

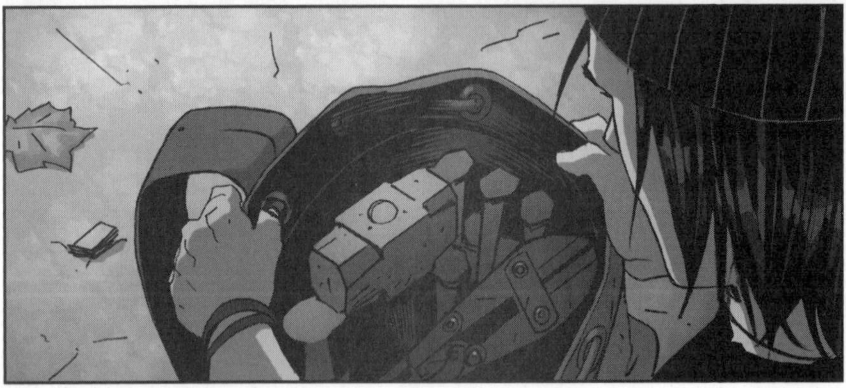

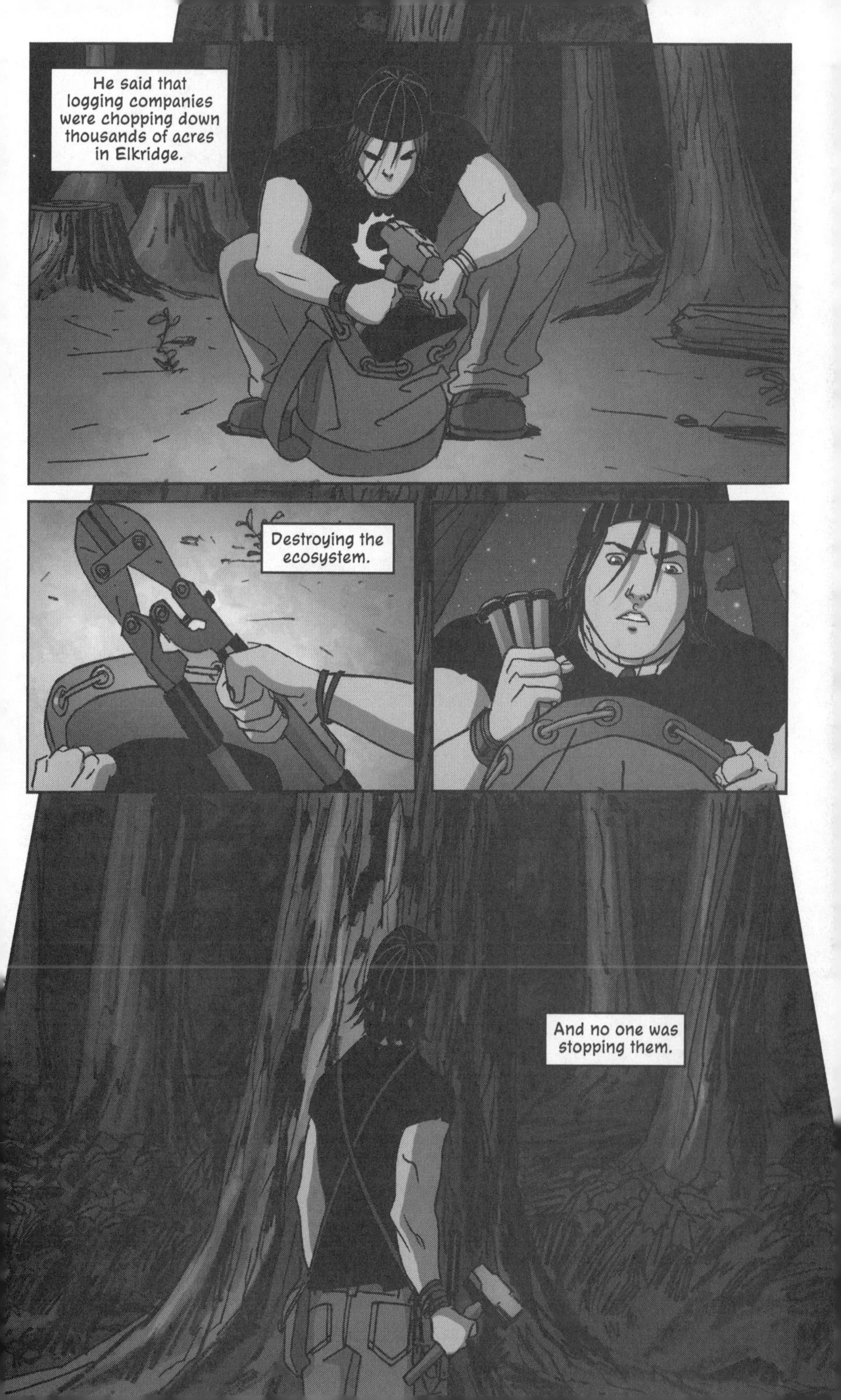
He said that logging companies were chopping down thousands of acres in Elkridge.
Destroying the ecosystem.
And no one was stopping them.

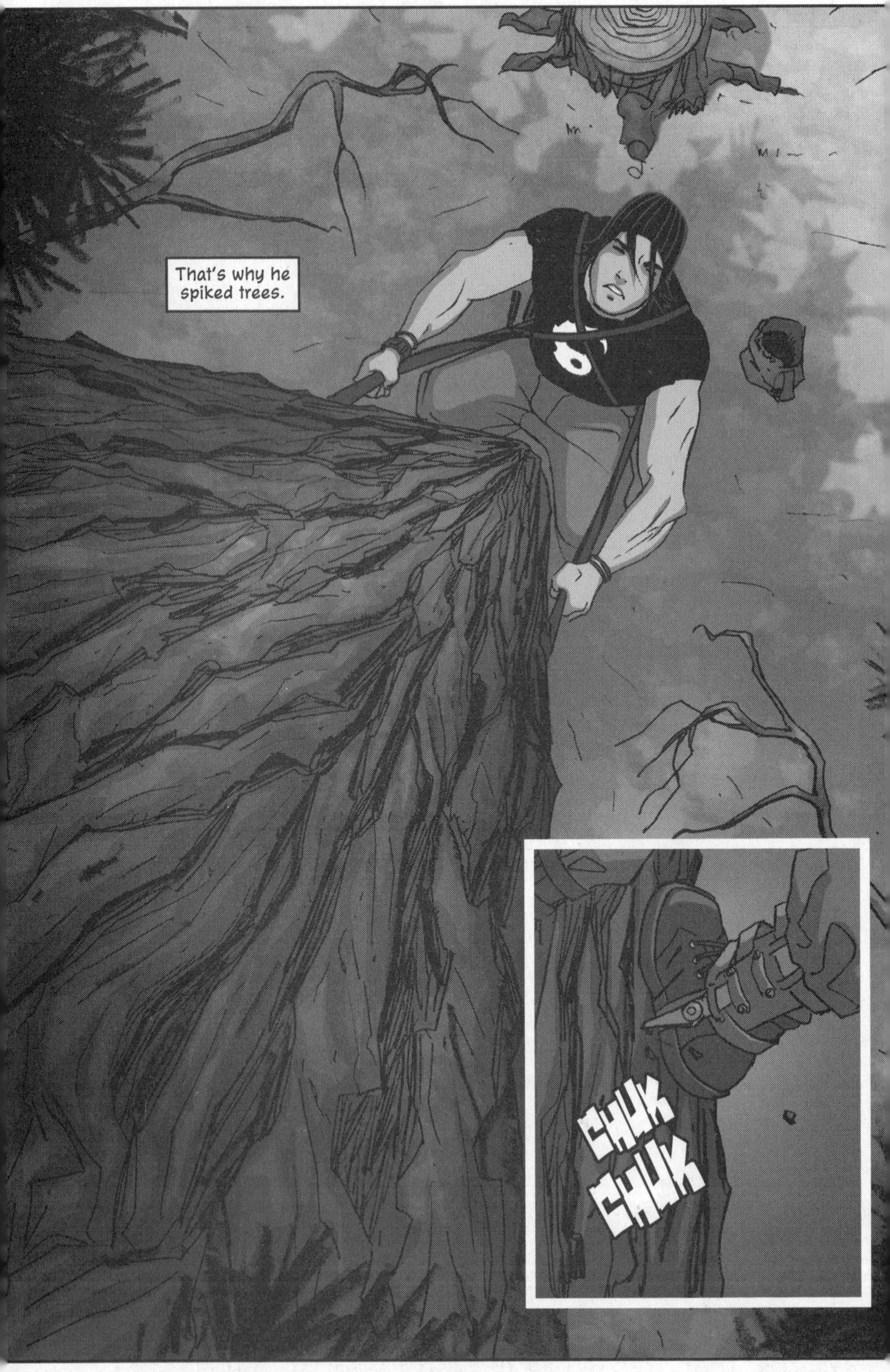
That's why he spiked trees.
CHUK
CHUK

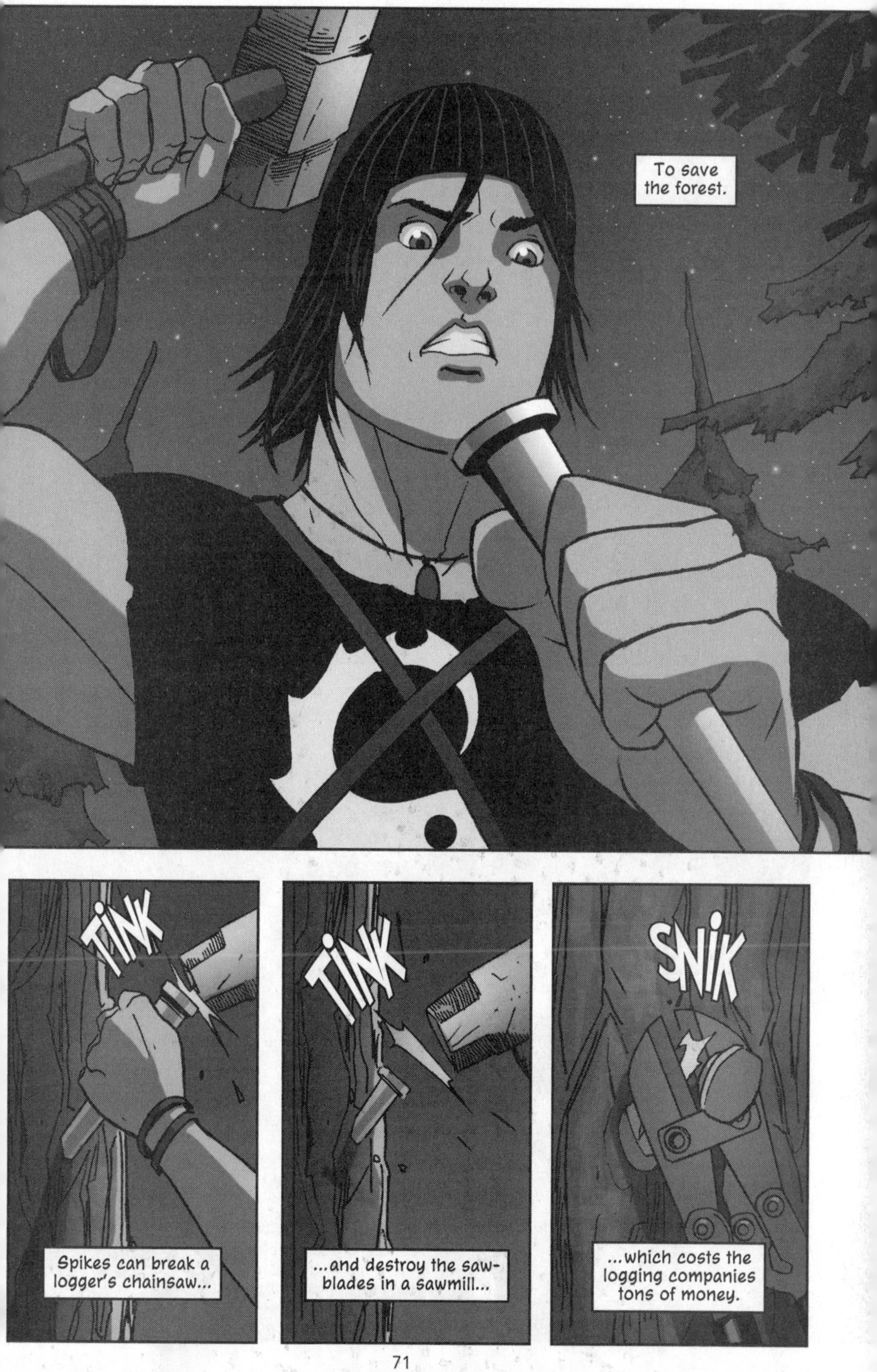
To save the forest.
TINK
Spikes can break a logger's chainsaw...
TINK
...and destroy the saw-blades in a sawmill...
SNIK
...which costs the logging companies tons of money.

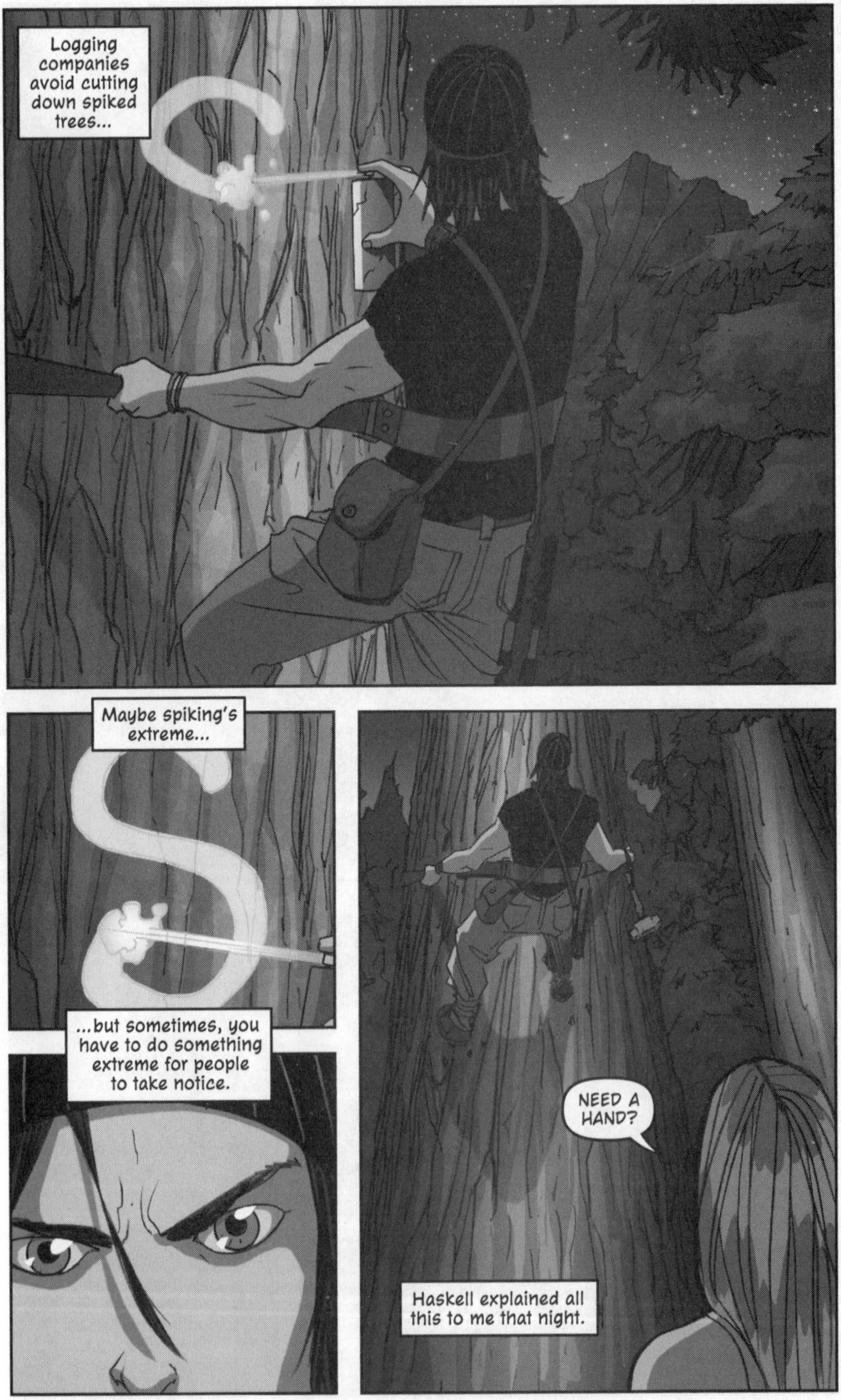
Logging companies avoid cutting down spiked trees...
Maybe spiking's extreme...
...but sometimes, you have to do something extreme for people to take notice.
NEED A HAND?
Haskell explained all this to me that night.

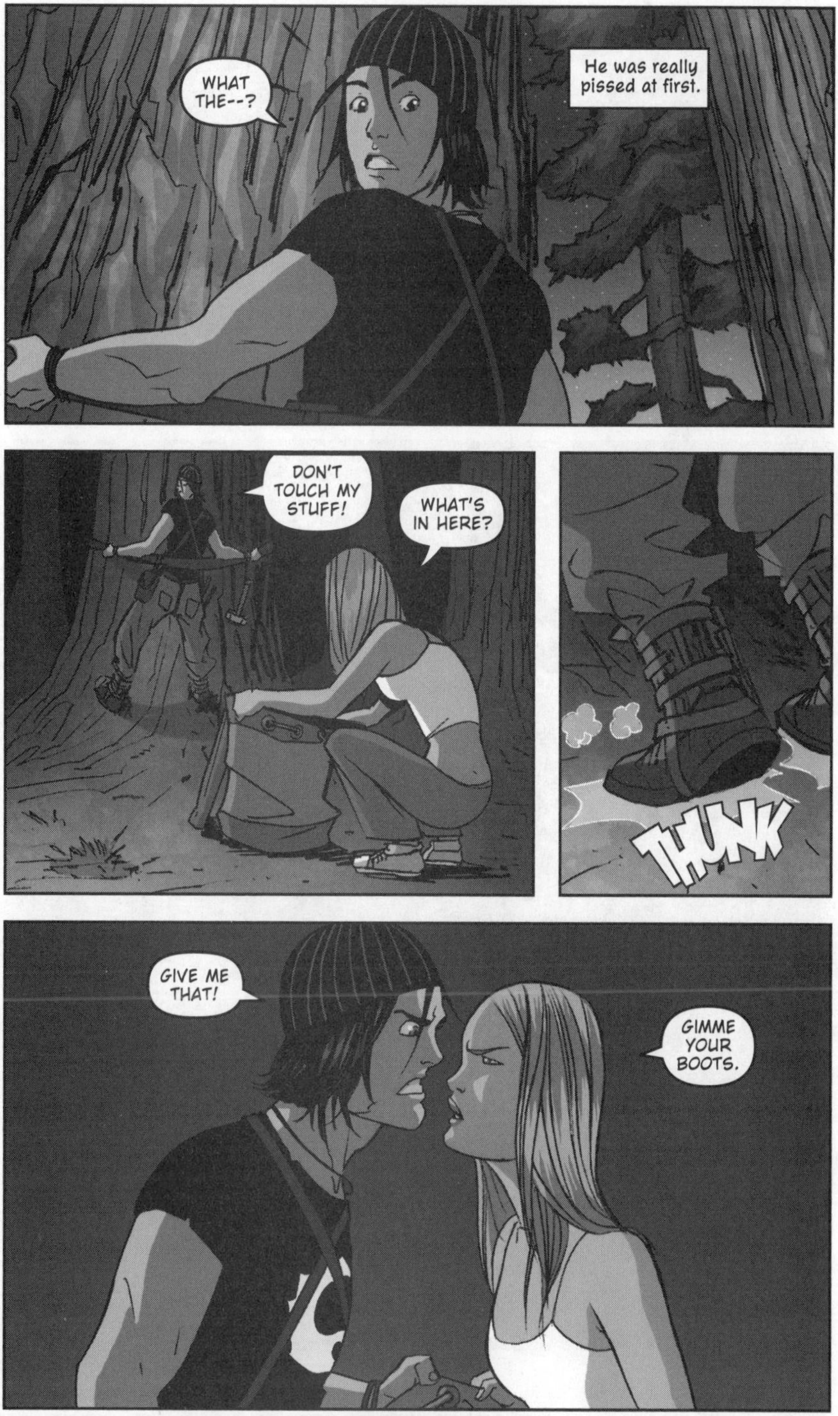
WHAT THE--?
He was really pissed at first.
DON'T TOUCH MY STUFF!
WHAT'S IN HERE?
THUNK
GIVE ME THAT!
GIMME YOUR BOOTS.

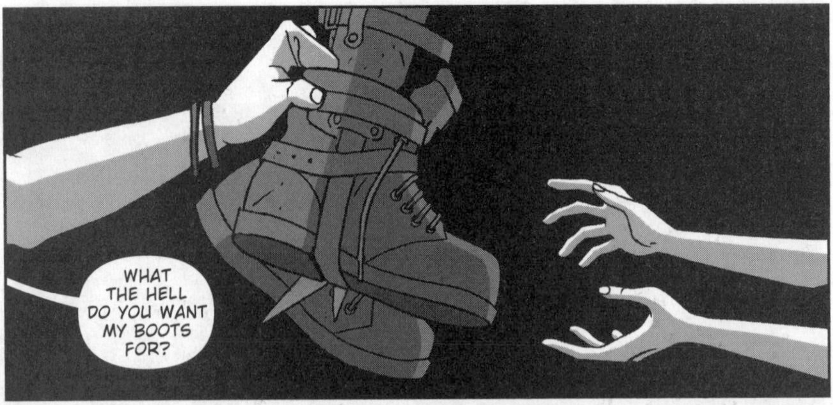
WHAT THE HELL DO YOU WANT MY BOOTS FOR?

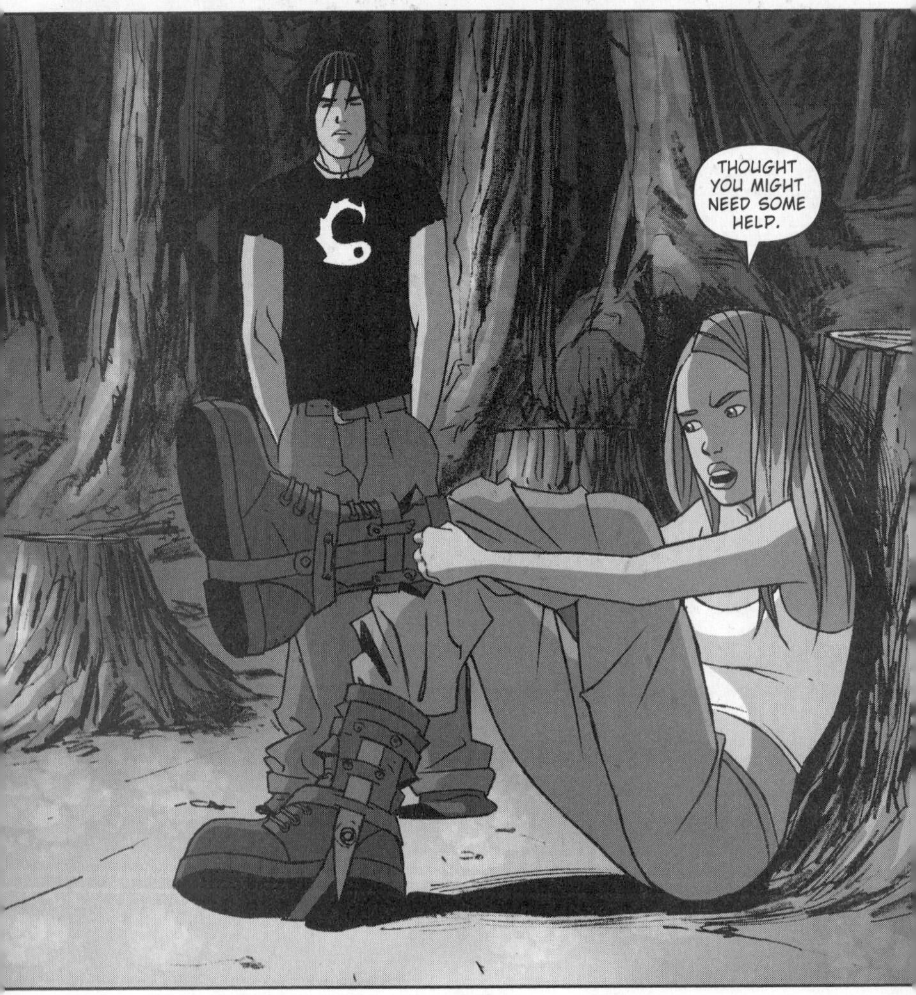
THOUGHT YOU MIGHT NEED SOME HELP.

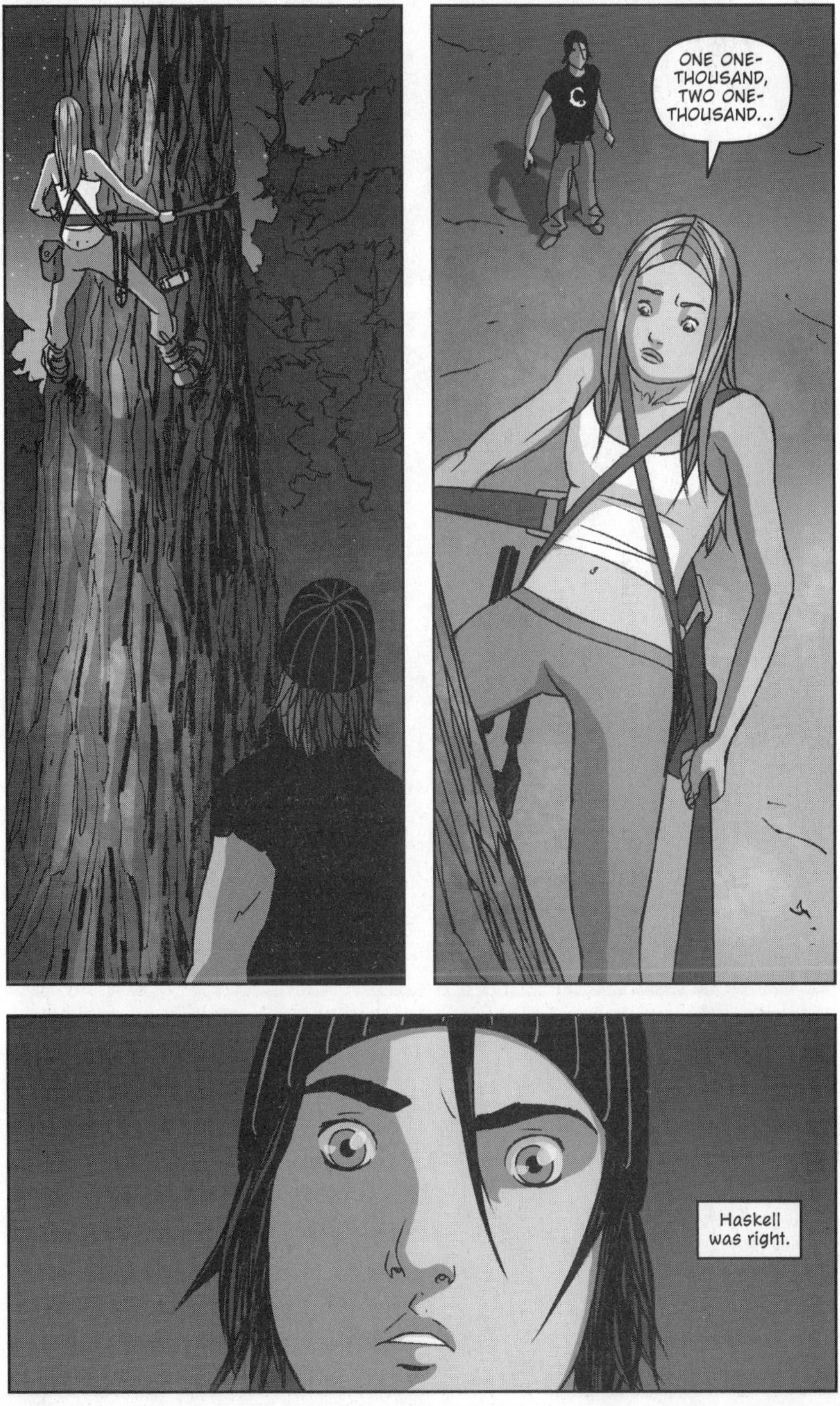
ONE ONE-THOUSAND, TWO ONE-THOUSAND...
Haskell was right.

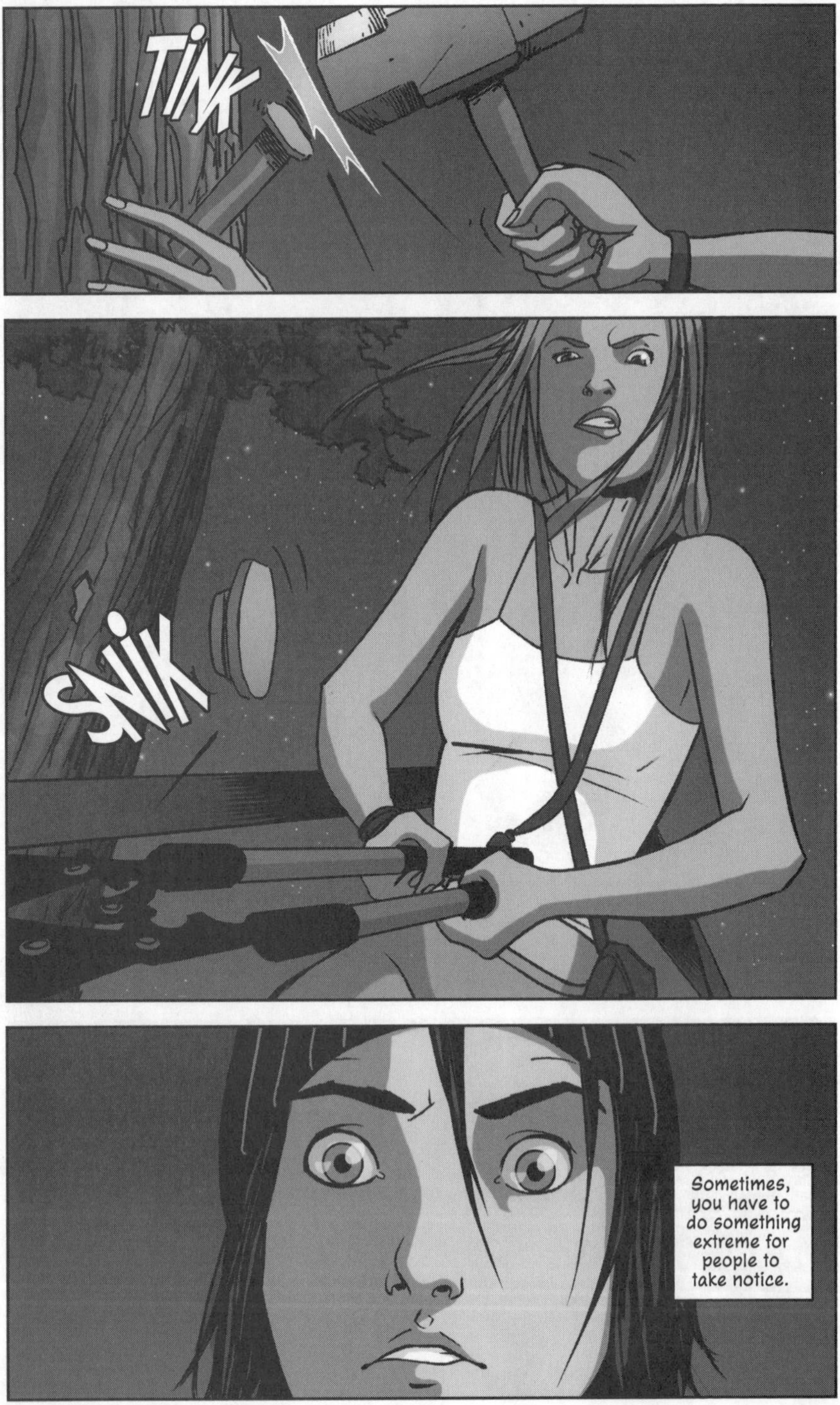
TINK
SNIK
Sometimes, you have to do something extreme for people to take notice.

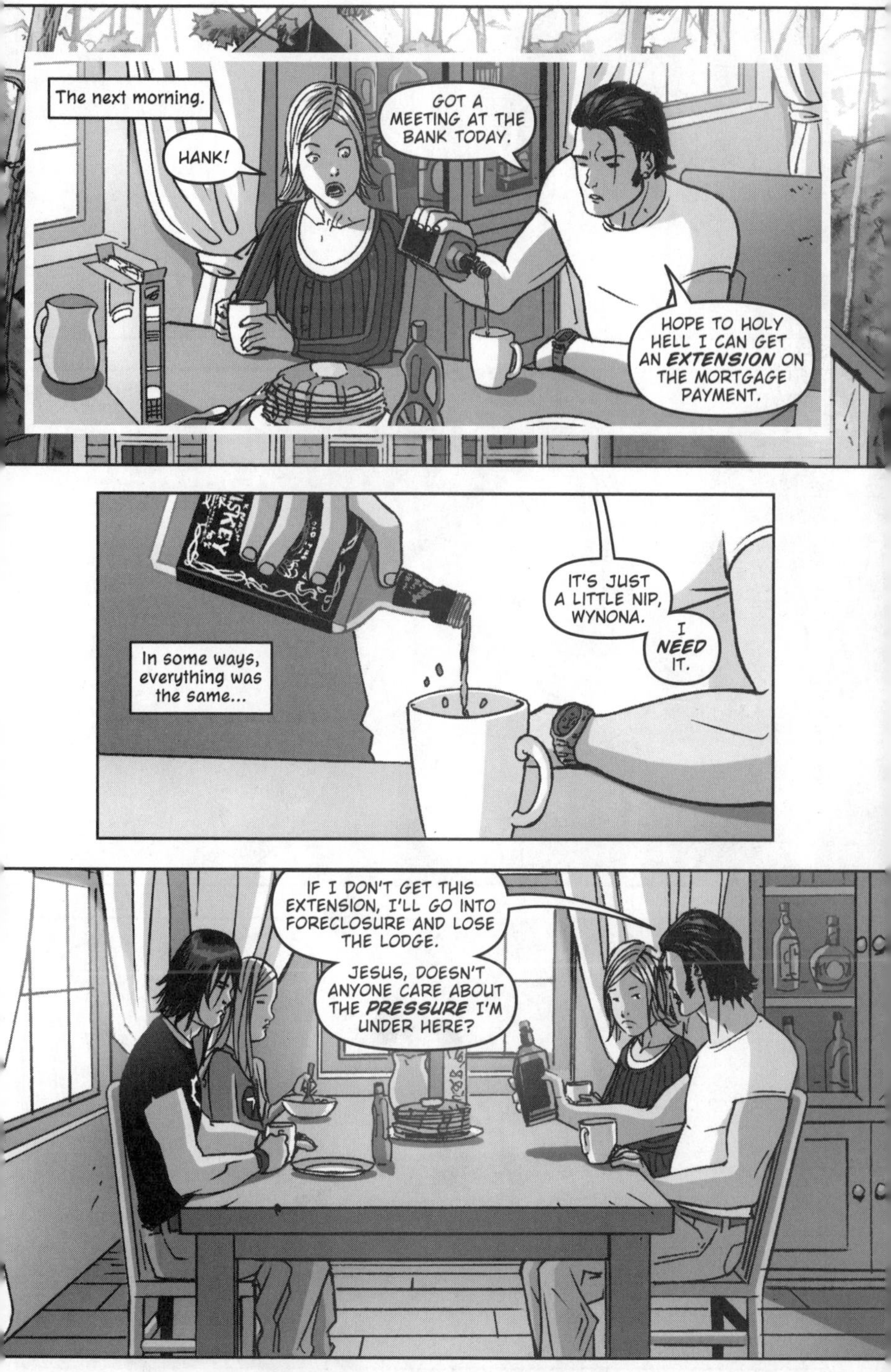
The next morning.
HANK!
GOT A MEETING AT THE BANK TODAY.
HOPE TO HOLY HELL I CAN GET AN *EXTENSION* ON THE MORTGAGE PAYMENT.
In some ways, everything was the same...
IT'S JUST A LITTLE NIP, WYNONA.
I *NEED* IT.
IF I DON'T GET THIS EXTENSION, I'LL GO INTO FORECLOSURE AND LOSE THE LODGE.
JESUS, DOESN'T ANYONE CARE ABOUT THE *PRESSURE* I'M UNDER HERE?

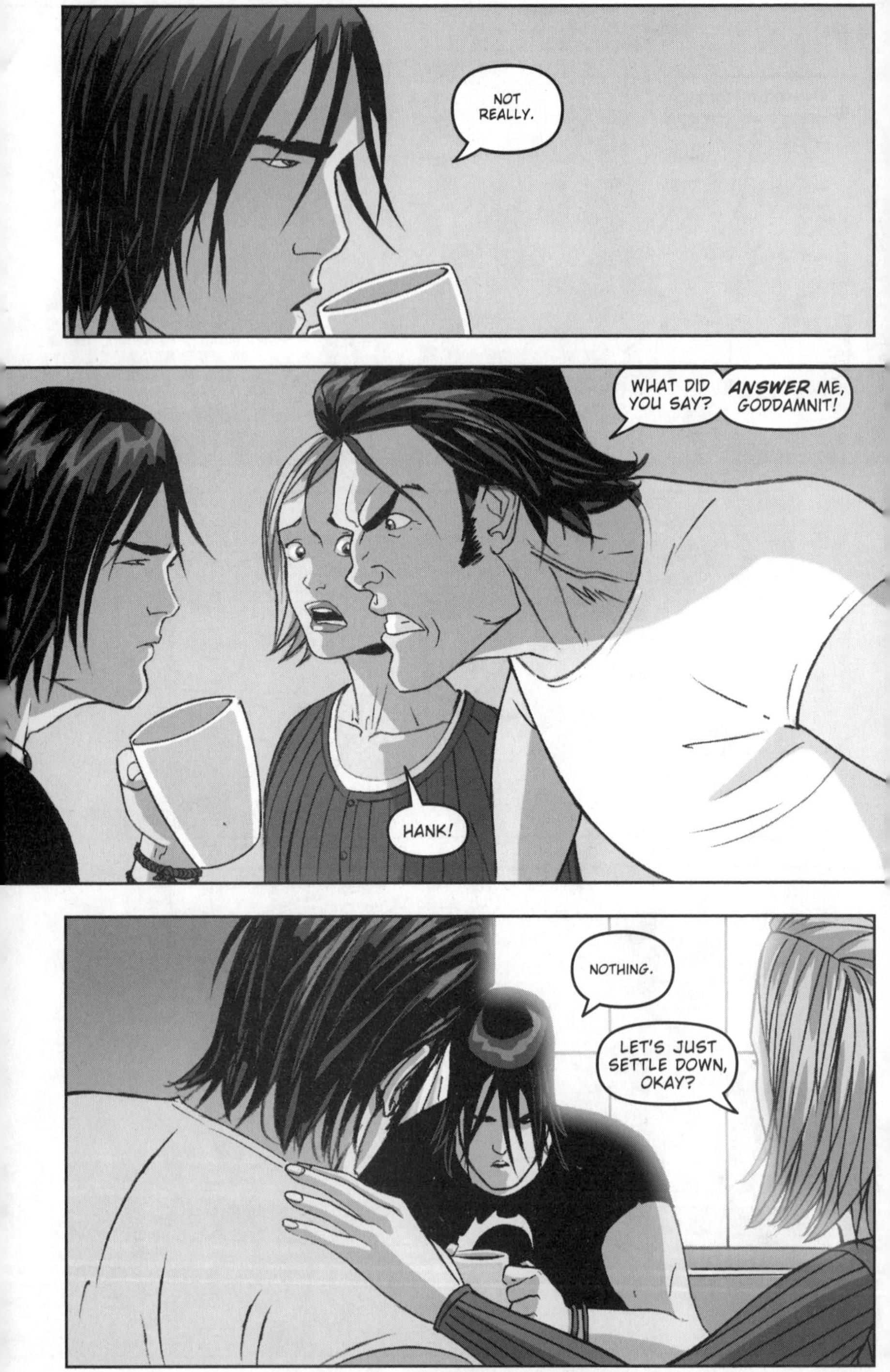
NOT REALLY.
WHAT DID YOU SAY?
ANSWER ME, GODDAMNIT!
HANK!
NOTHING.
LET'S JUST SETTLE DOWN, OKAY?

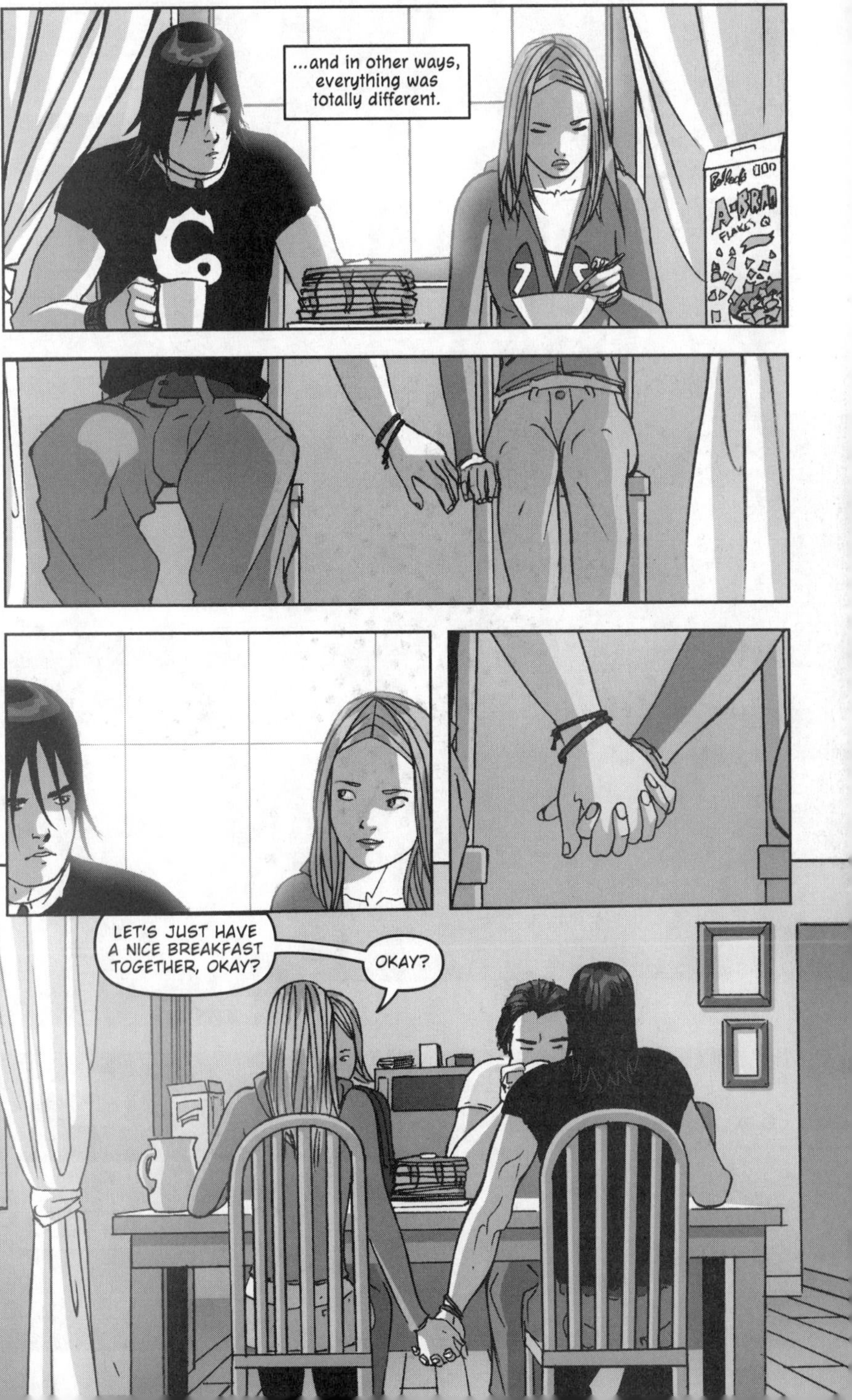
...and in other ways, everything was totally different.
A-BRAN FLAKES
LET'S JUST HAVE A NICE BREAKFAST TOGETHER, OKAY?
OKAY?

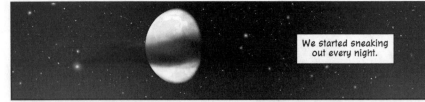

We started sneaking
out every night.

HEY, WAIT.
DON'T SPIKE
LOW.

TINK
TINK

WE ONLY
SPIKE
HIGH.

WHY?

JUST
TRUST
ME.

OKAY.

Haskell said
we should keep
a lookout for
forest rangers.

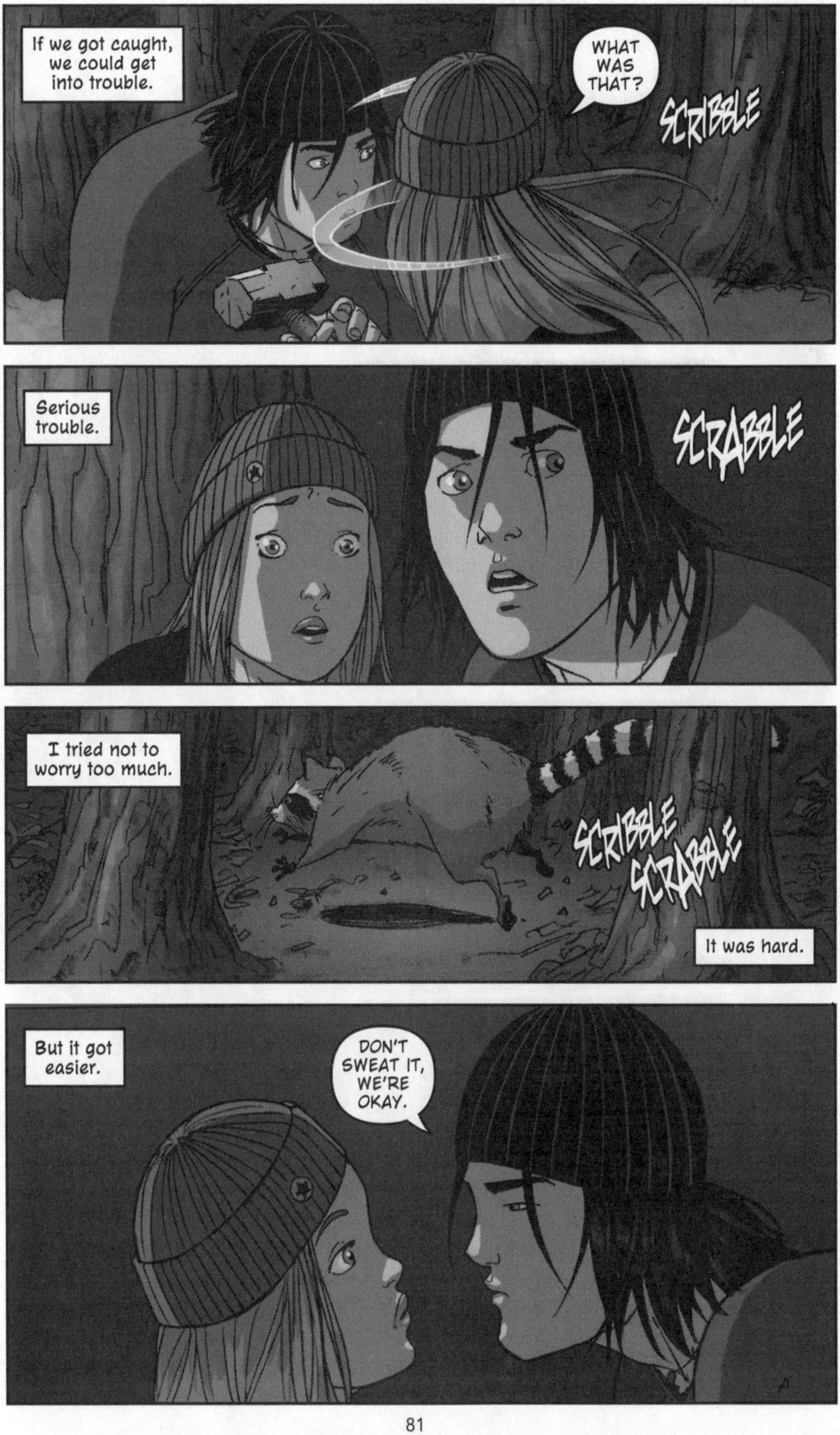
If we got caught, we could get into trouble.
WHAT WAS THAT?
SCRIBBLE
Serious trouble.
SCRABBLE
I tried not to worry too much.
SCRIBBLE
SCRABBLE
It was hard.
But it got easier.
DON'T SWEAT IT, WE'RE OKAY.

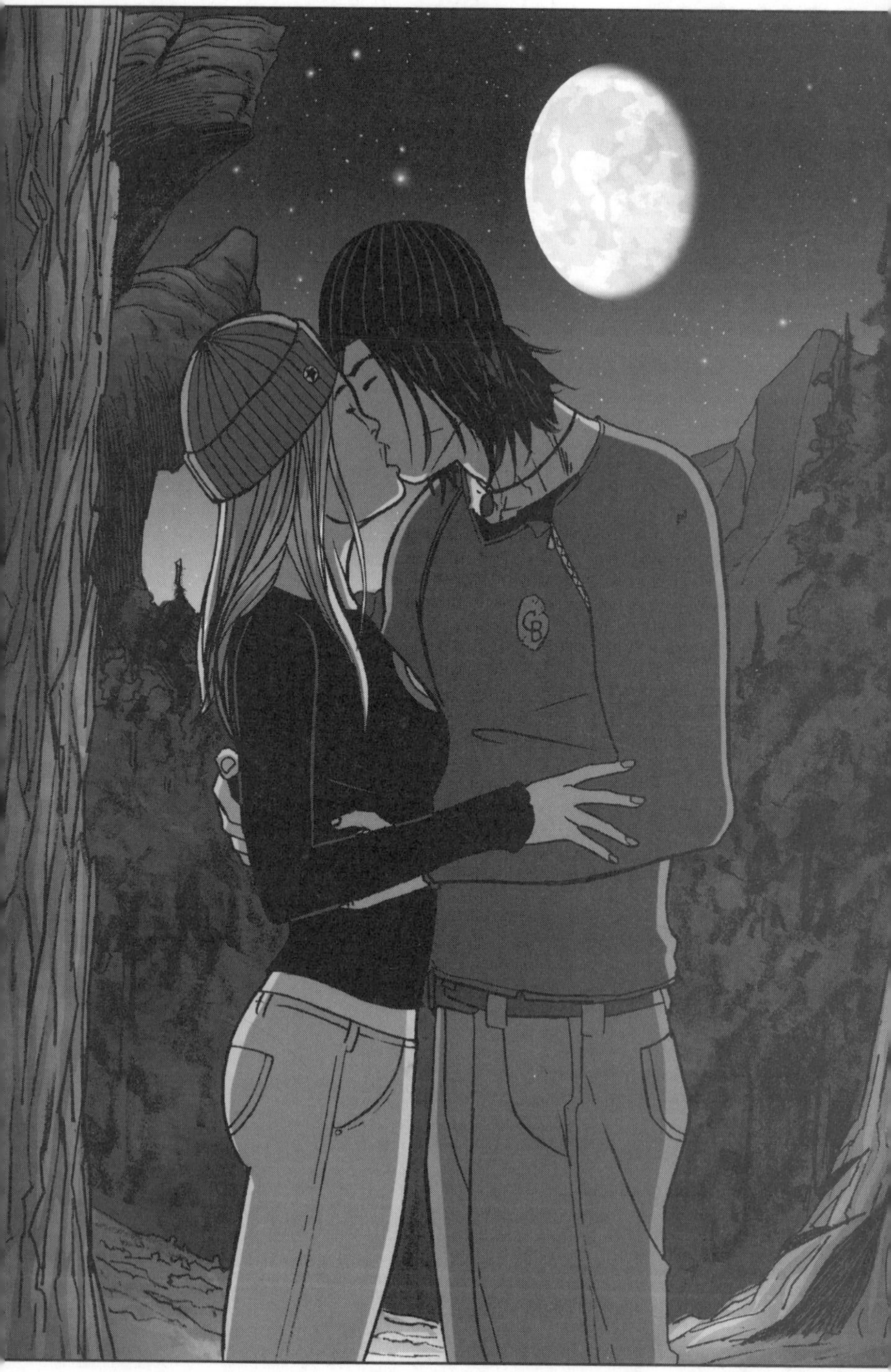

Danni-
Where
r u?
Back ● Send
New Message
Danni-
Where
r u?
Back ● Send
Hel-LO?
Back ● Send
New Message
Hel-LO?
Back ● Send
U r
such a
bitch!
Back ● Send
New Message
U r
such a
bitch!
Back ● Send

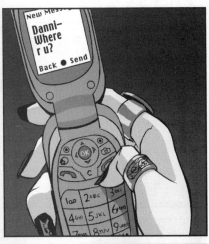

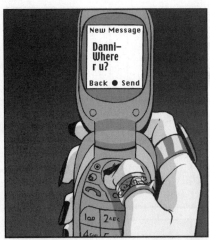

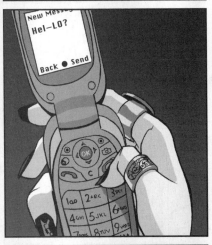

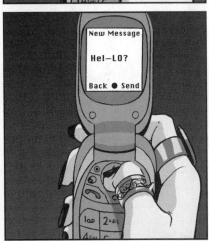

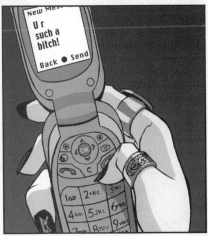

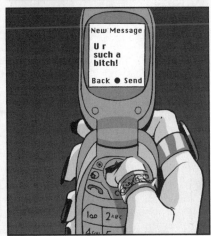

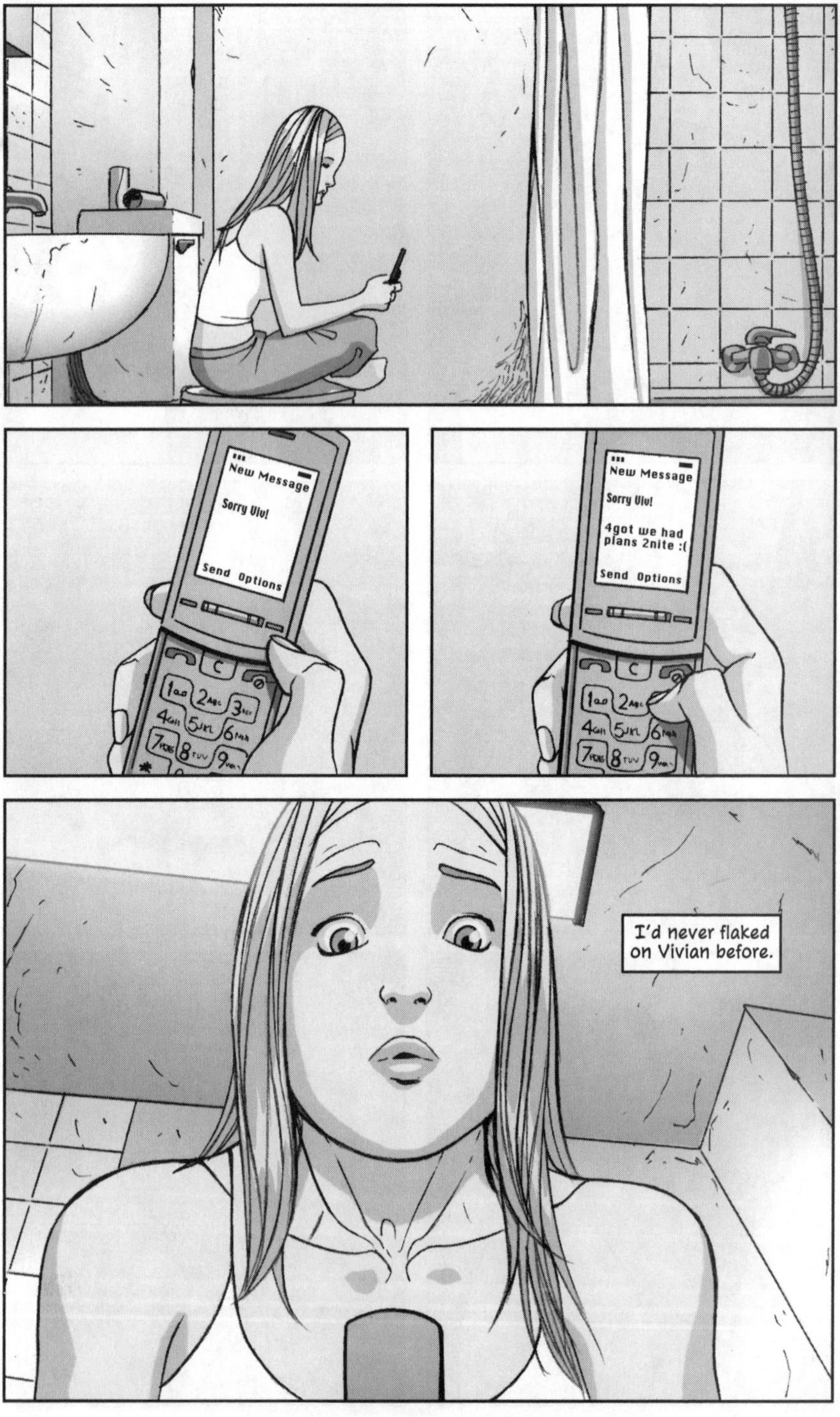
New Message
Sorry Viv!
Send Options
New Message
Sorry Viv!
4got we had plans 2nite :(
Send Options
I'd never flaked on Vivian before.

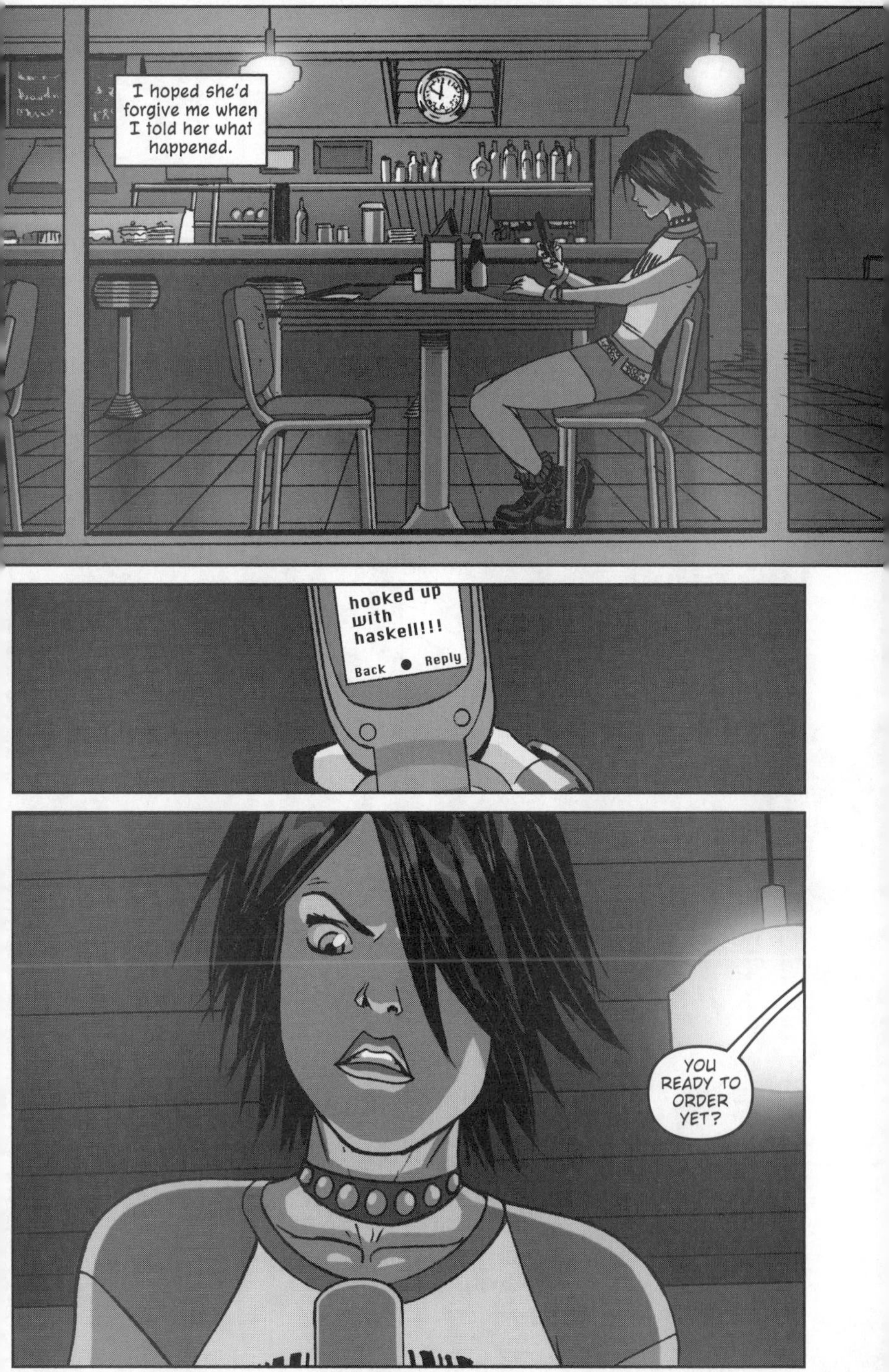
I hoped she'd forgive me when I told her what happened.
hooked up with haskell!!!
Back
Reply
YOU READY TO ORDER YET?

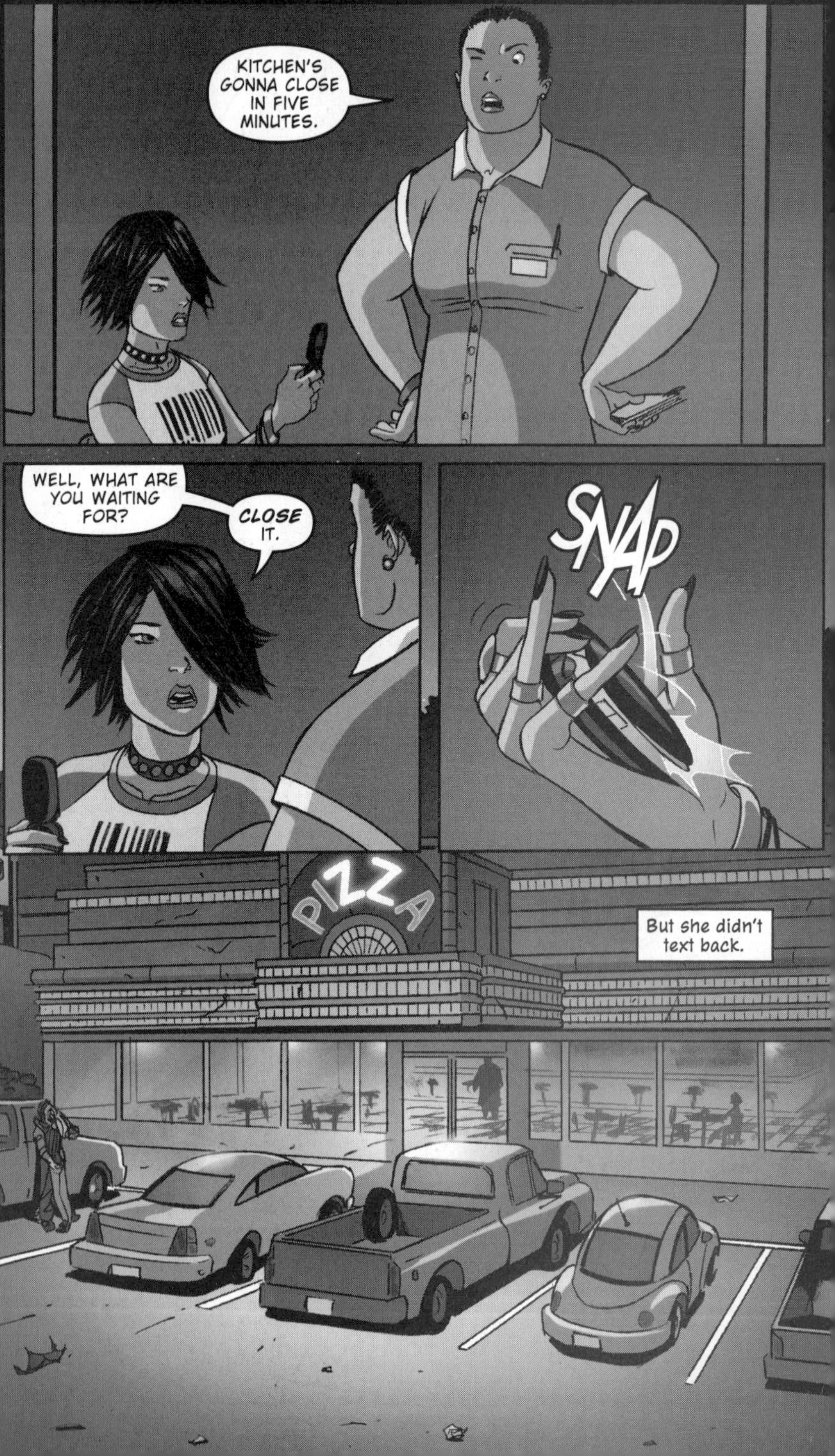

KITCHEN'S GONNA CLOSE IN FIVE MINUTES.
WELL, WHAT ARE YOU WAITING FOR?
CLOSE IT.
SNAP
PIZZA
But she didn't text back.

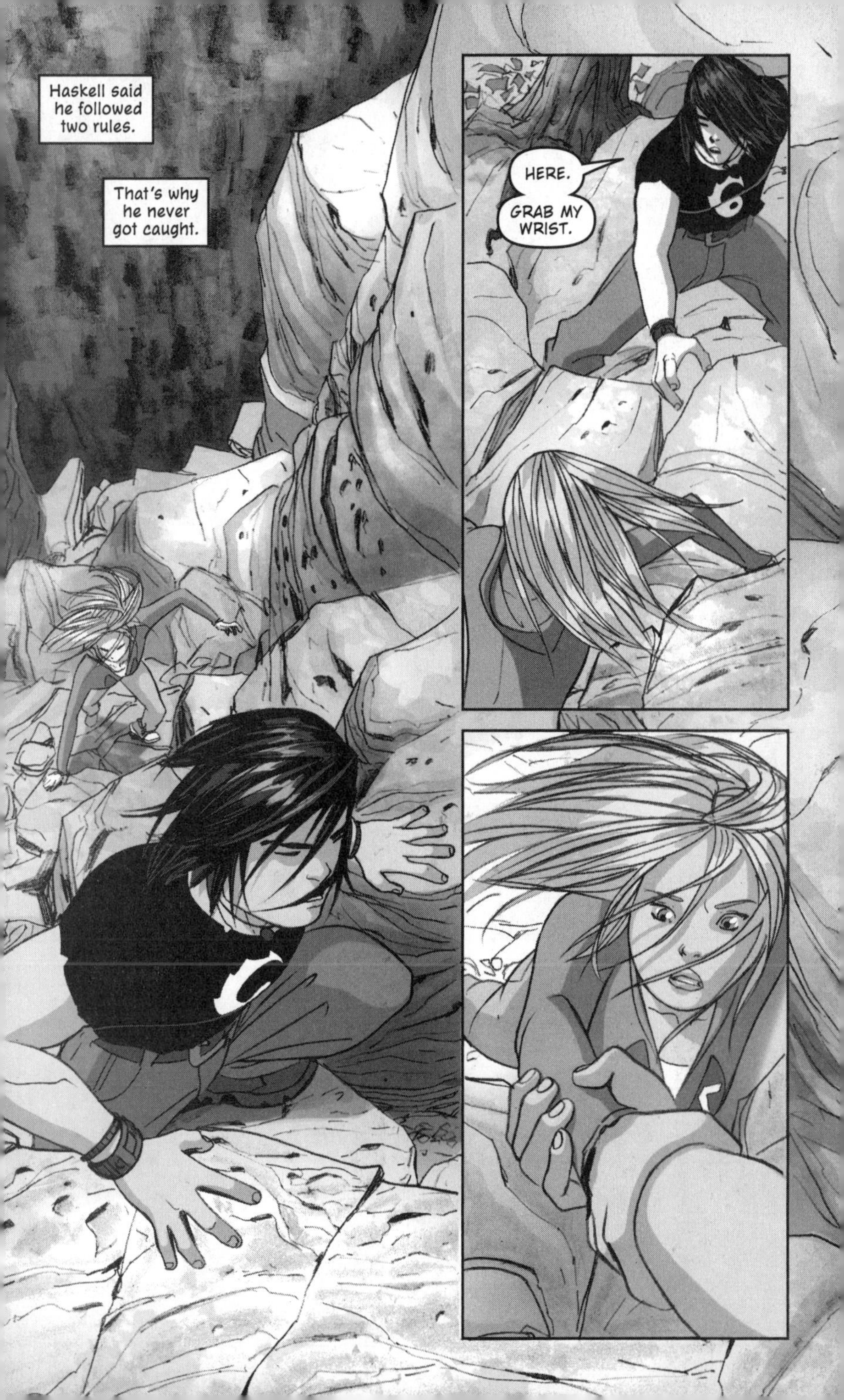
Haskell said he followed two rules.
That's why he never got caught.
HERE.
GRAB MY WRIST.

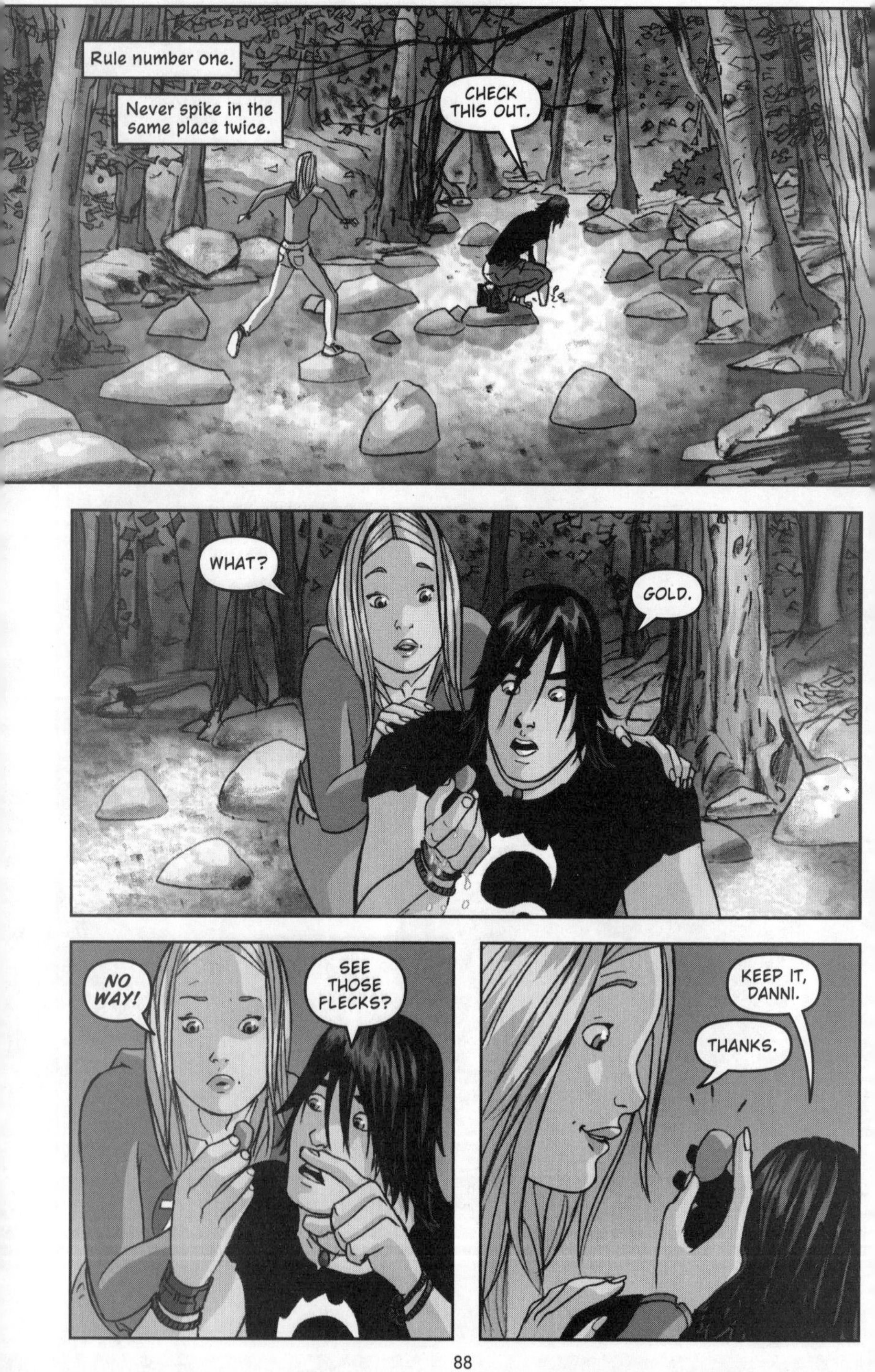
Rule number one.
Never spike in the same place twice.
CHECK THIS OUT.
WHAT?
GOLD.
NO WAY!
SEE THOSE FLECKS?
KEEP IT, DANNI.
THANKS.

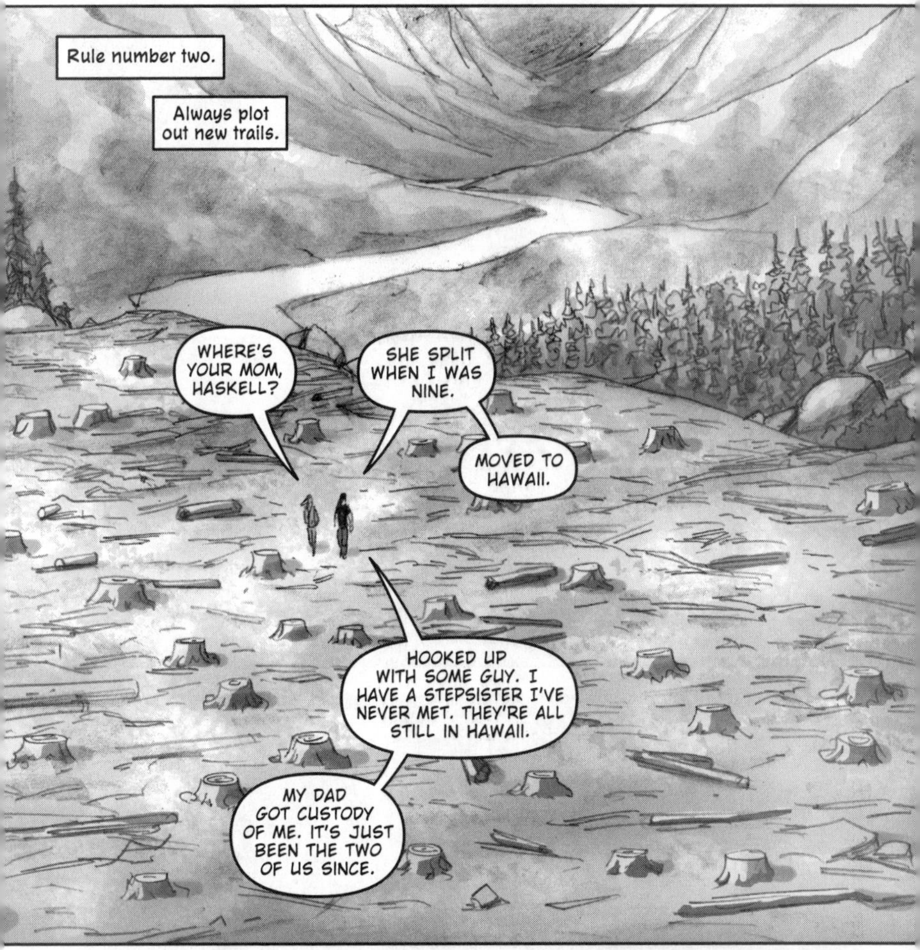
Rule number two.
Always plot out new trails.
WHERE'S YOUR MOM, HASKELL?
SHE SPLIT WHEN I WAS NINE.
MOVED TO HAWAII.
HOOKED UP WITH SOME GUY. I HAVE A STEPSISTER I'VE NEVER MET. THEY'RE ALL STILL IN HAWAII.
MY DAD GOT CUSTODY OF ME. IT'S JUST BEEN THE TWO OF US SINCE.

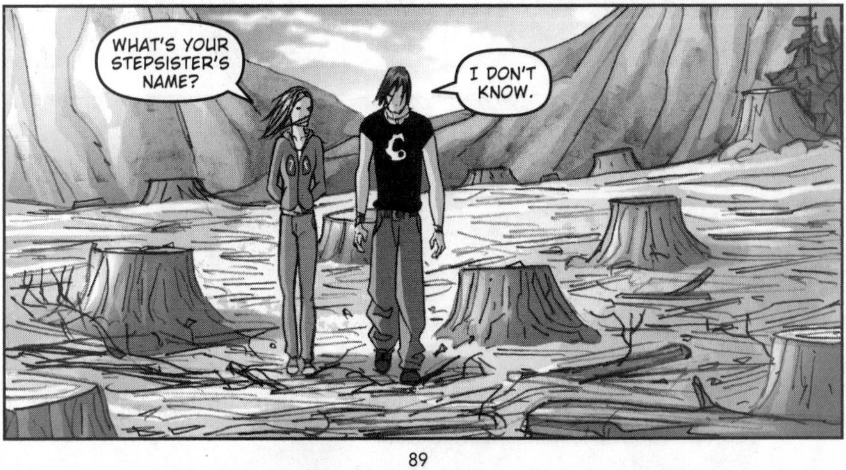
WHAT'S YOUR STEPSISTER'S NAME?
I DON'T KNOW.

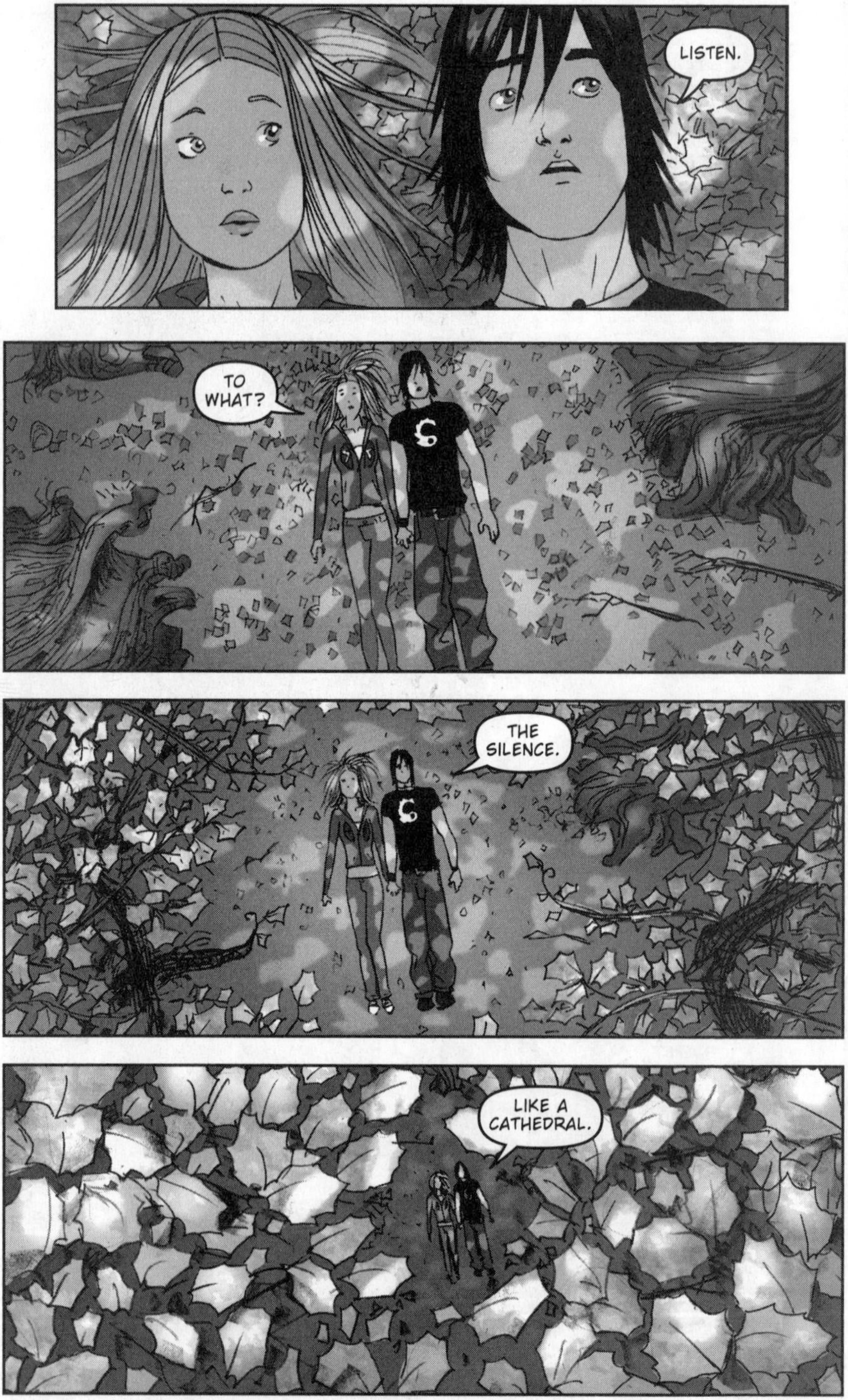
LISTEN.
TO WHAT?
THE SILENCE.
LIKE A CATHEDRAL.

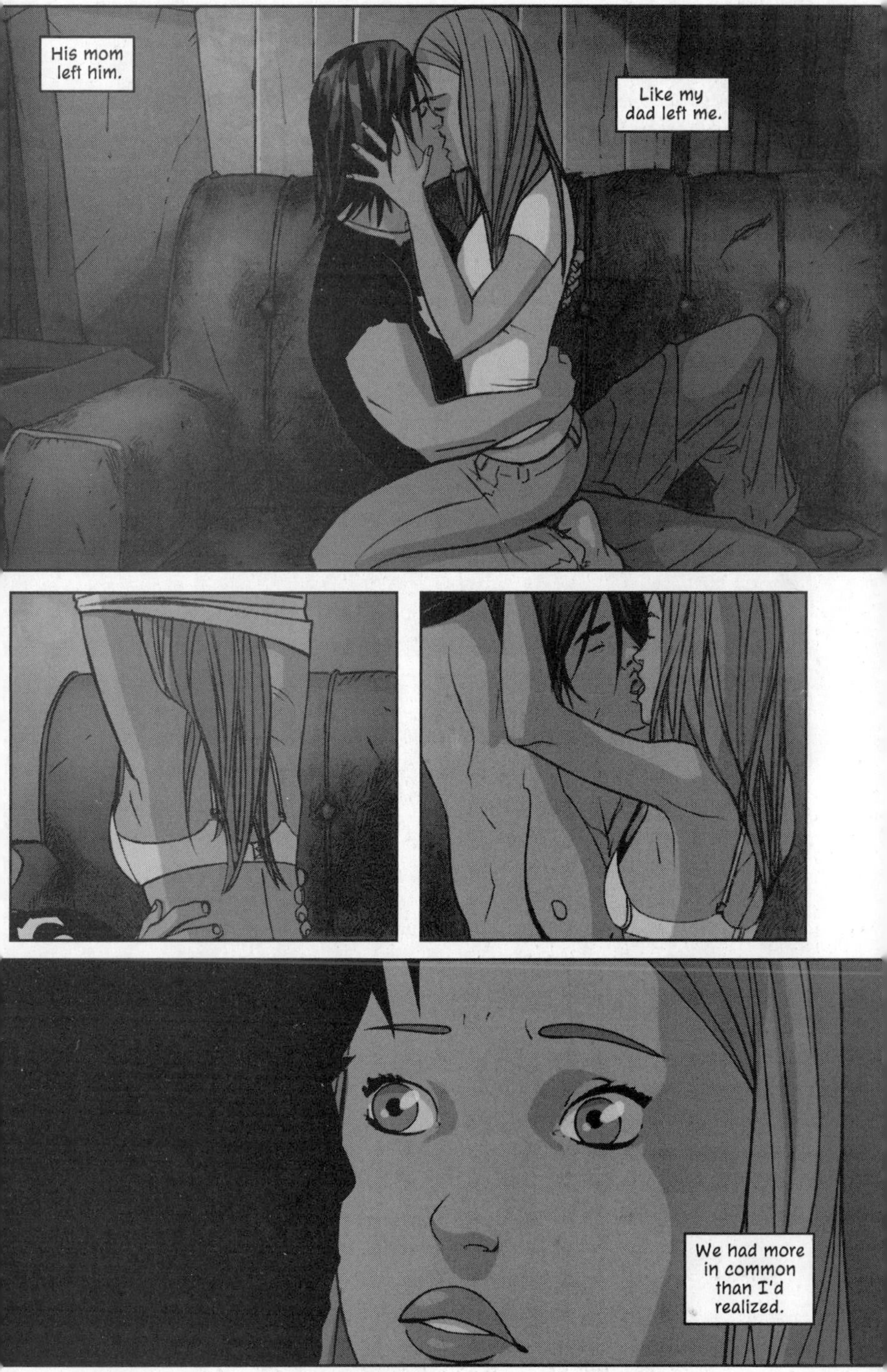
His mom left him.
Like my dad left me.
We had more in common than I'd realized.

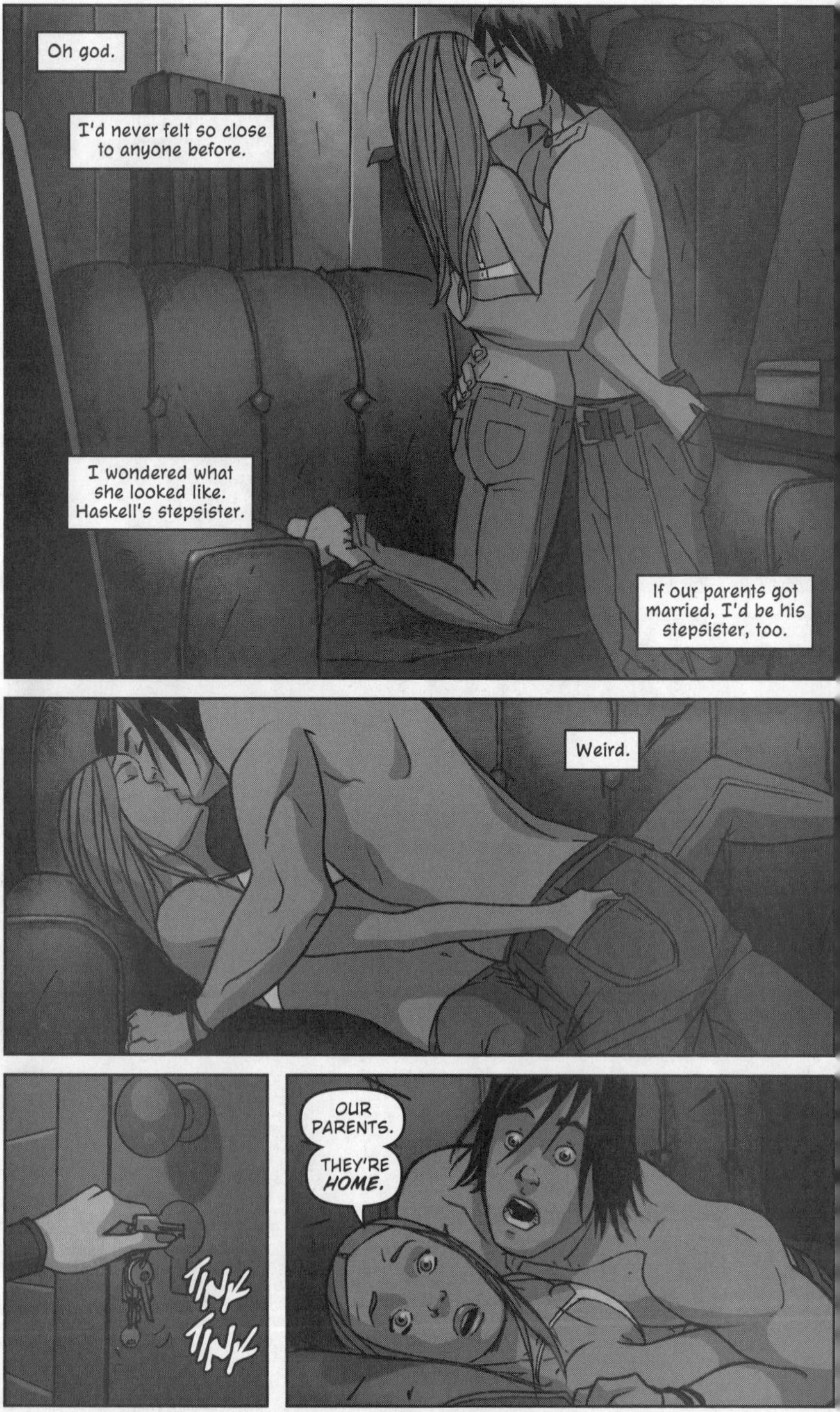
Oh god.
I'd never felt so close to anyone before.
I wondered what she looked like. Haskell's stepsister.
If our parents got married, I'd be his stepsister, too.
Weird.
TINK
TINK
OUR PARENTS.
THEY'RE *HOME.*

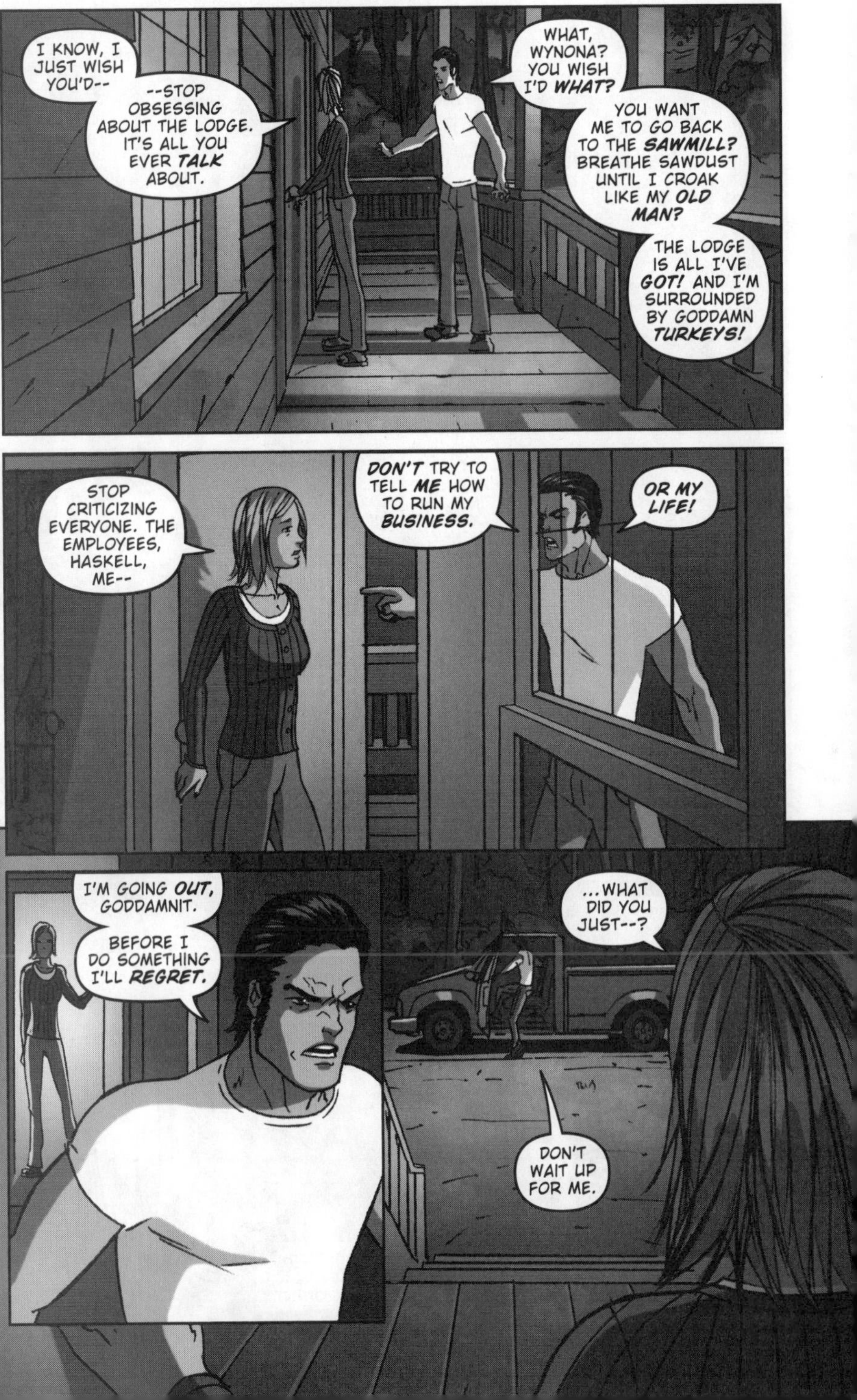
I KNOW, I JUST WISH YOU'D--
--STOP OBSESSING ABOUT THE LODGE. IT'S ALL YOU EVER TALK ABOUT.
WHAT, WYNONA? YOU WISH I'D WHAT?
YOU WANT ME TO GO BACK TO THE SAWMILL? BREATHE SAWDUST UNTIL I CROAK LIKE MY OLD MAN?
THE LODGE IS ALL I'VE GOT! AND I'M SURROUNDED BY GODDAMN TURKEYS!
STOP CRITICIZING EVERYONE. THE EMPLOYEES, HASKELL, ME--
DON'T TRY TO TELL ME HOW TO RUN MY BUSINESS.
OR MY LIFE!
I'M GOING OUT, GODDAMNIT.
BEFORE I DO SOMETHING I'LL REGRET.
...WHAT DID YOU JUST--?
DON'T WAIT UP FOR ME.

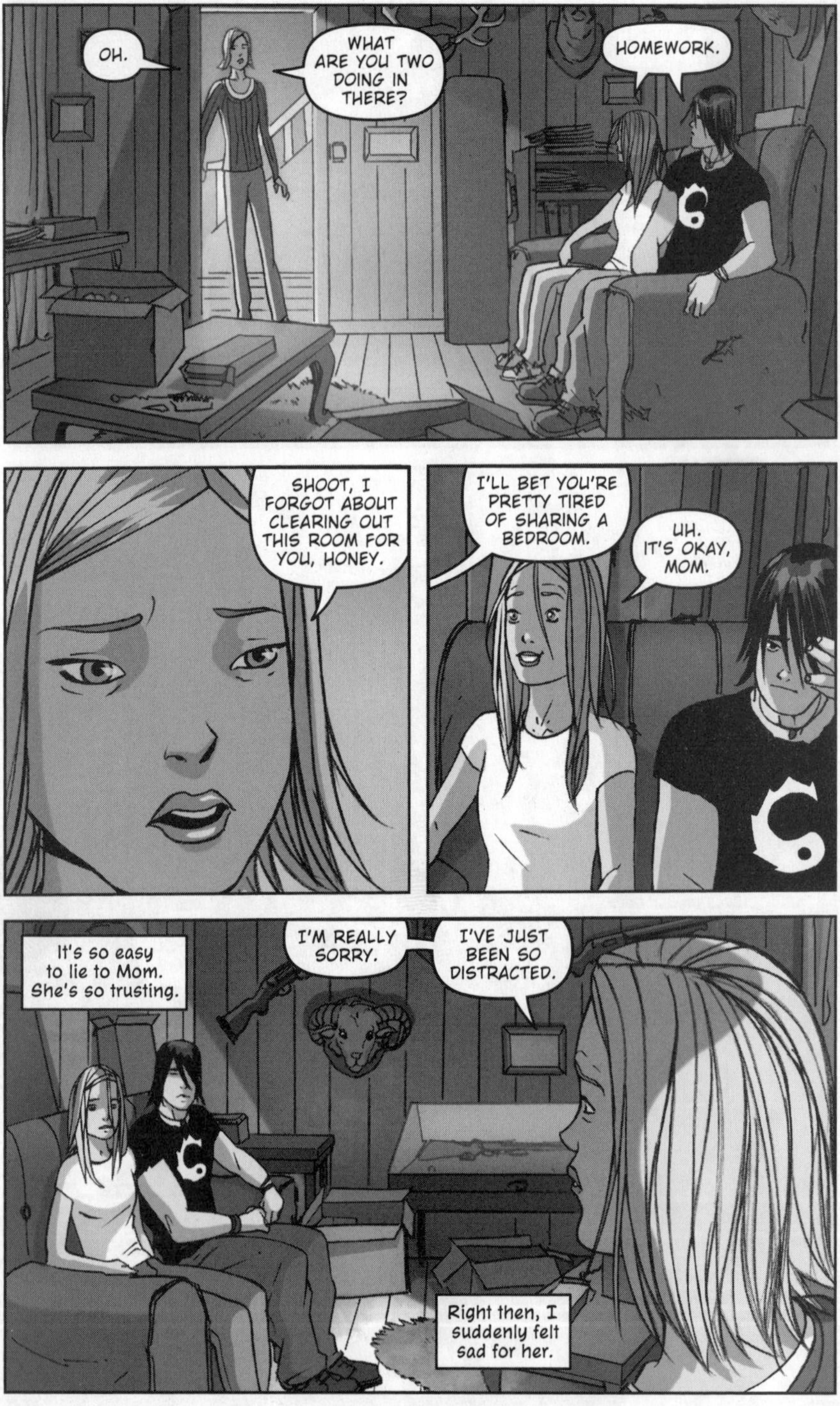
OH.
WHAT ARE YOU TWO DOING IN THERE?
HOMEWORK.
SHOOT, I FORGOT ABOUT CLEARING OUT THIS ROOM FOR YOU, HONEY.
I'LL BET YOU'RE PRETTY TIRED OF SHARING A BEDROOM.
UH. IT'S OKAY, MOM.
It's so easy to lie to Mom. She's so trusting.
I'M REALLY SORRY.
I'VE JUST BEEN SO DISTRACTED.
Right then, I suddenly felt sad for her.

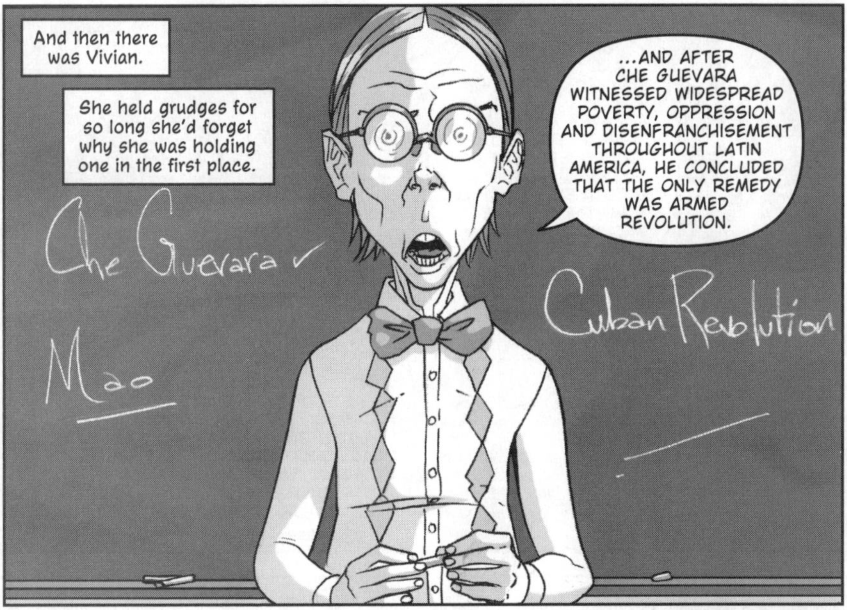
And then there was Vivian.
She held grudges for so long she'd forget why she was holding one in the first place.
...AND AFTER CHE GUEVARA WITNESSED WIDESPREAD POVERTY, OPPRESSION AND DISENFRANCHISEMENT THROUGHOUT LATIN AMERICA, HE CONCLUDED THAT THE ONLY REMEDY WAS ARMED REVOLUTION.
Che Guevara
Cuban Revolution
Mao

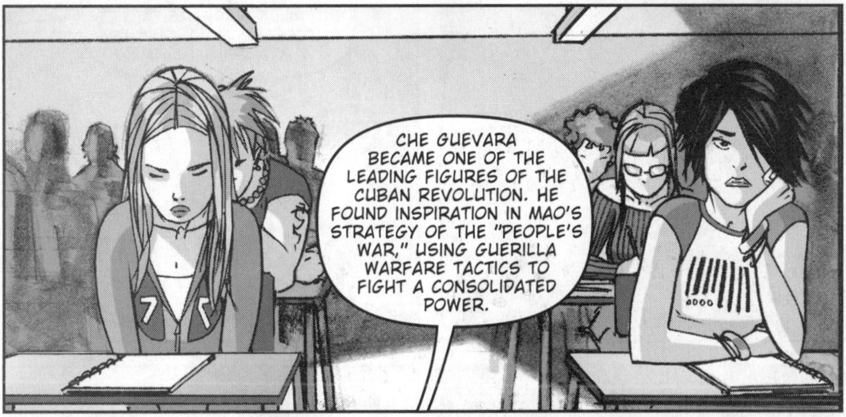
CHE GUEVARA BECAME ONE OF THE LEADING FIGURES OF THE CUBAN REVOLUTION. HE FOUND INSPIRATION IN MAO'S STRATEGY OF THE "PEOPLE'S WAR," USING GUERILLA WARFARE TACTICS TO FIGHT A CONSOLIDATED POWER.

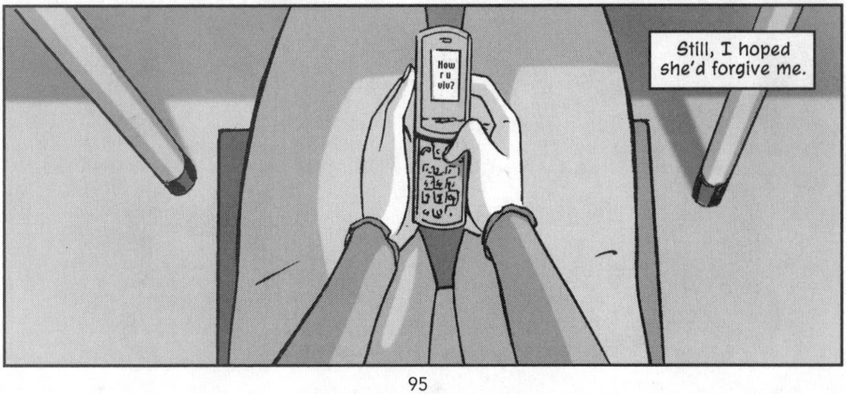
How r u vlu?
Still, I hoped she'd forgive me.

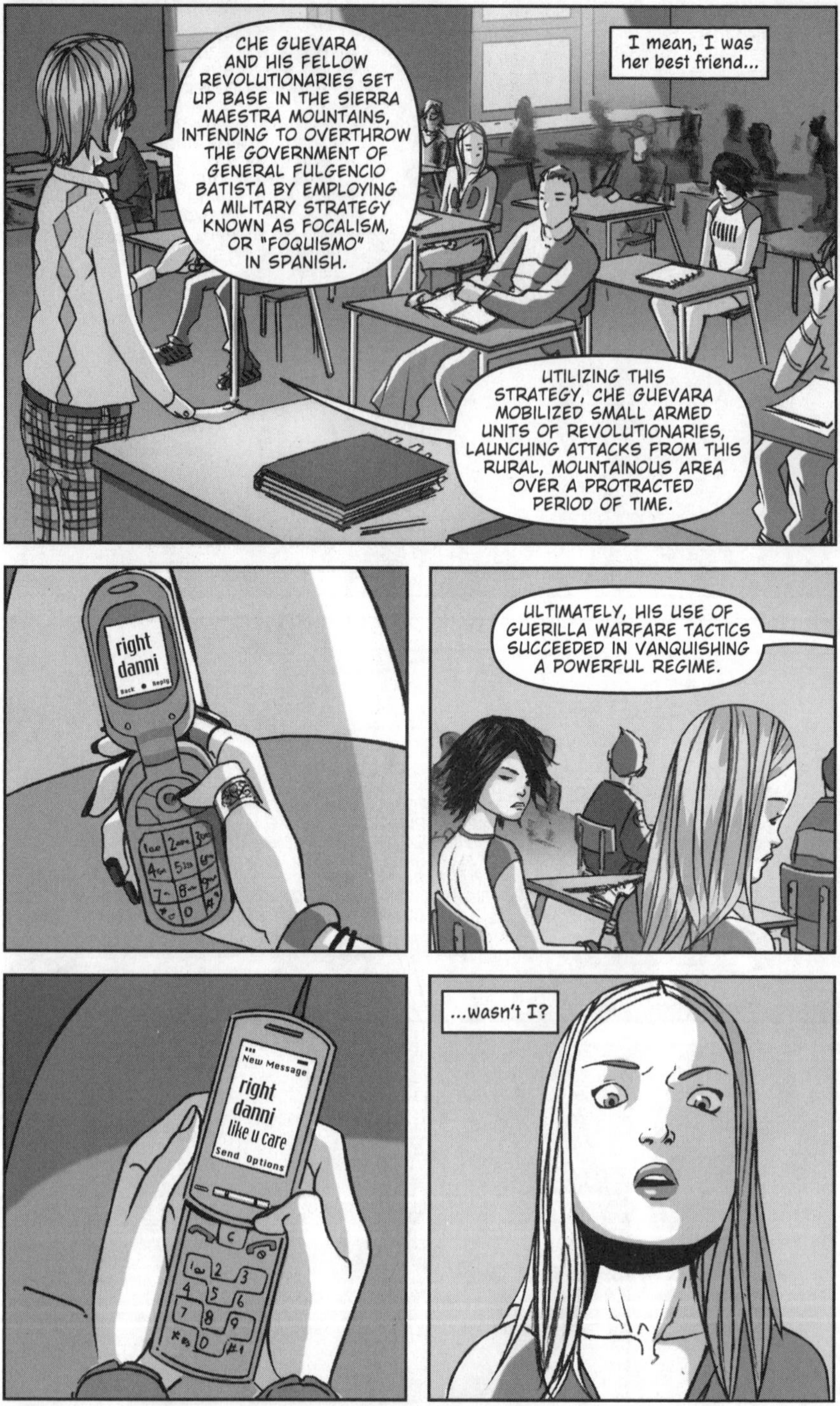
I mean, I was her best friend...
CHE GUEVARA AND HIS FELLOW REVOLUTIONARIES SET UP BASE IN THE SIERRA MAESTRA MOUNTAINS, INTENDING TO OVERTHROW THE GOVERNMENT OF GENERAL FULGENCIO BATISTA BY EMPLOYING A MILITARY STRATEGY KNOWN AS FOCALISM, OR "FOQUISMO" IN SPANISH.
UTILIZING THIS STRATEGY, CHE GUEVARA MOBILIZED SMALL ARMED UNITS OF REVOLUTIONARIES, LAUNCHING ATTACKS FROM THIS RURAL, MOUNTAINOUS AREA OVER A PROTRACTED PERIOD OF TIME.
right danni
Back Reply
ULTIMATELY, HIS USE OF GUERILLA WARFARE TACTICS SUCCEEDED IN VANQUISHING A POWERFUL REGIME.
New Message
right danni like u care
Send Options
...wasn't I?

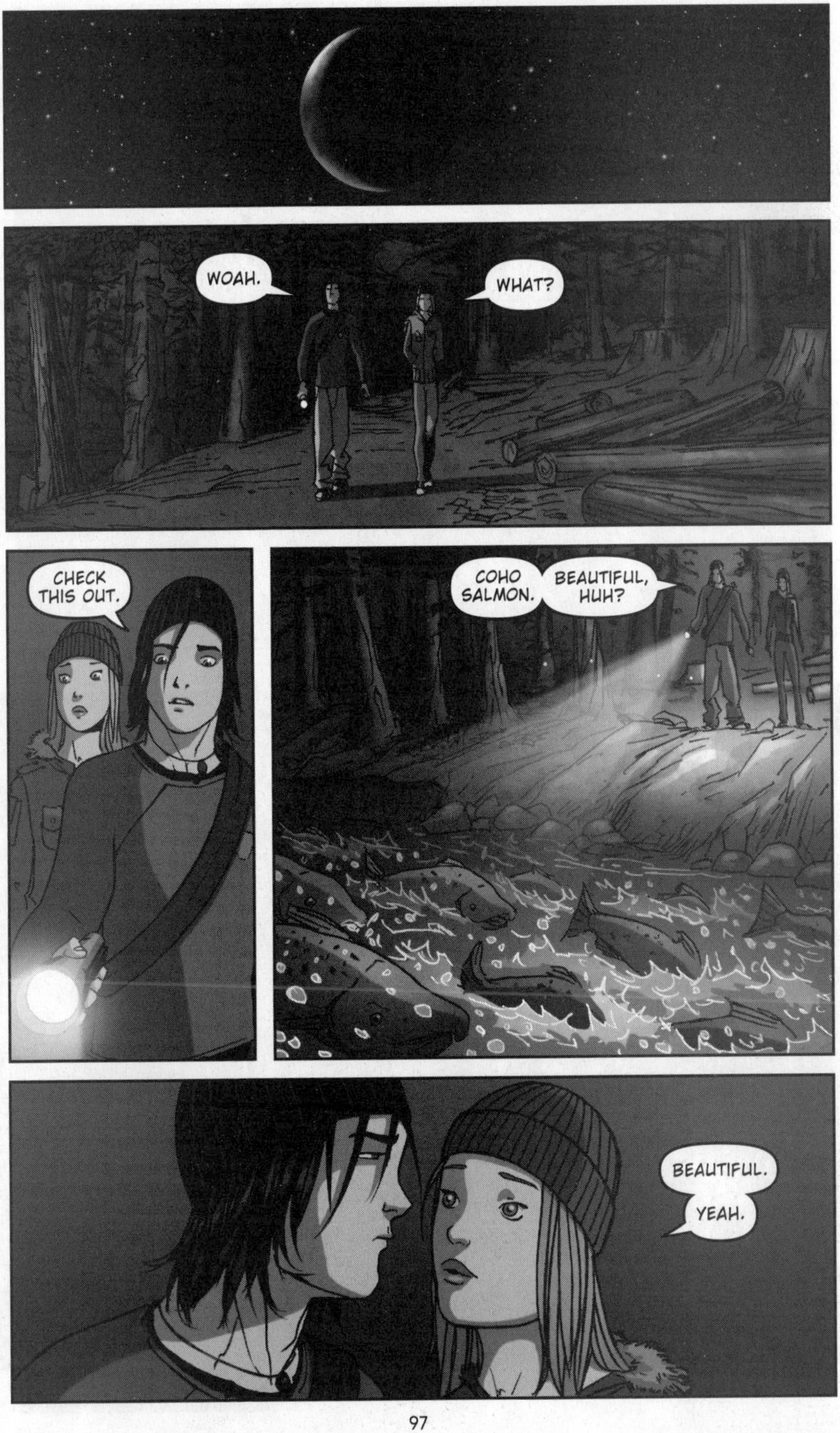
WOAH.
WHAT?
CHECK THIS OUT.
COHO SALMON.
BEAUTIFUL, HUH?
BEAUTIFUL.
YEAH.

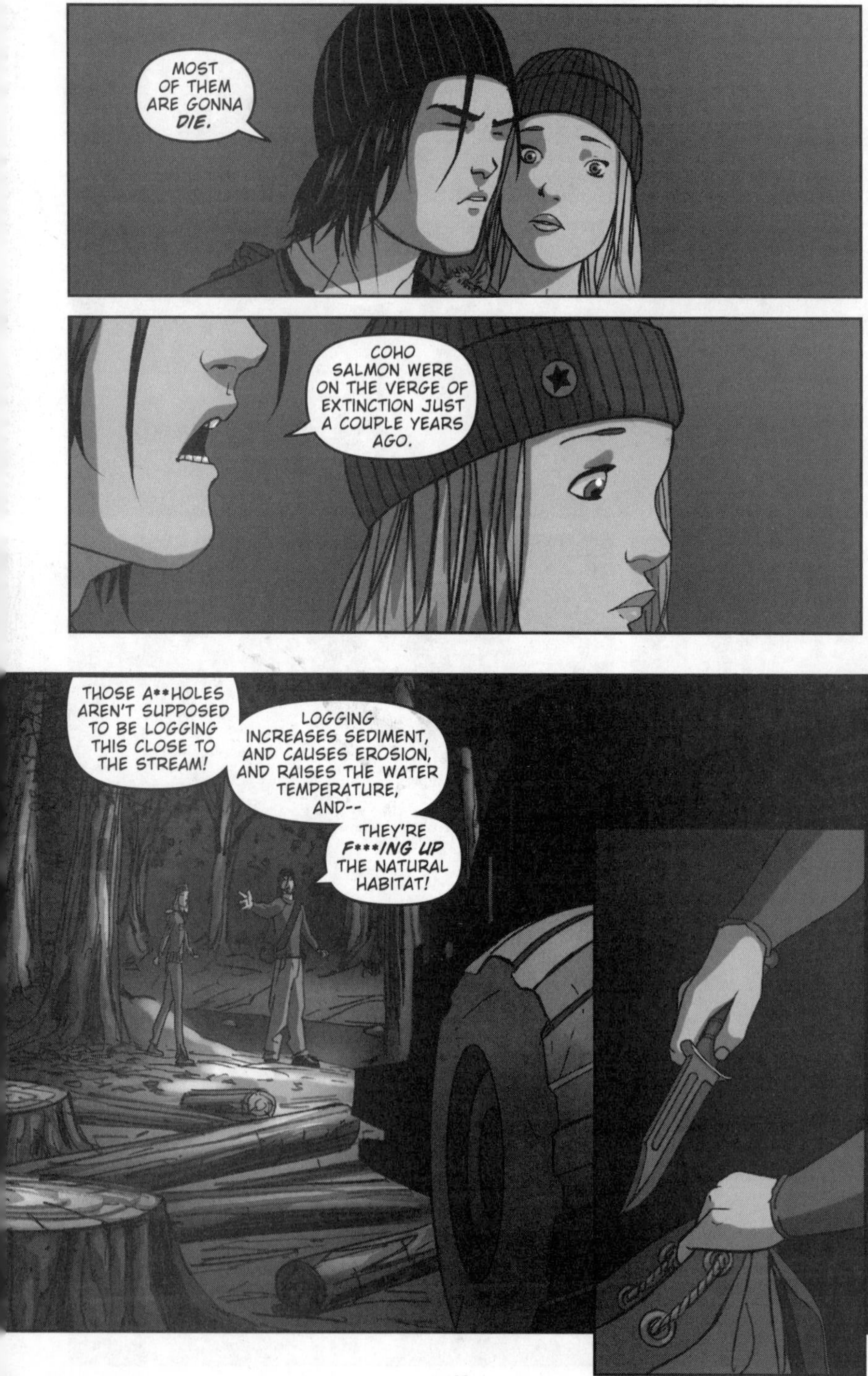
MOST OF THEM ARE GONNA *DIE.*
COHO SALMON WERE ON THE VERGE OF EXTINCTION JUST A COUPLE YEARS AGO.
THOSE A**HOLES AREN'T SUPPOSED TO BE LOGGING THIS CLOSE TO THE STREAM!
LOGGING INCREASES SEDIMENT, AND CAUSES EROSION, AND RAISES THE WATER TEMPERATURE, AND--
THEY'RE ***F***ING UP*** THE NATURAL HABITAT!

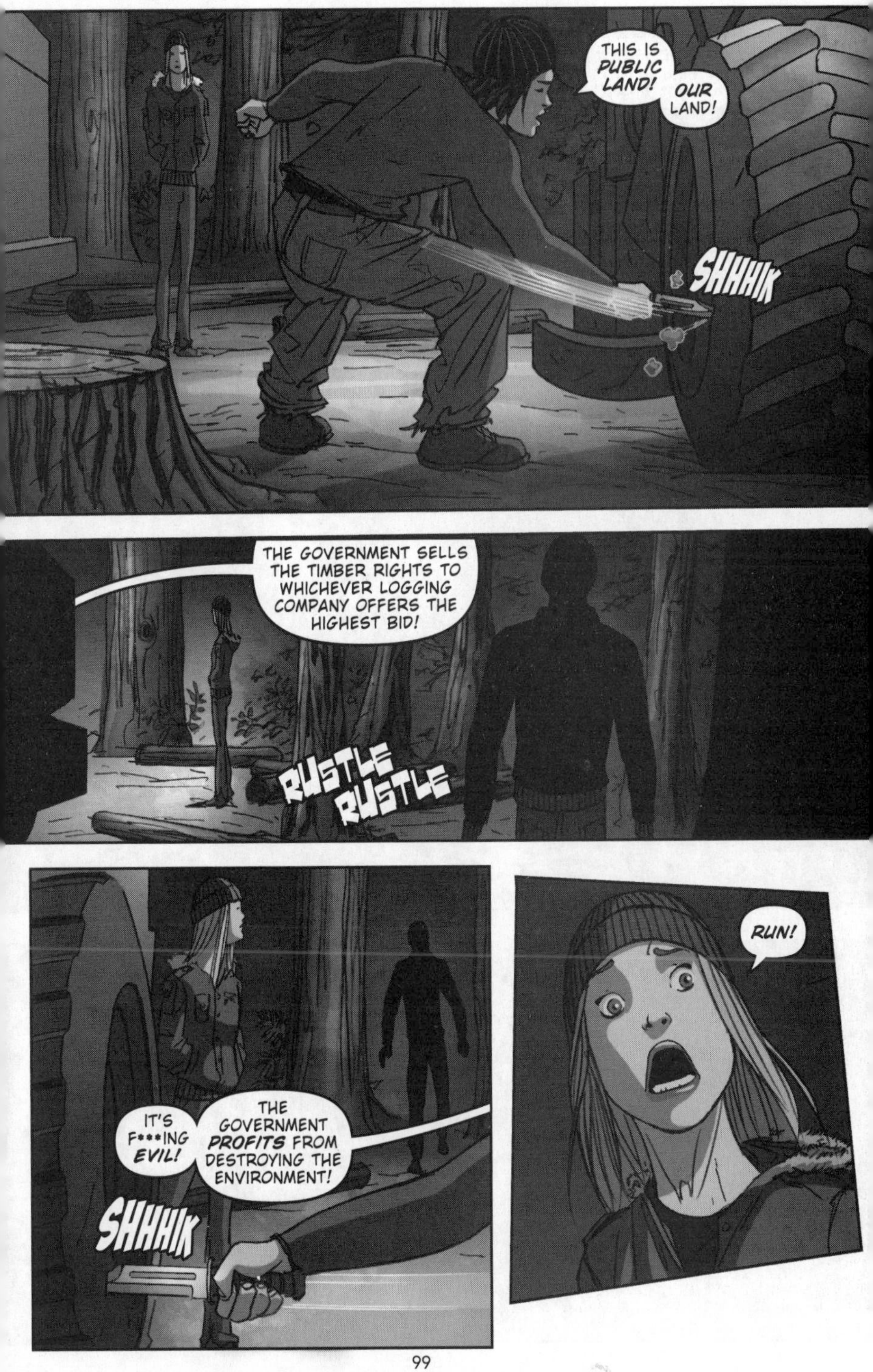
THIS IS PUBLIC LAND!
OUR LAND!
SHHHIK
THE GOVERNMENT SELLS THE TIMBER RIGHTS TO WHICHEVER LOGGING COMPANY OFFERS THE HIGHEST BID!
RUSTLE RUSTLE
IT'S F***ING EVIL!
THE GOVERNMENT PROFITS FROM DESTROYING THE ENVIRONMENT!
SHHHIK
RUN!

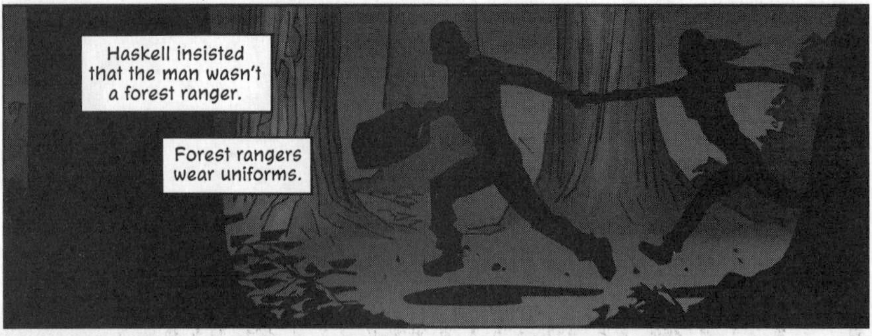
Haskell insisted that the man wasn't a forest ranger.
Forest rangers wear uniforms.

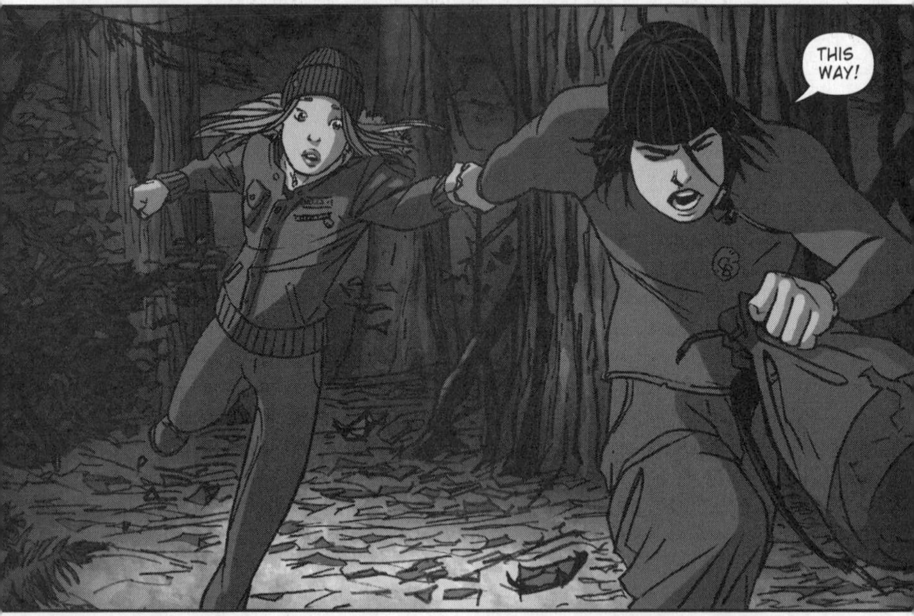
THIS WAY!

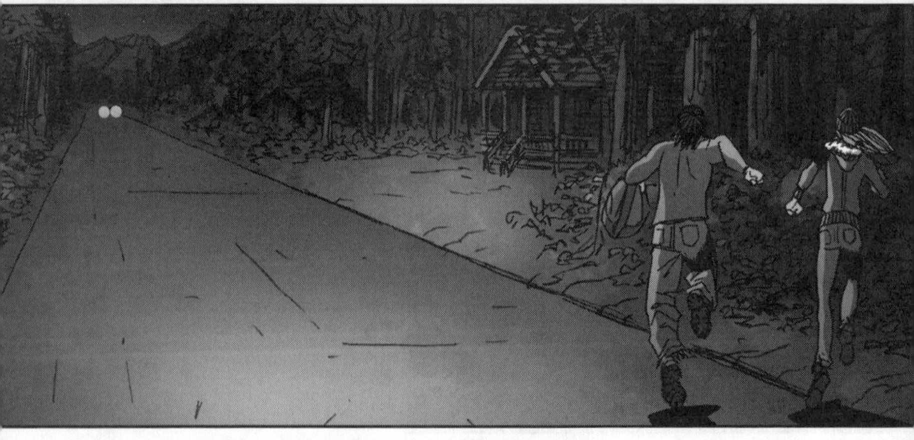

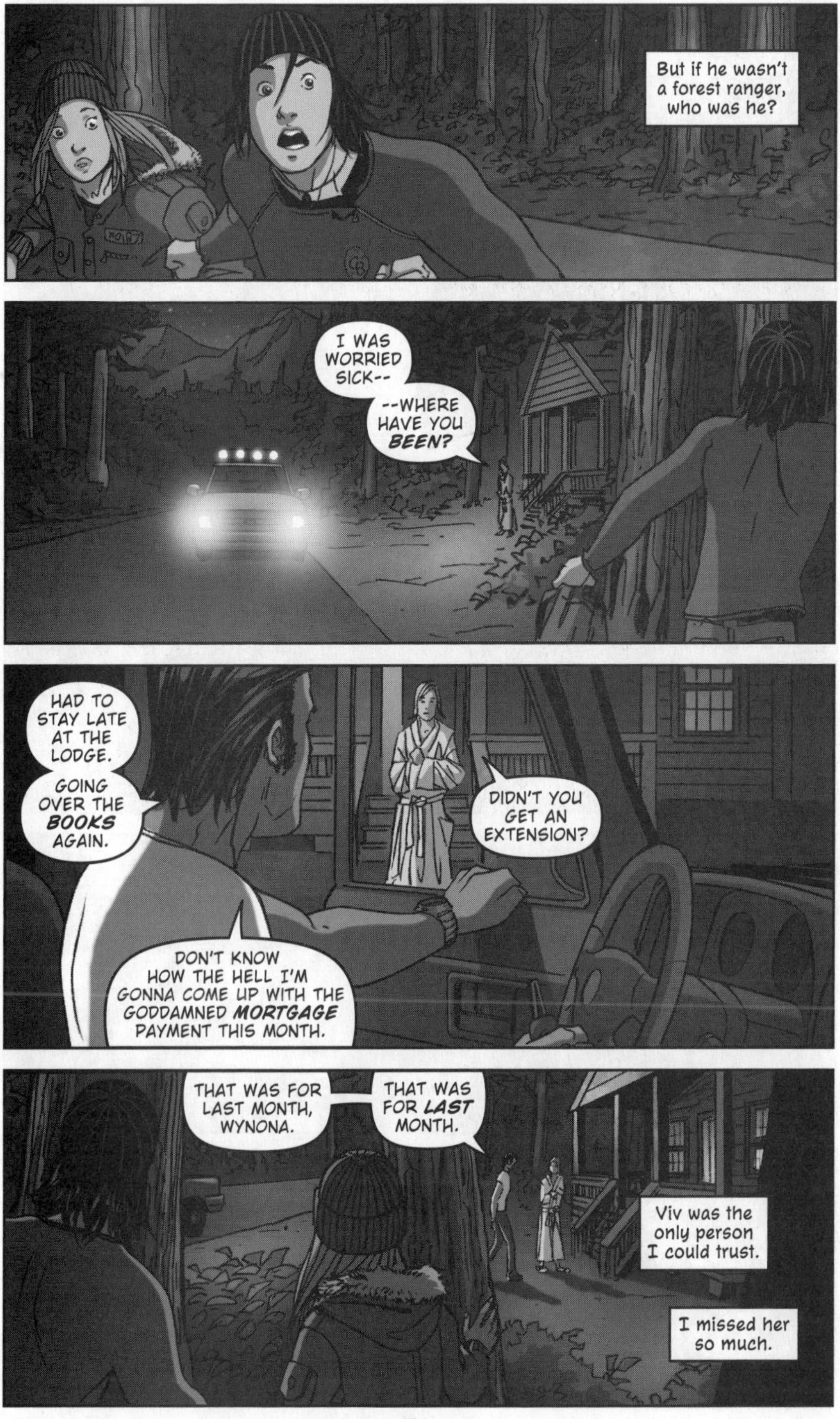

But if he wasn't a forest ranger, who was he?
I WAS WORRIED SICK--
--WHERE HAVE YOU BEEN?
HAD TO STAY LATE AT THE LODGE.
GOING OVER THE BOOKS AGAIN.
DIDN'T YOU GET AN EXTENSION?
DON'T KNOW HOW THE HELL I'M GONNA COME UP WITH THE GODDAMNED MORTGAGE PAYMENT THIS MONTH.
THAT WAS FOR LAST MONTH, WYNONA.
THAT WAS FOR LAST MONTH.
Viv was the only person I could trust.
I missed her so much.

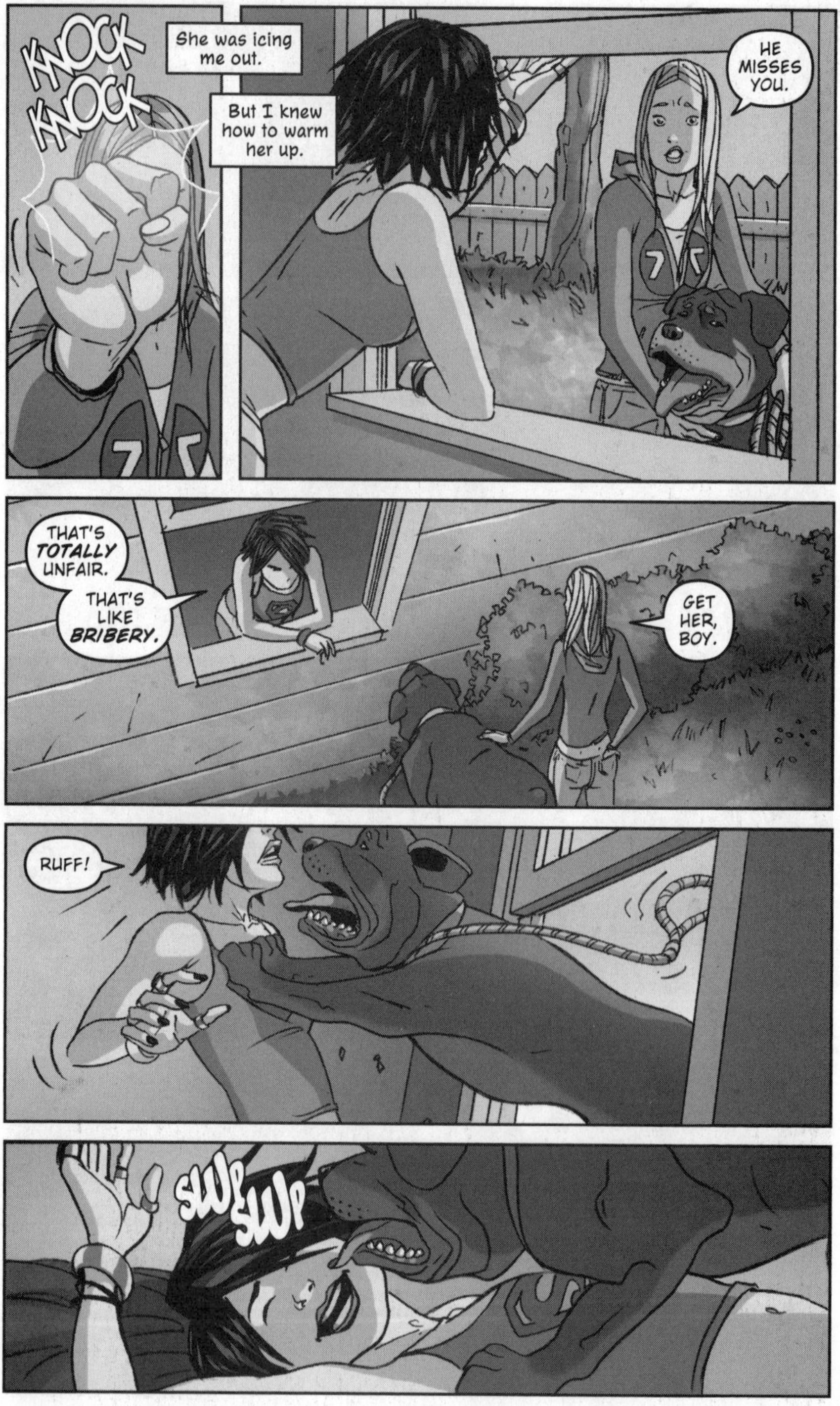
KNOCK KNOCK
She was icing me out.
But I knew how to warm her up.
HE MISSES YOU.
THAT'S TOTALLY UNFAIR.
THAT'S LIKE BRIBERY.
GET HER, BOY.
RUFF!
SLUP SLUP

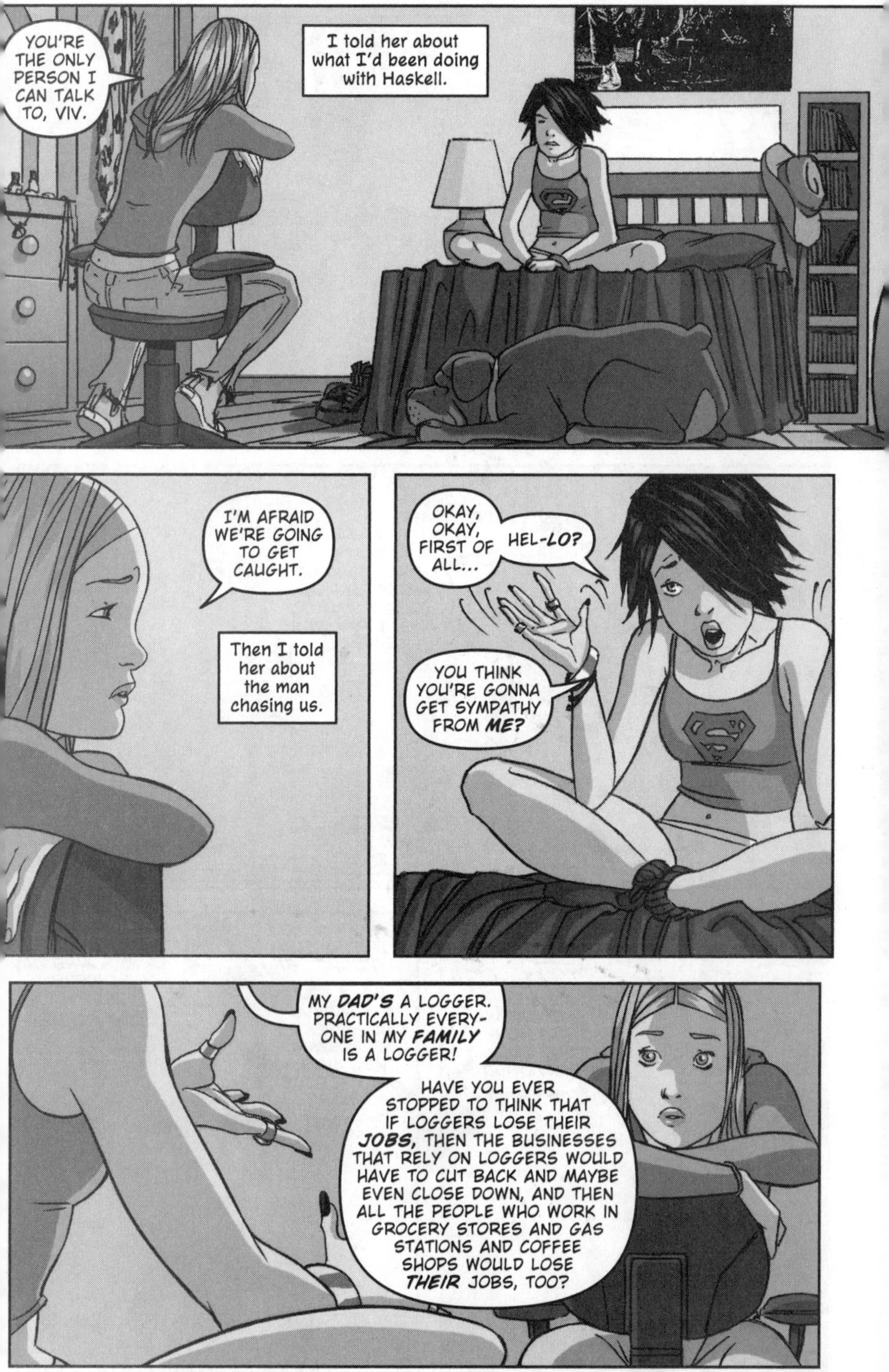
YOU'RE THE ONLY PERSON I CAN TALK TO, VIV.
I told her about what I'd been doing with Haskell.
I'M AFRAID WE'RE GOING TO GET CAUGHT.
Then I told her about the man chasing us.
OKAY, OKAY, FIRST OF ALL...
HEL-*LO?*
YOU THINK YOU'RE GONNA GET SYMPATHY FROM *ME?*
MY *DAD'S* A LOGGER. PRACTICALLY EVERY-ONE IN MY *FAMILY* IS A LOGGER!
HAVE YOU EVER STOPPED TO THINK THAT IF LOGGERS LOSE THEIR *JOBS,* THEN THE BUSINESSES THAT RELY ON LOGGERS WOULD HAVE TO CUT BACK AND MAYBE EVEN CLOSE DOWN, AND THEN ALL THE PEOPLE WHO WORK IN GROCERY STORES AND GAS STATIONS AND COFFEE SHOPS WOULD LOSE *THEIR* JOBS, TOO?

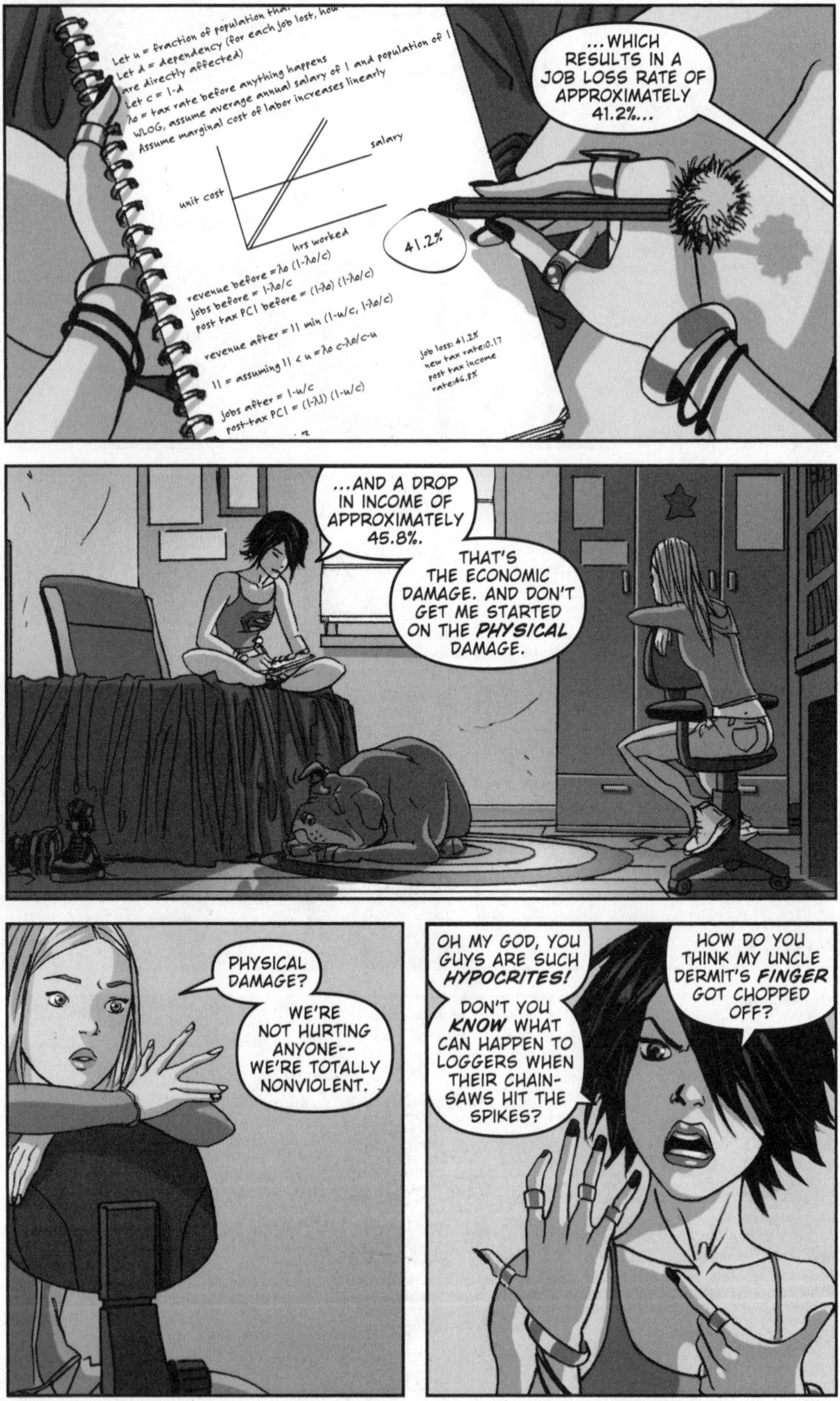
Let u = fraction of population
Let d = dependency (for each job lost, how
are directly affected)
Let c = 1-d
λo = tax rate before anything happens
WLOG, assume average annual salary of 1 and population of 1
Assume marginal cost of labor increases linearly
salary
unit cost
hrs worked
41.2%
revenue before = λo (1-λo/c)
jobs before = 1-λo/c
post tax PC1 before = (1-λo) (1-λo/c)
revenue after = λ1 min (1-u/c, 1-λo/c)
λ1 = assuming λ1 < u = λo c-λo/c-u
jobs after = 1-u/c
post-tax PC1 = (1-λ1) (1-u/c)
job loss: 41.2%
new tax rate: 0.17
post tax income
rate: 46.8%
...WHICH RESULTS IN A JOB LOSS RATE OF APPROXIMATELY 41.2%...
...AND A DROP IN INCOME OF APPROXIMATELY 45.8%.
THAT'S THE ECONOMIC DAMAGE. AND DON'T GET ME STARTED ON THE *PHYSICAL* DAMAGE.
PHYSICAL DAMAGE?
WE'RE NOT HURTING ANYONE-- WE'RE TOTALLY NONVIOLENT.
OH MY GOD, YOU GUYS ARE SUCH *HYPOCRITES!*
DON'T YOU *KNOW* WHAT CAN HAPPEN TO LOGGERS WHEN THEIR CHAIN-SAWS HIT THE SPIKES?
HOW DO YOU THINK MY UNCLE DERMIT'S *FINGER* GOT CHOPPED OFF?

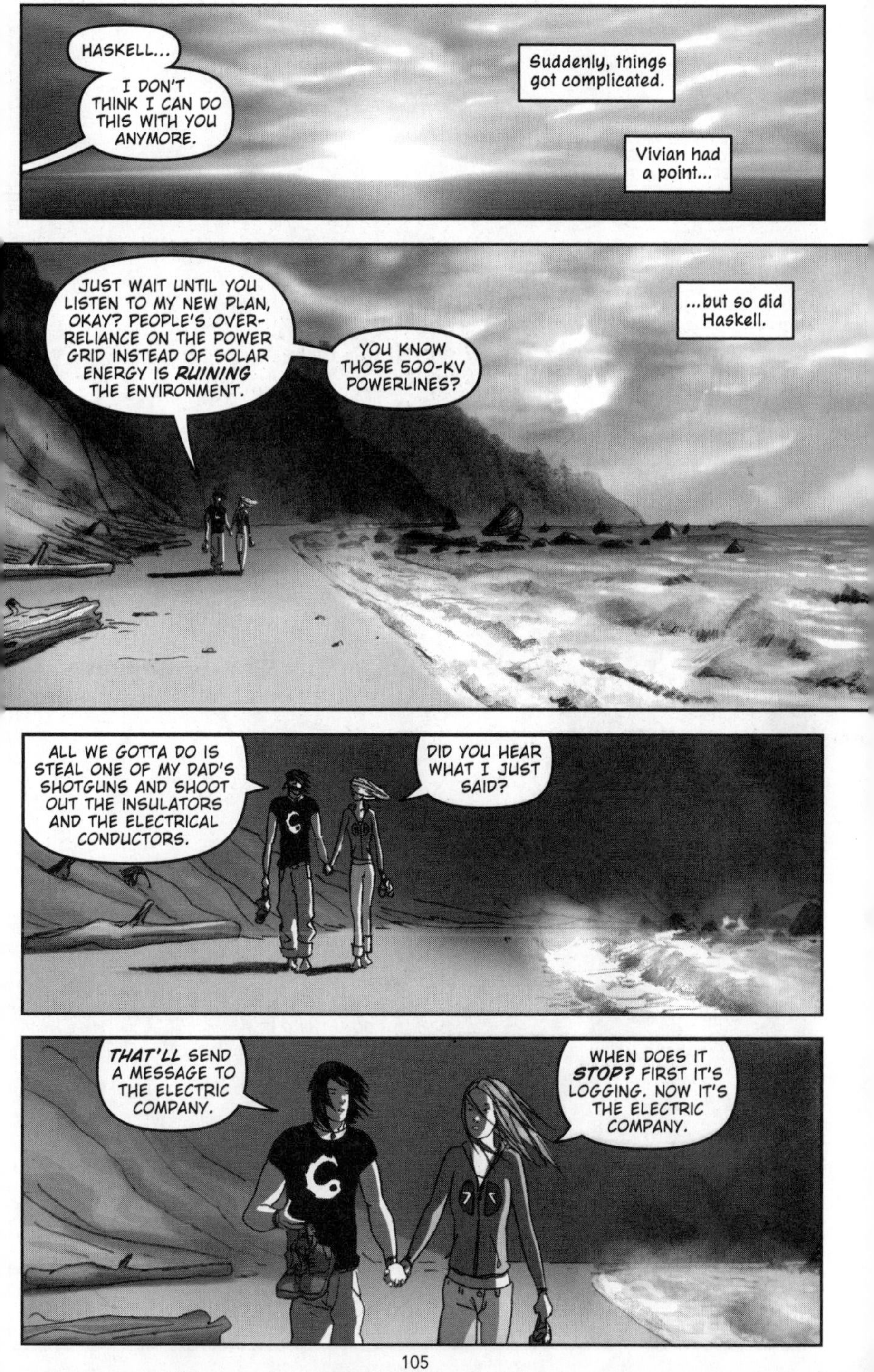
HASKELL...
I DON'T THINK I CAN DO THIS WITH YOU ANYMORE.
Suddenly, things got complicated.
Vivian had a point...
JUST WAIT UNTIL YOU LISTEN TO MY NEW PLAN, OKAY? PEOPLE'S OVER-RELIANCE ON THE POWER GRID INSTEAD OF SOLAR ENERGY IS RUINING THE ENVIRONMENT.
YOU KNOW THOSE 500-KV POWERLINES?
...but so did Haskell.
ALL WE GOTTA DO IS STEAL ONE OF MY DAD'S SHOTGUNS AND SHOOT OUT THE INSULATORS AND THE ELECTRICAL CONDUCTORS.
DID YOU HEAR WHAT I JUST SAID?
THAT'LL SEND A MESSAGE TO THE ELECTRIC COMPANY.
WHEN DOES IT STOP? FIRST IT'S LOGGING. NOW IT'S THE ELECTRIC COMPANY.

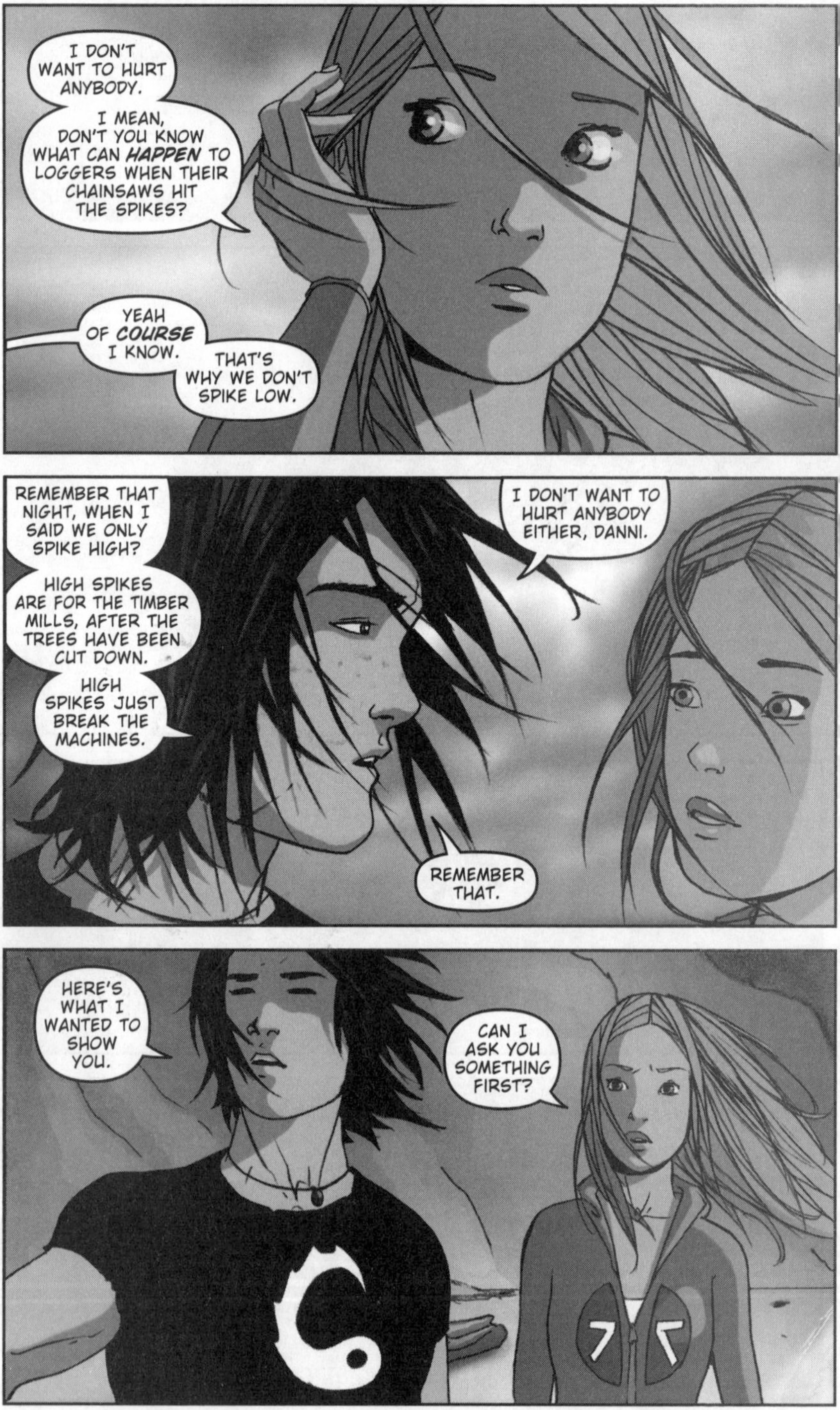
I DON'T WANT TO HURT ANYBODY.
I MEAN, DON'T YOU KNOW WHAT CAN *HAPPEN* TO LOGGERS WHEN THEIR CHAINSAWS HIT THE SPIKES?
YEAH OF *COURSE* I KNOW.
THAT'S WHY WE DON'T SPIKE LOW.
REMEMBER THAT NIGHT, WHEN I SAID WE ONLY SPIKE HIGH?
HIGH SPIKES ARE FOR THE TIMBER MILLS, AFTER THE TREES HAVE BEEN CUT DOWN.
HIGH SPIKES JUST BREAK THE MACHINES.
I DON'T WANT TO HURT ANYBODY EITHER, DANNI.
REMEMBER THAT.
HERE'S WHAT I WANTED TO SHOW YOU.
CAN I ASK YOU SOMETHING FIRST?

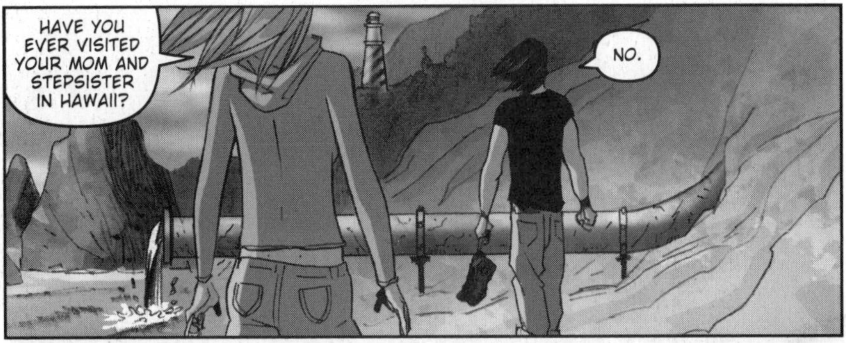
HAVE YOU EVER VISITED YOUR MOM AND STEPSISTER IN HAWAII?
NO.

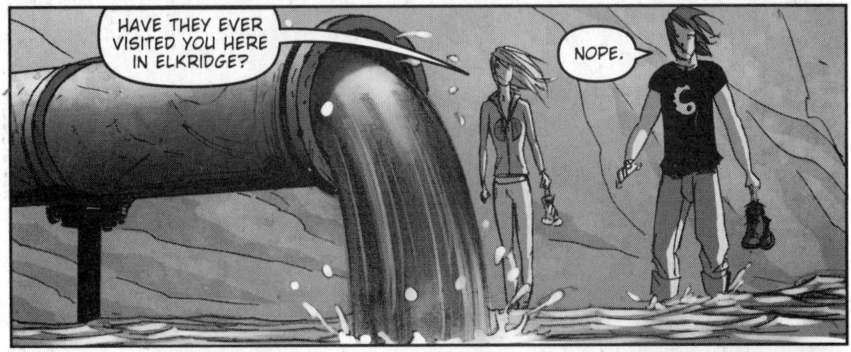
HAVE THEY EVER VISITED YOU HERE IN ELKRIDGE?
NOPE.

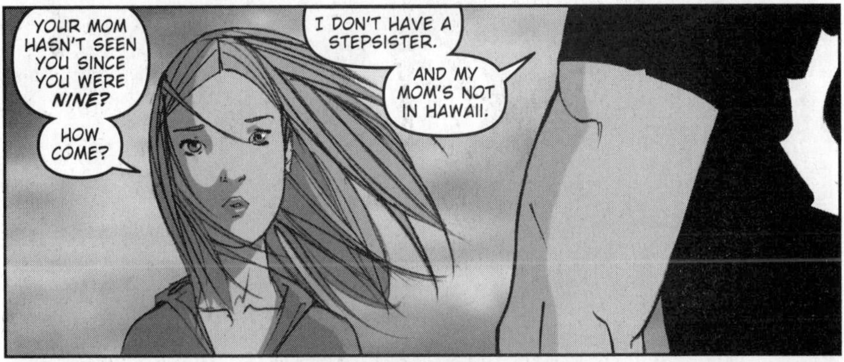
YOUR MOM HASN'T SEEN YOU SINCE YOU WERE ***NINE?***
HOW COME?
I DON'T HAVE A STEPSISTER.
AND MY MOM'S NOT IN HAWAII.

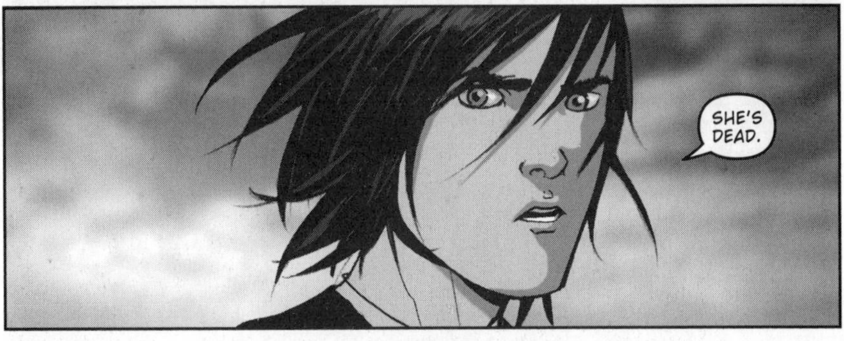
SHE'S DEAD.

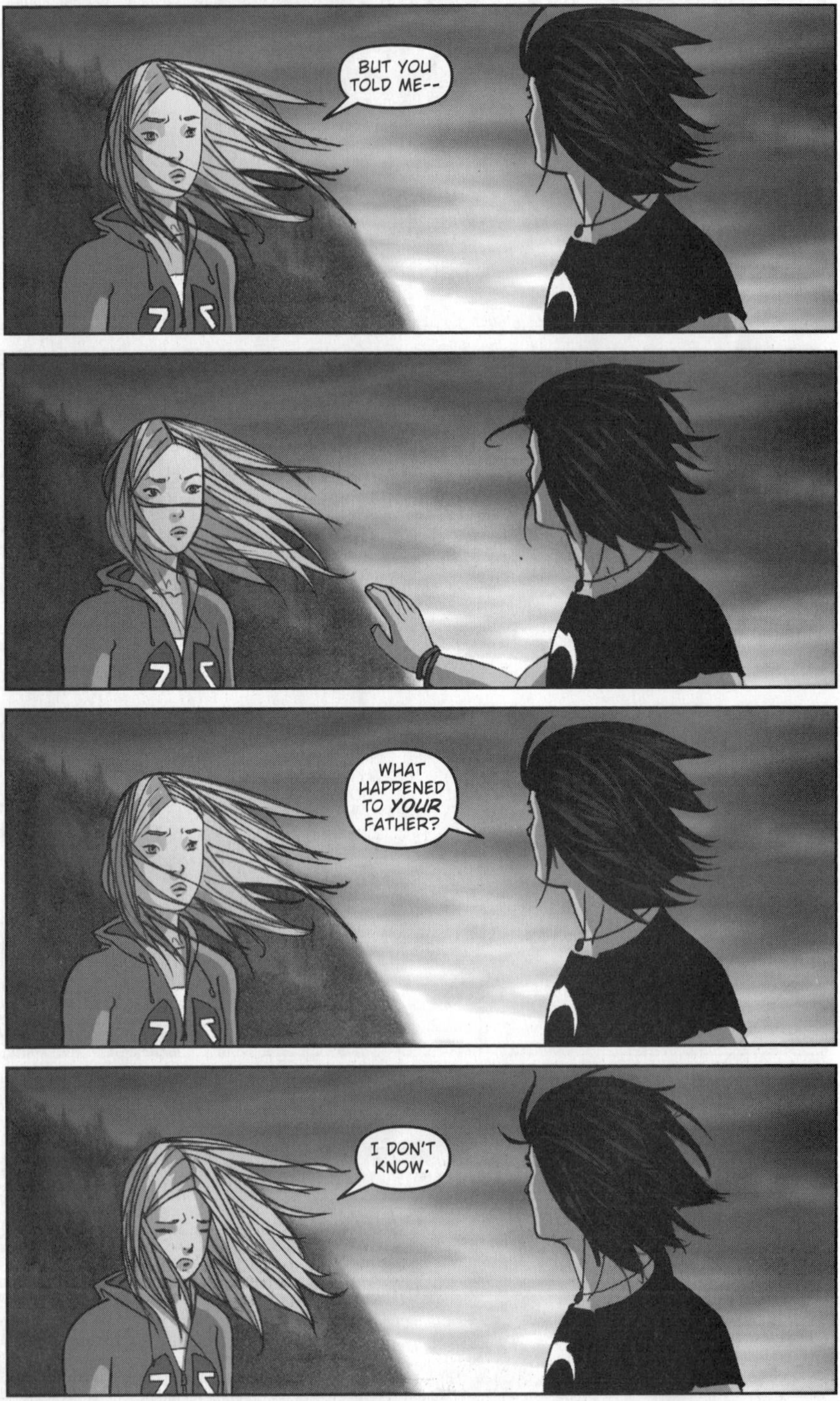
BUT YOU TOLD ME--
WHAT HAPPENED TO *YOUR* FATHER?
I DON'T KNOW.

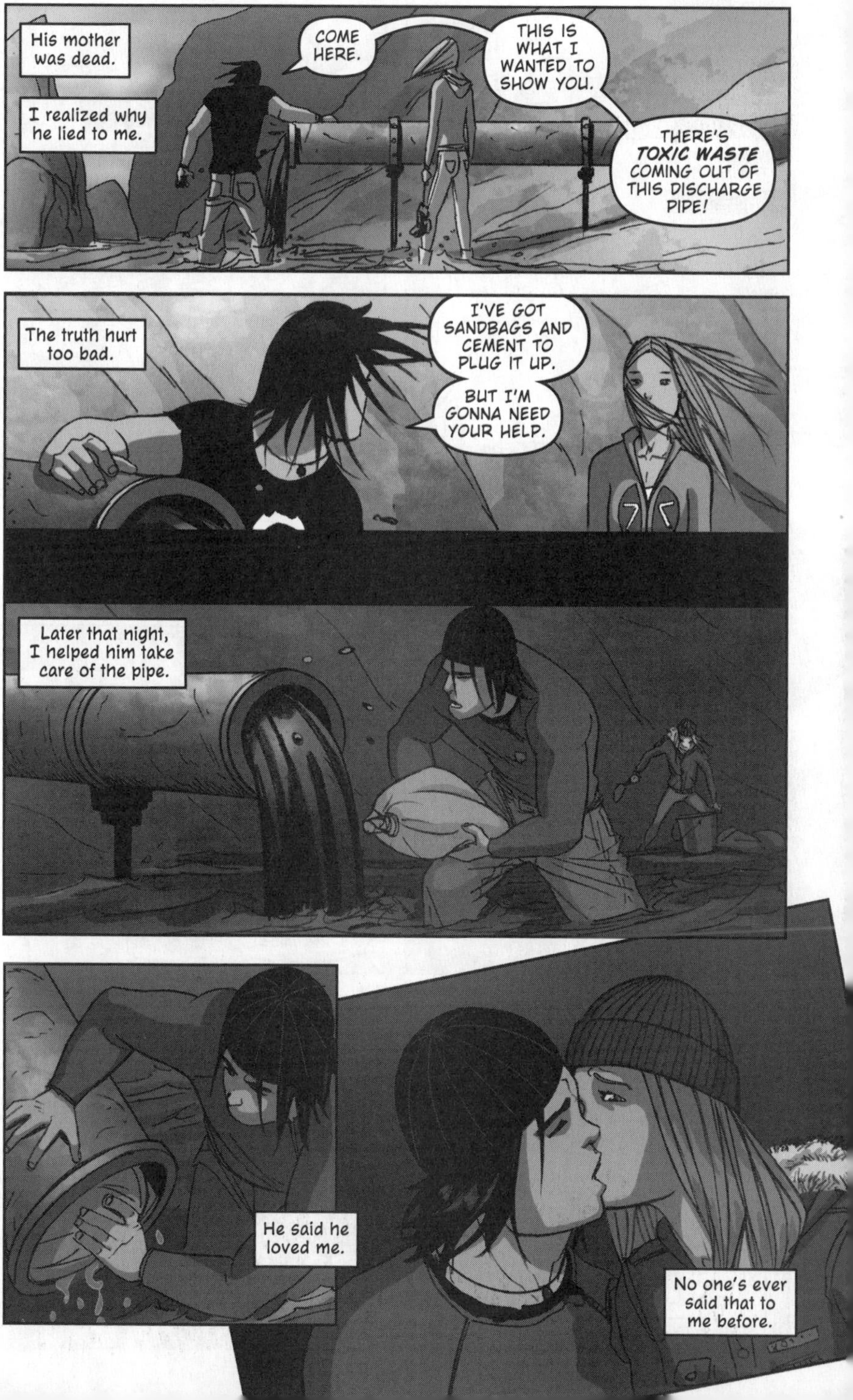
His mother was dead.
I realized why he lied to me.
COME HERE.
THIS IS WHAT I WANTED TO SHOW YOU.
THERE'S *TOXIC WASTE* COMING OUT OF THIS DISCHARGE PIPE!
The truth hurt too bad.
I'VE GOT SANDBAGS AND CEMENT TO PLUG IT UP.
BUT I'M GONNA NEED YOUR HELP.
Later that night, I helped him take care of the pipe.
He said he loved me.
No one's ever said that to me before.

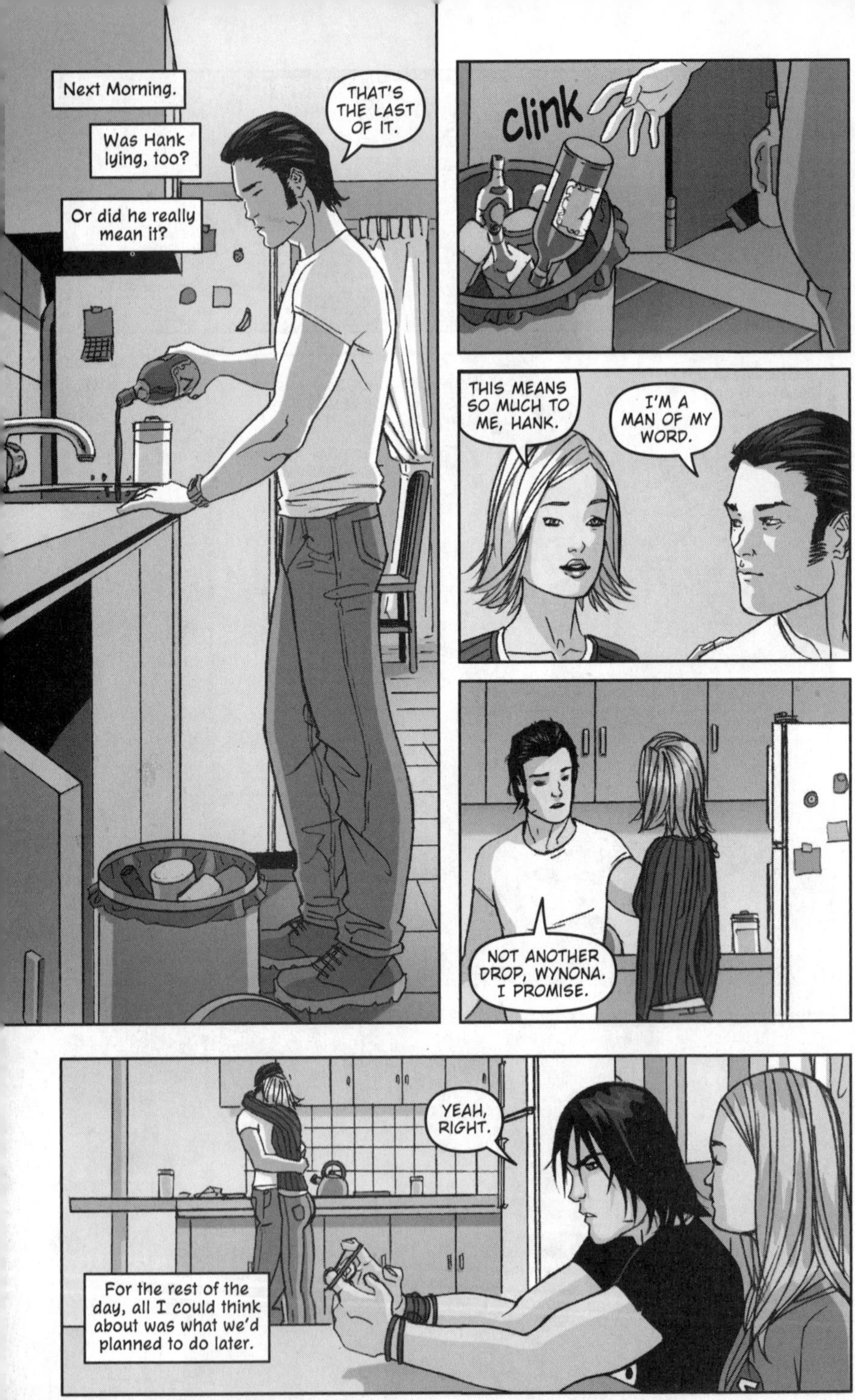
Next Morning.
Was Hank lying, too?
Or did he really mean it?
THAT'S THE LAST OF IT.
clink
THIS MEANS SO MUCH TO ME, HANK.
I'M A MAN OF MY WORD.
NOT ANOTHER DROP, WYNONA. I PROMISE.
YEAH, RIGHT.
For the rest of the day, all I could think about was what we'd planned to do later.

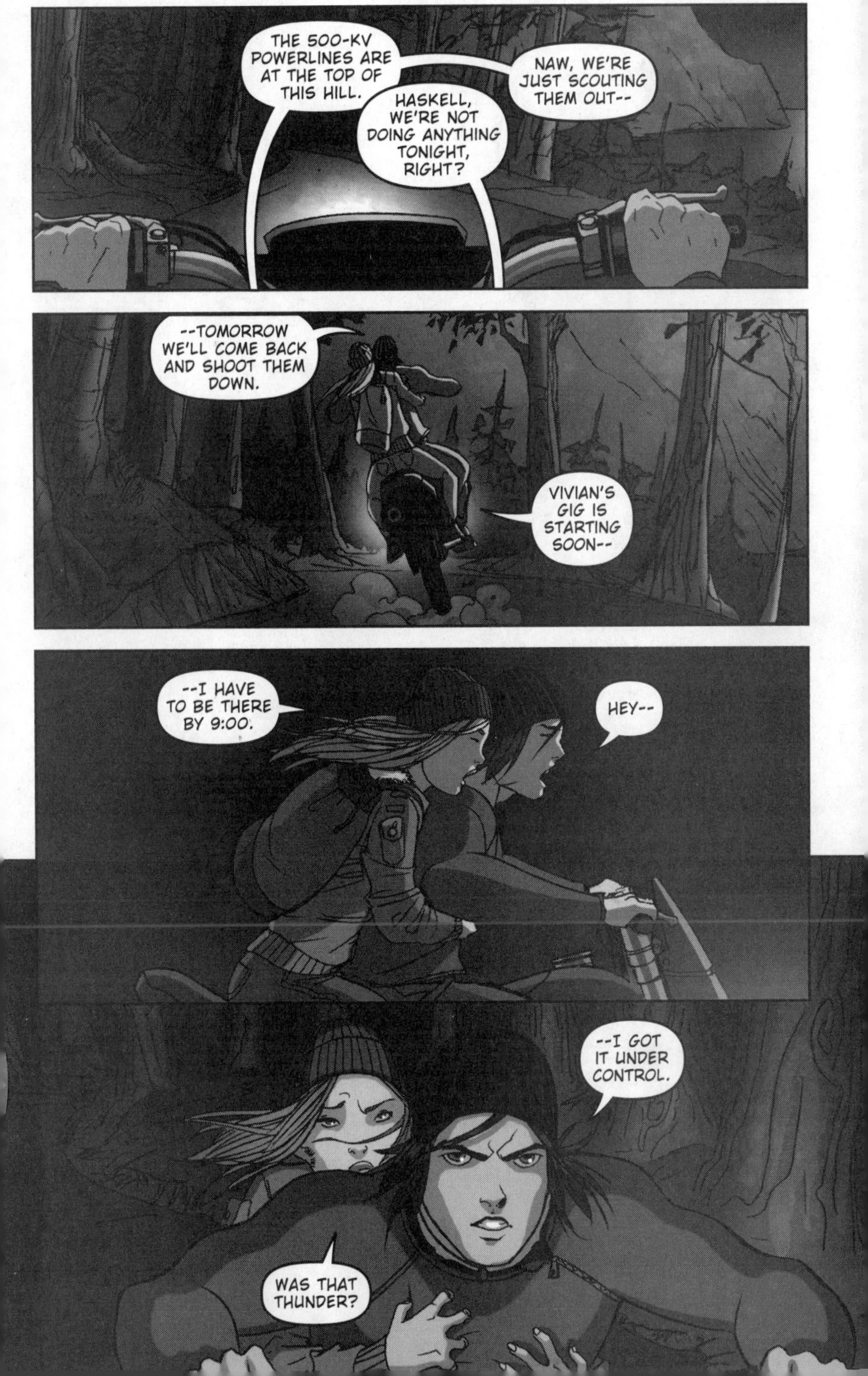
THE 500-KV POWERLINES ARE AT THE TOP OF THIS HILL.
NAW, WE'RE JUST SCOUTING THEM OUT--
HASKELL, WE'RE NOT DOING ANYTHING TONIGHT, RIGHT?
--TOMORROW WE'LL COME BACK AND SHOOT THEM DOWN.
VIVIAN'S GIG IS STARTING SOON--
--I HAVE TO BE THERE BY 9:00.
HEY--
--I GOT IT UNDER CONTROL.
WAS THAT THUNDER?

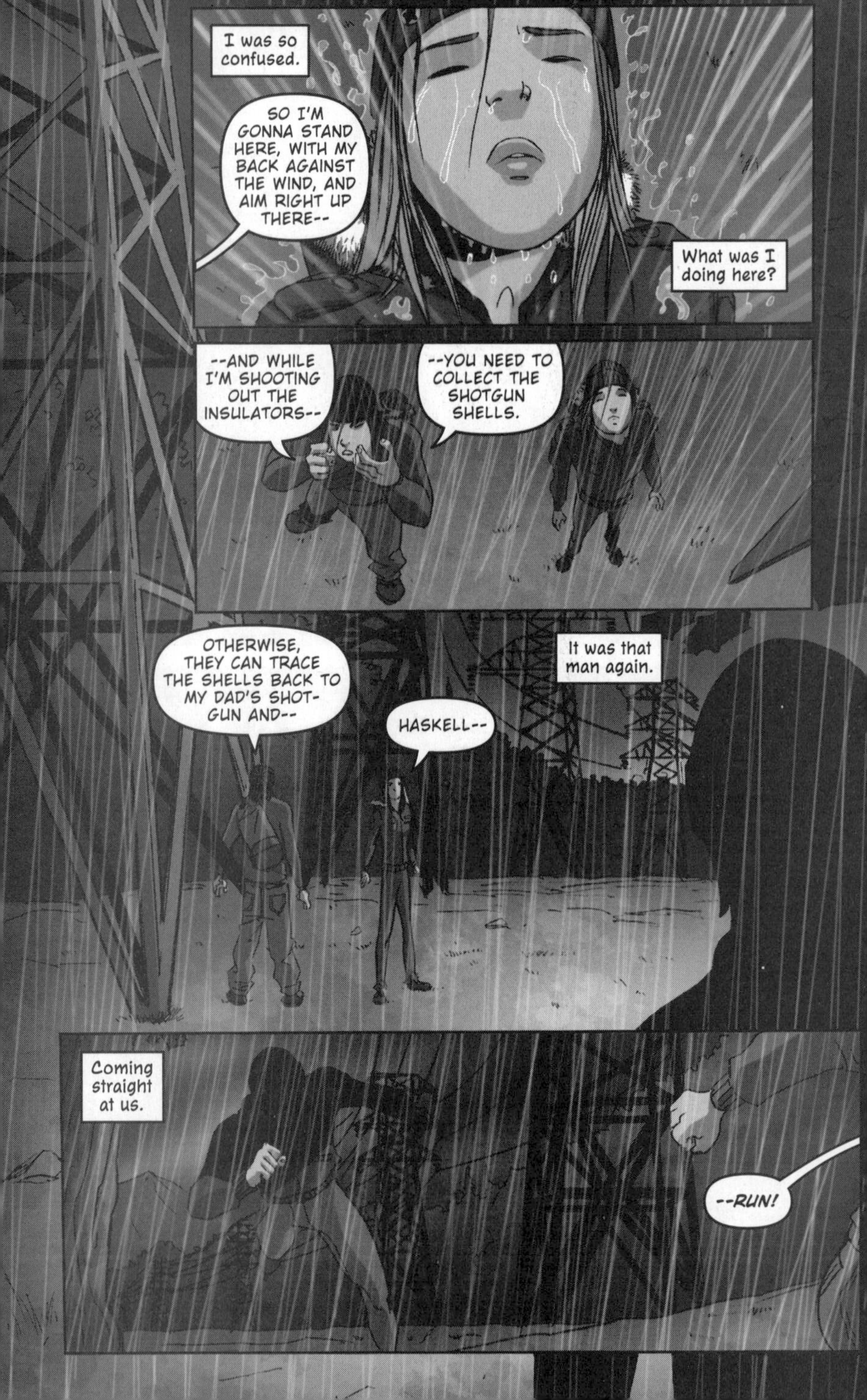

I was so confused.
SO I'M GONNA STAND HERE, WITH MY BACK AGAINST THE WIND, AND AIM RIGHT UP THERE--
What was I doing here?
--AND WHILE I'M SHOOTING OUT THE INSULATORS--
--YOU NEED TO COLLECT THE SHOTGUN SHELLS.
OTHERWISE, THEY CAN TRACE THE SHELLS BACK TO MY DAD'S SHOT-GUN AND--
HASKELL--
It was that man again.
Coming straight at us.
--RUN!

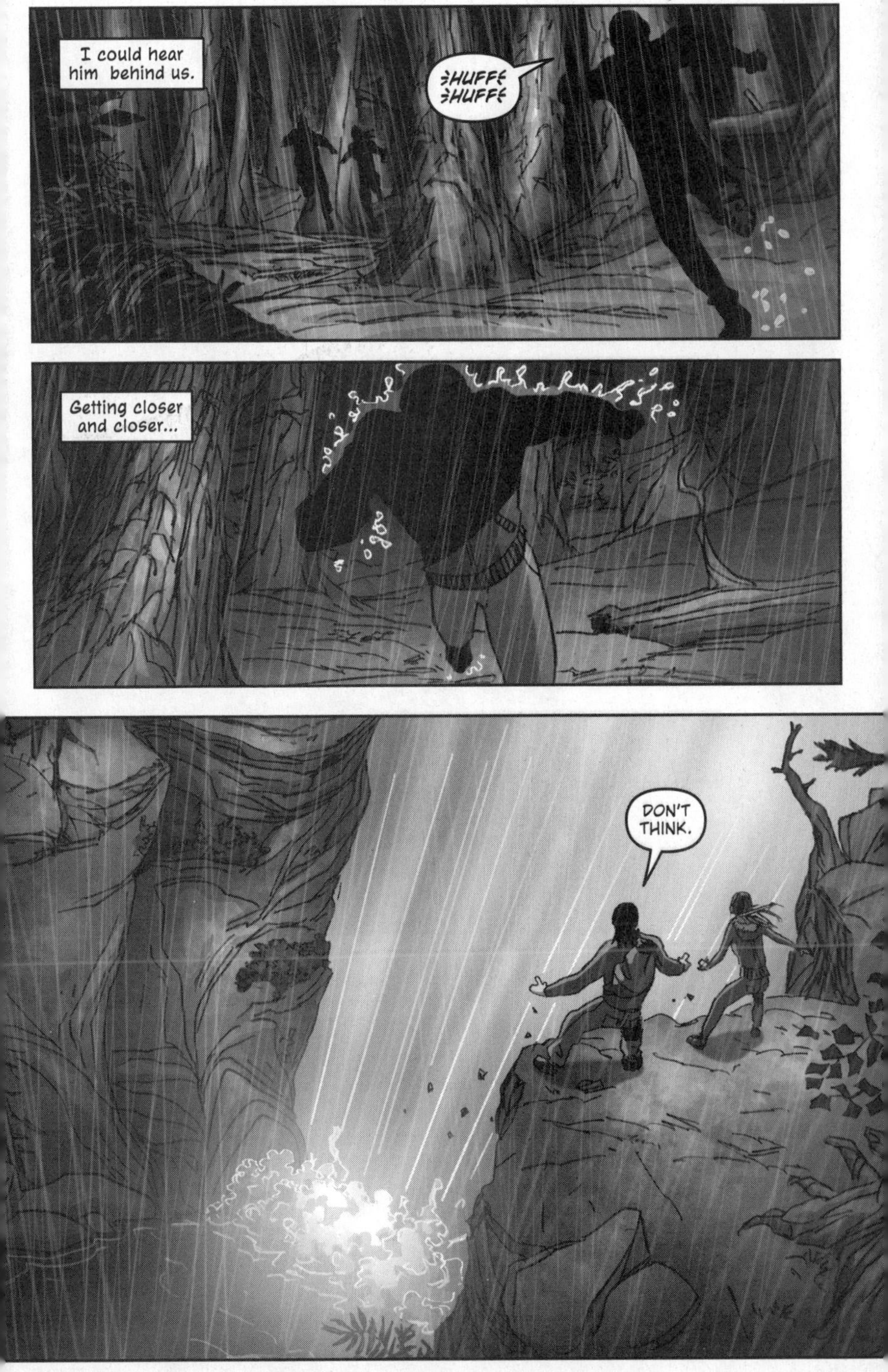
I could hear him behind us.
HUFF HUFF
Getting closer and closer...
DON'T THINK.

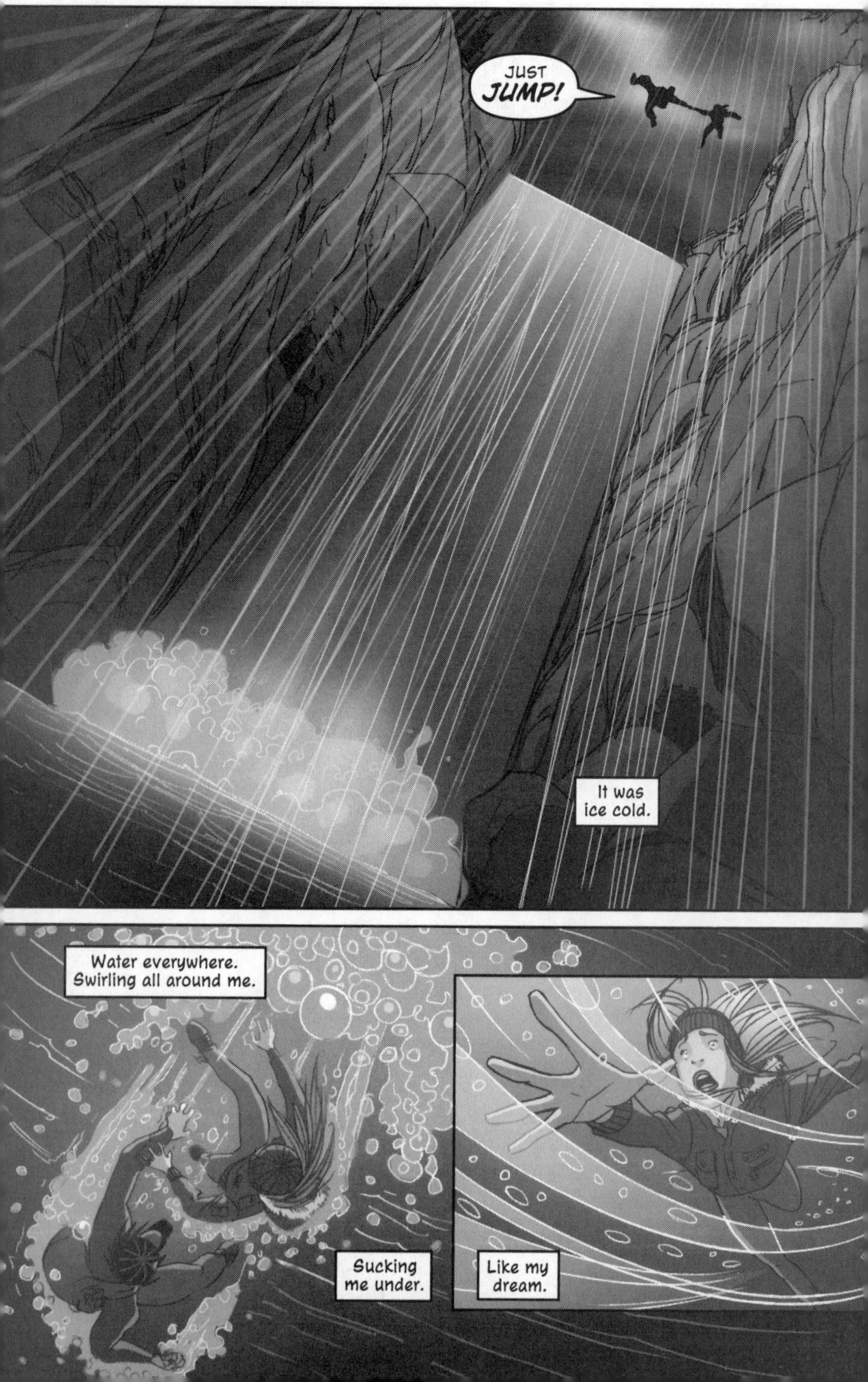
JUST JUMP!
It was ice cold.
Water everywhere. Swirling all around me.
Sucking me under.
Like my dream.

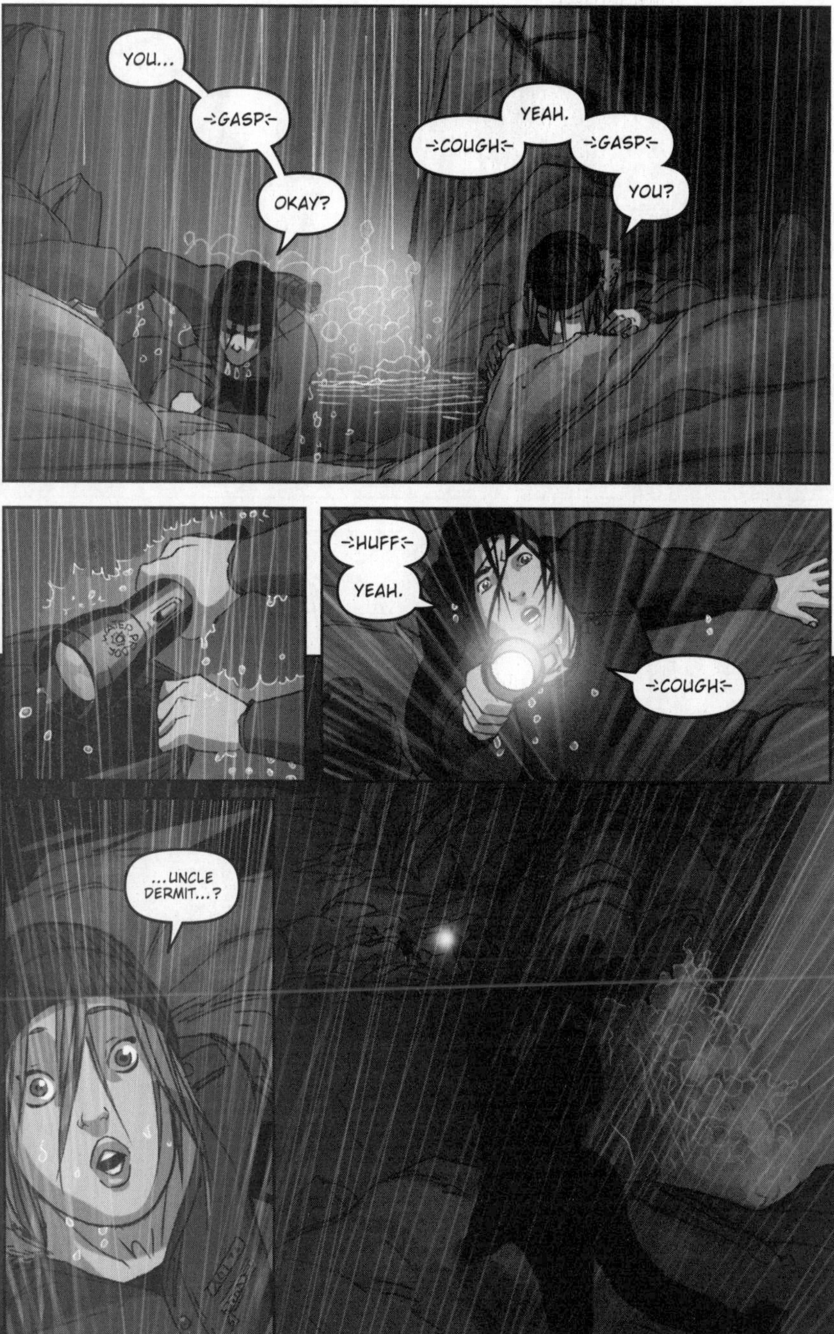
YOU...
-GASP-
OKAY?
-COUGH-
YEAH.
-GASP-
YOU?
-HUFF-
YEAH.
-COUGH-
...UNCLE DERMIT...?

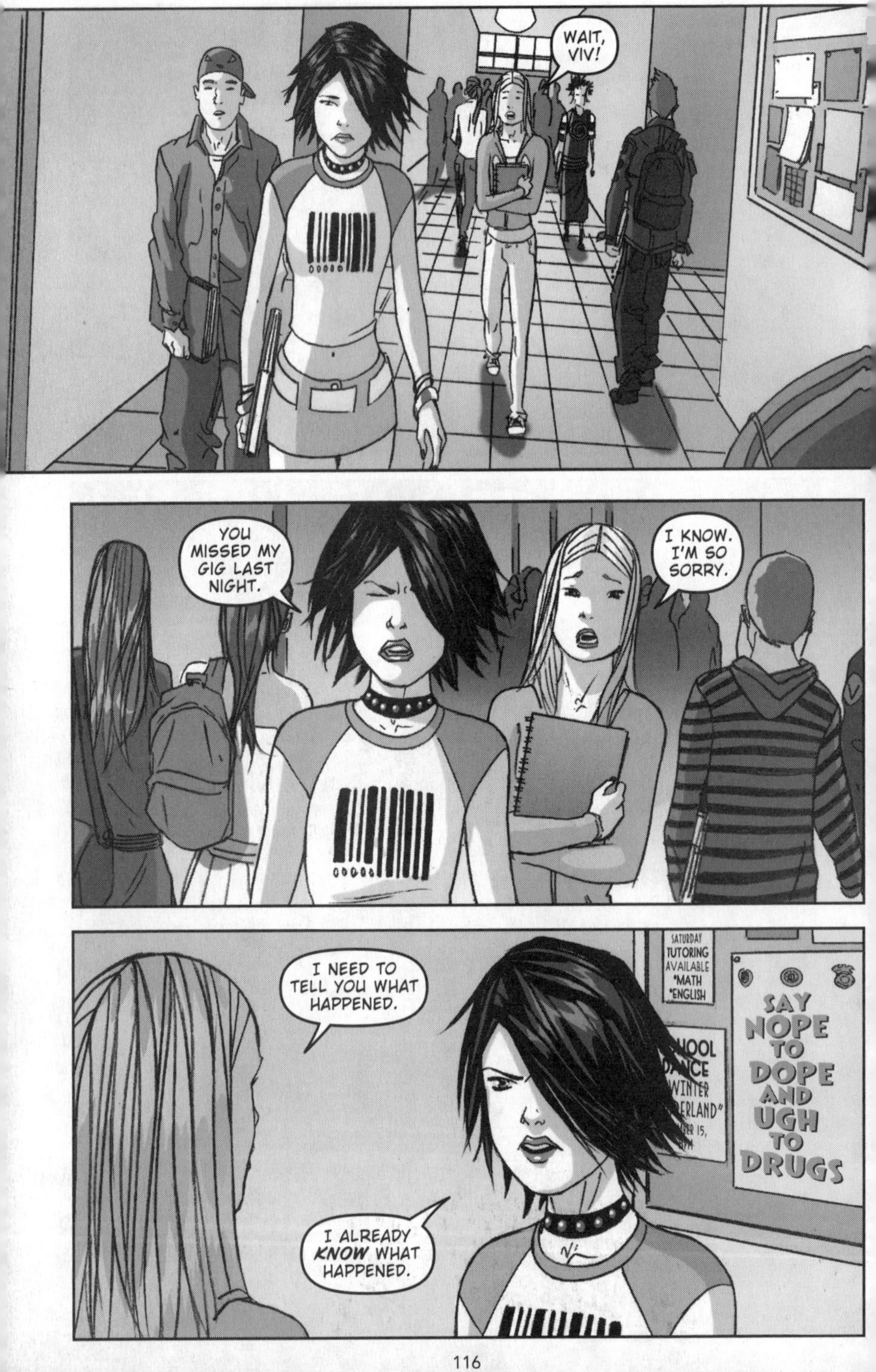
WAIT, VIV!
YOU MISSED MY GIG LAST NIGHT.
I KNOW. I'M SO SORRY.
SATURDAY TUTORING AVAILABLE *MATH *ENGLISH
SAY NOPE TO DOPE AND UGH TO DRUGS
I NEED TO TELL YOU WHAT HAPPENED.
I ALREADY *KNOW* WHAT HAPPENED.

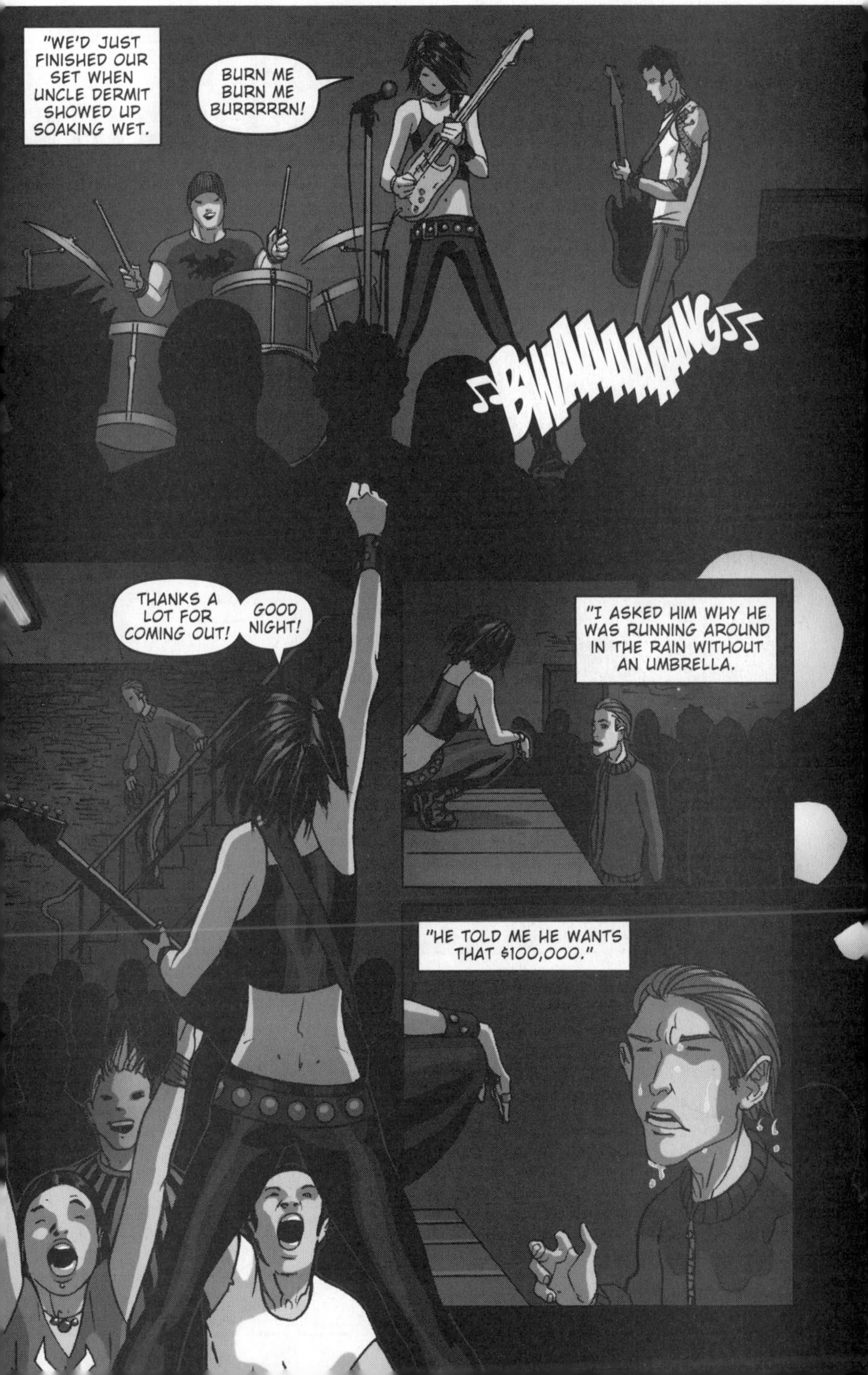
"WE'D JUST FINISHED OUR SET WHEN UNCLE DERMIT SHOWED UP SOAKING WET.
BURN ME BURN ME BURRRRRN!
BWAAAAAAANG
THANKS A LOT FOR COMING OUT!
GOOD NIGHT!
"I ASKED HIM WHY HE WAS RUNNING AROUND IN THE RAIN WITHOUT AN UMBRELLA.
"HE TOLD ME HE WANTS THAT $100,000."

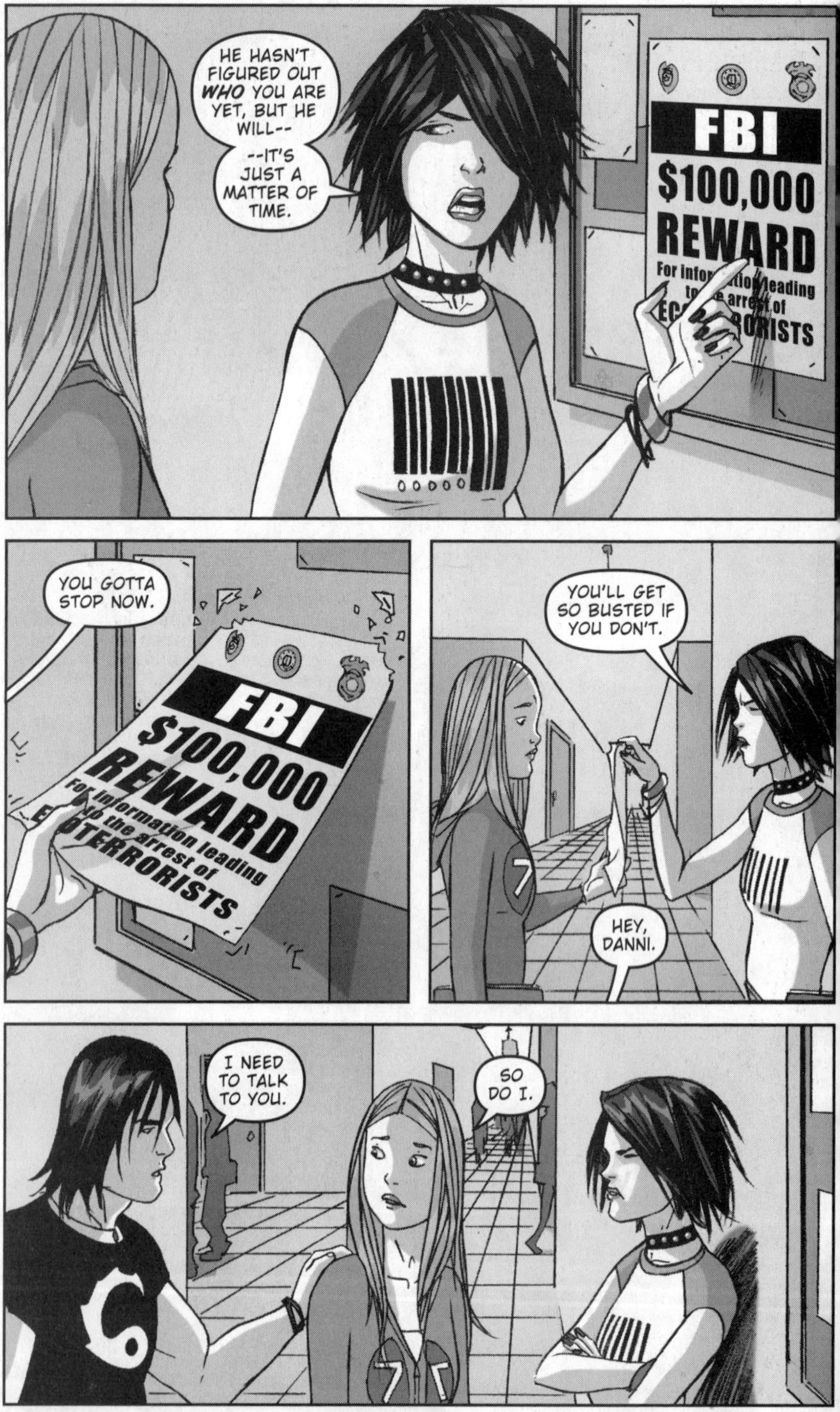
HE HASN'T FIGURED OUT WHO YOU ARE YET, BUT HE WILL--
--IT'S JUST A MATTER OF TIME.
FBI
$100,000
REWARD
YOU GOTTA STOP NOW.
FBI
$100,000
REWARD
YOU'LL GET SO BUSTED IF YOU DON'T.
HEY, DANNI.
I NEED TO TALK TO YOU.
SO DO I.

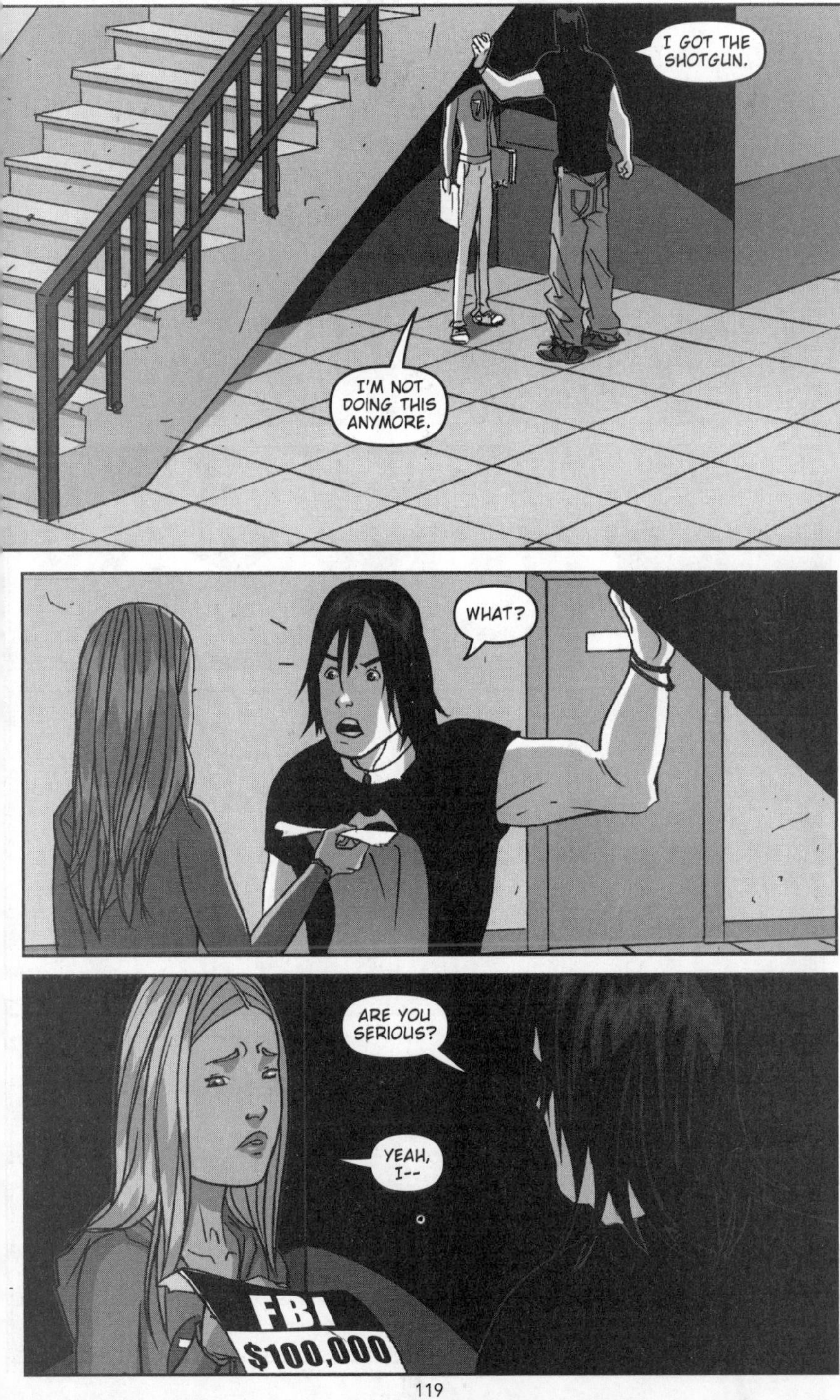
I GOT THE SHOTGUN.
I'M NOT DOING THIS ANYMORE.
WHAT?
ARE YOU SERIOUS?
YEAH, I--
FBI
$100,000

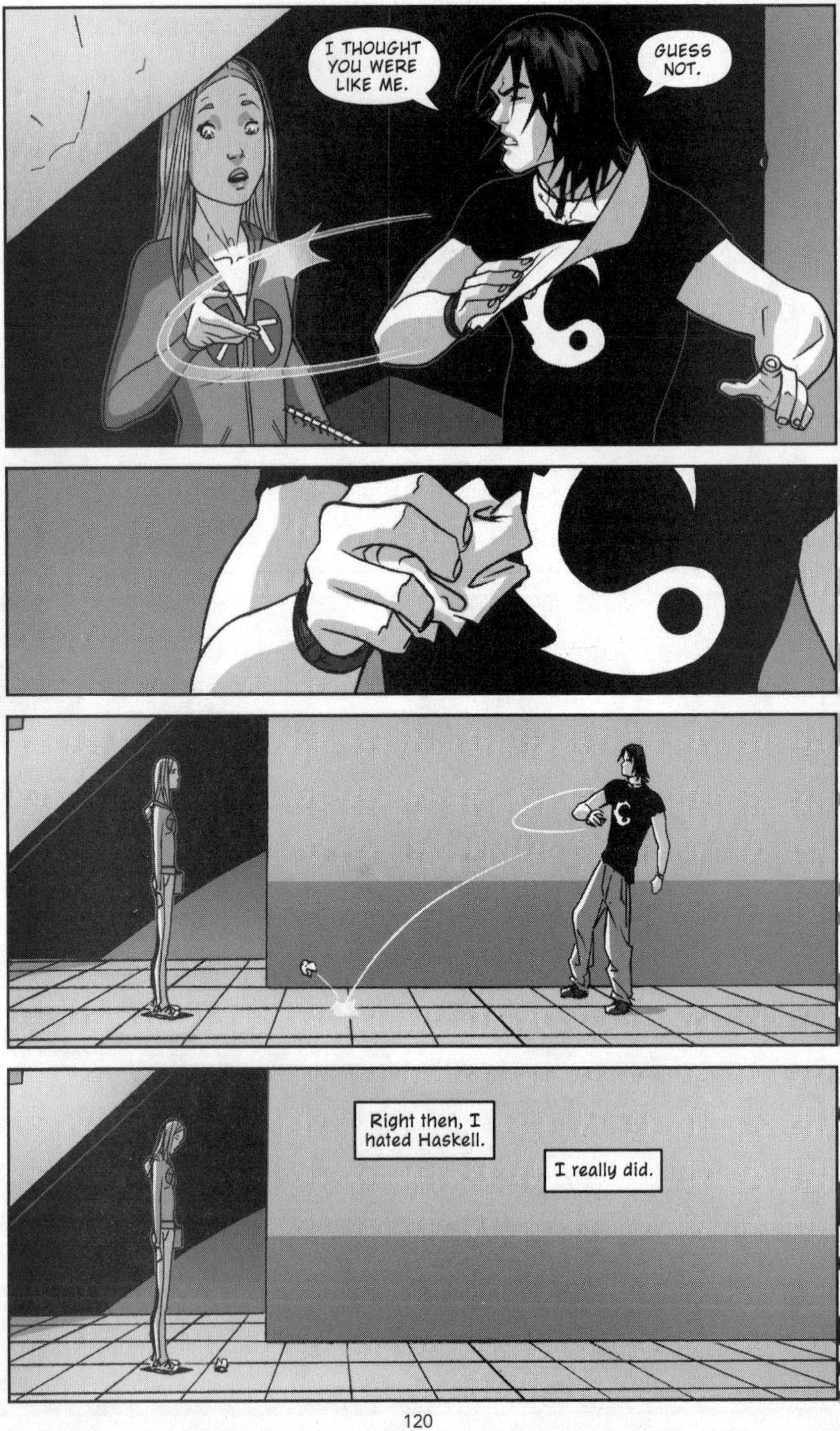

I THOUGHT YOU WERE LIKE ME.
GUESS NOT.
Right then, I hated Haskell.
I really did.

But I also loved him.

I couldn't let anything happen to him.

Even if he was right.

Even if I believed in what he was doing.

I couldn't waste any more time.

I had to stop him.

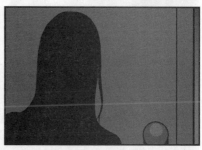

KNOCK KNOCK

121

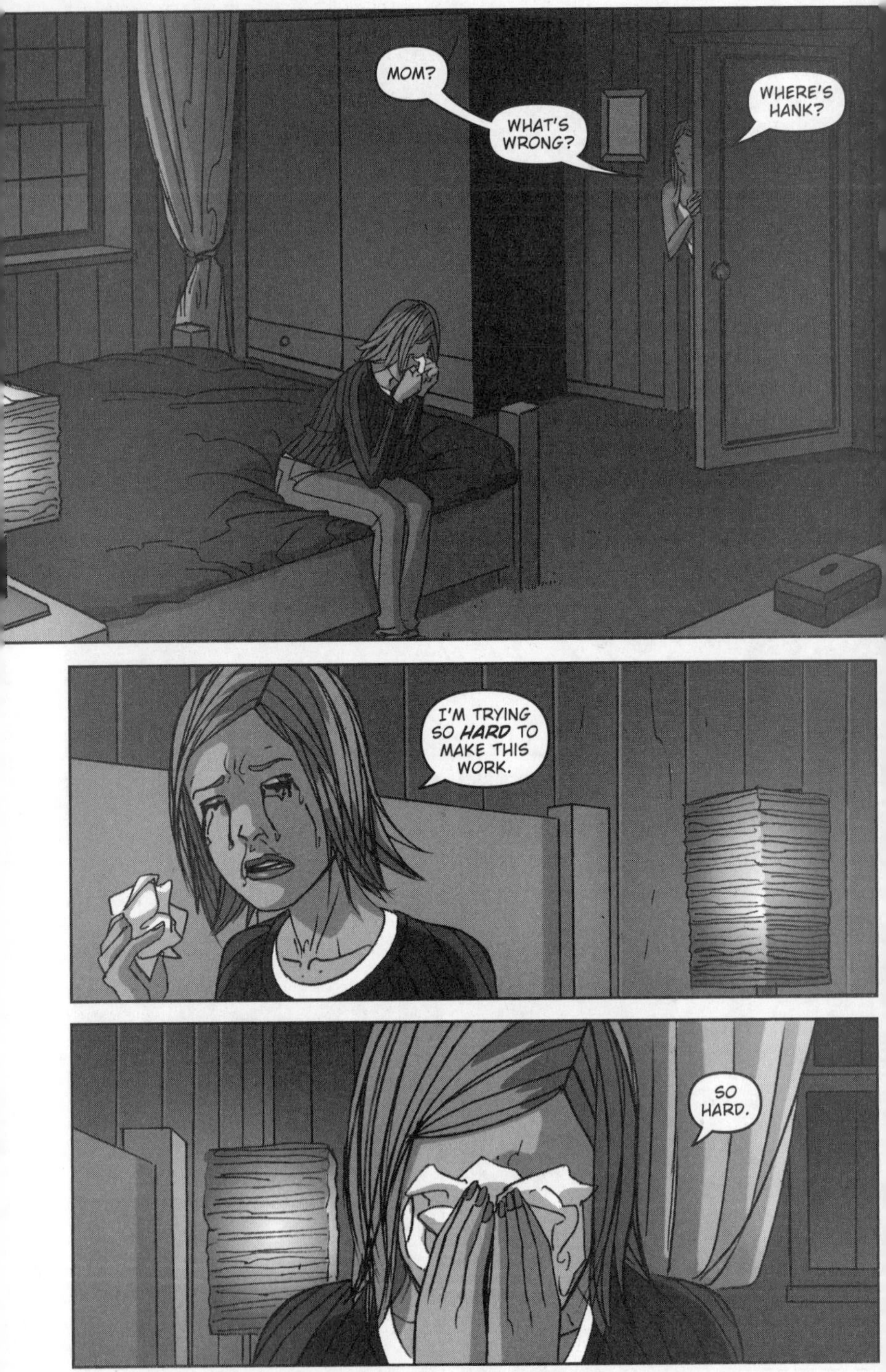
MOM?
WHAT'S WRONG?
WHERE'S HANK?
I'M TRYING SO HARD TO MAKE THIS WORK.
SO HARD.

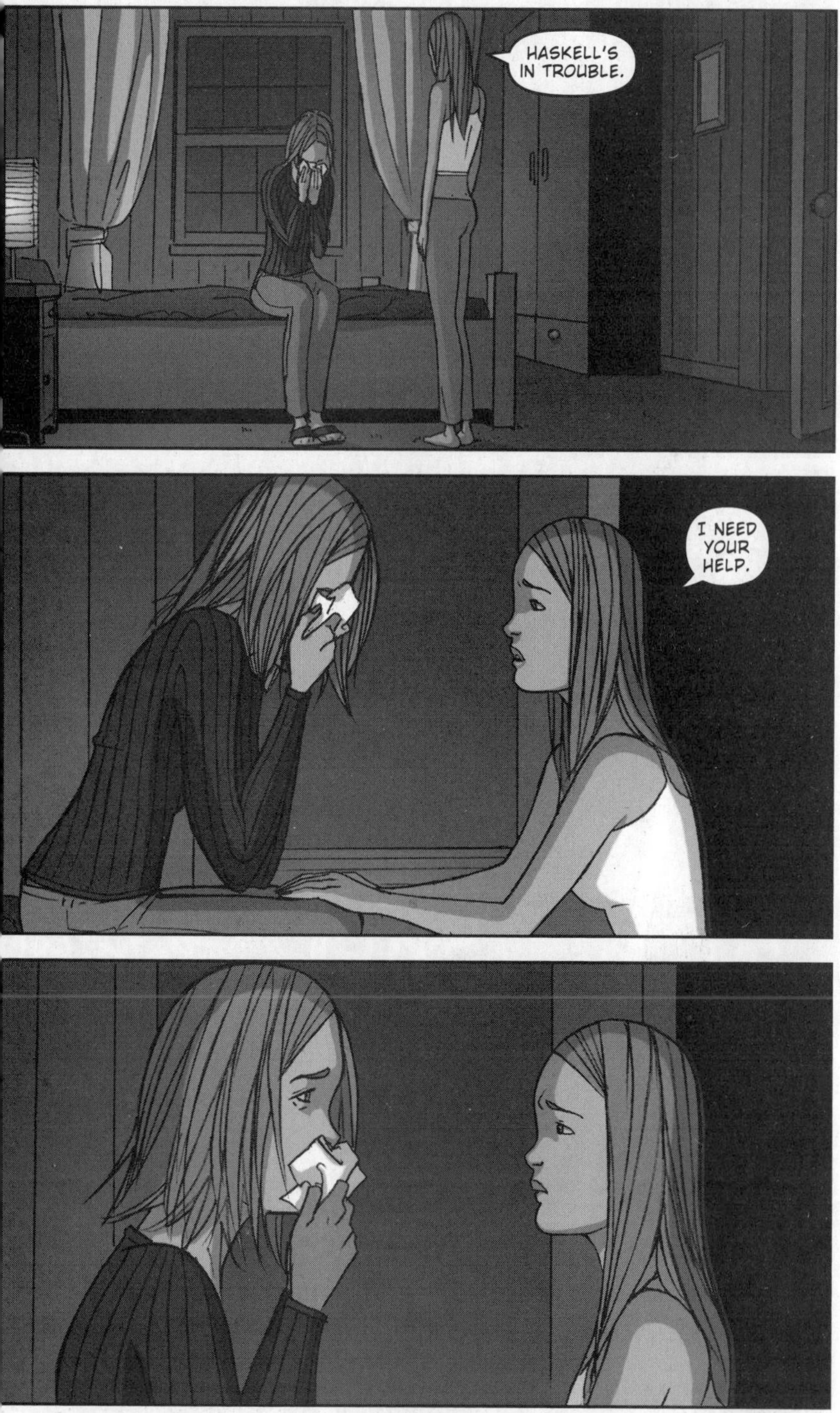
HASKELL'S IN TROUBLE.
I NEED YOUR HELP.

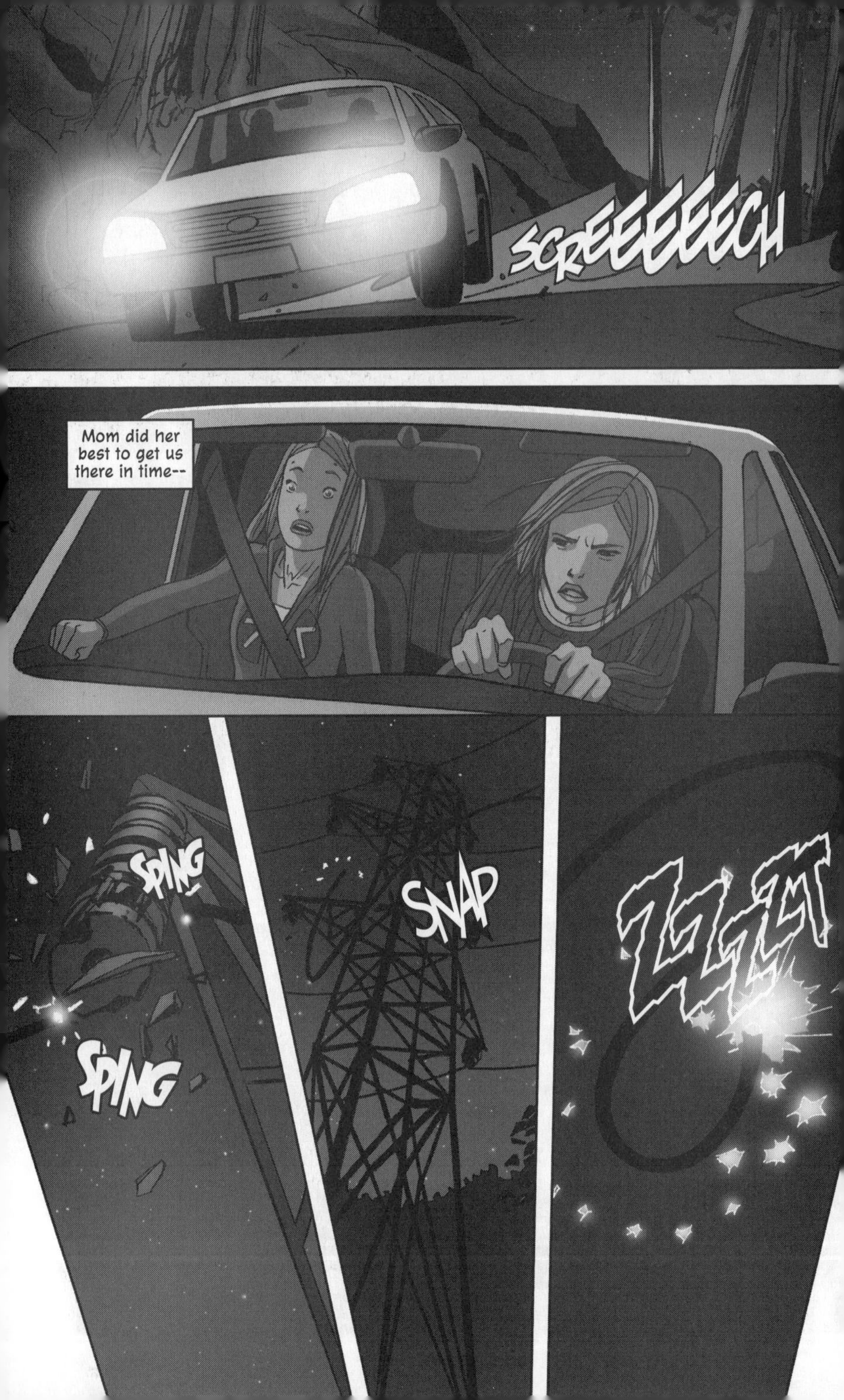
SCREEEEEECH
Mom did her best to get us there in time--
SPING
SPING
SNAP
ZZZZT

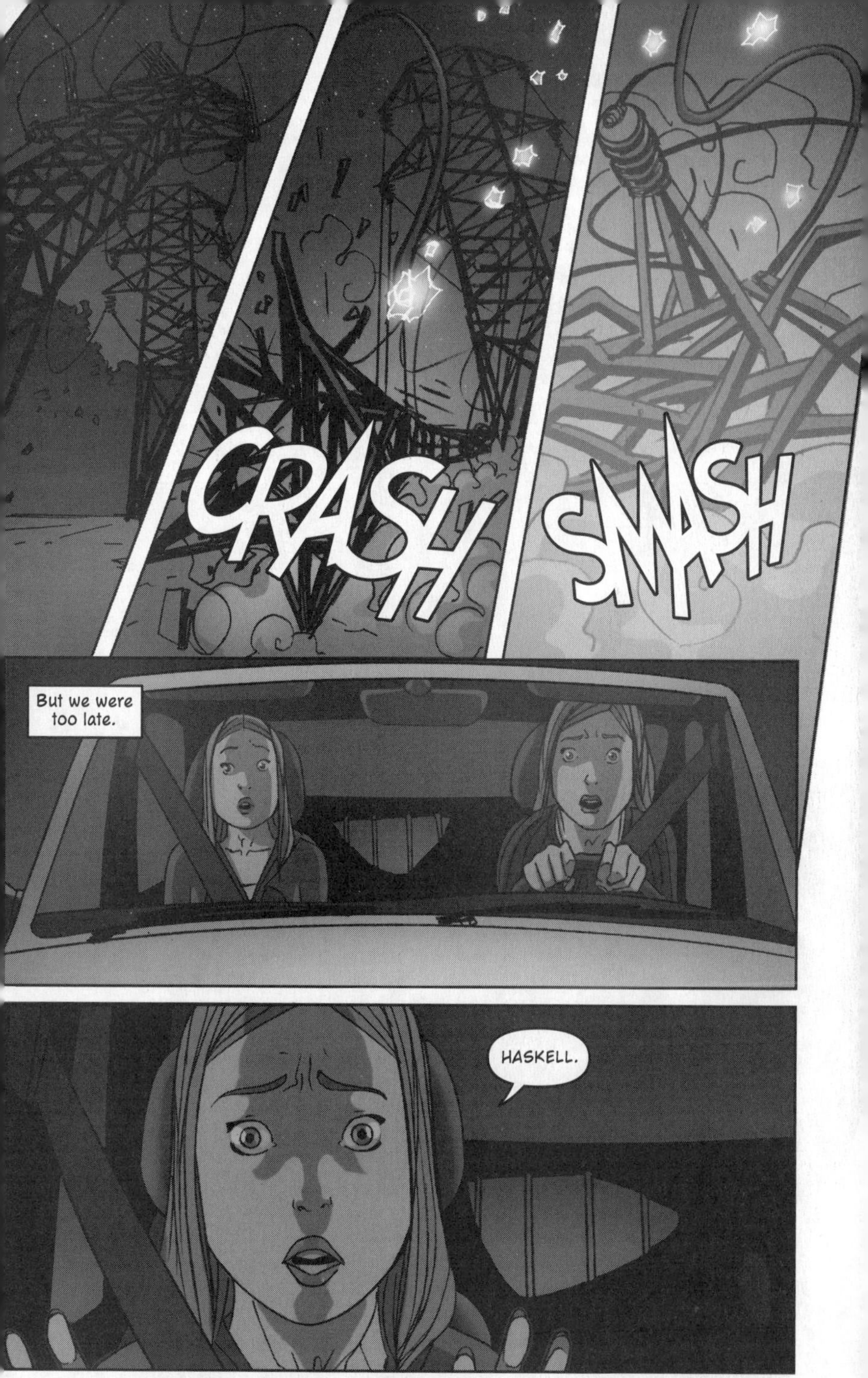
CRASH
SMASH
But we were too late.
HASKELL.

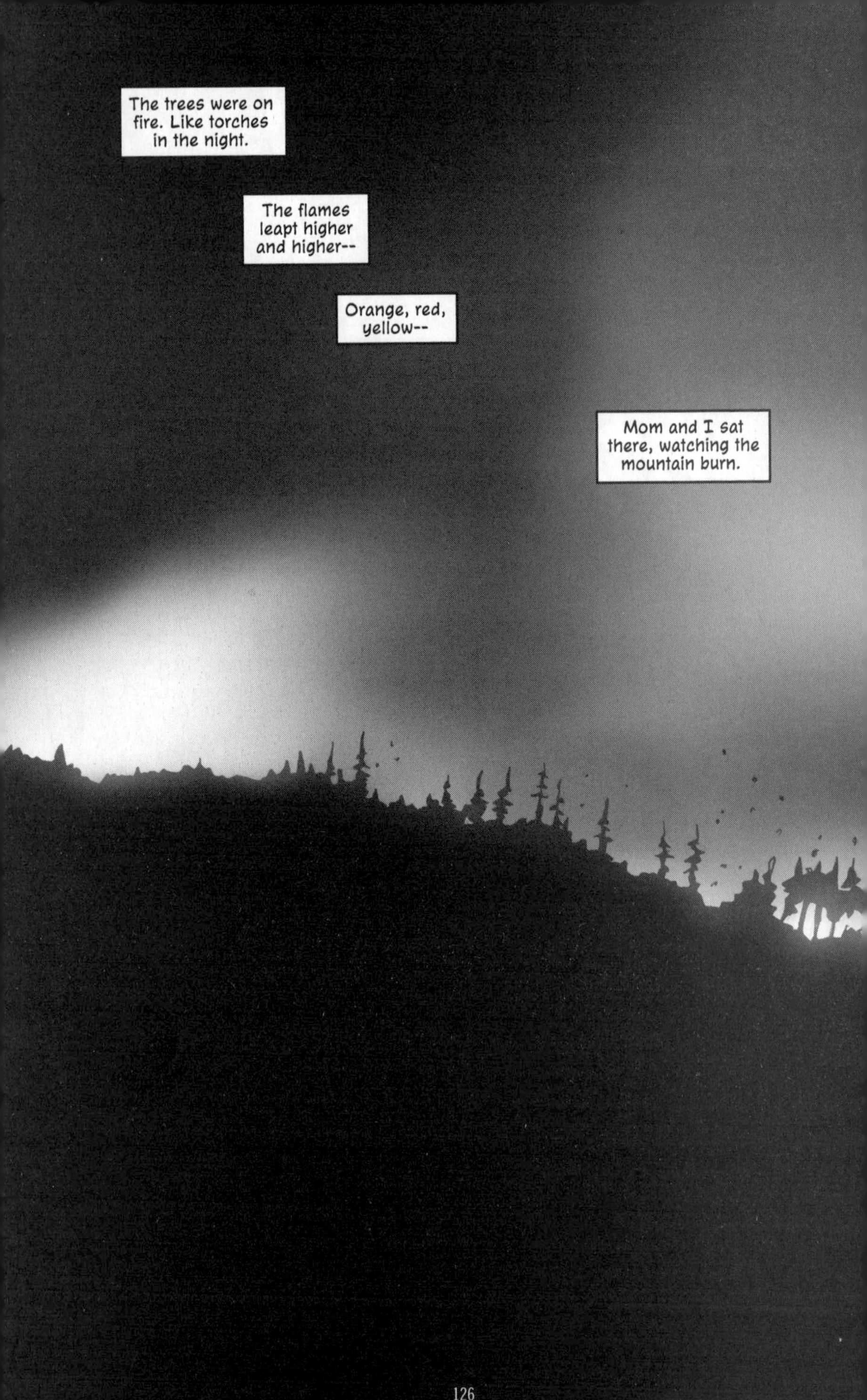
The trees were on fire. Like torches in the night.
The flames leapt higher and higher--
Orange, red, yellow--
Mom and I sat there, watching the mountain burn.

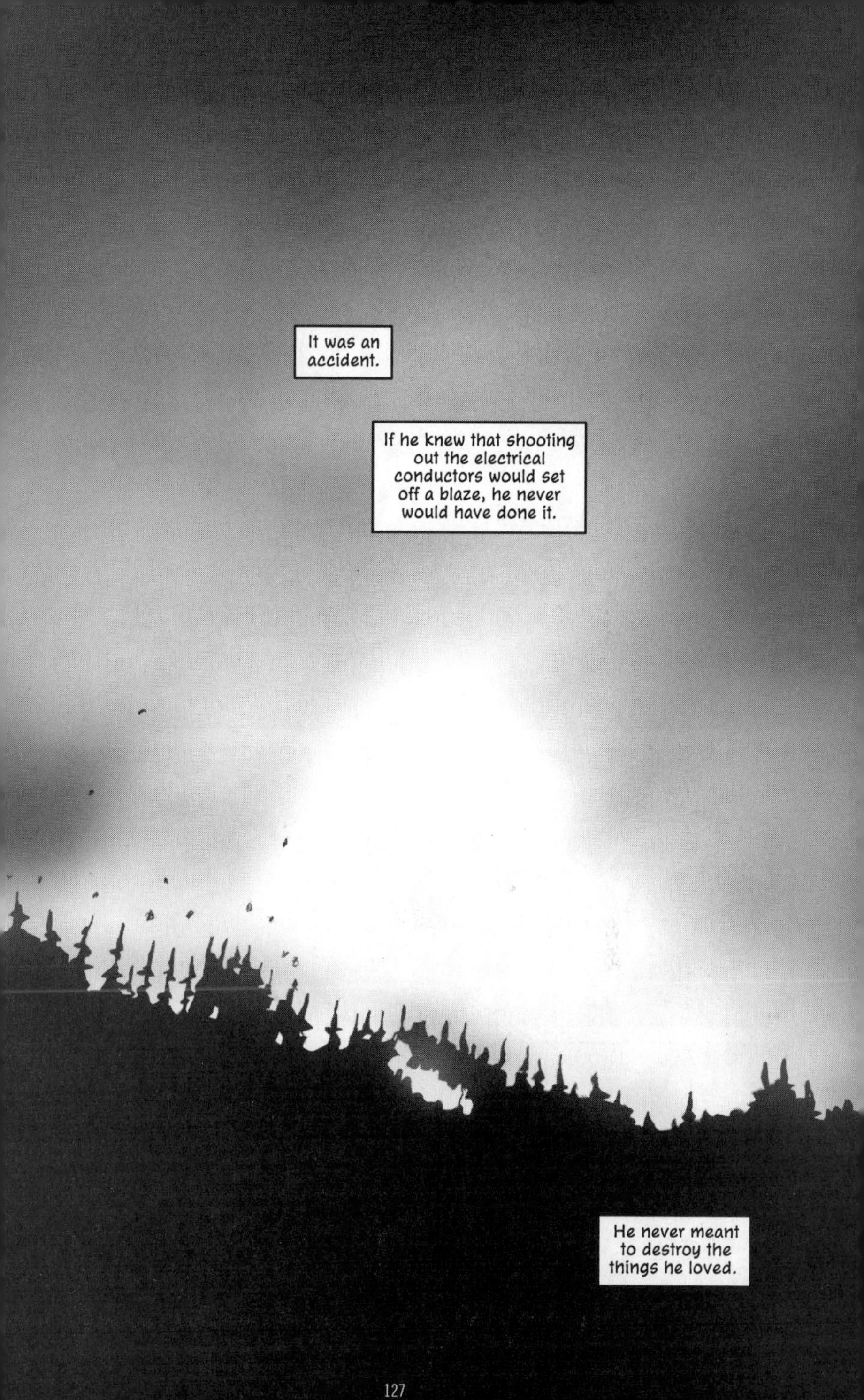
It was an accident.
If he knew that shooting out the electrical conductors would set off a blaze, he never would have done it.
He never meant to destroy the things he loved.

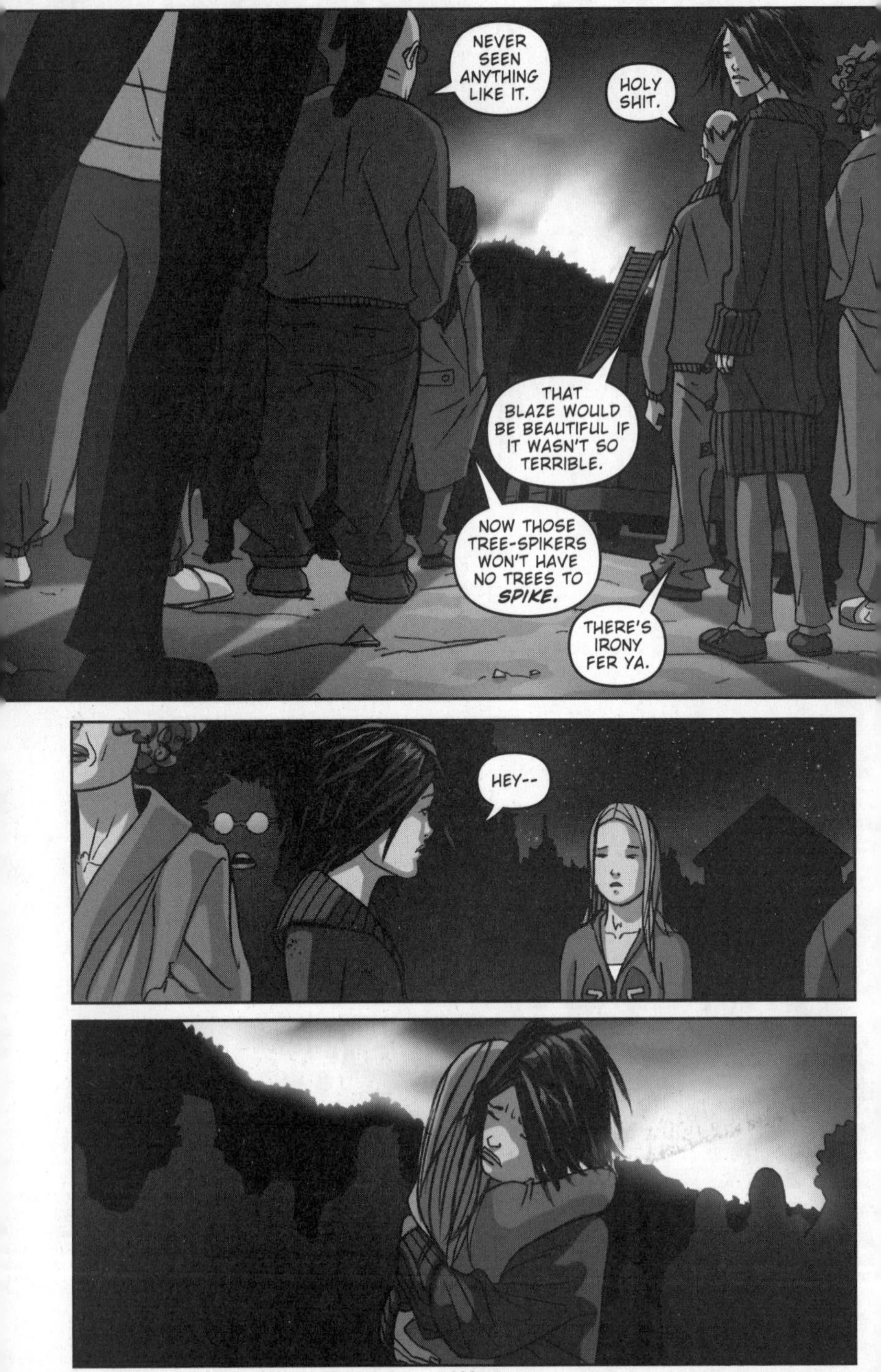
NEVER SEEN ANYTHING LIKE IT.
HOLY SHIT.
THAT BLAZE WOULD BE BEAUTIFUL IF IT WASN'T SO TERRIBLE.
NOW THOSE TREE-SPIKERS WON'T HAVE NO TREES TO **SPIKE.**
THERE'S IRONY FER YA.
HEY--

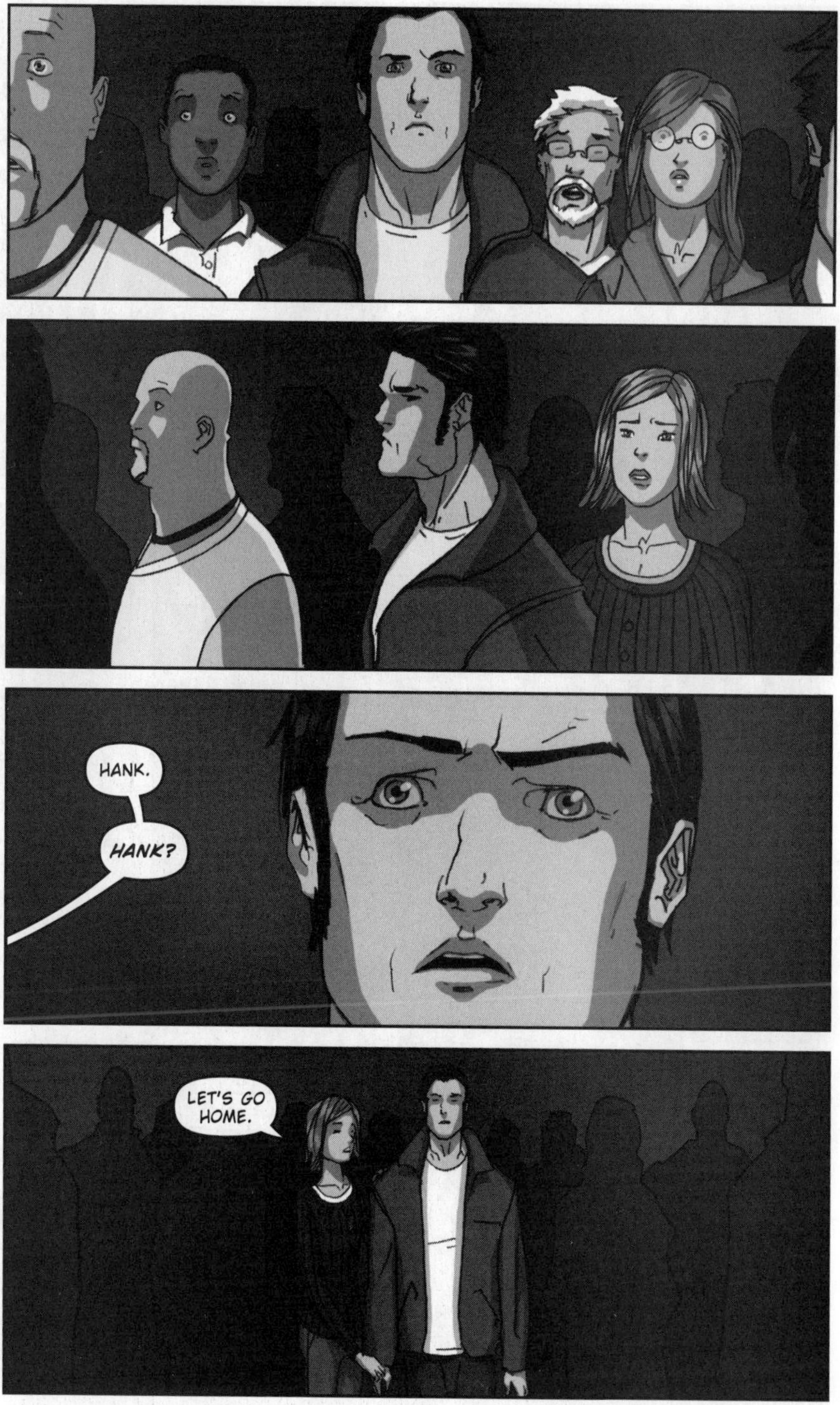
HANK.
HANK?
LET'S GO HOME.

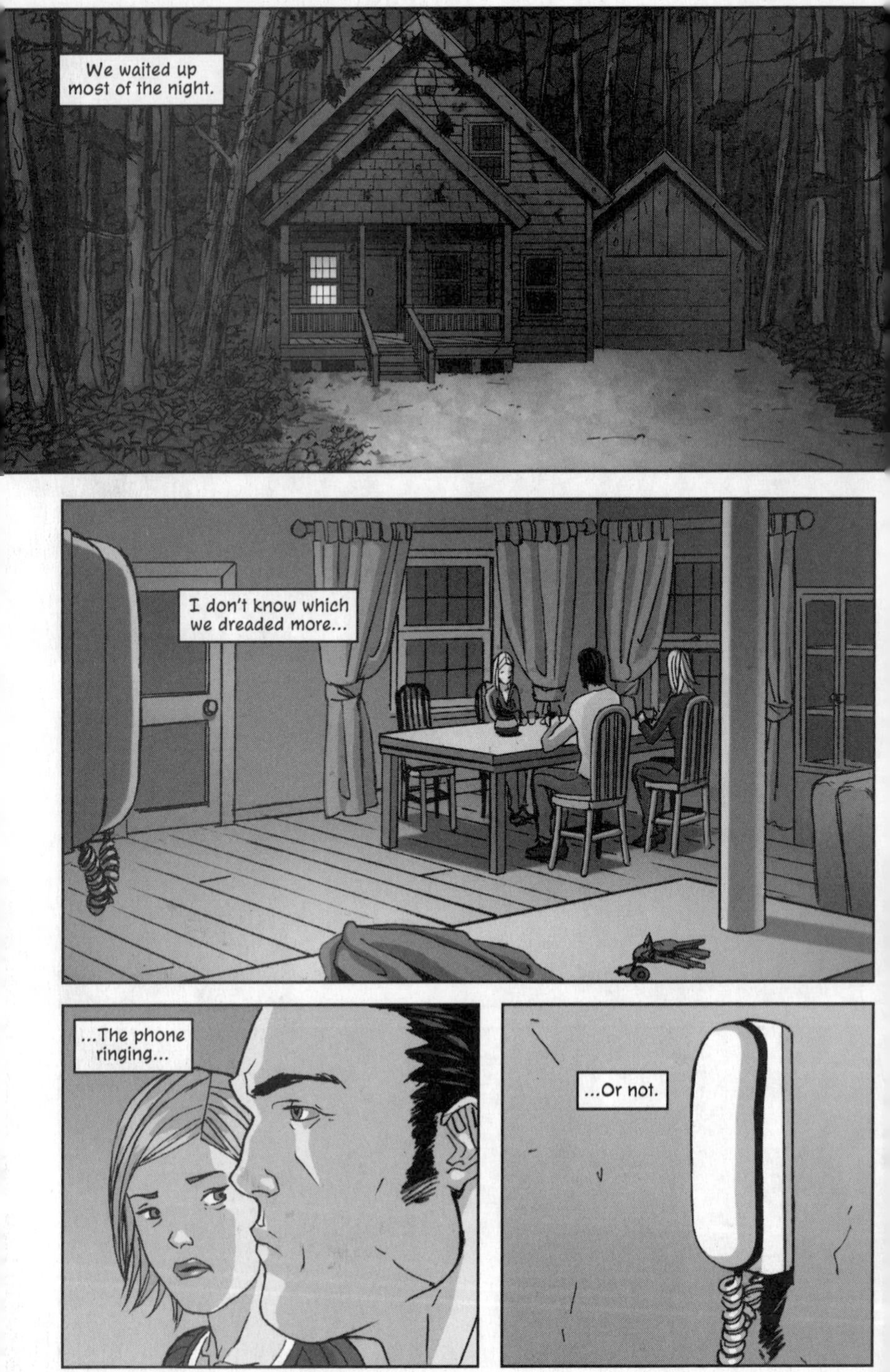
We waited up most of the night.
I don't know which we dreaded more...
...The phone ringing...
...Or not.

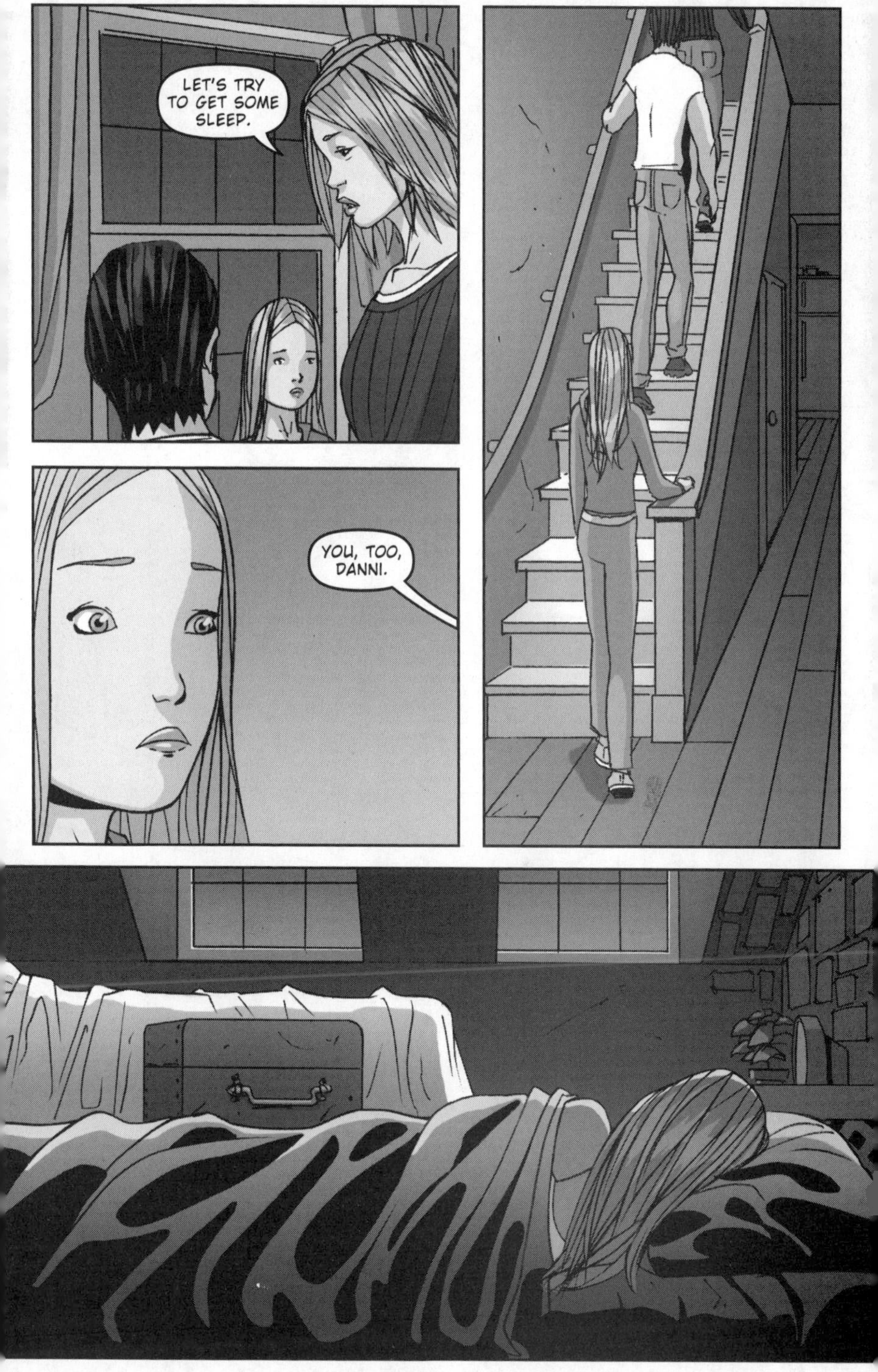
LET'S TRY TO GET SOME SLEEP.
YOU, TOO, DANNI.

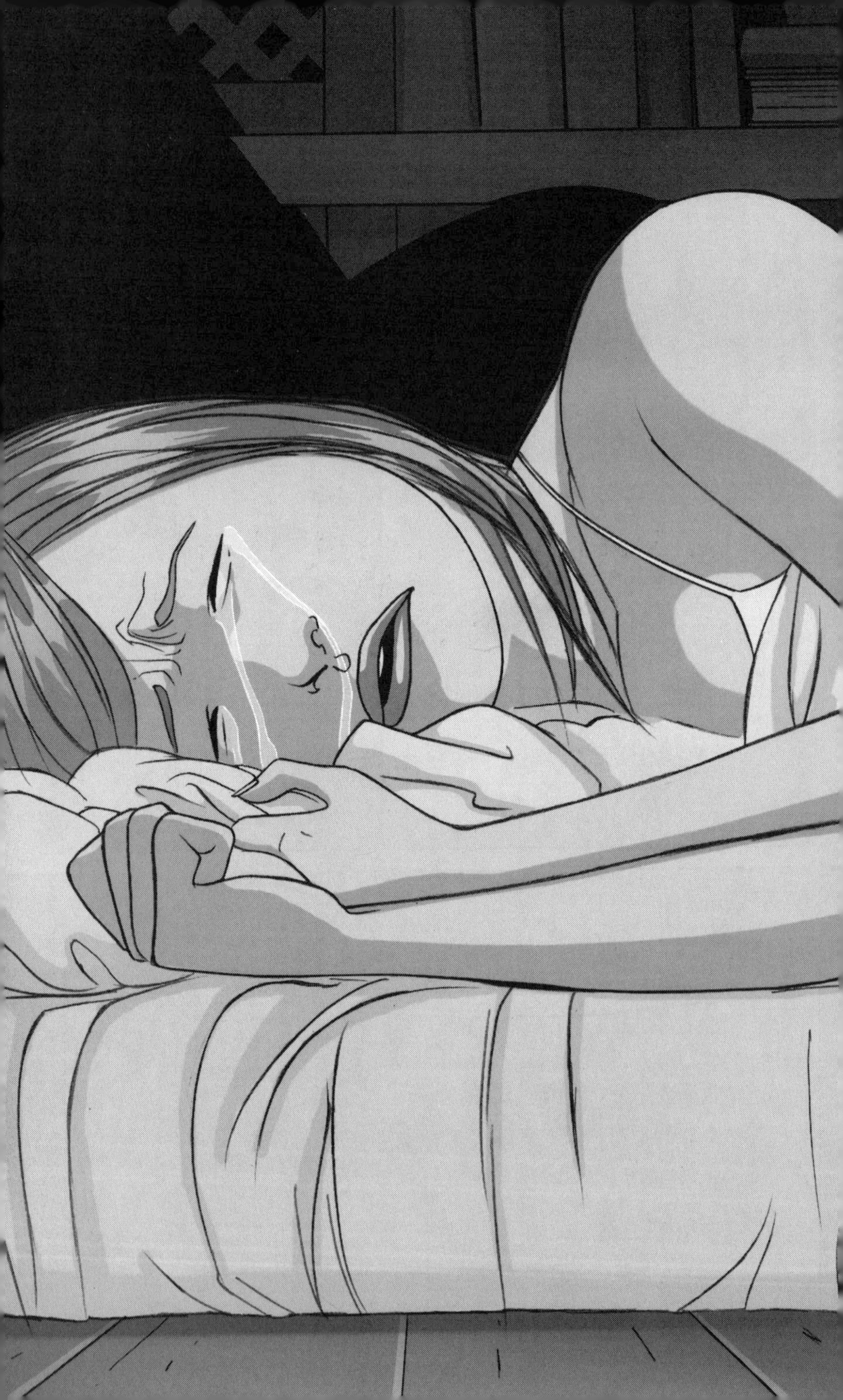

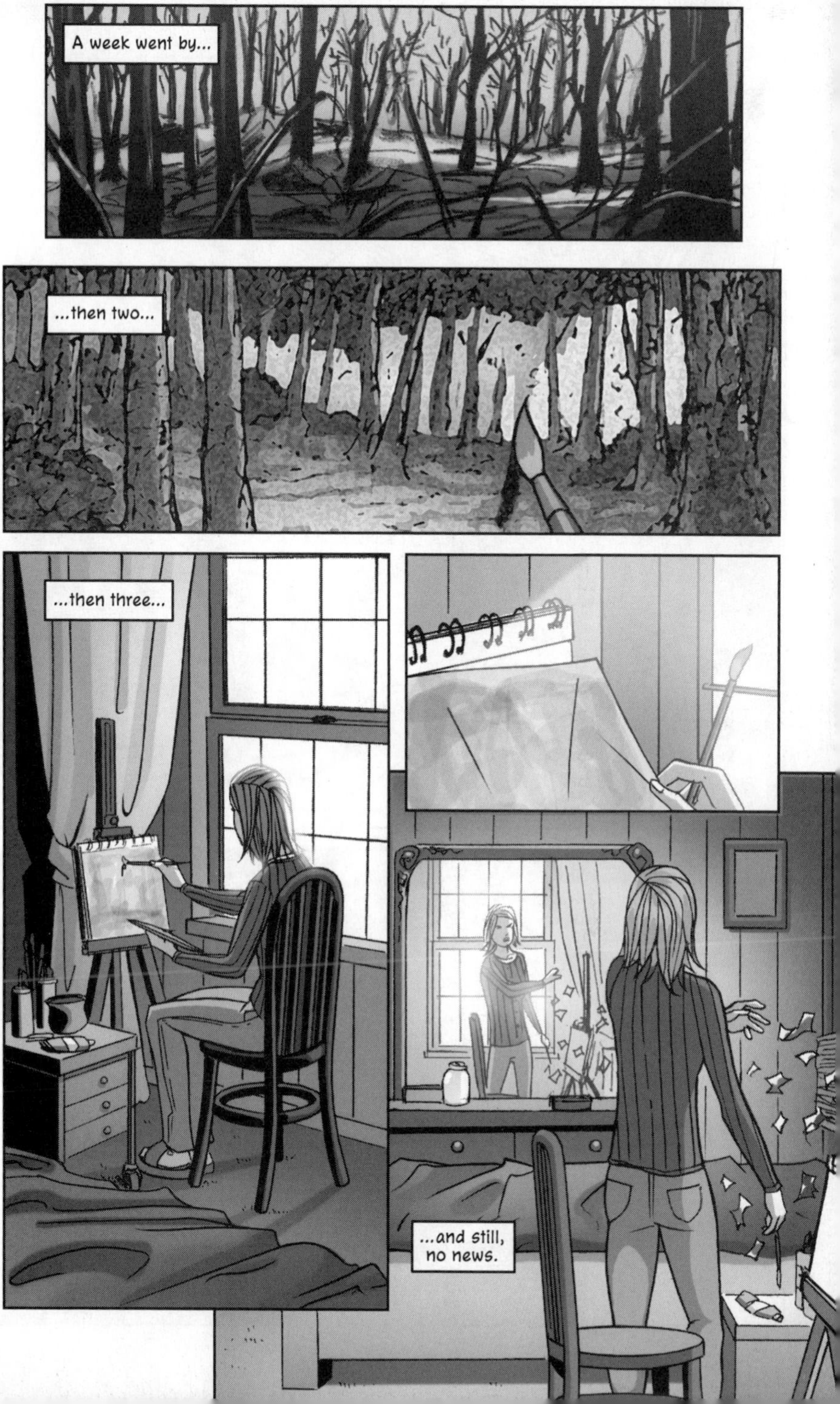

A week went by...
...then two...
...then three...
...and still, no news.

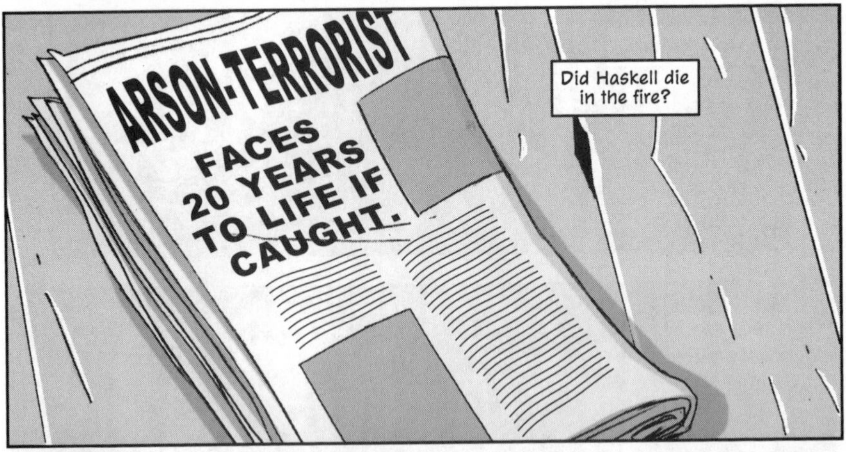
ARSON-TERRORIST
FACES 20 YEARS TO LIFE IF CAUGHT.
Did Haskell die in the fire?

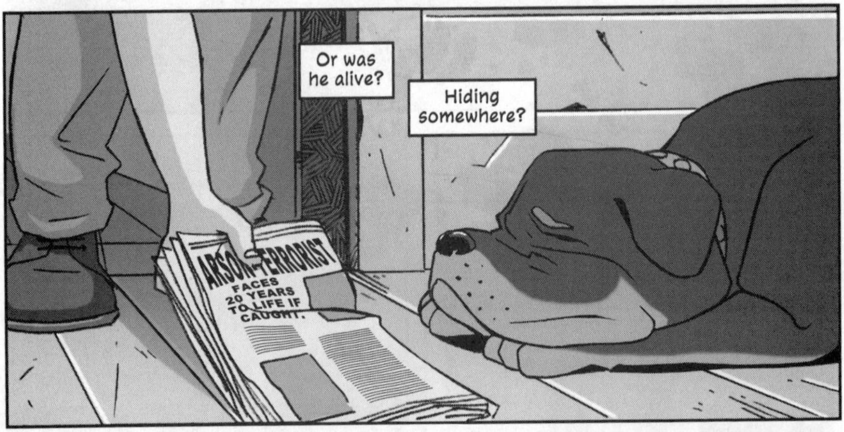
Or was he alive?
Hiding somewhere?
ARSON-TERRORIST
FACES 20 YEARS TO LIFE IF CAUGHT.

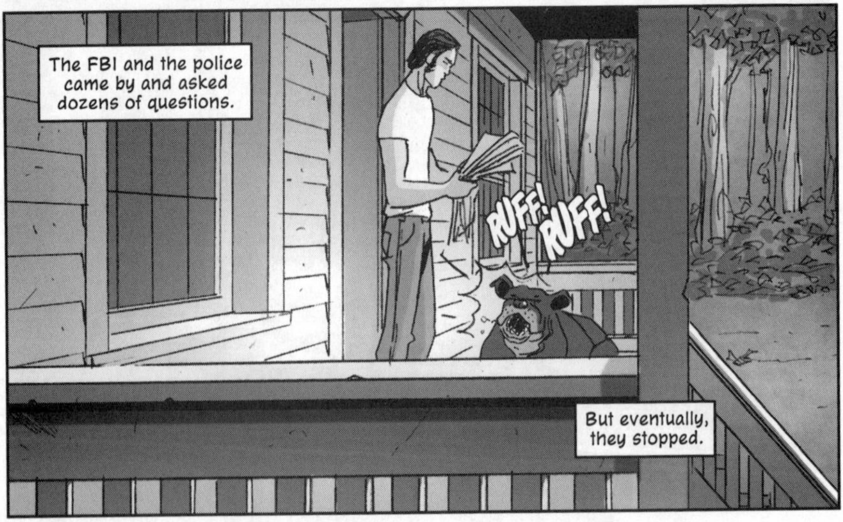
The FBI and the police came by and asked dozens of questions.
RUFF! RUFF!
But eventually, they stopped.

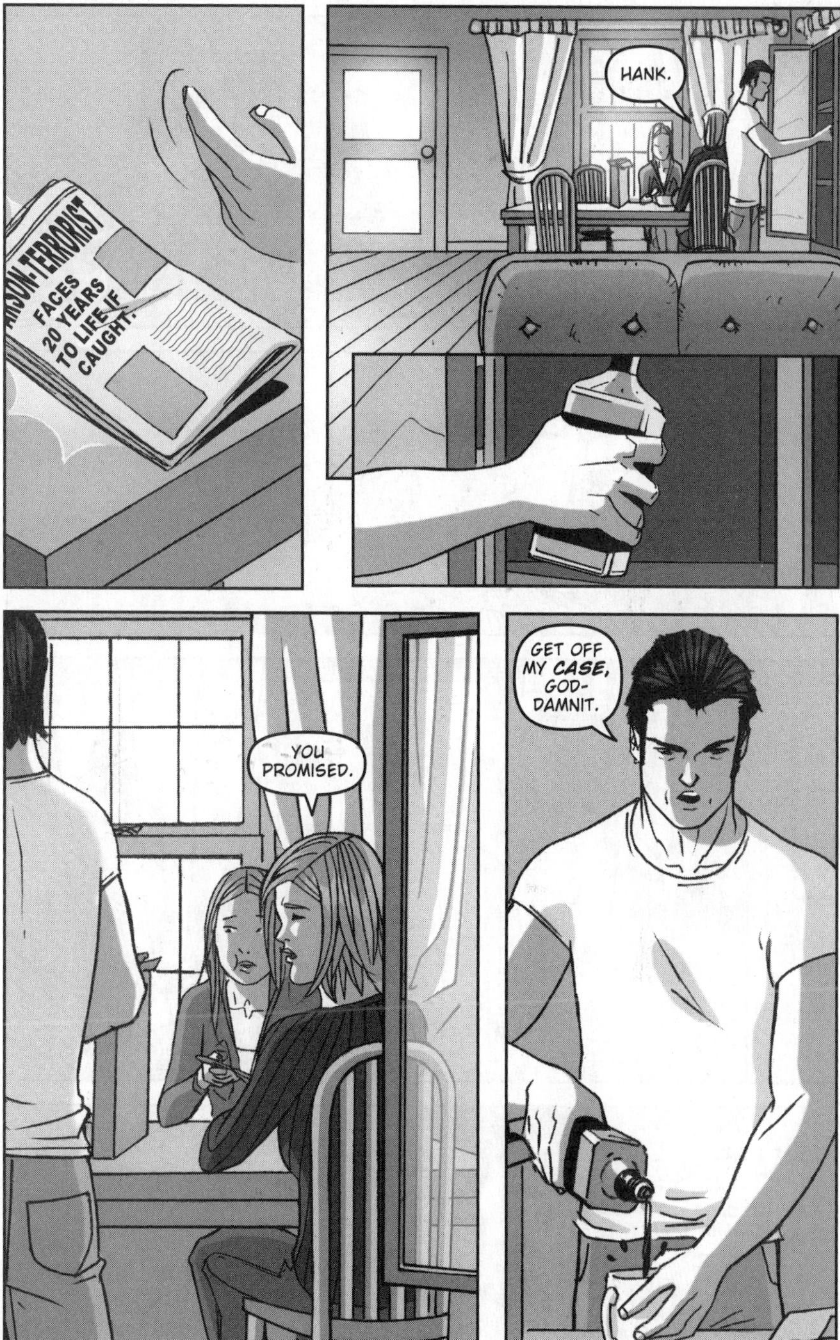
ARSON-TERRORIST
FACES 20 YEARS TO LIFE IF CAUGHT.
HANK.
YOU PROMISED.
GET OFF MY CASE, GOD-DAMNIT.

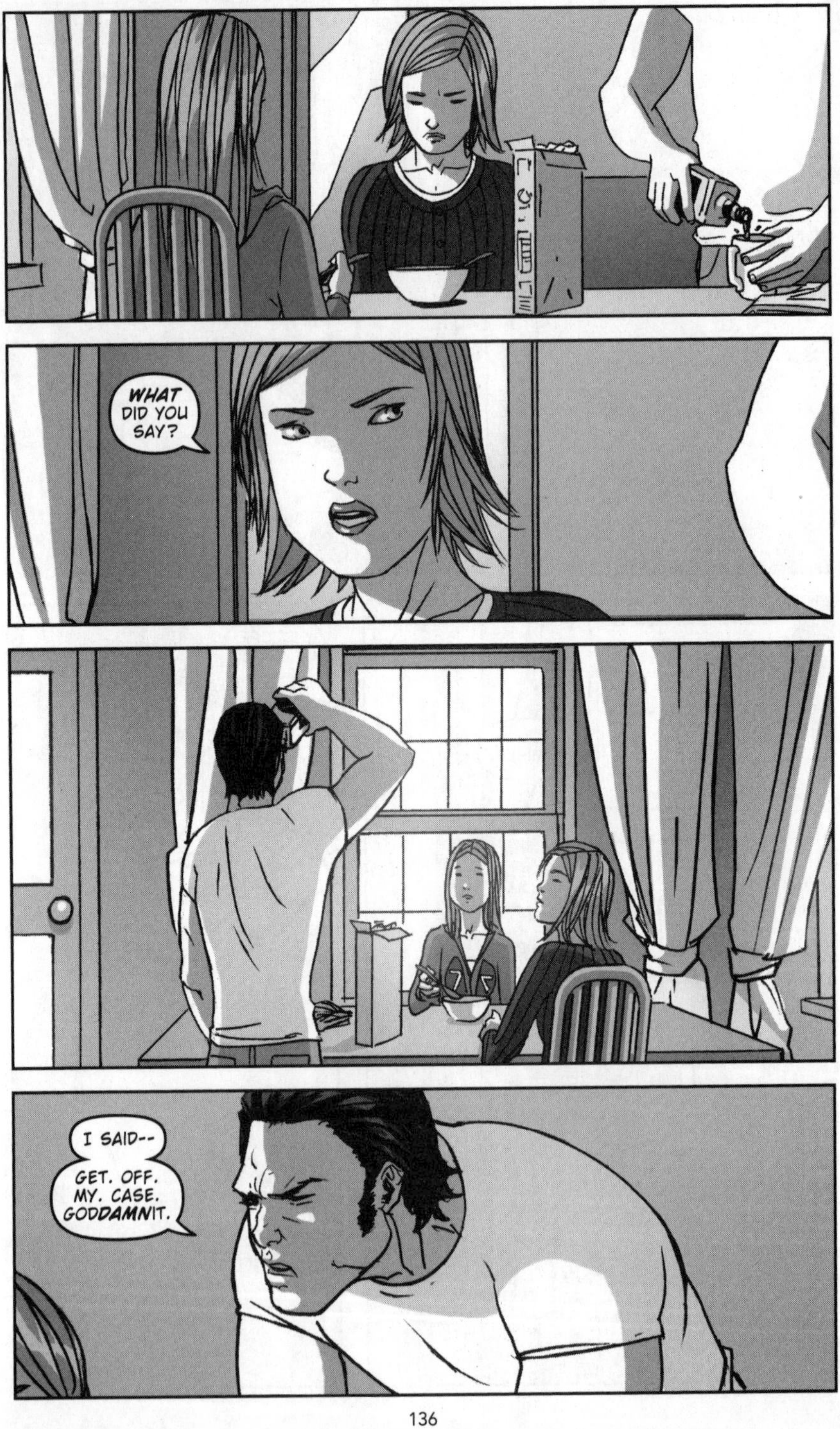
WHAT DID YOU SAY?
I SAID--
GET. OFF. MY. CASE. GODDAMNIT.

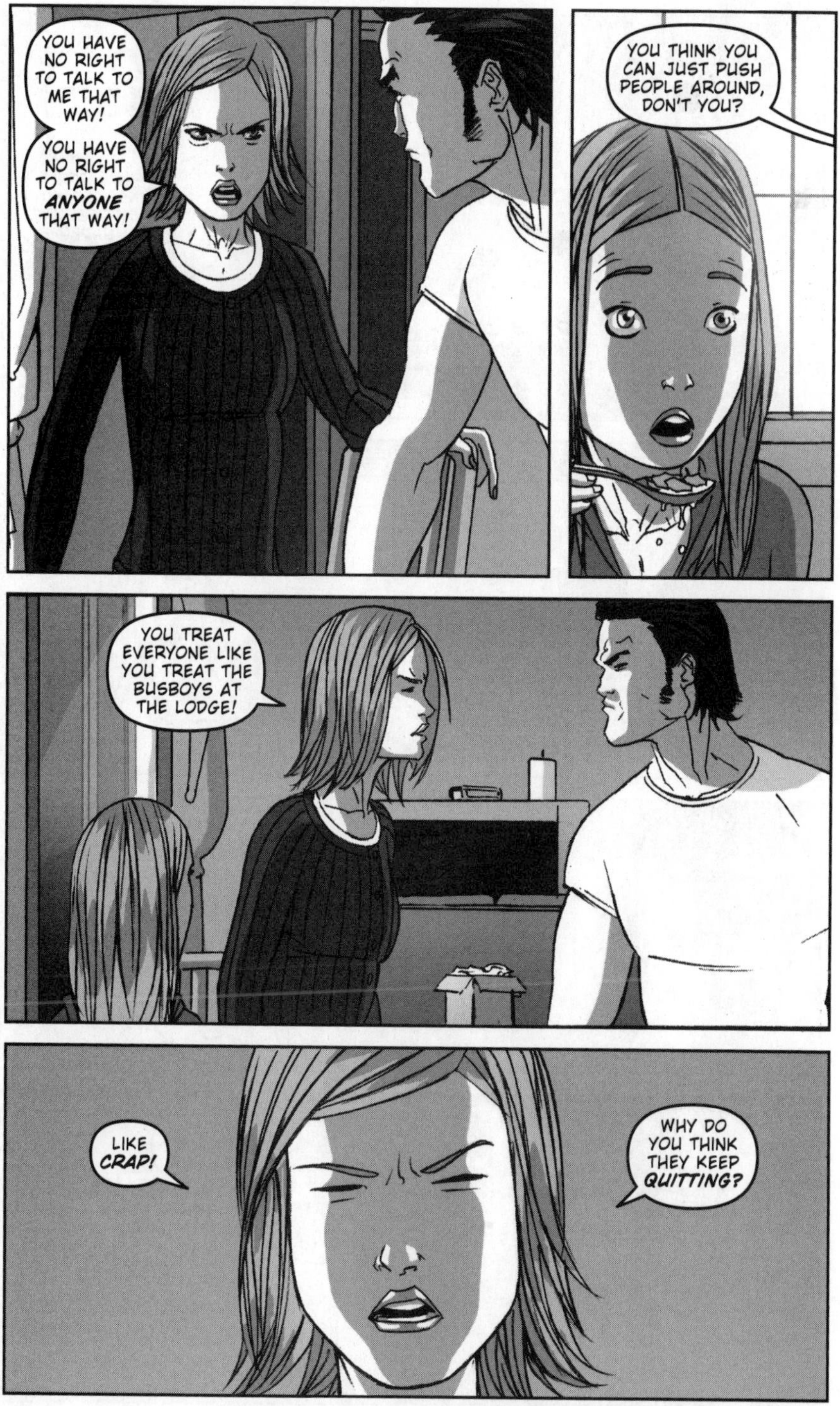

YOU HAVE NO RIGHT TO TALK TO ME THAT WAY!
YOU HAVE NO RIGHT TO TALK TO ANYONE THAT WAY!
YOU THINK YOU CAN JUST PUSH PEOPLE AROUND, DON'T YOU?
YOU TREAT EVERYONE LIKE YOU TREAT THE BUSBOYS AT THE LODGE!
LIKE CRAP!
WHY DO YOU THINK THEY KEEP QUITTING?

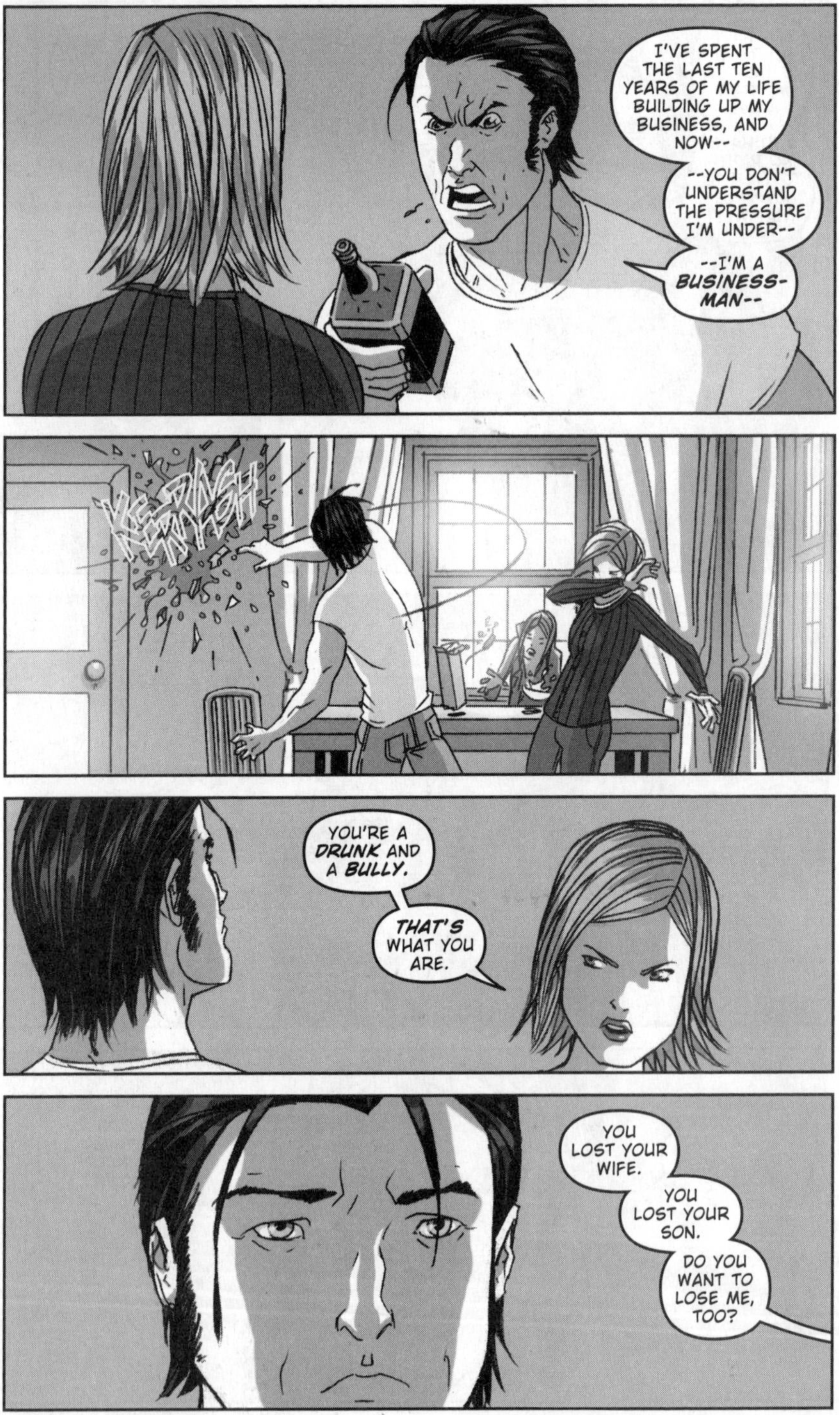
I'VE SPENT THE LAST TEN YEARS OF MY LIFE BUILDING UP MY BUSINESS, AND NOW--
--YOU DON'T UNDERSTAND THE PRESSURE I'M UNDER--
--I'M A **BUSINESS-MAN--**
YOU'RE A **DRUNK** AND A **BULLY.**
THAT'S WHAT YOU ARE.
YOU LOST YOUR WIFE.
YOU LOST YOUR SON.
DO YOU WANT TO LOSE ME, TOO?

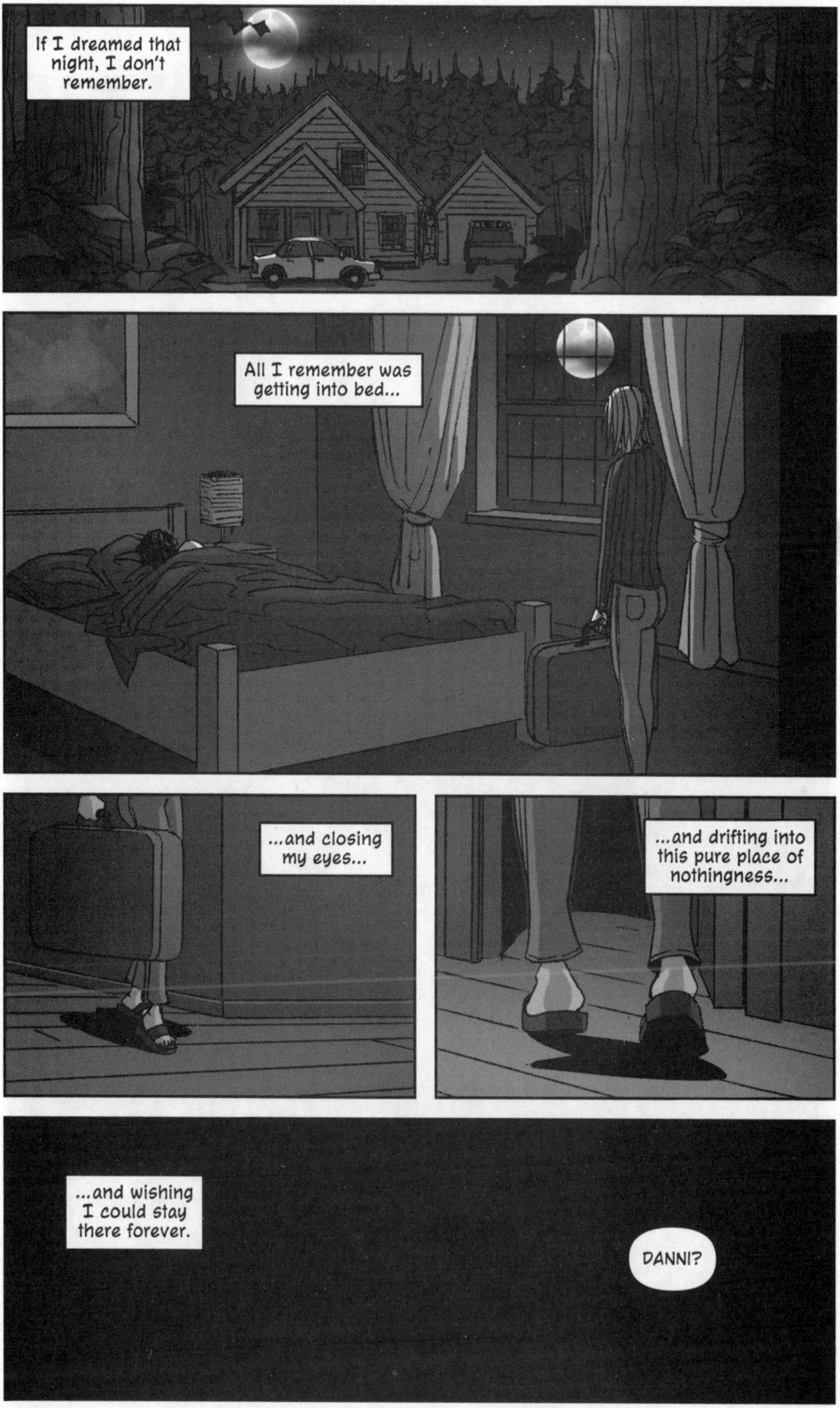
If I dreamed that night, I don't remember.
All I remember was getting into bed...
...and closing my eyes...
...and drifting into this pure place of nothingness...
...and wishing I could stay there forever.
DANNI?

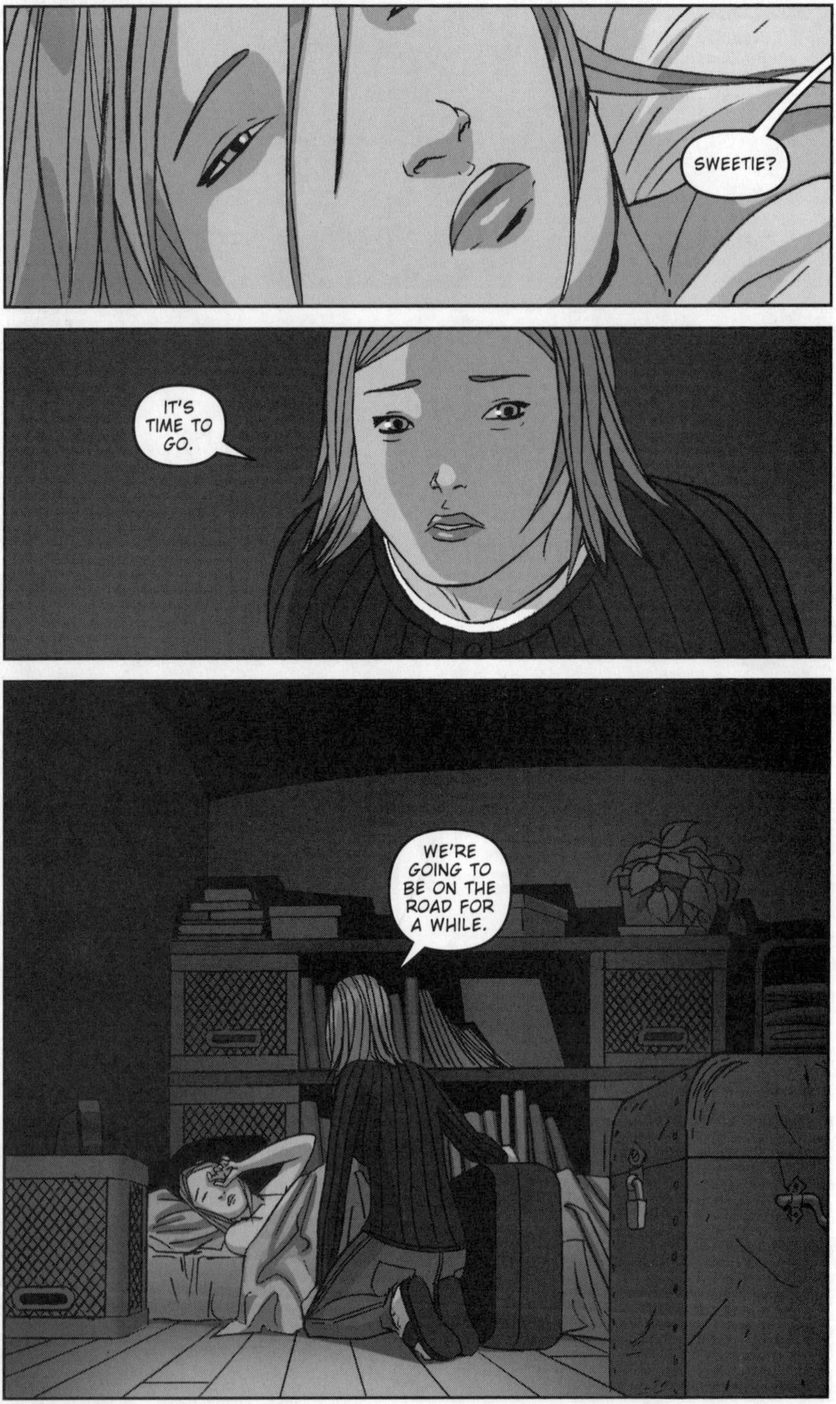
SWEETIE?
IT'S TIME TO GO.
WE'RE GOING TO BE ON THE ROAD FOR A WHILE.

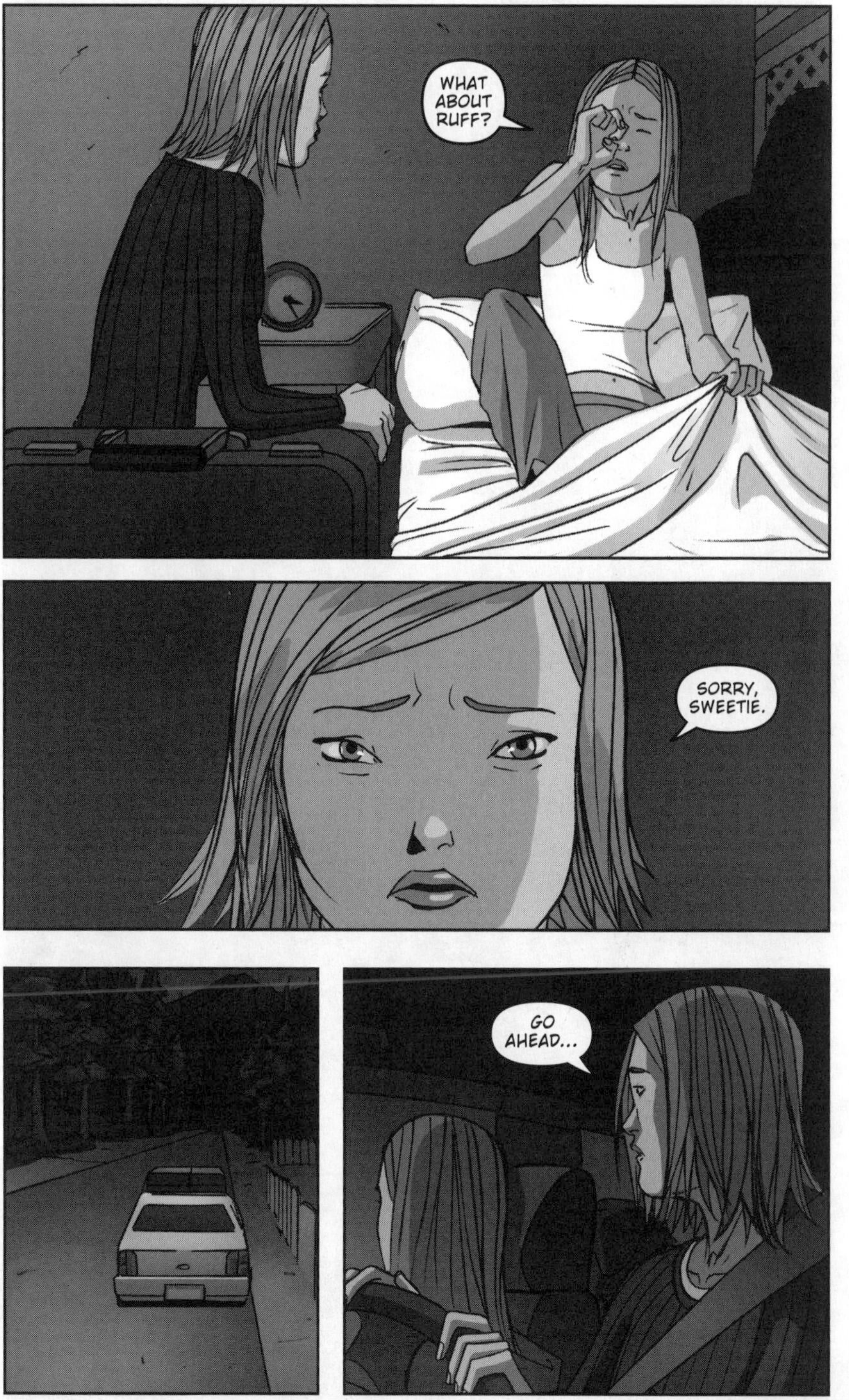
WHAT ABOUT RUFF?
SORRY, SWEETIE.
GO AHEAD...

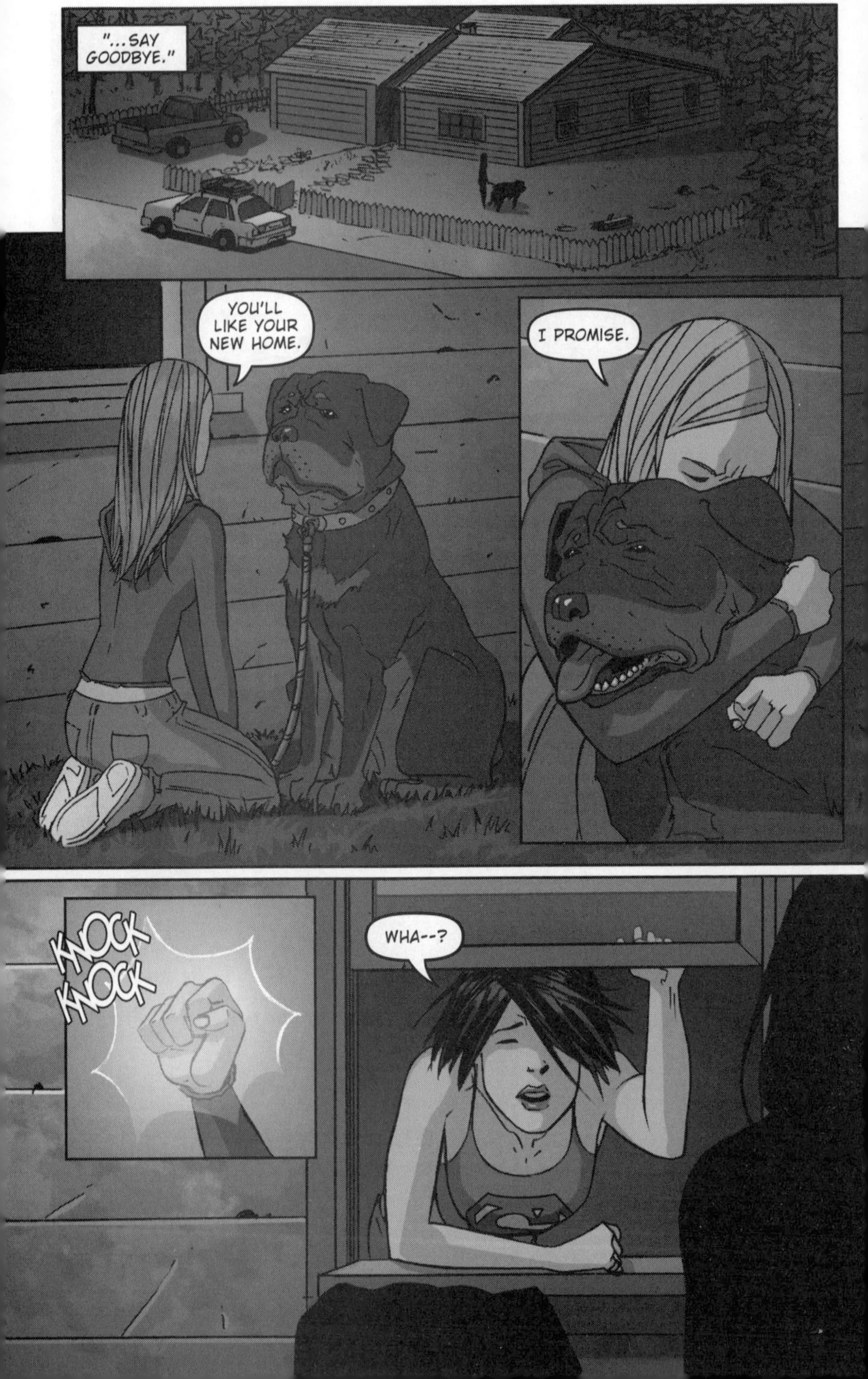
"...SAY GOODBYE."
YOU'LL LIKE YOUR NEW HOME.
I PROMISE.
KNOCK KNOCK
WHA--?

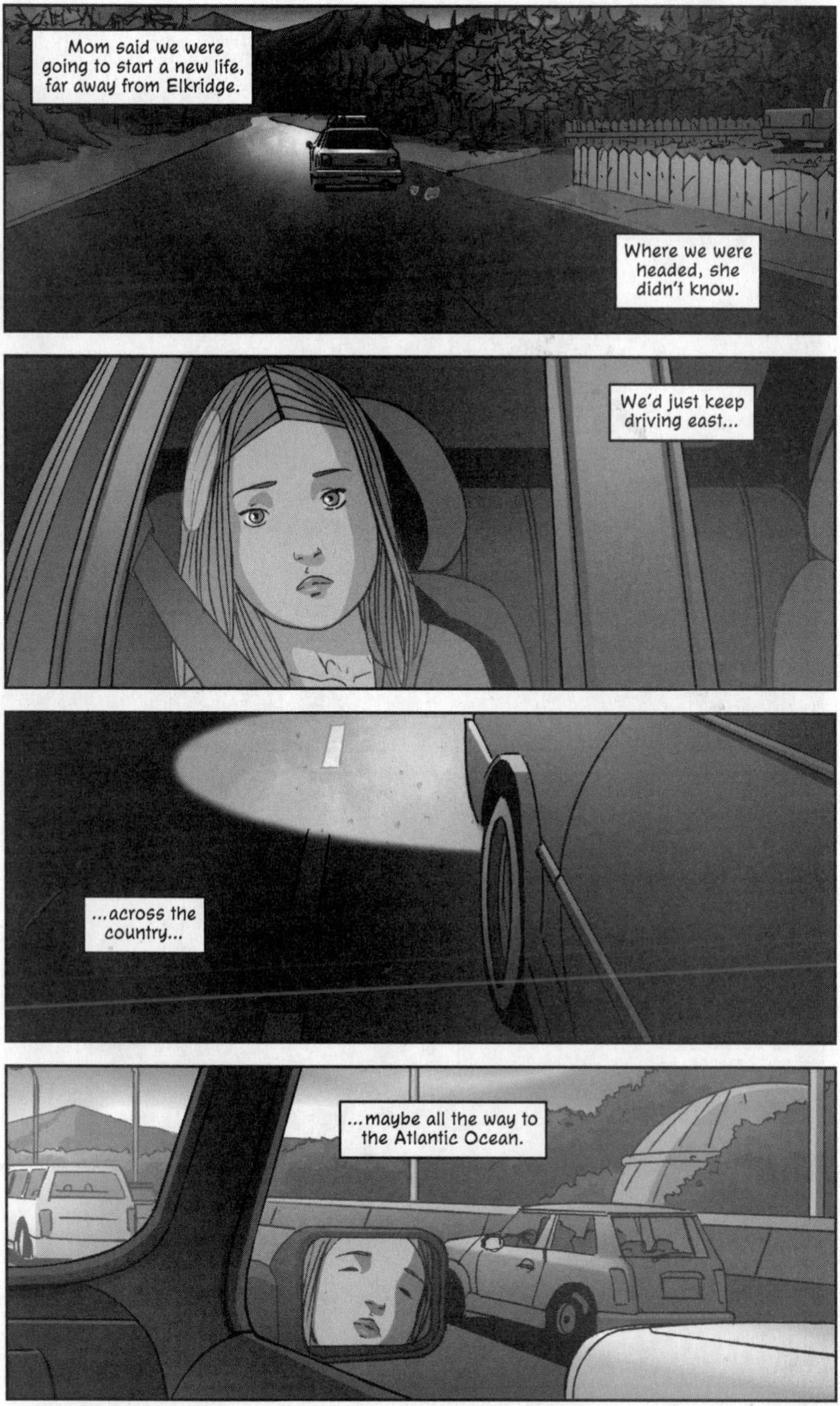
Mom said we were going to start a new life, far away from Elkridge.
Where we were headed, she didn't know.
We'd just keep driving east...
...across the country...
...maybe all the way to the Atlantic Ocean.

MOTEL
VACANCY

I couldn't believe it.

We were starting over.

From scratch.

Again.

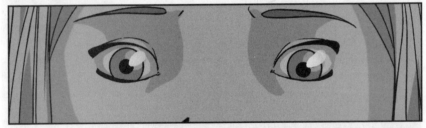

"SEE THOSE FLECKS?"

"GOLD."

"KEEP IT, DANNI."

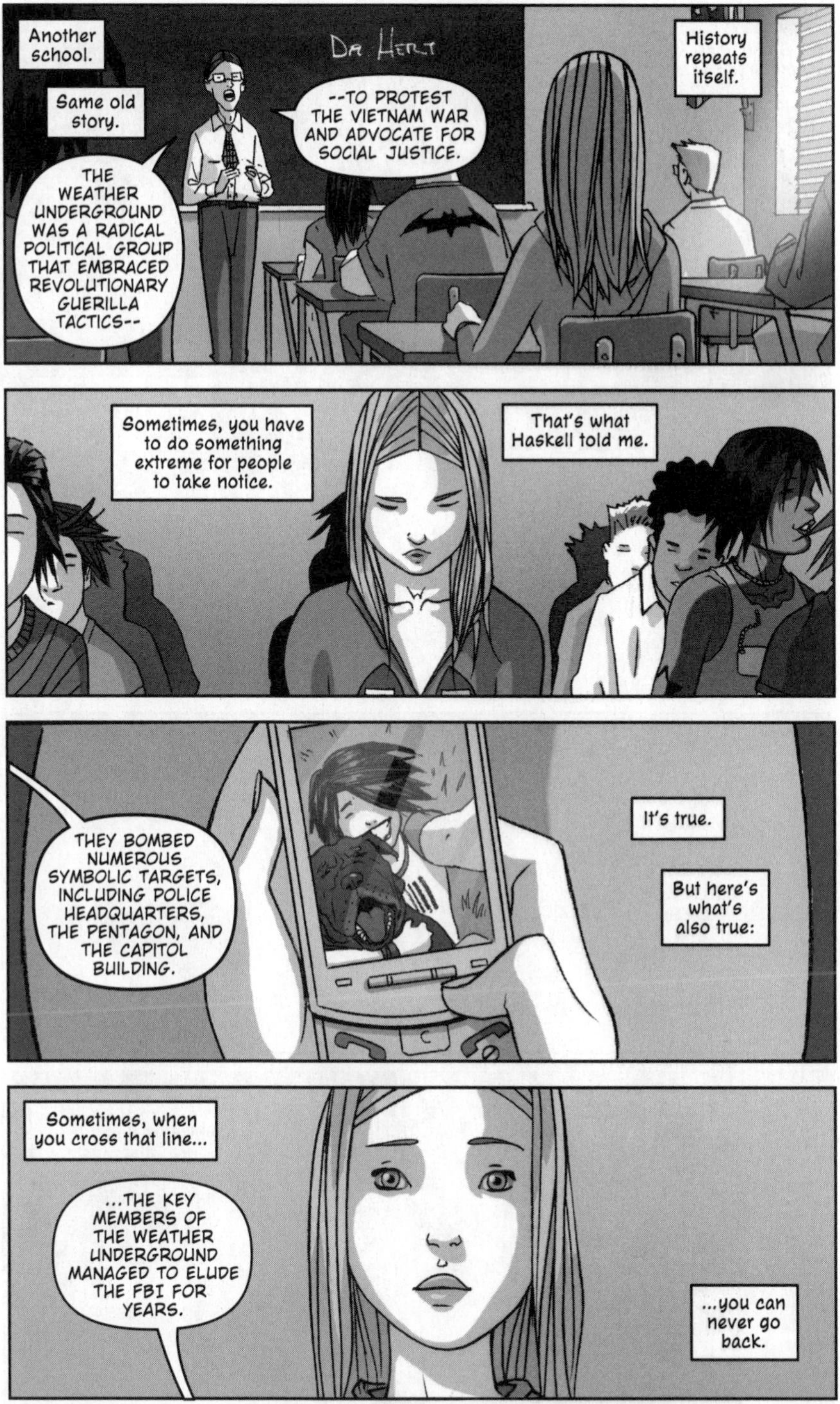
Another school.
DR. HERT
Same old story.
History repeats itself.
THE WEATHER UNDERGROUND WAS A RADICAL POLITICAL GROUP THAT EMBRACED REVOLUTIONARY GUERILLA TACTICS--
--TO PROTEST THE VIETNAM WAR AND ADVOCATE FOR SOCIAL JUSTICE.
Sometimes, you have to do something extreme for people to take notice.
That's what Haskell told me.
THEY BOMBED NUMEROUS SYMBOLIC TARGETS, INCLUDING POLICE HEADQUARTERS, THE PENTAGON, AND THE CAPITOL BUILDING.
It's true.
But here's what's also true:
Sometimes, when you cross that line...
...THE KEY MEMBERS OF THE WEATHER UNDERGROUND MANAGED TO ELUDE THE FBI FOR YEARS.
...you can never go back.

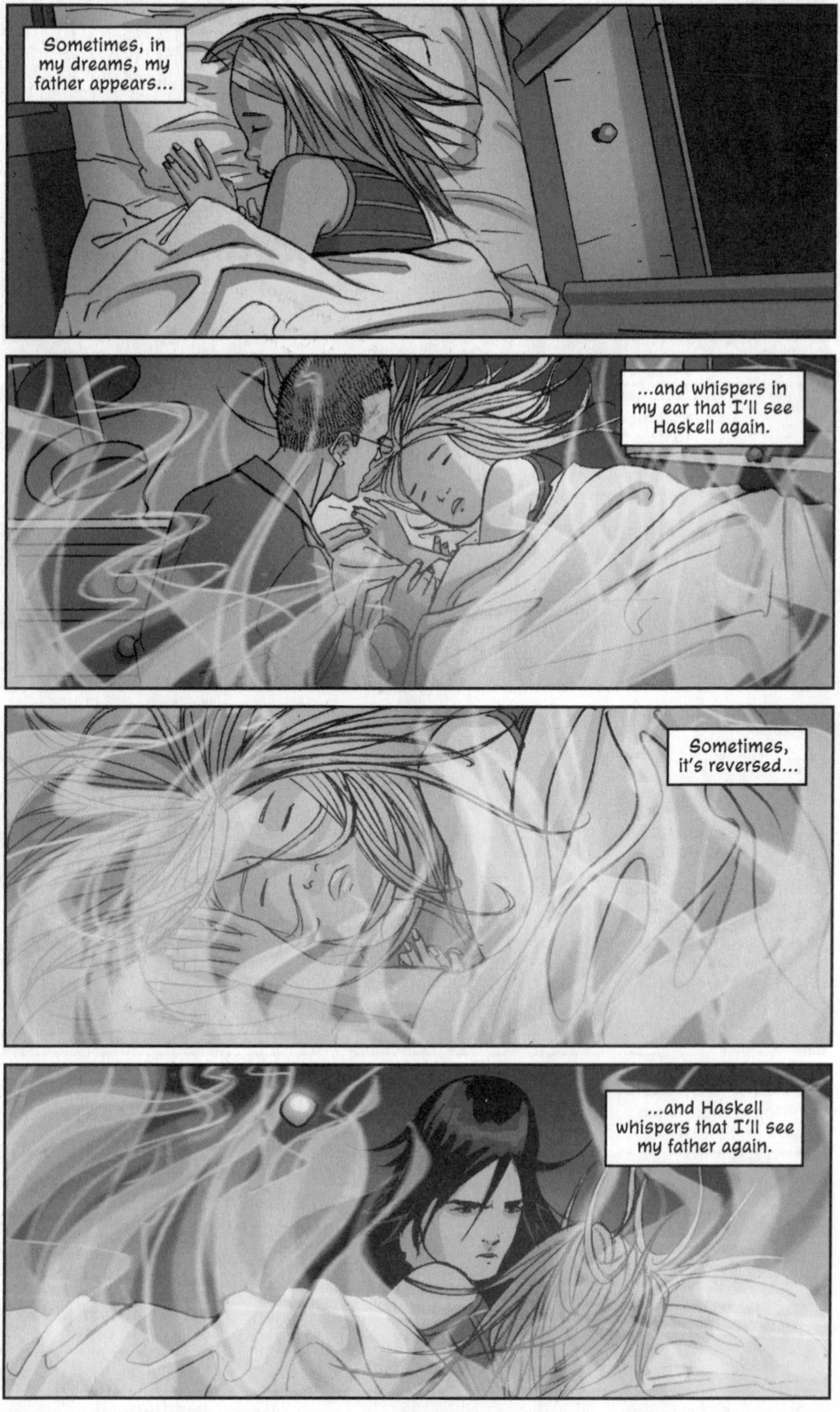
Sometimes, in my dreams, my father appears...
...and whispers in my ear that I'll see Haskell again.
Sometimes, it's reversed...
...and Haskell whispers that I'll see my father again.

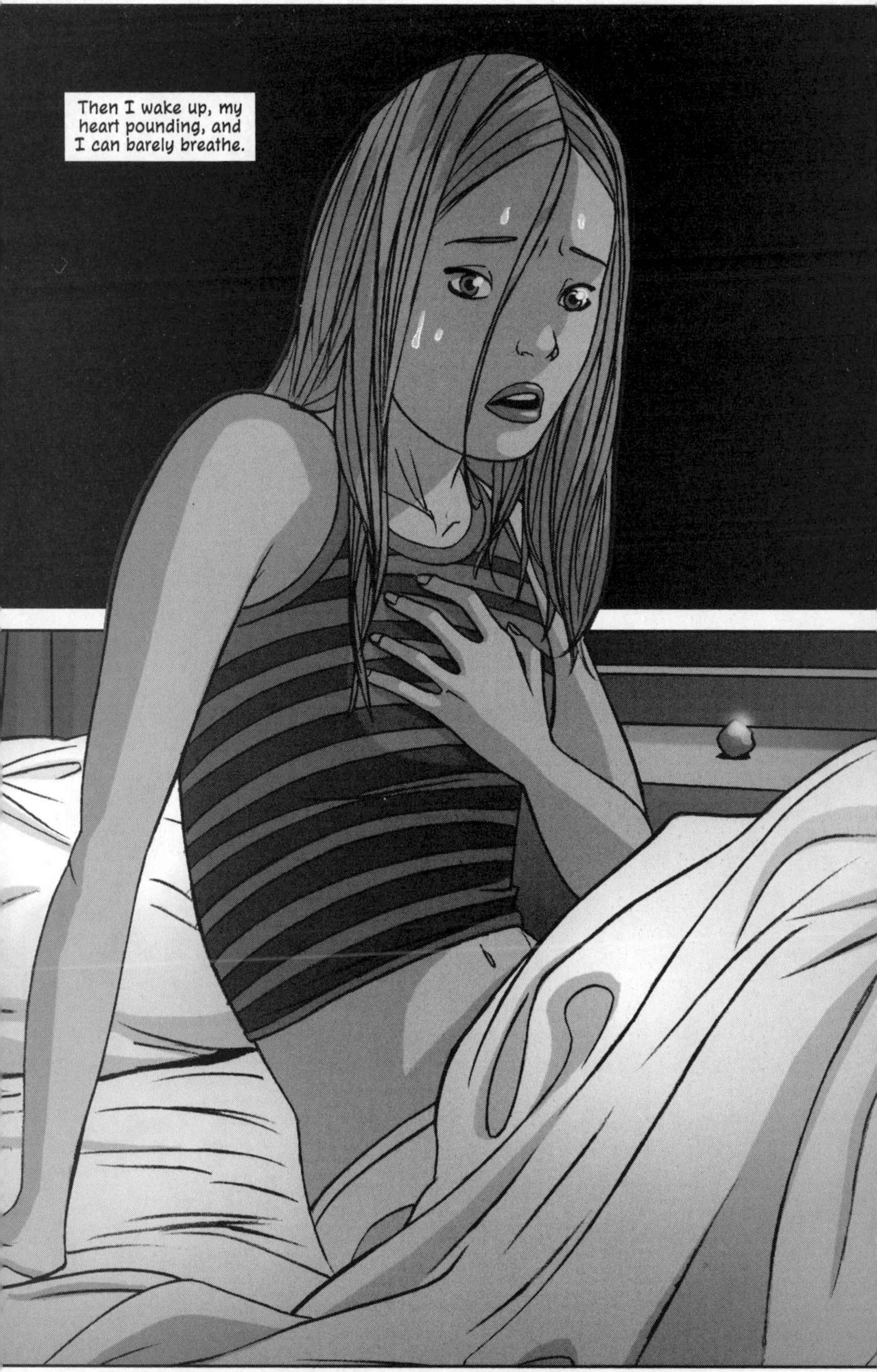
Then I wake up, my heart pounding, and I can barely breathe.

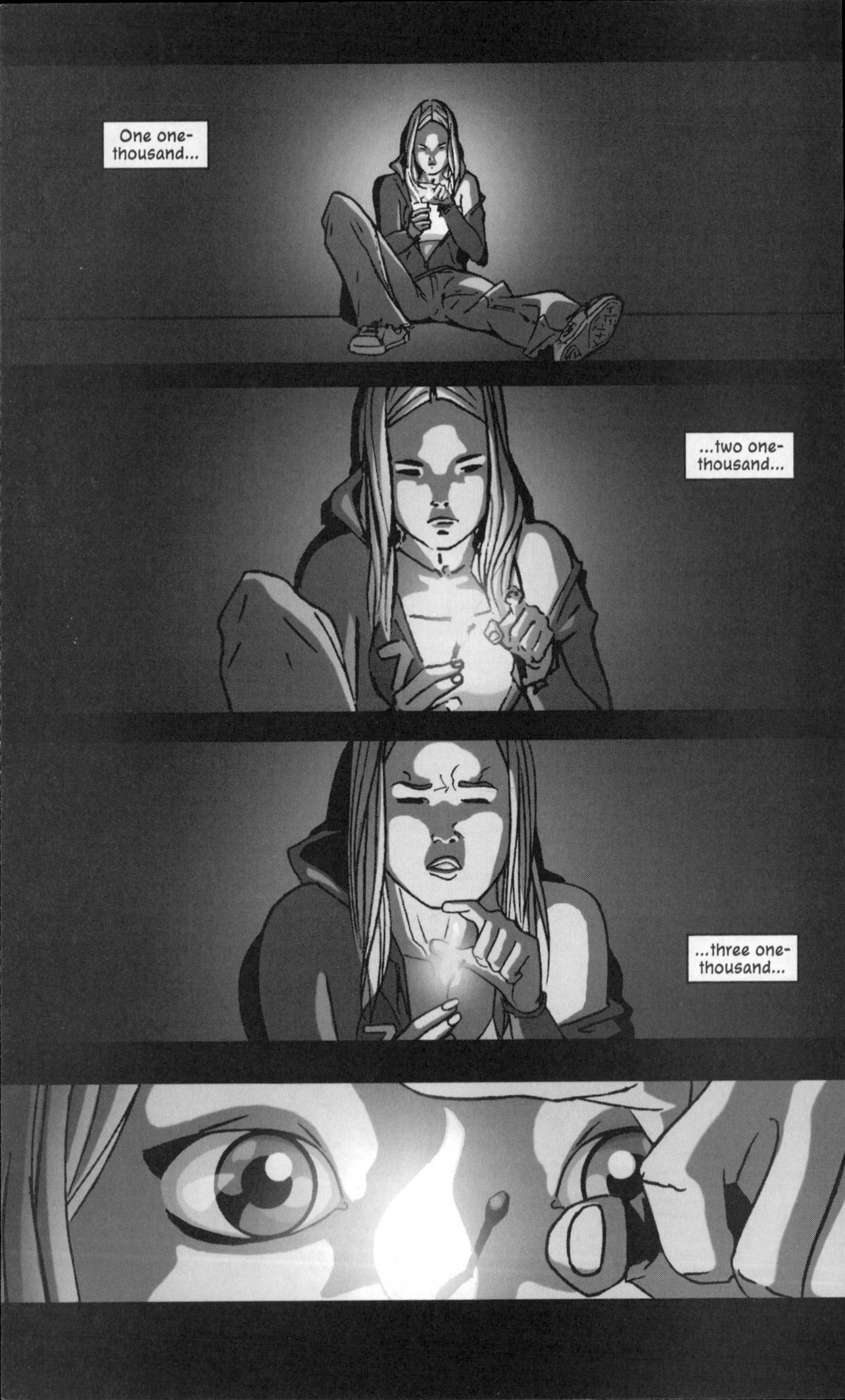
One one-thousand...
...two one-thousand...
...three one-thousand...

REBECCA DONNER

Rebecca was born in Canada but grew up in a Section 8 apartment building in Los Angeles, an experience that inspired her critically acclaimed novel *Sunset Terrace*. Her stories, book reviews, and essays have appeared in numerous publications, and she has taught writing at Wesleyan and Barnard. Rebecca also wrote and directed two short films, wrote three plays that were produced in Los Angeles and New York, sings in a rock band, and is actively resisting the ridiculous notion that you have to focus on one thing in life. She lives in the East Village in New York City and is writing her third novel.

INAKI MIRANDA

Inaki was born in Argentina, spent part
of his childhood in California and finally
established his bones in Madrid, Spain,
where he attended the Complutense
University and earned a degree in
fine arts. After testing the waters of
animation and videogames, he made
himself a place in the comics industry
by illustrating *2000AD*'s *Judge Dredd*,
The Lexian Chronicles, *The Chase*
and a story in VERTIGO'S multiple
Eisner Award-winning series FABLES.
He likes long walks in the rain and
popping bubble wrap whenever he
gets the chance.

EVA DE LA CRUZ

Having acquired experience from
working in the animation and videogame
industries, Eva made her professional
comics debut in the pages of *2000AD*
coloring *Judge Dredd*. She also
colored a *Judge Dredd* strip which ran
for six months in UK's *Metro* newspaper.
Eva currently resides in the Spanish
capital but would happily renounce
the chaotic streets of Madrid for the
abundant beauty of the Northern
Canadian wilderness.

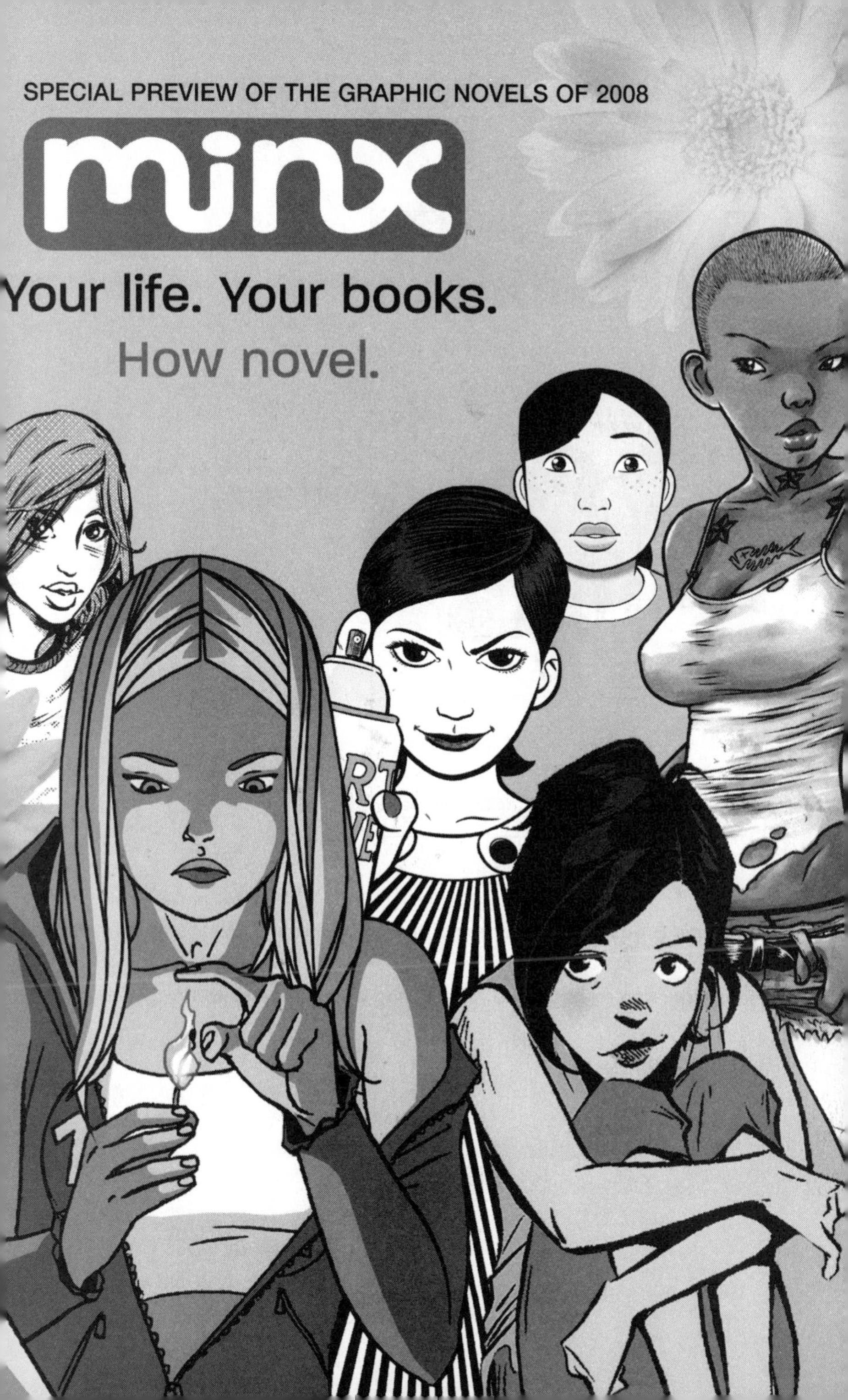
SPECIAL PREVIEW OF THE GRAPHIC NOVELS OF 2008
minx
Your life. Your books.
How novel.

WATER BABY

Ross Campbell

By two-time Eisner Award nominee
ROSS CAMPBELL

Surfer girl Brody just got her leg bitten off by a shark. What's worse?

Her shark of an ex-boyfriend is back, and when it comes to Brody's couch,

he's not budging.

By ROSS CAMPBELL
AVAILABLE IN JUNE ■ Read on.
But please note: The following pages are not sequential.

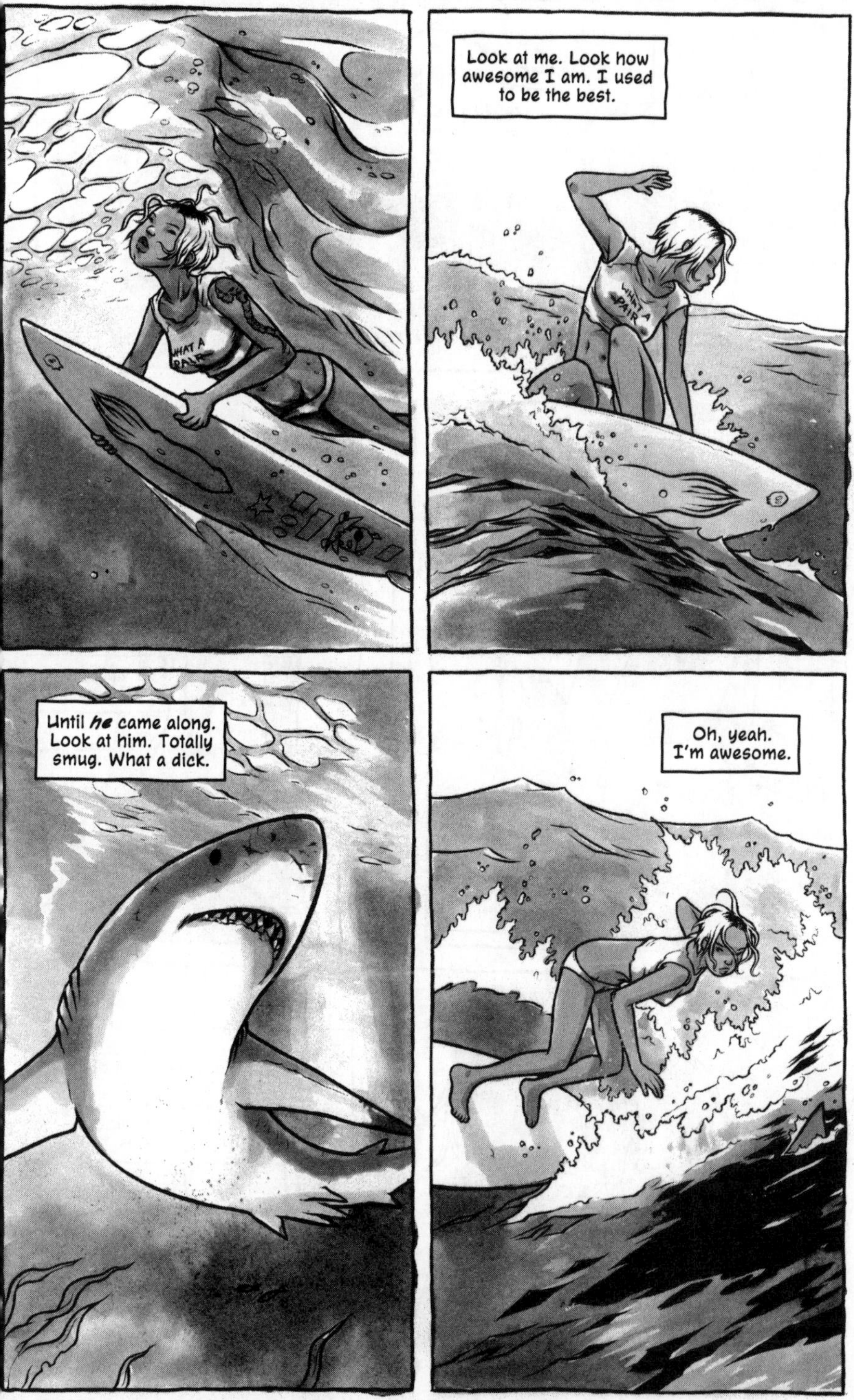
WHAT A PAIR
Look at me. Look how awesome I am. I used to be the best.
WHAT A PAIR
Until *he* came along. Look at him. Totally smug. What a dick.
Oh, yeah. I'm awesome.

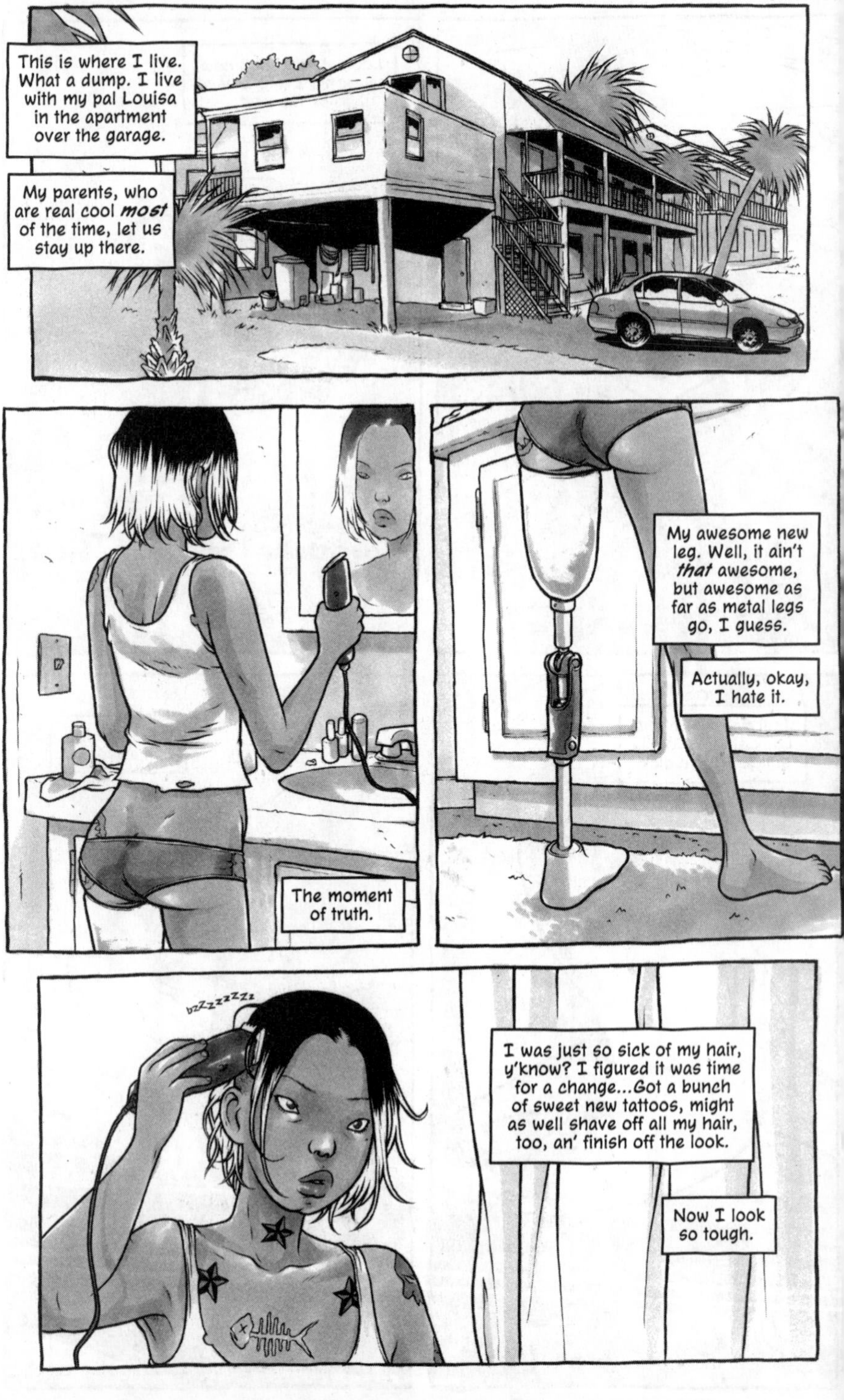
This is where I live. What a dump. I live with my pal Louisa in the apartment over the garage.
My parents, who are real cool *most* of the time, let us stay up there.
The moment of truth.
My awesome new leg. Well, it ain't *that* awesome, but awesome as far as metal legs go, I guess.
Actually, okay, I hate it.
bzzzzzzzz
I was just so sick of my hair, y'know? I figured it was time for a change...Got a bunch of sweet new tattoos, might as well shave off all my hair, too, an' finish off the look.
Now I look so tough.

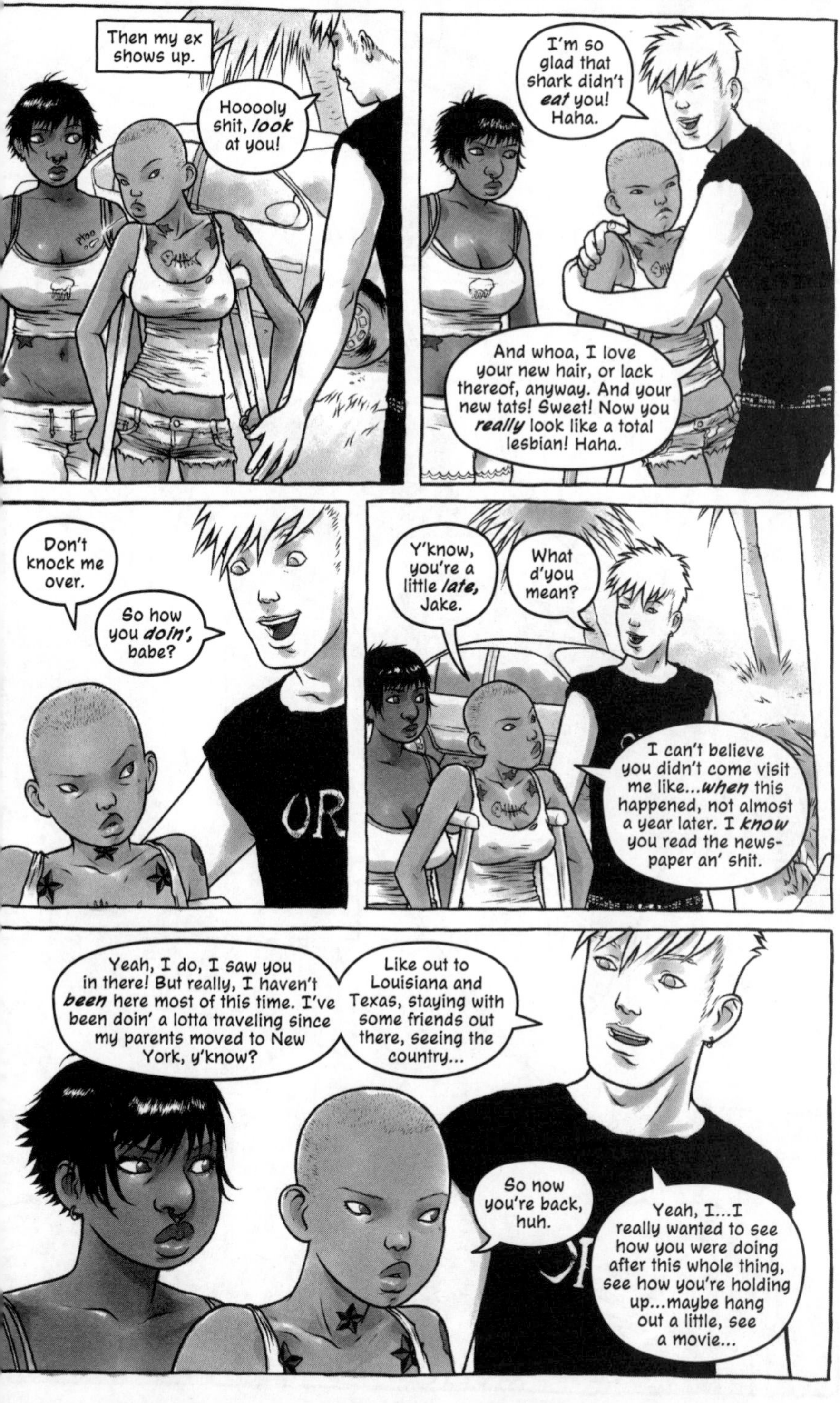
Then my ex shows up.
Hoooooly shit, *look* at you!
I'm so glad that shark didn't *eat* you! Haha.
And whoa, I love your new hair, or lack thereof, anyway. And your new tats! Sweet! Now you *really* look like a total lesbian! Haha.
Don't knock me over.
So how you *doin',* babe?
Y'know, you're a little *late,* Jake.
What d'you mean?
I can't believe you didn't come visit me like...*when* this happened, not almost a year later. I *know* you read the news-paper an' shit.
Yeah, I do, I saw you in there! But really, I haven't *been* here most of this time. I've been doin' a lotta traveling since my parents moved to New York, y'know?
Like out to Louisiana and Texas, staying with some friends out there, seeing the country...
So now you're back, huh.
Yeah, I...I really wanted to see how you were doing after this whole thing, see how you're holding up...maybe hang out a little, see a movie...

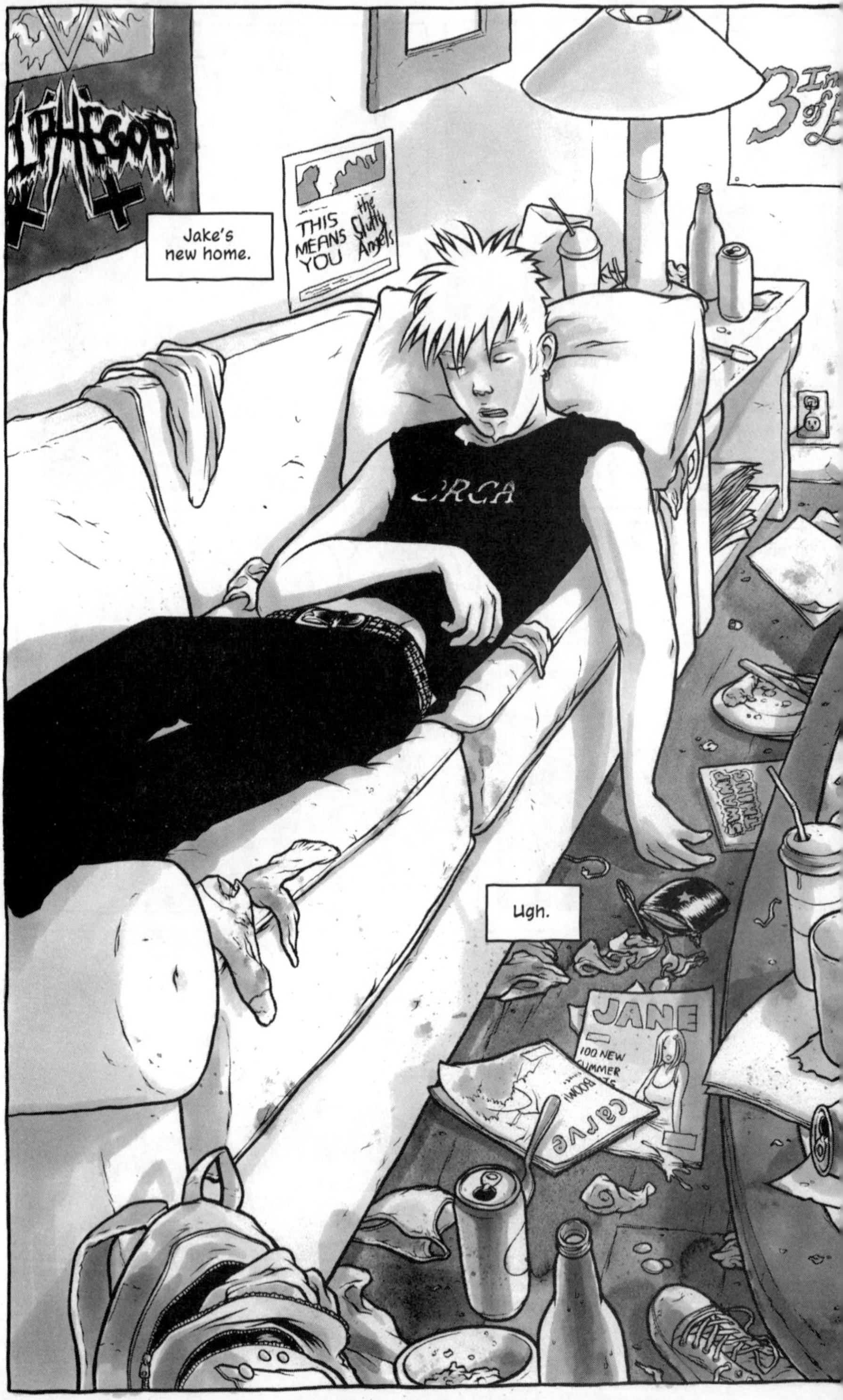
Jake's new home.
THIS MEANS YOU
the Slutty Angels
SWAMP THING
Ugh.
JANE
100 NEW SUMMER
Carve
BOOM!

Downtown only
4
The New York Four
Brian Wood + Ryan Kelly

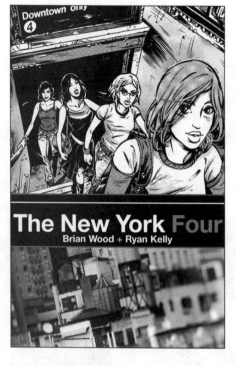

Written by multiple Eisner Award nominee/Indie icon BRIAN WOOD

Experience New York City through the eyes of Riley, a shy, almost reclusive straight-A student who convinces three other NYU freshmen to join a research group to earn extra money.

As the girls become fast friends, two things complicate what should be the greatest time of Riley's life: connecting with her arty, estranged older sister and having a mysterious online crush on a guy known only as "sneakerfreak."

Will Riley be able to balance new relationships with academics and her stuffy literati parents as the intensity of her secret romance threatens to unravel everything?

By BRIAN WOOD & RYAN KELLY

AVAILABLE IN JULY ■ Read on.

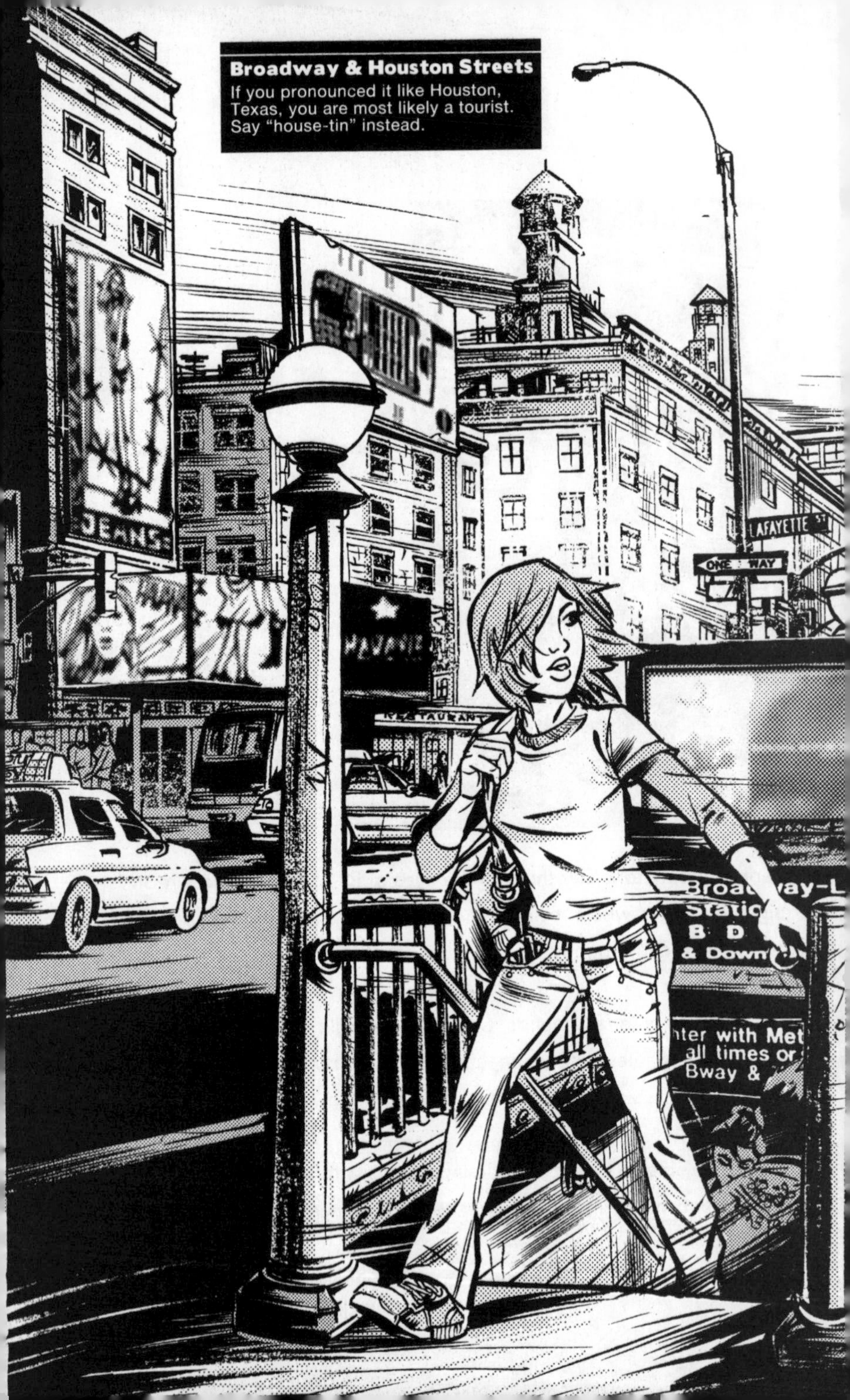
Broadway & Houston Streets
If you pronounced it like Houston, Texas, you are most likely a tourist. Say "house-tin" instead.
JEANS
RESTAURANT
LAFAYETTE ST
ONE WAY

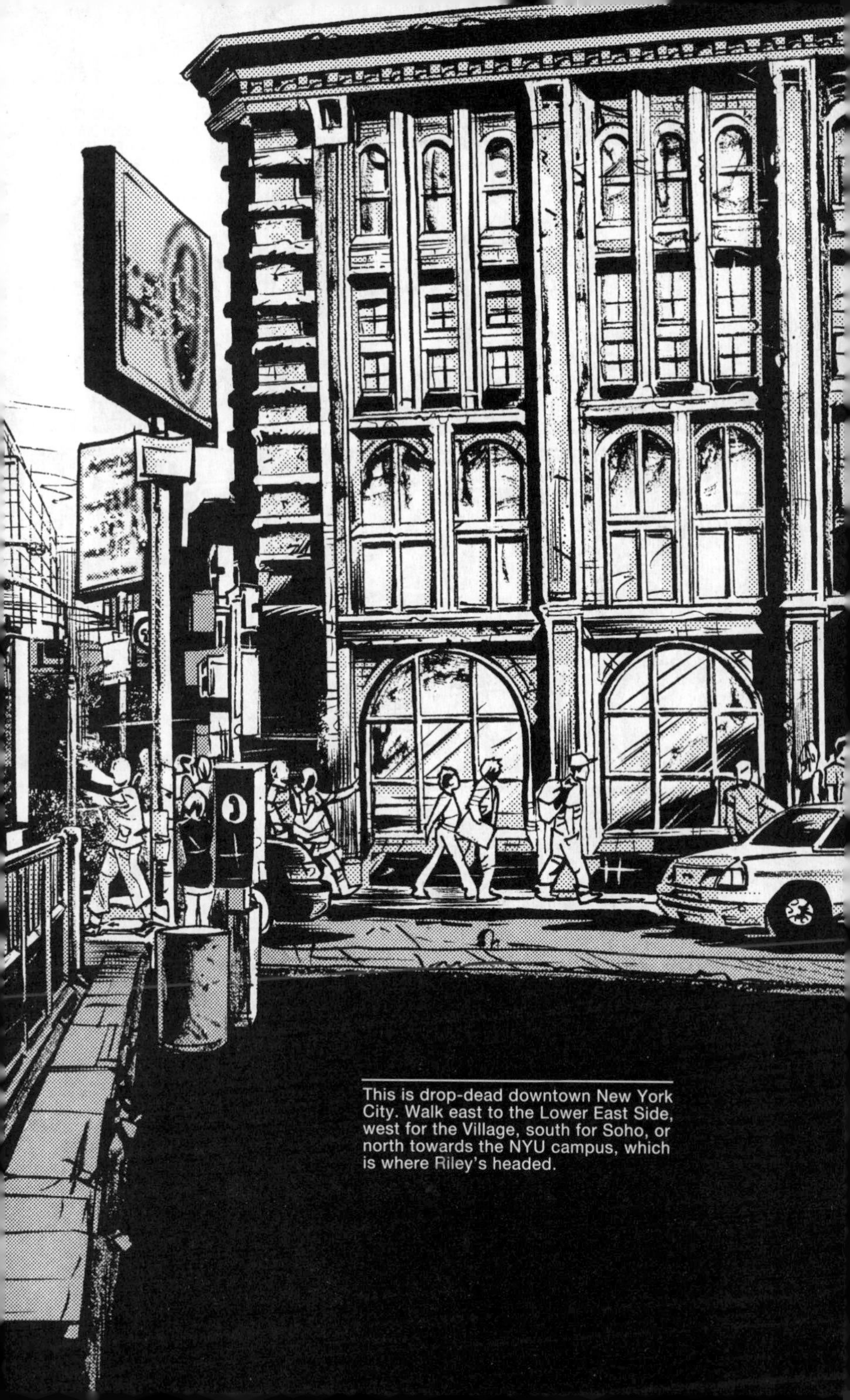
This is drop-dead downtown New York City. Walk east to the Lower East Side, west for the Village, south for Soho, or north towards the NYU campus, which is where Riley's headed.

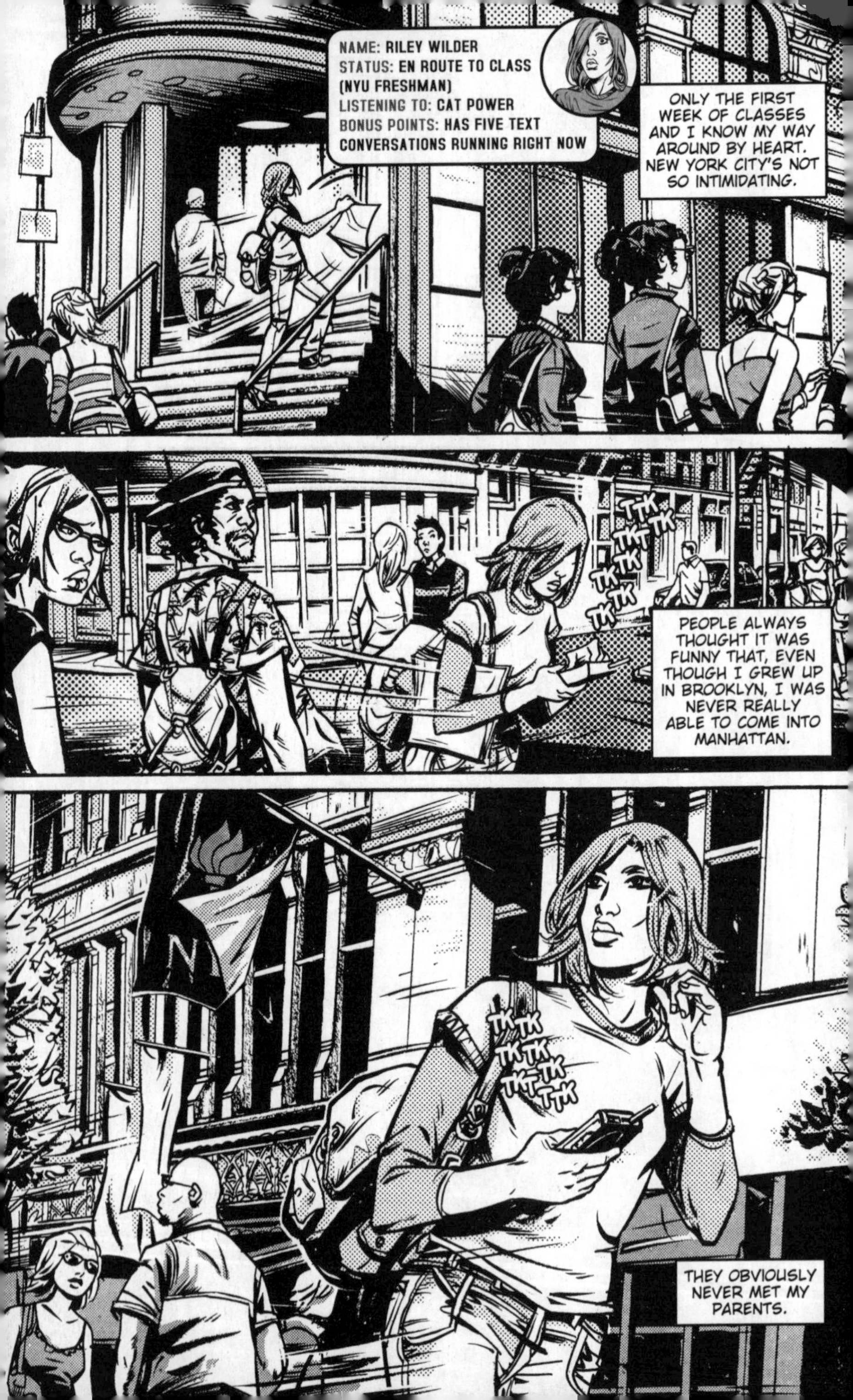
NAME: RILEY WILDER
STATUS: EN ROUTE TO CLASS
(NYU FRESHMAN)
LISTENING TO: CAT POWER
BONUS POINTS: HAS FIVE TEXT
CONVERSATIONS RUNNING RIGHT NOW
ONLY THE FIRST WEEK OF CLASSES AND I KNOW MY WAY AROUND BY HEART. NEW YORK CITY'S NOT SO INTIMIDATING.
TK TK TK TK TK TK TK TK
PEOPLE ALWAYS THOUGHT IT WAS FUNNY THAT, EVEN THOUGH I GREW UP IN BROOKLYN, I WAS NEVER REALLY ABLE TO COME INTO MANHATTAN.
TK TK TK TK TK TK TK TK
THEY OBVIOUSLY NEVER MET MY PARENTS.

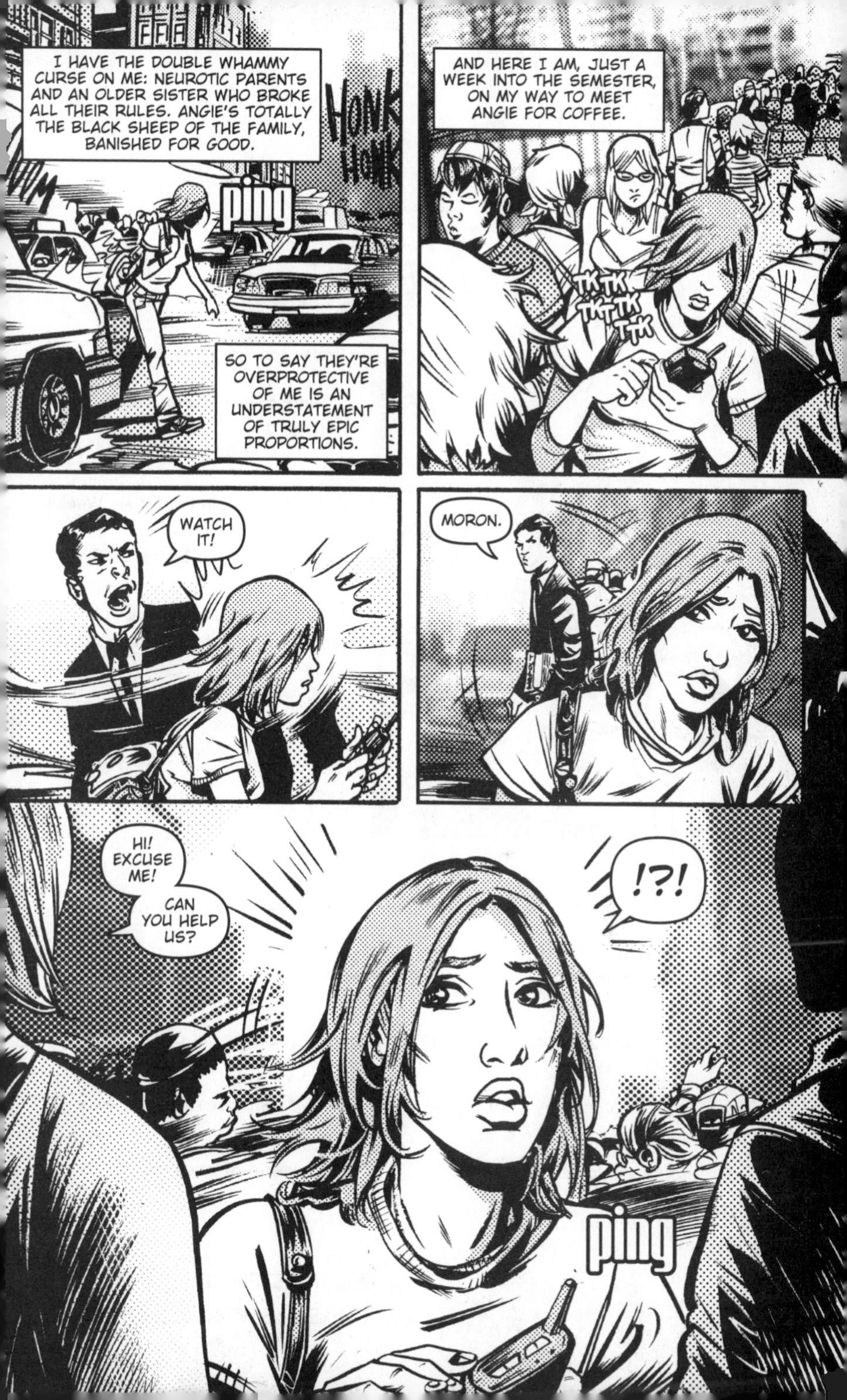
I HAVE THE DOUBLE WHAMMY CURSE ON ME: NEUROTIC PARENTS AND AN OLDER SISTER WHO BROKE ALL THEIR RULES. ANGIE'S TOTALLY THE BLACK SHEEP OF THE FAMILY, BANISHED FOR GOOD.
HONK HONK
ping
SO TO SAY THEY'RE OVERPROTECTIVE OF ME IS AN UNDERSTATEMENT OF TRULY EPIC PROPORTIONS.
AND HERE I AM, JUST A WEEK INTO THE SEMESTER, ON MY WAY TO MEET ANGIE FOR COFFEE.
TK TK TK TK TK TK
WATCH IT!
MORON.
HI! EXCUSE ME!
CAN YOU HELP US?
!?!
ping

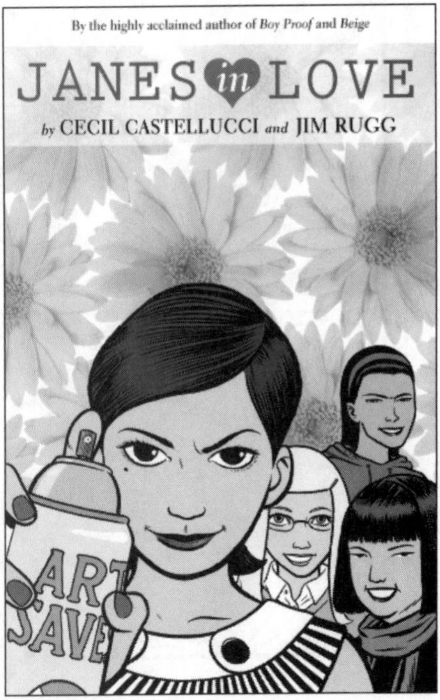
By the highly acclaimed author of Boy Proof and Beige
JANES in LOVE
by CECIL CASTELLUCCI and JIM RUGG
ART SAVE

Praise for *The Plain Janes*:

"Thought-provoking....absolutely engaging..."
—Booklist, Starred review

Starred review in Publishers Weekly

Washington Post Best of 2007 pick

Included in The New York Public Library's Books for the Teen Age 2008

The second title in the PLAIN JANES series finds the coolest clique of misfits playing cupid and becoming entangled in the affairs of the heart. P.L.A.I.N., People Loving Art In Neighborhoods, goes global once the art gang procures a spot in the Metro City Museum of Modern Art contest. And the girls will discover that in art and in love, general rules don't often apply.

By CECIL CASTELLUCCI & JIM RUGG
AVAILABLE IN SEPTEMBER ▪ Read on.

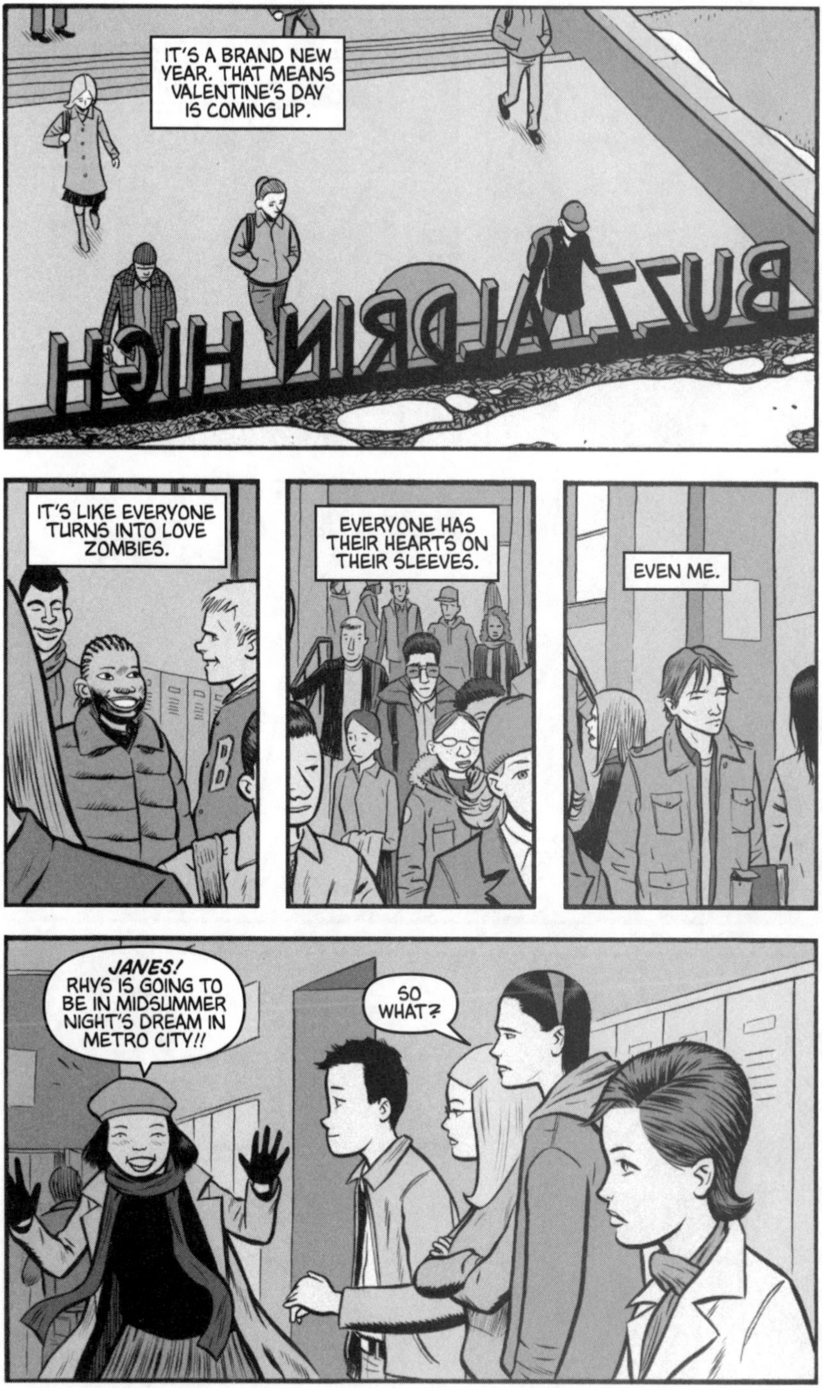
IT'S A BRAND NEW YEAR. THAT MEANS VALENTINE'S DAY IS COMING UP.
BUZZ ALDRIN HIGH
IT'S LIKE EVERYONE TURNS INTO LOVE ZOMBIES.
EVERYONE HAS THEIR HEARTS ON THEIR SLEEVES.
EVEN ME.
JANES! RHYS IS GOING TO BE IN MIDSUMMER NIGHT'S DREAM IN METRO CITY!!
SO WHAT?

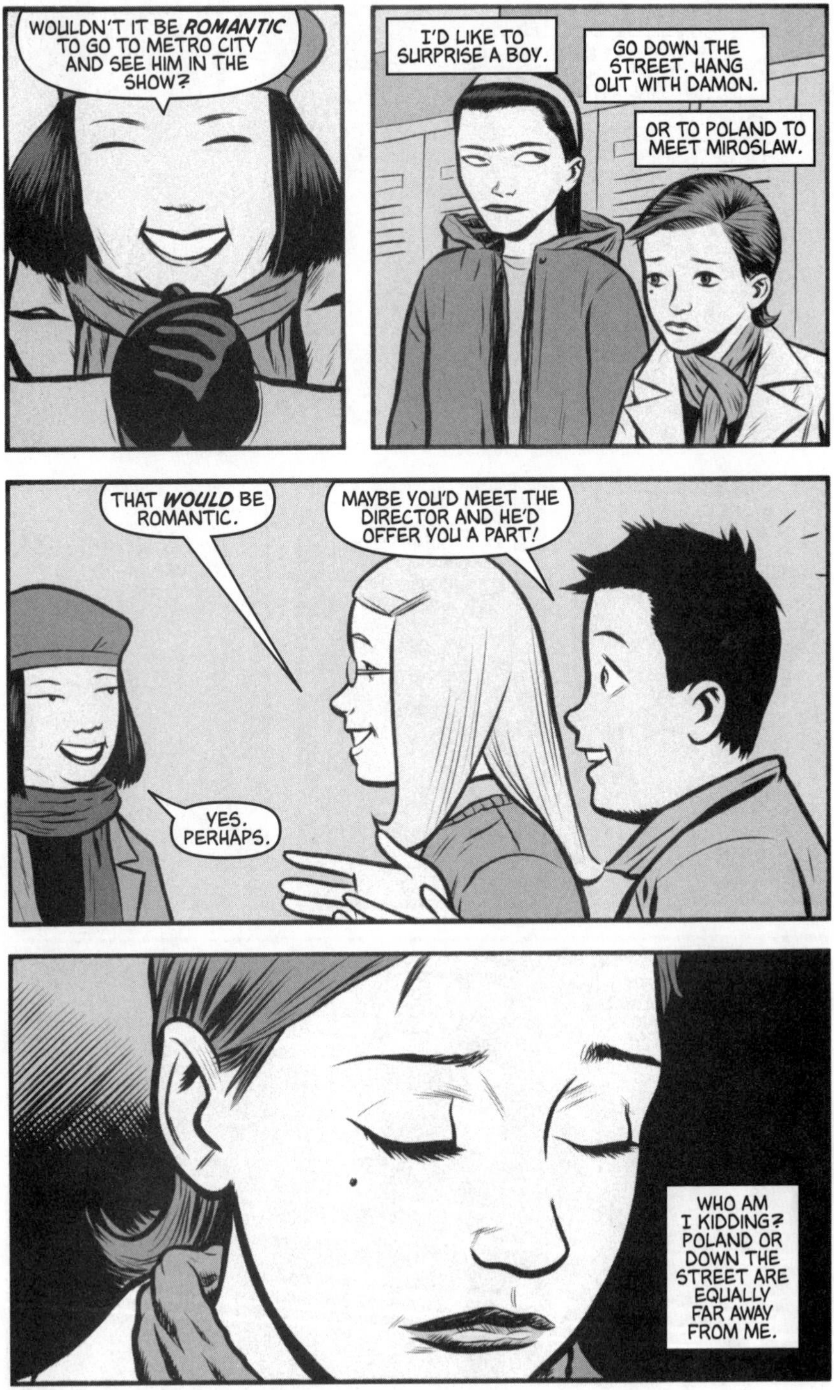
WOULDN'T IT BE *ROMANTIC* TO GO TO METRO CITY AND SEE HIM IN THE SHOW?
I'D LIKE TO SURPRISE A BOY.
GO DOWN THE STREET. HANG OUT WITH DAMON.
OR TO POLAND TO MEET MIROSLAW.
THAT *WOULD* BE ROMANTIC.
MAYBE YOU'D MEET THE DIRECTOR AND HE'D OFFER YOU A PART!
YES. PERHAPS.
WHO AM I KIDDING? POLAND OR DOWN THE STREET ARE EQUALLY FAR AWAY FROM ME.

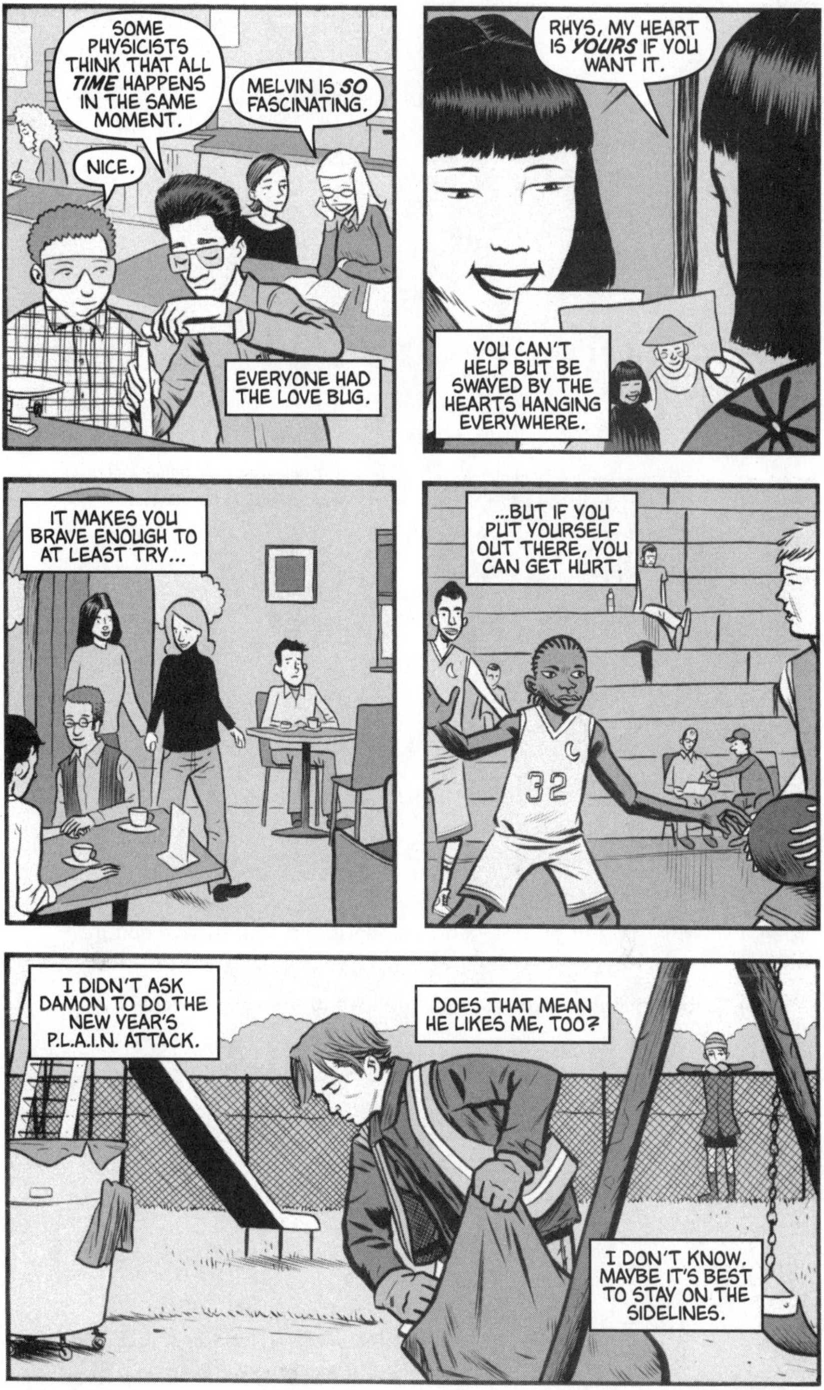
SOME PHYSICISTS THINK THAT ALL TIME HAPPENS IN THE SAME MOMENT.
MELVIN IS SO FASCINATING.
NICE.
EVERYONE HAD THE LOVE BUG.
RHYS, MY HEART IS YOURS IF YOU WANT IT.
YOU CAN'T HELP BUT BE SWAYED BY THE HEARTS HANGING EVERYWHERE.
IT MAKES YOU BRAVE ENOUGH TO AT LEAST TRY...
...BUT IF YOU PUT YOURSELF OUT THERE, YOU CAN GET HURT.
32
I DIDN'T ASK DAMON TO DO THE NEW YEAR'S P.L.A.I.N. ATTACK.
DOES THAT MEAN HE LIKES ME, TOO?
I DON'T KNOW. MAYBE IT'S BEST TO STAY ON THE SIDELINES.

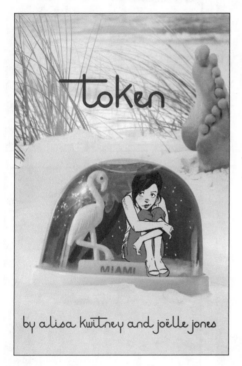

Written by noted comics author
and novelist ALISA KWITNEY

Can a Jewish "girl out of time" and a Spanish old soul survive culture

clashes and criminal records to find true love in the sun-drenched,

sequined miasma that was South Beach in the Big '80s?

By ALISA KWITNEY & JOËLLE JONES
AVAILABLE IN OCTOBER ■ Read on.

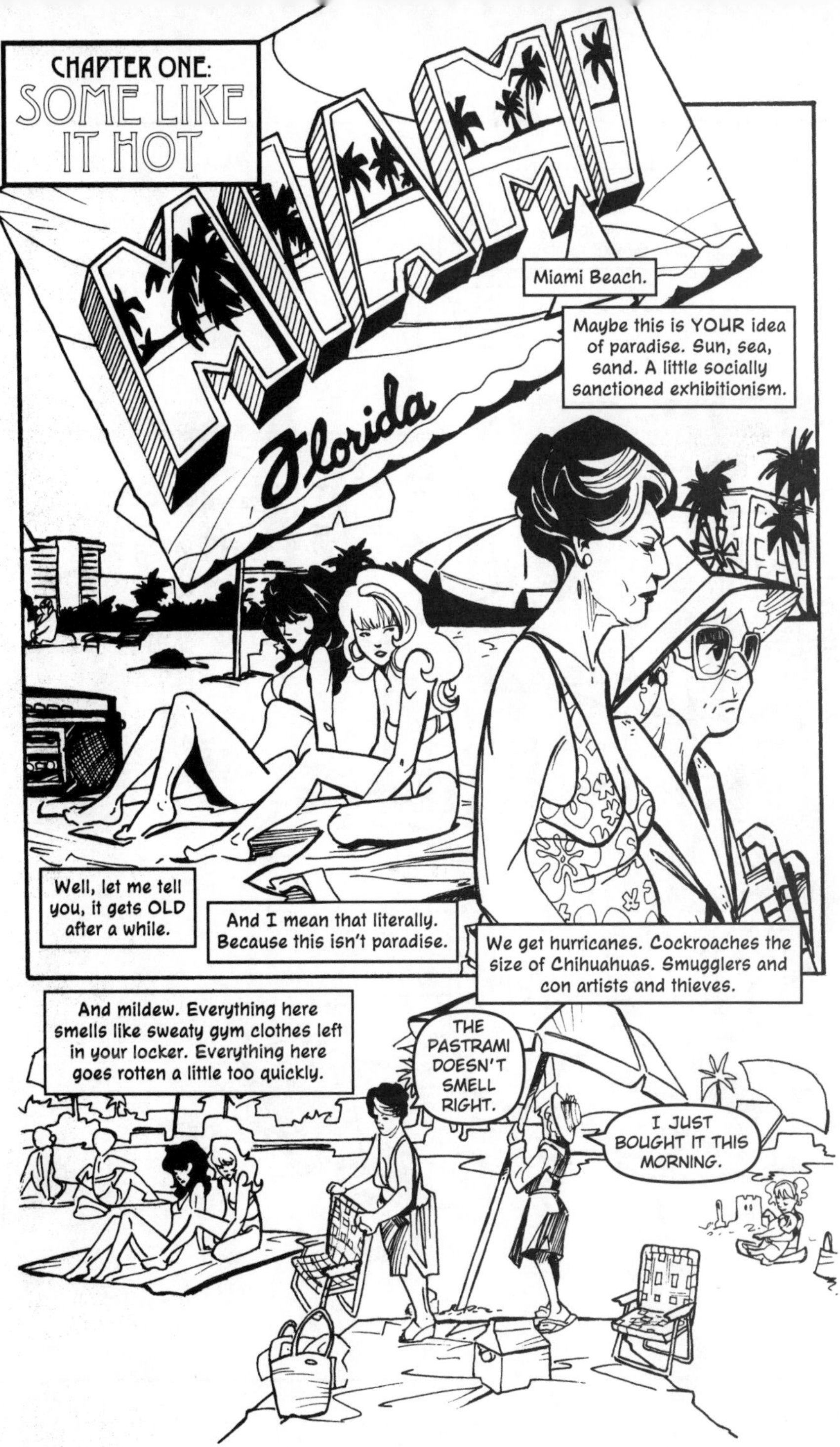
CHAPTER ONE:
SOME LIKE IT HOT
MIAMI
Florida
Miami Beach.
Maybe this is YOUR idea of paradise. Sun, sea, sand. A little socially sanctioned exhibitionism.
Well, let me tell you, it gets OLD after a while.
And I mean that literally. Because this isn't paradise.
We get hurricanes. Cockroaches the size of Chihuahuas. Smugglers and con artists and thieves.
And mildew. Everything here smells like sweaty gym clothes left in your locker. Everything here goes rotten a little too quickly.
THE PASTRAMI DOESN'T SMELL RIGHT.
I JUST BOUGHT IT THIS MORNING.

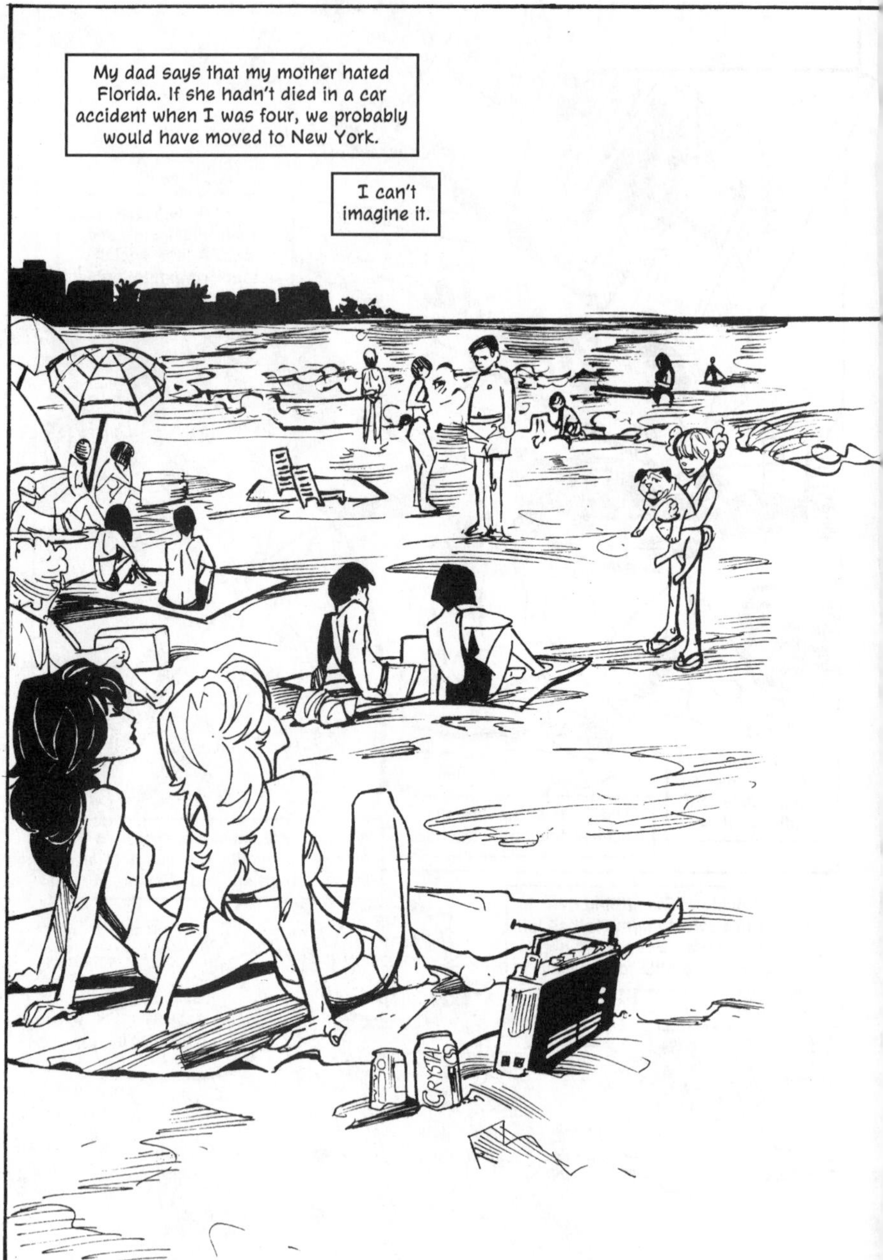
My dad says that my mother hated Florida. If she hadn't died in a car accident when I was four, we probably would have moved to New York.
I can't imagine it.
CRYSTAL

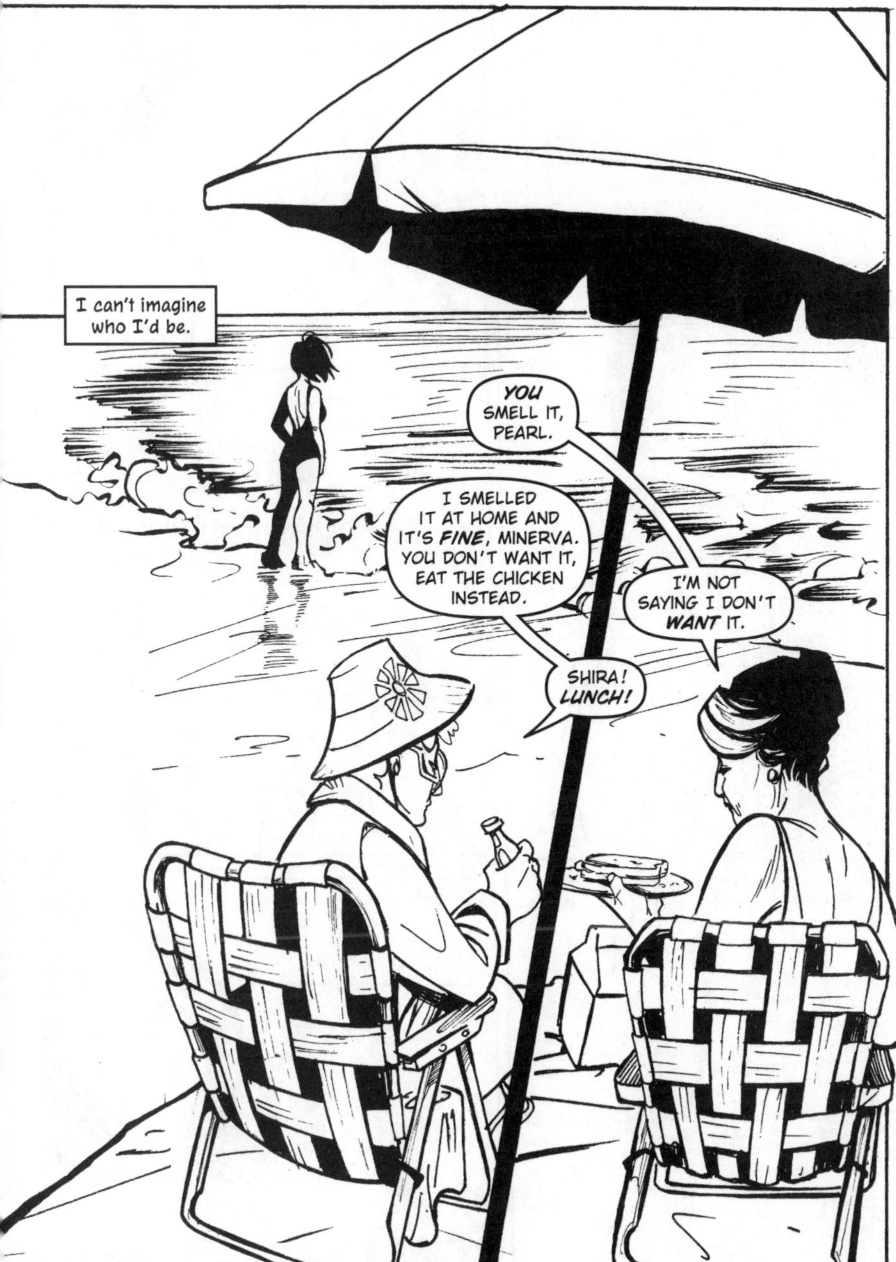
I can't imagine who I'd be.
YOU SMELL IT, PEARL.
I SMELLED IT AT HOME AND IT'S FINE, MINERVA. YOU DON'T WANT IT, EAT THE CHICKEN INSTEAD.
I'M NOT SAYING I DON'T WANT IT.
SHIRA! LUNCH!

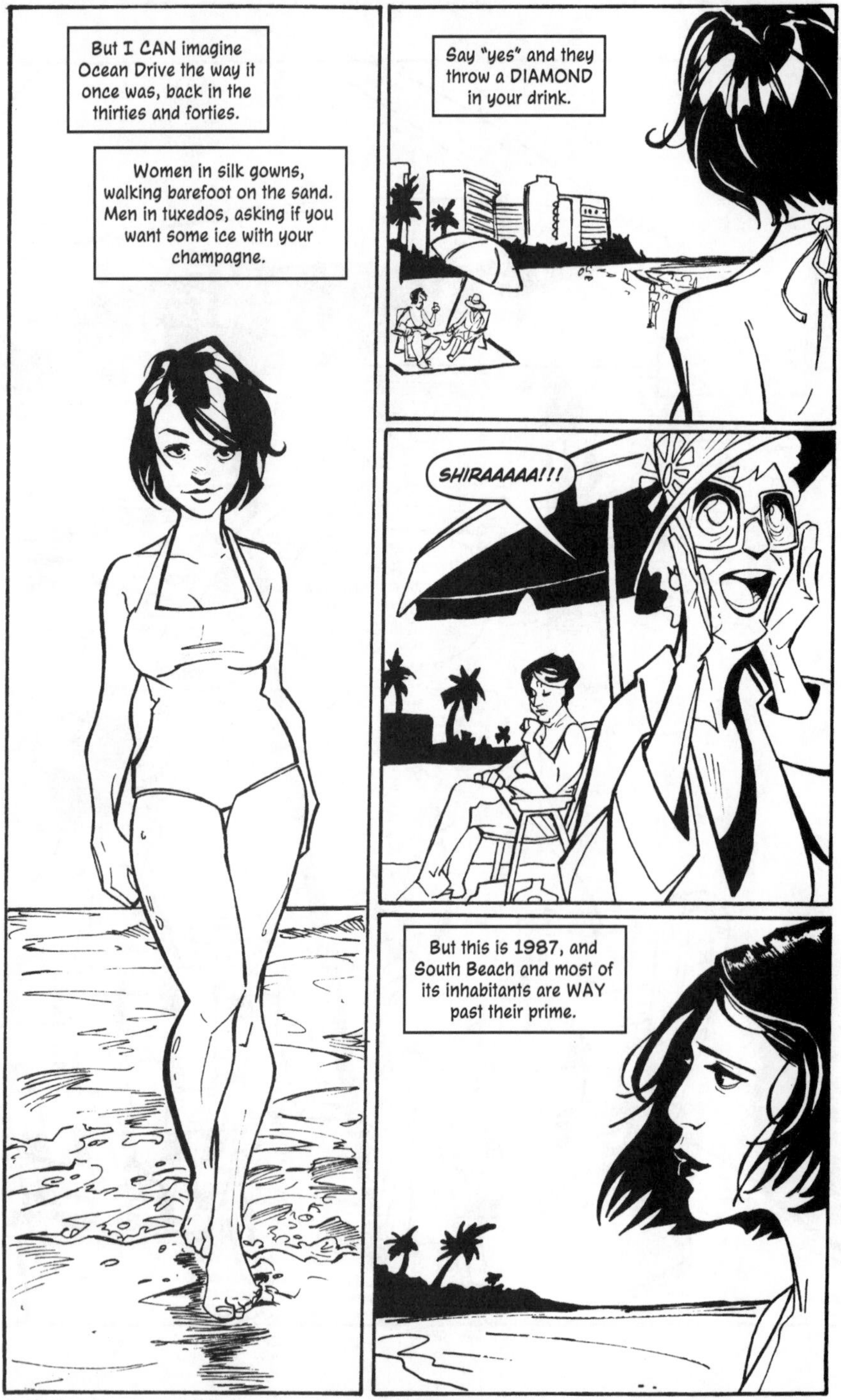
But I CAN imagine Ocean Drive the way it once was, back in the thirties and forties.
Women in silk gowns, walking barefoot on the sand. Men in tuxedos, asking if you want some ice with your champagne.
Say "yes" and they throw a DIAMOND in your drink.
SHIRAAAAA!!!
But this is 1987, and South Beach and most of its inhabitants are WAY past their prime.

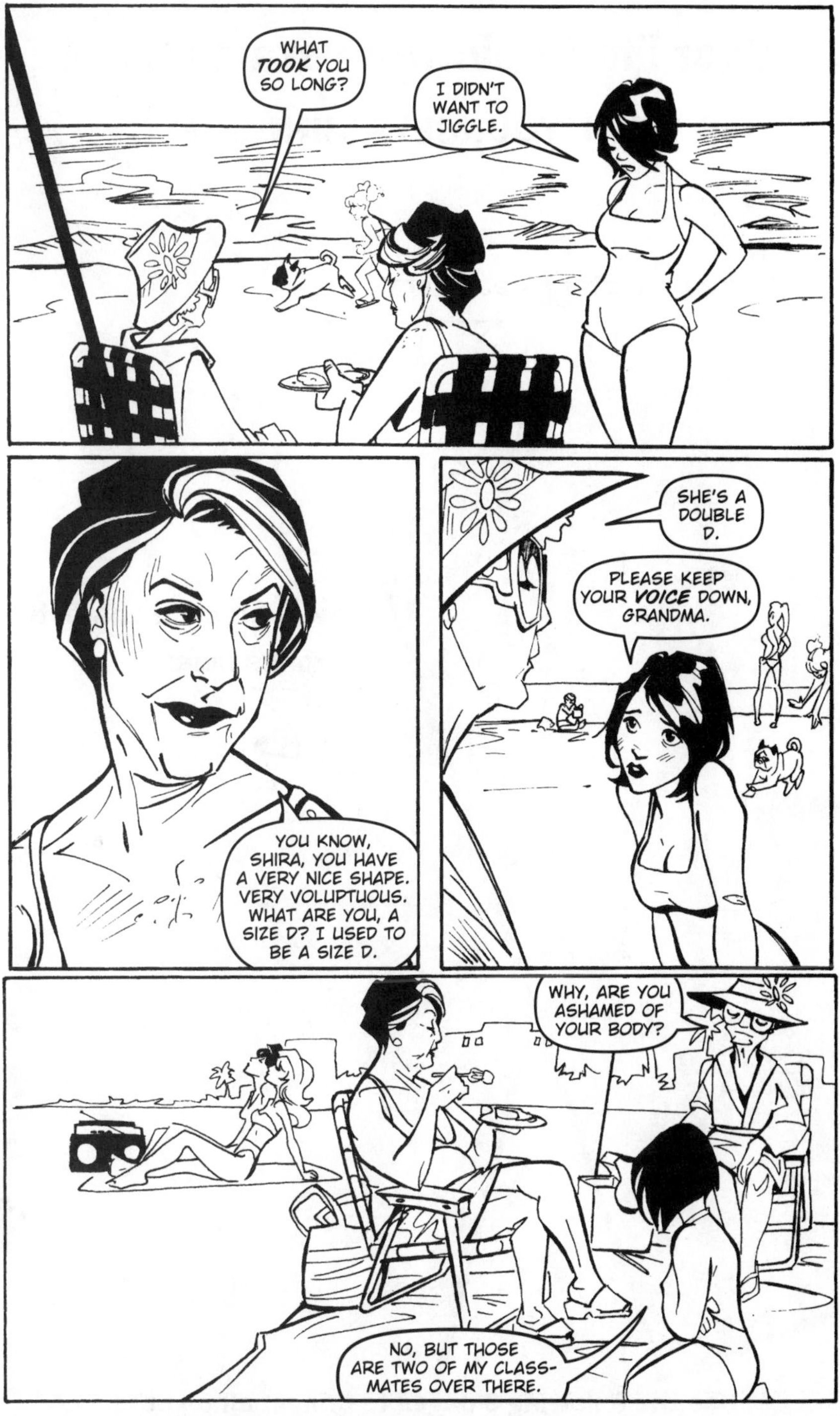
WHAT **TOOK** YOU SO LONG?
I DIDN'T WANT TO JIGGLE.
YOU KNOW, SHIRA, YOU HAVE A VERY NICE SHAPE. VERY VOLUPTUOUS. WHAT ARE YOU, A SIZE D? I USED TO BE A SIZE D.
SHE'S A DOUBLE D.
PLEASE KEEP YOUR **VOICE** DOWN, GRANDMA.
WHY, ARE YOU ASHAMED OF YOUR BODY?
NO, BUT THOSE ARE TWO OF MY CLASS-MATES OVER THERE.

Your life in pictures starts here!

~A DO-IT YOURSELF MINI COMIC~

Write your story ideas here:

Draw your main character sketches here:

Use the following 3 pages to bring it all together.

TITLE: BY:

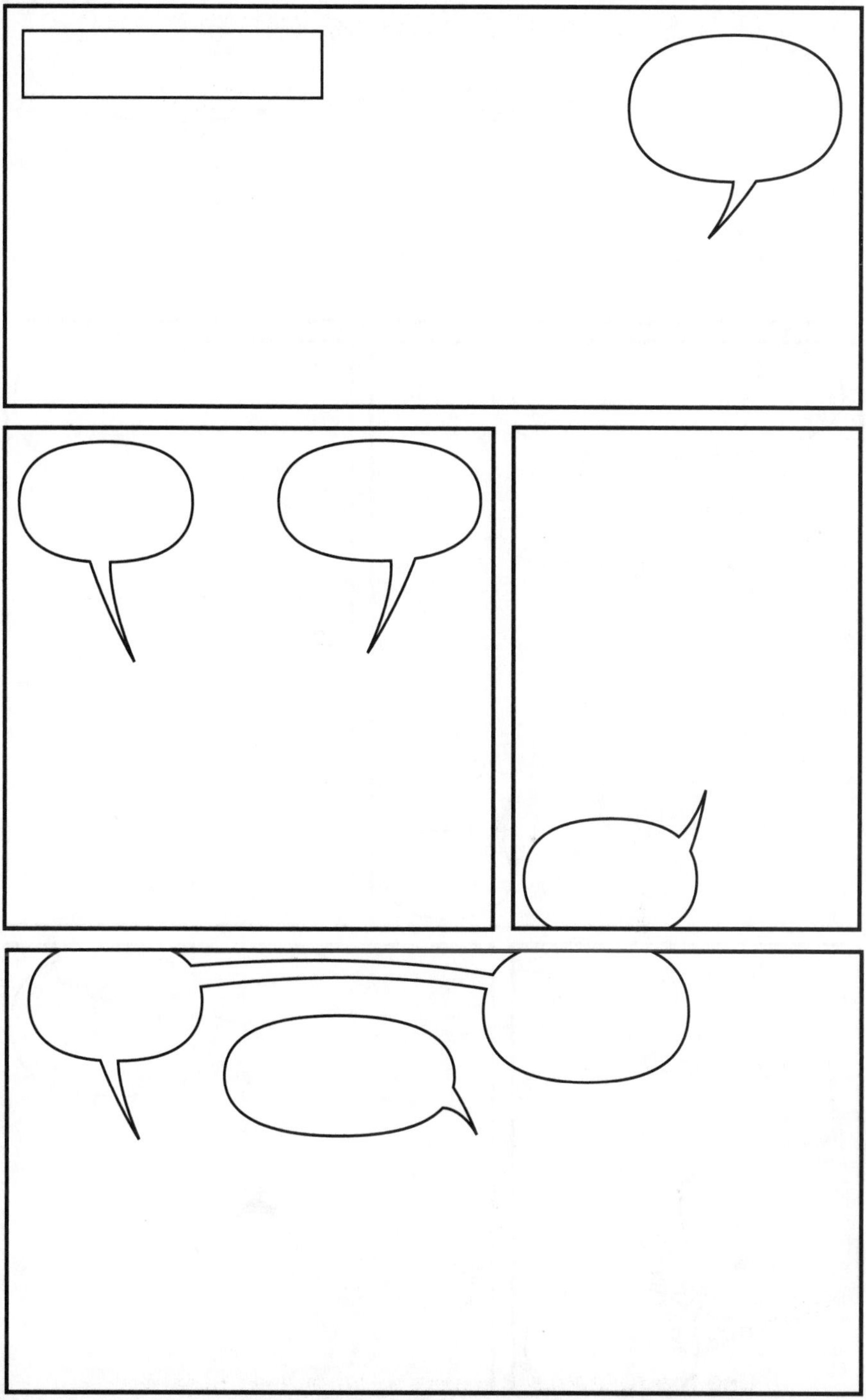

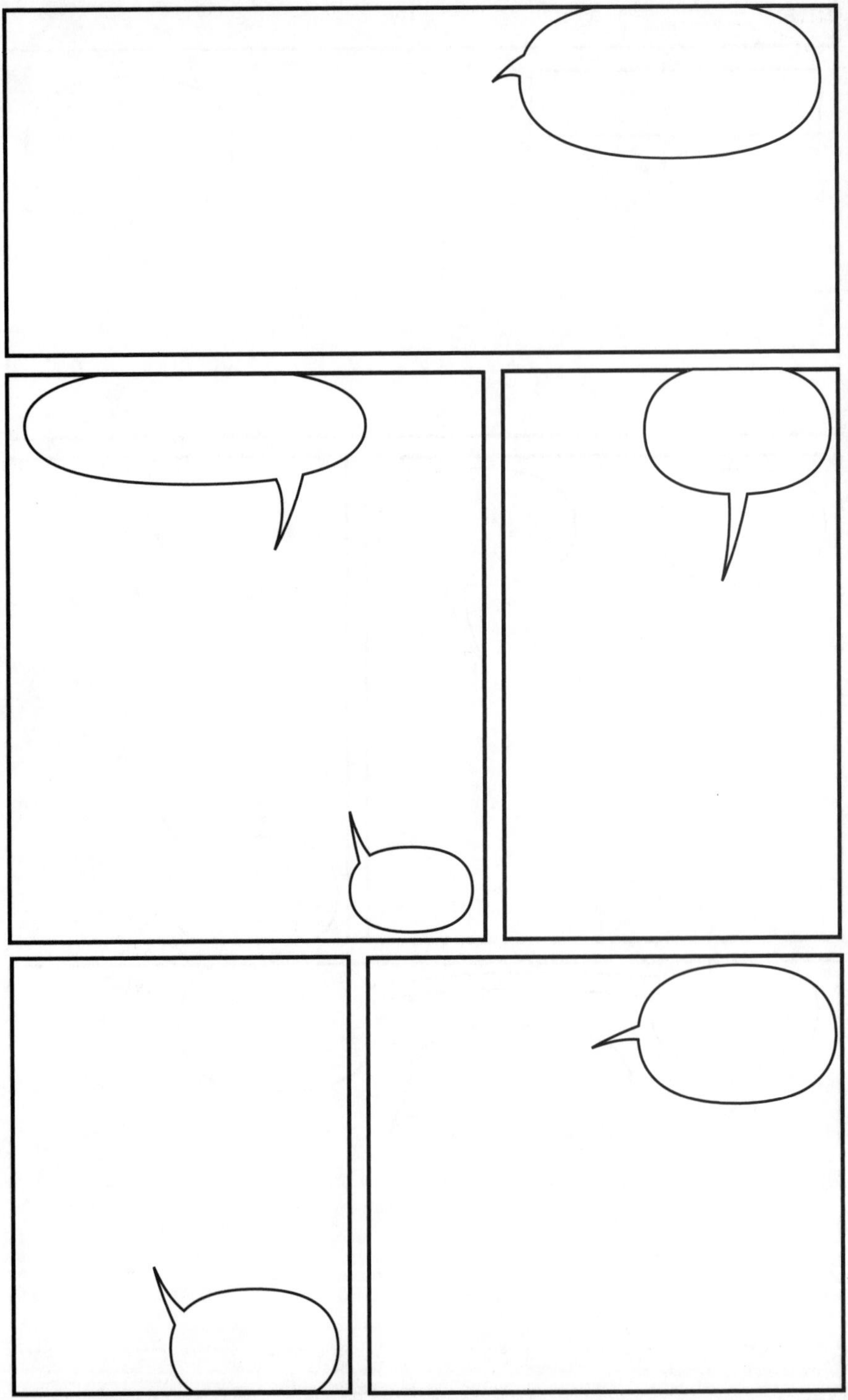

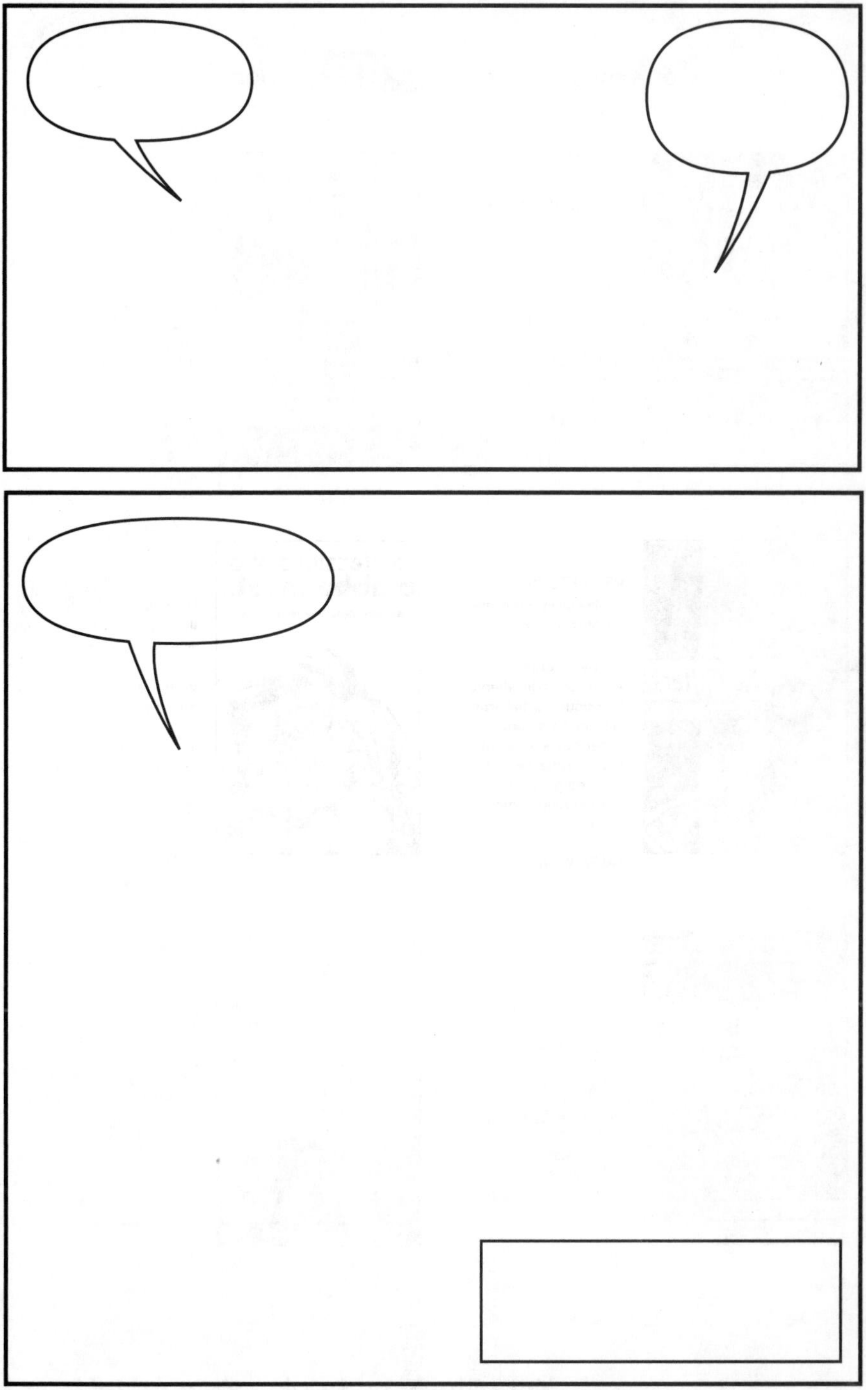

CHECK OUT STORYTELLING TIPS FROM TOP WRITERS AND ARTISTS AT MINXBOOKS.NET

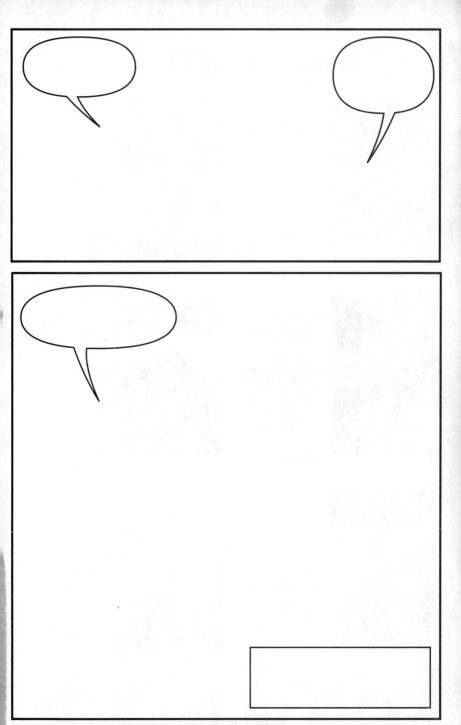

Don't miss any of the minx books:

By the highly acclaimed author of Boy Proof and The Queen of Cool
THE PLAIN JANES
CECIL CASTELLUCCI
and JIM RUGG

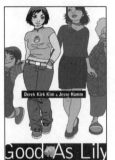

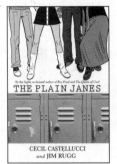

THE PLAIN JANES
By Cecil Castellucci
and Jim Rugg

Four girls named Jane are anything but ordinary once they form a secret art gang called P.L.A.I.N. — People Loving Art In Neighborhoods. But can art attacks really save the hell that is high school?

Derek Kirk Kim & Jesse Hamm
Good As Lily

GOOD AS LILY
By Derek Kirk Kim
and Jesse Hamm

What would you do if versions of yourself at 6, 29 and 70 suddenly appear and wreak havoc on your already awkward existence?

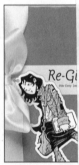

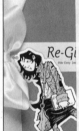

ONFESSIONS OF A
LABBERMOUTH
Mike and Louise Carey
d Aaron Alexovich

hen Tasha's mom brings ome a creepy boyfriend d his deadpan daughter, dysfunctional family is eaded for a complete eltdown. By the father-ughter writing team.

cluded in The New York ublic Library's Books for the Teen Age 2008

clubbing
Andi Watson
Josh Howard

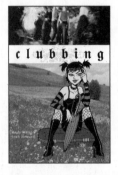

CLUBBING
By Andi Watson
and Josh Howard

A spoiled, rebellious London girl takes on the stuffy English countryside when she solves a murder mystery on the 19th hole of her grandparents' golf course.

kimmie66
AARON ALEXOVICH

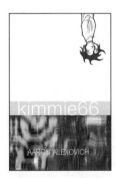

KIMMIE66
By Aaron Alexovich

This high-velocity, virtual reality ghost story follows a tech-savvy teenager on a dangerous quest to save her best friend, the world's first all-digital girl.

"Neuromancer for the Hello Kitty crowd."
—*Village Voice*

Your life. Your books. ***How novel.***
minxbooks.net